CA-Clipper 5.2
Step-by-Step

CORIOLIS GROUP BOOK

CA-Clipper 5.2
Step-by-Step

Dan Gutierrez

John Wiley & Sons, Inc.
New York • Chichester • Brisbane • Toronto • Singapore

This text is printed on acid-free paper.

Copyright © 1994 by John Wiley & Sons, Inc.

All rights reserved. Published simultaneously in Canada.

Reproduction or translation of any part of this work beyond that permitted by section 107 or 108 of the 1976 United States Copyright Act without the written permission of the copyright owner is unlawful. Requests for permission or further information should be addressed to the Permissions Department, John Wiley & Sons, Inc.

Words in this publication in which the Author and Publisher believe trademark or other proprietary rights may exist have been designated as such by use of Initial Capital Letters. However, in so designating or failing to designate such words, neither the Author nor the Publisher intends to express any judgment on the validity or legal status of any proprietary right that may be claimed in the words.

Library of Congress Cataloging-in-Publication Data

Gutierrez, Dan D.
    CA-Clipper 5.2 : step-by-step / Dan Gutierrez.
      p. cm.
    Includes index.
    ISBN 0-471-55499-5 (alk. paper)
     1. Compilers (Computer programs) 2. Clipper (Computer Program Language) I. Title.
QA76.76.C65G88   1994
005.75'65--dc20   93-27511
                                                                      CIP

Printed in the United States of America

10 9 8 7 6 5 4 3 2 1

Contents

Chapter 1   The Clipper Programming Environment — 1
   Hard Disk Organization — 2
   DOS Environment Variables — 5
   Compilers versus Interpreters — 5
   The Development Cycle — 6
   Compiling with CA-Clipper — 8
      .CLP Files — 12
   LINKING — 12
   RMAKE — 14
   Program Execution — 16
   Clipper Utilities — 16
      DBU — 17
      RL — 18
      PE — 19
      Third-Party Utilities — 19
   The Debugger — 21
      Debugger Features — 22
      Debugger Basics — 22
   The Norton Guides — 28
   Summary — 29

Chapter 2   Language Basics — 31
   The Clipper Coding Style — 32
   Data Types — 35
   FIELD/MEMVAR Statements — 37
   The Assignment Operator — 38
   Other Operators — 38
   Relational Operators — 40
   The Fall of Macros — 41
   Extended Expressions — 41
   Alias Functions — 42
   An Improved IF Statement — 43

    The DO WHILE Looping Structure   44
    The FOR/NEXT Looping Structure   46
    The DO CASE/ENDCASE Control Structure   46
    The BEGIN/END SEQUENCE Control Structure   47
    Screen Input/Output   51
        @ SAY GET   51
        @ BOX   52
        Simple Menuing with @ Prompt   54
        Saving/Restoring Screen Contents   55
        Buffered Screen Output   57
        DEVOUT()   57
        DEVOUTPIC()   57
        DEVPOS()   57
        DISPBOX()   58
        DISPCOUNT()   58
        DISPOUT()   58
        Stuffing the Keyboard   59
    Summary   60
    Exercise   61
        Answer   61

Chapter 3   The Preprocessor   63

    A Preprocessor Defined   64
    Manifest Constants   68
    Include Files   73
    Conditional Compilation   76
    Pseudo Functions   80
    Other Features   82
    Assertions   83
    Summary   85
    Exercises   85
        Answers   85

Chapter 4   User-Defined Commands   87

    An Intelligent Search and Replace   89
    Preprocessor Operations   89
    Match Markers   91
        Word Match Marker   92
        Regular Match Marker   93
        Extended Expression Match Marker   94
        Optional Clauses   95

List Match Marker	97
Restricted Match Marker	98
Wild Match Marker	100
Result Markers	101
Regular Result Marker	101
Dumb Stringify Result Marker	102
Smart Stringify Result Marker	102
Logify Result Marker	103
Blockify Result Marker	103
Normal Stringify Result Marker	104
Repeating Clauses	105
Examples from COMMON.CH	106
Summary	108
Exercise	109
Answer	109

Chapter 5 Subprograms — 111

Programs Units	112
Procedures	113
Functions	117
Scope and Lifetime	119
Private Scope	120
Local Scope	123
Public Scope	125
Static Scope	127
Global Scope	129
Static Functions and Procedures	129
Comparison of Scopes and Lifetimes	130
Announce and Request	131
INIT and EXIT Procedures	133
Summary	137
Exercise	138
Answer	138

Chapter 6 Code Blocks — 139

What Is a Code Block?	140
Definition	141
Evaluation	141
Programming Applications	143
Code Block Parameter Passing	146
Get/Set Block Functions	147

FIELDBLOCK()	147
FIELDWBLOCK()	148
MEMVARBLOCK()	149
Summary	150
Exercise	150
Answer	150

Chapter 7 Arrays — 151

Why Are Clipper's Arrays So Special	152
Declaring and Using Arrays	153
Literal Declarations	154
Fixed-Size Declarations	155
Dynamic Declarations	155
Assigning Values to Array Elements	156
Array References	156
Comparing Arrays	157
Applying Arrays in Everyday Coding	158
Array Functions	159
A Brief Tour	159
Array Manipulation	160
User Interface	165
Database Related	167
Code Block Related	169
Environment	169
Jump Tables	171
Passing Arrays as Parameters	172
Array Return Values	173
Recursion	174
Global Variables	175
Summary	176
Exercises	176
Answers	177

Chapter 8 Database Access — 179

Accessing Databases with CA-Clipper	180
RDD Technology	182
Replaceable Database Driver Architecture Overview	182
RDD Terminology	184
Order Management System	186
Using the DBFNTX RDD	187
Using the DBFNDX RDD	187

Using the DBFMDX RDD	188
Using the DBFCDX RDD	189
Using the DBPX RDD	190
Installing RDD Files	192
Linking with RDDs	192
Database Commands	192
APPEND FROM	193
COPY TO	193
GO	194
INDEX	195
SEEK	196
SET INDEX TO	197
SET ORDER TO	198
Database Functions	199
ALIAS()	199
DBAPPEND()	199
DBCLEARFILTER()	200
DBCLEARINDEX()	200
DBCLEARRELATION()	201
DBCLOSEALL()	201
DBCLOSEAREA()	202
DBCOMMIT()	202
DBCOMMITALL()	202
DBCREATE()	202
DBCREATEINDEX()	203
DBDELETE()	204
DBEVAL()	204
DBFILTER()	204
DBGOBOTTOM()	205
DBGOTO()	205
DBGOTOP()	205
DBRECALL()	206
DBREINDEX()	206
DBRELATION()	206
DBRSELECT()	207
DBSEEK()	207
DBSELECTAREA()	208
DBSETDRIVER()	208
DBSETFILTER()	208
DBSETINDEX()	209
DBSETORDER()	209

DBSETRELATION()	210
DBSKIP()	210
DBUNLOCK()	210
DBUNLOCKALL()	211
DBUSEAREA()	211
HEADER()	211
INDEXEXT()	211
INDEXKEY()	212
INDEXORD()	212
LASTREC()	213
RECNO()	213
RECSIZE()	213
RDD Commands	214
DELETE TAG	214
RDD Functions	214
DBRLOCK()	214
DBRLOCKLIST()	215
DBRUNLOCK()	216
ORDBAGEXT()	216
ORDBAGNAME()	217
ORDCREATE()	217
ORDDESTROY()	218
ORDFOR()	219
ORDKEY()	219
ORDLISTADD()	220
ORDLISTCLEAR()	220
ORDLISTREBUILD()	220
ORDNAME()	221
ORDNUMBER()	221
ORDSETFOCUS()	222
RDDLIST()	222
RDDNAME()	223
RDDSETDEFAULT()	223
The Importance of Code Blocks	225
Database Traversal and DBEVAL()	225
Setting Relations	228
The Many-to-Many Relation	230
Listing 8.1 Establishing a "Supplier-by-Part" M:M Relationship	232
Listing 8.2 Program using "Suppliers-by-Part" M:M Orientation	235

Summary	237
Exercise	237
Answer	237

Chapter 9 Memo Fields — 239

Memo Technology Revisited	240
Memo Field Basics	242
Memo Field/Character String Functions	243
MEMOEDIT()	250
An Introduction to MEMOEDIT()	250
The User Function	252
Simple Memo Field Access	253
Getting Memo Fields	255
Editing Text Disk Files	256
Converting Summer '87 Memo Fields	260
Summary	262
Exercise	263
Answer	263

Chapter 10 Standard Classes — 265

Object-Based Technology: General Terms	266
Classes and Objects: The Basics	268
Instance Variables	269
Method Functions	272
Sending Messages	275
Clipper's OOP Limitations	275
Clipper Class Extensions Products	276
Summary	276
Exercise	277
Answer	277

Chapter 11 TBrowse — 279

The TBrowse and TBColumn Classes	280
TBrowse Requirements	281
A Complete TBrowse	287
Speeding Up a TBrowse	289
Customizing a TBrowse	290
Formatting Data	290
Freezing Columns	291
Using Color	291
Limiting the Scope	291

Array Browsing	293
Browsing Text Files	298
Other Topics	300
Summary	300
Exercise	300
Answer	301

Chapter 12 Low-Level File Functions — 303

A Review of the Functions	304
Create/Open DOS Files	304
Moving through the Data	307
Reading Data	309
Writing Data	309
FILEIO.PRG	311
Low-Level File Example for Beginners	311
Summary	314
Exercise	314
Answer	314

Chapter 13 Applications — 317

Data Entry CA-Clipper Style	318
Entry()	319
GetScr()	320
InitVars()	321
SetVars()	322
ReplVars()	323
Menu()	323
The GET System	325
Listing 13.1 Data Entry UDF Collection	325
Basic Reporting	331
A Formula for Reporting	331
A Simple Style of Report	333
Listing 13.2 Multi-Table Report Program	335
Summary	340
Exercises	340
Answers	341

Index — 355

Preface

From its early beginnings with the dBASE II product from Ashton-Tate, the Xbase language has attracted thousands of application developers throughout the world by offering a powerful, easy-to-use programming environment. This environment, laced with database hooks, was designed to ease the task of providing the means to build applications that access data stored in disk based files. Nantucket Corporation, early on, became a renowned supplier of an Xbase compatible product called Clipper that took one important step forward, namely compiling Xbase code into the form of a standalone executable file; an .EXE file. But Nantucket did much more than simply provide for a means of compiling Xbase code. Indeed, it added extensions to the language in its compiler that were so desirable that many Xbase programmers gave up previously sought after dBASE compatibility in favor of writing programs in an often simpler, and certainly more powerful, manner. This evolutionary product plan followed all the releases of Clipper, but not until the release of Clipper 5, did the differences and ultimate power excel to such great proportions.

The Clipper 5 language represented a very different flavor of Xbase programming. To be sure, one can still compile older dBASE III Plus code with a high degree of compatibility. But this was not the primary goal the developers of Clipper 5 had in mind. On the contrary, Clipper 5 has so many new and exciting features that if you were to write Clipper 5 optimized code (which is exactly what you will write after reading this book), much of it would barely resemble its Xbase roots. What with new operators, a preprocessor, an advanced array structure, code blocks, and predefined classes, the resulting code is a distant relative to the old dBASE II/III and even dBASE IV code still operating today. At one point, Nantucket attempted to divorce themselves from the Xbase marketplace completely, stating that they were not Xbase, but rather a new and very different language alogether. From a marketing point of view, this didn't make much sense since there were, as we said earlier, thousands upon thousands of Xbase developers out there who could gain benefit from using the new and improved Clipper 5 language.

There were unforeseen problems, however, relating to this target market for the Clipper 5 compiler. Just who is it for? Is it for Xbase programmers looking for a better way? Is it for old Summer '87 release (the release prior to Clipper 5) programmers trying to keep on track with current offerings? Or is it just for non-database programmers coming from BASIC, C, or other high-level languages? The answer to this question doesn't really matter to what we hope to achieve in this book. The one common denominator among all of the above groups is this: Many developers who attempt to make the move to Clipper 5 are often frustrated at the sheer number of new concepts and features that must be mastered before getting productive. Nantucket delivered an excellent application development environment to the programming community, but it never told anyone how to use it, at least properly. Now that Computer Associates, Inc. has taken the reins of the product (now formally called *CA-Clipper*), we've already seen several product updates and improved documentation.

There are quite a few good books available that describe the language (written by wonderfully capable Clipper gurus worldwide), but for the most part they focus on seasoned programmers who are looking for somewhat advanced techniques and good code examples. None of these books, to my knowledge, set out to educate the *Clipper beginner*. This is therefore the goal of this book: to bring the enormously powerful CA-Clipper language to the masses.

I have already done much in this regard: teaching the *CA-Clipper as a Software Development Platform* class at UCLA Extension, writing the *Clipper Basics* column for Data Based Advisor magazine, conducting CA-Clipper training seminars in the Los Angeles area, and founding a Virtual Clipper User Group on AMULET:vc (a collection of virtual communities). These are some of the ways I've been able to see firsthand the difficulties with learning the language. In the process, I've developed my own favorite methods for teaching beginners how to program with CA-Clipper. This book is the culmination of these efforts.

Who Should Read This Book

This book is written specifically for several diverse groups of application developers. First, this book is for Xbase programmers wishing to become conversant in the CA-Clipper language. This would include people who currently write programs in Borland International's dBASE III Plus or dBASE IV, Microsoft's FoxPro, or any other Xbase dialect. The book is also for Clipper programmers who have until now resisted the move to CA-Clipper and still use the Summer '87 release. It is a very good idea for the Summer '87 crowd to come aboard the CA-Clipper bandwagon in light of future developments with the product. Plus, there is a lot of work out in the field for performing Summer '87 to CA-Clipper conversions! In the most general sense, however, this book is for programmers knowledgeable in another computer programming language and who have a need to learn the Clipper language. These individuals recognize CA-Clipper to be a robust, heavy weight programming language with database hooks that may be used for developing serious applications.

As far as prerequisite knowledge goes, however, we do assume the reader has programmed in an Xbase language before and is familiar with the programming basics in this environment, such as the database file system, screen input/output, and basic language constructs. We'll take you from there and make you CA-Clipper proficient.

We will start at the very beginning, presenting language features that will progressively give the programmer a bigger and bigger picture of what Clipper offers and will ultimately give the programmer a sizable repertoire of techniques to use the language effectively, in other words, to write *CA-Clipper optimized code.*

Prerequisite Items

Before we get started, we should make sure that you have all the tools required to write programs in CA-Clipper. The following short list gives the bare essentials. There is quite a sizable third party market for the Clipper language and additional aids, such as libraries, linkers, and utilities of every kind can be acquired after you master the basics.

- CA-CLIPPER compiler, Release 5.2c or later from Computer Associates, Inc.
- PC Compatible computer with a recommended configuration of at least a 386SX processor, 2Mb RAM, 40Mb hard disk, floppy disk drive, and VGA display
- Programmer's Editor of your choice; although Clipper comes with a simple editor, PE (which is actually written in Clipper), we highly recommend that you purchase a third party product

A Quick Review of the Chapters

Chapter 1: The Clipper Programming Environment begins the learning process with an introduction on how to "tool up" for writing programs with CA-Clipper. This chapter discusses all of the basic components you'll encounter when using CA-Clipper: the compiler (and its command-line switches), the RTLINK linker, RMAKE, and the Debugger. We'll also take a look at a typical CA-Clipper installation.

Chapter 2: Language Basics presents all of the new and revised language constructs found in CA-Clipper. Topics in this chapter include: data types, operators, expressions, comments, and basic commands and statements. We also include a complete discussion of Clipper's screen input and output capabilities.

Chapter 3: The Preprocessor illustrates the use of the various directives understood by the preprocessor, a unique component of CA-Clipper that allows the source code to be "prepared" before the actual Clipper compiler begins the translation process.

Chapter 4: User-Defined Commands completes the discussion of the preprocessor by showing how CA-Clipper allows the modification of existing command syntax as well as the creation of new commands. We'll see how UDCs are the part of the preprocessor that holds many of the secrets of the CA-Clipper language.

Chapter 5: Subprograms defines how CA-Clipper handles calling and passing parameters to two different types of subprograms: procedures and user-defined functions. In addition, we'll demonstrate the importance of understanding CA-Clipper's contemporary variable scoping and lifetime rules.

Chapter 6: Code Blocks simplifies the use of code blocks, usually considered the most mysterious part of the CA-Clipper language. This chapter brings a fundamental understanding of this special program data type to the reader and shows how to utilize them in everyday programming tasks.

Chapter 7: Arrays explores CA-Clipper's "ragged arrays," which are often thought of as the most improved part of the language. We'll see that with CA-Clipper's flexible array capabilities, any type of data structure with any type of "topology" can be realized.

Chapter 8: Database Access focuses on the basics of accessing data residing in database files. You'll learn how data can be handled in a very different manner than in other Xbase products and even prior releases of Clipper. You will also examine the full complement of database functions that do the work previously done by commands like USE, SEEK, and CLOSE. We'll also cover all of the recent additions in the 5.2x release in the form of *RDD* access commands and functions, as well as the new Order Management system. Finally, we'll provide information on the pseudo-relational aspects of CA-Clipper such as linking databases and one-to-many and many-to-many relationships.

Chapter 9: Memo Fields explains the effective use of Memo fields, the one area that has not changed much since the Summer '87 release. We'll also provide a complete discussion of how the old Memo field technology is still intact in CA-Clipper but receives a facelift if other CA-Clipper features are applied.

Chapter 10: Standard Classes defines the bold new feature in CA-Clipper that most likely has the farthest reaching effects, namely *object orientation*. The CA-Clipper language was designed with object orientation in mind. This chapter describes, in brief terms, the four predefined CA-Clipper classes and the terminology that surrounds them.

Chapter 11: TBrowse applies the concepts defined in Chapter 10, using two of the predefined classes found in CA-Clipper, TBrowse and TBColumn as an example. We'll see how to apply object-oriented programming when using the revamped Browse system.

Chapter 12: Low Level File Functions illustrates how to perform low level access to DOS disk files directly from a Clipper program.

Chapter 13: Applications shows how to begin the construction of complete CA-Clipper applications by examining two generic application groups: *data entry* and *reporting*.

A Look to the Future

Now that Computer Associates, Inc. is the keeper of the Clipper family of products, the future of Clipper looks quite favorable. CA is firmly entrenched in corporate America, a place Clipper has traditionally found difficult to break into. Developers are hopeful that the Fortune 1000s will now look at Clipper and its future derivatives as a viable application development alternative. Moreover, with the object-oriented slant of both the current product and future products such as Visual Objects for Clipper, Computer Associates, Inc. is definitely following and keeping close ties with industry trends. It's a good time to learn the Clipper language, and after you've finished reading this book, you'll be firmly set to take advantage of all its current and future benefits. Good luck!

Contacting the Author

The author welcomes questions and/or comments pertaining to this book. I can be reached in Cyberspace via CompuServe at: 73317,646 or from the Internet via CompuServe at 73317.646@compuserve.com. In addition, the author welcomes all interested parties to join me and many colleagues in our special virtual community by calling AMULET:vc (Santa Monica, California in physical reality) where the first *Virtual Clipper User Group* regularly meets. Just call the data line (310) 453-7705 to gain free access.

Acknowledgments

I would like to thank the wonderful professionals at *Data Based Advisor* magazine who first allowed me to realize my desire to bring Clipper programming to the masses by presenting beginning level material through my "Clipper Basics" column. Since April 1992 when the series began, I have been contacted by new Clipper enthusiasts from throughout the world expressing their thanks for this introductory material. I am also indebted to the new Clipper programmers who have went through my seminar series and my students at UCLA Extension, who provided me with the insight on how to provide answers to even the most simple questions. I'd also like to thank the people I've met on the conference circuit who also gave their appreciation for my magazine column and provided me with new ideas. It is by way of encouragement from those various groups of people that I found the focus necessary to put this book together. This book is for you!

The Clipper Programming Environment

Hard Disk Organization ➤ 2

DOS Environment Variables ➤ 5

Compilers versus Interpreters ➤ 5

The Development Cycle ➤ 6

Compiling with CA-Clipper ➤ 8

LINKING ➤ 12

RMAKE ➤ 14

Program Execution ➤ 16

Clipper Utilities ➤ 16

The Debugger ➤ 21

The Norton Guides ➤ 28

Summary ➤ 29

Before we begin our study of the Clipper programming language, it is first necessary to describe the development environment in which we will be working. By development environment, we mean the basic hardware requirements, software tools, hard disk organization, and DOS environment settings that must be established in order for the Clipper software development process to proceed.

In this chapter, we will present the basic ingredients of the CA-Clipper Xbase compiler with which you may begin to write programs. Necessarily, we will assume you are using CA-Clipper 5.2 or later, .RTLink (the linker that comes packaged with the product) and a programmer's editor of your choice. In addition, you'll also need a fresh (or at least reliable) install of the product on your hard disk. CA-Clipper's install program is simple and straightforward as it prompts you for answers to questions regarding how the product is to be installed. Since install programs are release dependent, we will not discuss installation in this book, but rather refer you to the latest Computer Associates, Inc. documentation.

Hard Disk Organization

We will begin with a short discussion about the hard disk organization of the Clipper programming environment. When CA-Clipper is first installed the directory structure shown in Figure 1.1 is produced. This configuration corresponds to a *full install* option consisting of system files, utilities, sample programs and online documentation (Norton Guides). When first trying out CA-Clipper, a full install is recommended so that you may view the product in its entirety.

Figure 1.1 Your hard disk should include these directories when you request a full installation.

\CLIPPER5
\CLIPPER5\BIN
\CLIPPER5\LIB
\CLIPPER5\SOURCE
\CLIPPER5\SOURCE\DBU
\CLIPPER5\SOURCE\PE
\CLIPPER5\SOURCE\RL
\CLIPPER5\SOURCE\SAMPLE
\CLIPPER5\SOURCE\SYS
\CLIPPER5\INCLUDE
\CLIPPER5\PLL
\CLIPPER5\OBJ
\NG

After you become more conversant with CA-Clipper, you may remove directories containing source code for the sample programs and CA-Clipper utilities. This would include all subdirectories under \SOURCE except \SYS, which you may require when your skills become better developed.

For learning purposes now, we should carefully examine the contents of \CLIPPER5\SOURCE\SAMPLE to see the kind of coding techniques Computer Associates, Inc. advocates. The source code for the Clipper utilities DBU, RL and PE which are supplied in their own directories under \CLIPPER5\SOURCE, are written in a quasi-CA-Clipper stylized form and may aid in your learning process. The PE editor utility specifically illustrates a reasonably complex application of the MEMOEDIT() editing facility that we will cover in Chapter 9.

Before we move on, let's first describe each of the hard disk directories that the CA-Clipper installation program sets up:

- **\CLIPPER5**

  This directory is the main hard disk directory in which the various pieces of the CA-Clipper compiler reside.

- **\CLIPPER5\BIN**

  This directory is the location of all CA-Clipper executable files such as CLIPPER.EXE (the compiler itself) and .RTLink (the linker program). After the install program automatically compiles the Clipper utiltiy programs, the resulting .EXE files should be copied into the \BIN subdirectory in order for them to be accessible at any time.

- **\CLIPPER5\LIB**

  This directory is where the CA-Clipper library files are located. Library files, which you will beome more familiar with when we discuss the linking process, play an important part in building the .EXE file for your program. You should also consider placing your favorite third party libraries in the \LIB subdirectory in order for the linker to have easy access to them.

- **\CLIPPER5\SOURCE**

  This directory is in turn composed of several subdirectories containing the various source code groups that come with CA-Clipper.

- **\CLIPPER5\SOURCE\DBU**

  This directory contains the source code for the *Database utility* program that is similar

- **\CLIPPER5\SOURCE\PE**

  in nature to the dBASE III Plus Assistant. When you compile these source code files, the DBU.EXE program results. You may use DBU to create database and index files, as well as browse through records.

  This directory contains the source code for the *programmer's editor*. Compiling these source code files yields the PE.EXE program, a simple to use, though not feature rich programmer's editor which may be used to enter and modify CA-Clipper program files.

- **\CLIPPER5\SOURCE\RL**

  This directory contains the source code for the *report and label designer* utility program. When you compile these source code files, the RL.EXE program results, which simulates the CREATE/MODIFY REPORT and LABEL commands in dBASE III Plus.

- **\CLIPPER5\SOURCE\SAMPLE**

  All CA-Clipper sample programs are located in this directory. For beginning CA-Clipper programmers, these files may prove to be excellent hunting grounds for useful coding techniques.

- **\CLIPPER5\SOURCE\SYS**

  For advanced programmers, the code found in this directory may shed insight into the internal workings of CA-Clipper. The code for the *Get System* and the *Error System* can be found here.

- **\CLIPPER5\INCLUDE**

  This directory contains all the standard Clipper header (.CH) files used by the preprocessor at compile time. We will discuss the contents of this subdirectory in depth in Chapters 3 and 4.

- **\CLIPPER5\PLL**

  The pre-linked libraries are built by the installation process and then placed in this subdirectory for regular use by the linker.

- **\CLIPPER5\OBJ**

  This is the directory where the linker searches for object files (.OBJ) during the creation of an executable (.EXE).

- **\CLIPPER5\NG** In this directory, you'll find the *Norton Guides* files that describe various portions of the CA-Clipper product in a fashion similar to the CA-Clipper Users Manual.

DOS Environment Variables

The installation process will also define several DOS environment variables as additions to your AUTOEXEC batch file. These variables are used to locate various types of files necessary for a successful compile and link. These are shown in Figure 1.2.

Notice in the DOS PATH command that the \CLIPPER5\BIN directory is inserted. This addition is useful since you are then able to run all CA-Clipper related executables, including the compiler, linker, and utilities, from any working directory. Both the standard directories and DOS variables are recommended for your first try at Clipper programming. These and other attributes may be changed or customized later when your experience grows.

Compilers versus Interpreters

Before we get into the specifics of applying the CA-Clipper compiler technology, we should say a few words regarding why compilers are advantageous over interpretive products. This topic should interest those developers making the transition from dBASE IV and FoxPro. First, the issue of speed comes into play when comparing these technologies. Generally speaking, compiled programs run faster than interpretive ones. This benefit is not entirely clear cut these days, because of hybrid interpretive products. This type of hybrid no longer repeatedly interprets the source as the program executes, but instead first generates pseudo-code and then uses that code as the basis of execution. Although these products (dBASE IV and FoxPro) do allow for the further translation to an .EXE file, they do so by wrapping a huge run-time system inside the .EXE yielding 1 to 2 Mb executables (Clipper's executables are much smaller and more optimized). The bottom line is that CA-Clipper stacks up well in terms of speed with other database products in the industry, both interpretive and compiled.

Figure 1.2 The Clipper DOS environment variables.

PATH C:\CLIPPER5\BIN;C:\NG
SET INCLUDE=C:\CLIPPER5\INCLUDE
SET LIB=C:\CLIPPER5\LIB
SET OBJ=C:\CLIPPER5\OBJ
SET PLL=C:\CLIPPER5\PLL

Second, we have the issue of packaging and distribution. Interpretive products have always had the annoying requirement that all users had to purchase and install a copy of the database product in order for programs to execute. The cost in terms of dollars and time comes heavily into play when networks are concerned. Incremental LAN modules must be acquired from the vendors each time you wish to add more users of your application when it runs on a network. With CA-Clipper however, not only do you *not* have to have Clipper present on the PC, workstation, or file server when your program runs, but on a network, you still only need the single copy of the compiled program, the .EXE file, installed on the file server. This simplifies the distribution and installation process significantly. Moreover, you only have to deliver the .EXE file to a customer (instead of numerous program .PRG files).

The security of source code is another positive aspect of compiled environments. Once you've compiled your code, it is protected from revealing proprietary company techniques that went into the program's design because your source code never touches the customer's hard disk. Currently there are no *reverse compiler* products on the market for CA-Clipper (although several exist for the Summer '87 release) so your source code is well protected.

> **Note**
>
> The sole function of a compiler is to *translate* a source code program into an object file (with an .OBJ file extension). This form of the program *is not executable*. It's the job of the linker to produce an .EXE.

The Development Cycle

When using a compiler of any type, the programmer follows the typical application development cycle. This Clipper development cycle involves the following steps:

- Entering/editing the program with your favorite programmer's editor
- Compiling the source into object files using the CA-Clipper compiler
- Linking the object files with any additional libraries to produce an executable file using your favorite linker or the standard CA-Clipper linker, .RTLink
- Executing the program from the DOS prompt
- Performing various debugging techniques, most notably with the Clipper Debugger (CLD)
- Repeating the process as many times as needed until the program operates properly

Let's take some time to detail these steps. In order to enter and/or edit the program source code files (.PRGs) you need a good programmer's editor. Clipper comes with an editor called PE (automatically compiled and linked, yielding PE.EXE during the full installation process, as are the other Clipper utility programs) that is written in Clipper, but it is rather short on features. More appropriate is any one of several quality programmer's editors, either commercially available or through shareware. In the Clipper community, there are many favorites. You should consult a trade publication for current availability. You may also find the standard DOS 5 or 6 editor quite acceptable as it has mouse capabilities and recognizes various video modes. Of course, with all the notoriety received by Microsoft Windows, many quality editors are now available, containing all the usual pleasures found in Windows applications. Plus, these Windows editors allow the programmer to launch the CA-Clipper compiler, linker, debugger, as well as the program itself right from inside the editor. Being able to perform the entire development cycle all from one central place is very convenient, especially in a graphical environment.

Compiling a program involves activating Clipper to translate the source code .PRG files into .OBJ object files. As we mentioned earlier, some editors allow you to launch the various development cycle tasks directly from the editor. You may also set up a few batch files to perform compiles and links and then execute them on an "as-needed" basis. One such batch file might be: C.BAT, which you might use to simply compile a single program module. C.BAT would contain the following:

```
clipper %1 /n /m /w /p /b
```

Another batch file you might consider creating is CL.BAT, which would compile and link. CL.BAT would contain the following:

```
clipper %1 /n /m /w /p /b
rtlink fi %1 /pll:base52
```

We will detail the structure of these commands shortly. To run these batch files, you would enter C <progname> and CL <progname> respectively at the DOS prompt.

Still another alternative for building your application is to use CA-Clipper's RMAKE utility, a topic covered later in this chapter.

The link step involves invoking a utility program that combines the .OBJ files built by the compiler with the standard CA-Clipper libraries and any third-party libraries. This is the step in the development cycle that yields an executable .EXE file. Bear in mind that CA-Clipper is not a *native code compiler* but instead a *pseudo-code compiler* that packages the pseudo code and run-time system inside of an .EXE (but in a manner unlike competing database products). The resulting .EXE, however, may be run standalone from the DOS prompt without CA-Clipper being present.

The final step in the cycle requires you to run the program. There are two ways to do this. First, you can simply execute the program from the DOS prompt by entering its name and pressing Enter. The program may run perfectly the first time (however this is highly unlikely!) and if so, your job is done.

If, on the other hand, the program exhibits strange or unruly behavior, it's time to debug it. The easiest way to debug a Clipper program is to utilize the CA-Clipper debugger, a utility program that allows you to control the execution of your program. We provide the details of the debugger later on in this chapter. For now, let's just say that the debugger helps you determine the causes of errors. You must then take that knowledge and repeat the development cycle, starting again with the programmer's editor.

Compiling with CA-Clipper

Compiling with CA-Clipper is a simple task. Once you finish entering the program code into one or more .PRG files with your editor, the compiler's job is to translate these program files into an .OBJ file. An .OBJ file is a machine language version of your Clipper program, but it is not in a form that can directly execute from the DOS prompt. To compile a program you enter the command

```
clipper <sourceFile>
```

at the DOS prompt. The accepted standard filename extension for Clipper programs is .PRG. If you use this extension, you do not have to include it when compiling. What happens now is unique with CA-Clipper compared to other Xbase products. First, the preprocessor scans your code, applying *preprocessor directives* as required. The result is an intermediate form (consisting largely of calls to special Clipper low-level functions) that will be passed along to the actual compiler. The compiler then diagnoses any syntax errors and reports them to you. If there are any errors, you'll have to look up the messages in the *Error Messages and Appendices Guide* that comes with the CA-Clipper product, return to your editor to fix the problems, and try to compile again. After a few iterations of this, you should have weeded out all compiler errors and an .OBJ file results.

At this point, we need to discuss the various available *compiler switches* that allow you to customize how Clipper processes your source code. Table 1.1 provides is a complete list of all switches and a description of their use.

As you can see, there are many compiler switches, but only a few are recommended for regular use. With these switches in mind, the way you should compile most of your Clipper programs, at least to begin with, would be with the following command:

```
clipper <sourceFile> /n /w /a /p /b
```

Here is another Clipper DOS environment variable that is available and saves you time when you find yourself using the same compiler switches all the time.

```
set clippercmd=/n /w /a /p /b
```

Table 1.1 Compiler Switches

Switch	Description
/a	Use /a to avoid ambiguity between variables and database fields; this option will automatically declare all variables appearing in a `PRIVATE`, `PUBLIC`, or `PARAMETERS` statement as memory variables.
/b	In order to use the Clipper source-level debugger, you must use the /b option to request that debugging information be embedded in the object file. Never use the /l option (which eliminates line numbers from the object file) with /b since the debugger also needs line numbers to reference specific lines in the program.
/d	The /d switch allows for manifest constant definition, used by the preprocessor. The format for specifying a manifest constant using the /d switch is: `/d<identifier>[=<text>]` where <identifier> is an legal manifest constant name and <text> is optional text to which the constant is mapped at compile-time. If your program requires more than one manifest constant defined in this manner, you may include multiple /d switches for a single compile. Chapter 3 contains more information concerning this feature and manifest constants.
/ES /ES0 /ES1 /ES2	The /ES series of compiler switches provide for a way to affect the DOS error level upon exit. /ES and /ES0 provide compability with Clipper 5.0x by not setting the DOS error level if warnings are encountered during compilation (i.e. /W was specified). /ES1 specifies an exit severity level of 1 if warnings are encountered. /ES2 specifies an exit severity level of 2 if warnings are encountered; in addition, an object file is not generated. /ES2 thus treats warnings in the same manner as errors. By having the compiler set the DOS error level, more intelligent batch files may be written.
/i	The /i switch also relates to the preprocessor by allowing for you to specify a hard disk directory to be searched first when looking for header files. You may specify more than one /i switch to provide access to multiple directories containing header files. The format for specifying a header file directory using the /i switch is: `/i<pathname>` where <pathname> is any legal DOS path name. Chapter 3 contains more information about this feature and header files.
/l	The /l switch *eliminates* all line numbers which are embedded into the compiled program by default. The debugger needs embedded line numbers to provide reference points. In addition, run-time error messages include line number references if embedded, thus helping you pinpoint the error.

Table 1.1 Compiler Switches (Continued)

Switch	Description
	During the development stage, the /l switch *should not be used*. However, when the program is fully debugged and you are ready to distribute the application for production use, there is a trade-off to consider. On one hand, using the /l switch reduces the overall size of your .EXE file. This may be helpful, especially if the software is to run on a network where RAM is tight. An advantage to leaving out /l is that if and when your program aborts while in use, a potentially useful few lines of information will display on the PC's screen indicating the precise line number at which point the program failed; with /l specified, you are left to figure this out on your own.
/m	The /m switch causes the Clipper compiler to only compile the program module (.PRG file) referenced on the command line. Normally, Clipper performs an automatic search for referenced program modules in order to resolve external references. This means that without /m, Clipper also compiles any additional modules referenced by a DO statement, SET FORMAT, or SET PROCEDURE commands. Clipper, however, does not automatically compile functions and procedures called using the function style mechanism described in Chapter 5. Using /m becomes useful when you have just entered a long source code file and wish to do a quick syntax check (although an object file is still generated; see the /s switch entry).
/n	This switch eliminates the automatic definition of a procedure name which is the same as the name of the .PRG file you are compiling. One reason for using /n is to enable the use of file-wide static variables. Another reason is to promote the use of Clipper as a purely procedural language where each program unit, including the main routine, is built as a function. We will discuss this in greater depth later.
/o	The /o switch provides for two functions: specify an object filename that is different than the .PRG filename, or specify a directory in which the object file is to be placed. The format for this feature is /O\<objectFile>|\<objectDirectory> where \<objectFile> is any valid DOS filename (the .OBJ extension is assumed) and \<objectDirectory> is a pathname ending with a backslash character.
/p	The /p option will save the output of the preprocessor in a file of the same name as the .PRG except with a .PPO extension. It is advisable to always use /p when learning Clipper programming. Viewing .PPO files will give you insight into how Clipper truly works. We'll speak more about .PPO files in Chapter 3.
/q	Normally, a Clipper program displays line numbers as it processes your program during a compile. Adding /q to your command turns off this feature, making for a more "quiet" display. You may consider using /q if

Table 1.1 Compiler Switches (Continued)

Switch	Description
	you are echoing the compilation process to a printer (otherwise the line numbers overprint the same line).
/r	Using /r, you may inform the linker program in which library file to search for unresolved external references in your program and embed the name in the object file. The format for using this option is `/r[<libraryname>]` where `<libraryname>` is a library file (with a .LIB extension). Note that this parameter is optional, and if not specified, will cause no libraries to be referenced in the resulting object file (the default embedded requests are CLIPPER.LIB, EXTEND.LIB and DBFNTX.LIB). You may use multiple /r switches.
/s	The /s switch performs a *syntax-only* check on a .PRG file. When compiling a new .PRG file for the first time, you may consider using the /s switch, which also disables object file generation. Coupled with the /m switch, only the .PRG file referenced is checked.
/t	Use /t to specify a directory where temporary files are to be placed during compilation; /t overrides the TMP DOS environment variable.
/u	If you wish to specify an alternate standard header file to be used by the preprocessor for recognizing valid CA-Clipper command syntax, use the /u switch. If you do not specify /u, the standard STD.CH is used. The format for this option is `/u[<standardHeaderfile>]` where `<standardHeaderfile>` is a file with the .CH extension containing UDC definitions. Note that this filename is optional and if not specified causes no header file to be used during compilation. *Chapter 4* contains more information about this feature and UDCs.
/v	Use /v to view all undeclared or unaliased variable names as PUBLIC or PRIVATE variables. This is contrary to the default assumption that such references are database fields.
/w	This option promotes the declaration of all variables in a program. With /w, warning messages are generated for each occurrence of an undeclared variable or unaliased reference to a database field. Using /w will provide for cleaner code. Don't worry about the multitude of messages that result when you first start using /w; you'll get used to it. If you get a clean compile when using /w, you can have the peace of mind that many potential errors have already been foregone.
/z	The /z switch turns off the otherwise automatic *shortcutting optimizations* that the Clipper compiler performs on logical operators .AND. and .OR.

With CLIPPERCMD set, the specified switches are appended after the CLIPPER command, thus if these switches are in effect and you enter

```
CLIPPER <sourceFile> /m
```

at the DOS prompt, it would be as if you entered

```
CLIPPER <sourceFile> /m /n /w /a /p /b
```

.CLP Files

It is often convenient when compiling an application that is composed of several .PRG files to produce a single .OBJ file instead of several individual ones. This is possible with the use of .CLP (pronounced "clip") files. For example let's say you have a group of report programs all called from a single menu program. It would make sense to build a single .OBJ containing all the report programs. To do this, you create an ASCII text file REPORTS.CLP containing something like:

REPMENU
IS
BS
AGING
TRIALBAL

Here, each line represents a .PRG file to include in the .OBJ file. To direct Clipper to the .CLP file you would enter

```
CLIPPER @REPORTS
```

LINKING

The link step may be a new concept for Xbase developers who have previously only used interpretive products such as dBASE IV or FoxPro. If you are a developer that has only used interpretive or run-time based database products then the concept of linking is new. The linker's job is to take one or more .OBJ files, resolve any *external references* (i.e. when you call a function or procedure subprogram) by combining portions of standard and third-party libraries and build an .EXE file. The .EXE executes standalone from the DOS prompt without Clipper even being on the hard disk.

The linker that comes with CA-Clipper is called .RTLink and is developed by Pocket Soft Inc. There are several other linkers available from other third-party vendors. To start a link, you must first have successful compiles of all programs in your application. This is to say that you receive no compiler errors and preferably no warnings (with the /w compiler switch). Then you can call the linker by entering

```
rtlink fi <objList>
```

where <objList> is a series of .OBJ files that comprise your application. For example you might enter

```
rtlink fi mmenu, entry, reports
```

In this case, if there are no link-time errors, an .EXE file with the name MMENU will be created. The .EXE file always takes the name of the first .OBJ file listed. A shorthand method would involve entering the .OBJ file names in an ASCII text file as in:

```
MMENU
ENTRY
REPORTS
```

If this link file is named MMENU.LNK then you would enter the following command at the DOS prompt to perform the link:

```
rtlink @MMENU
```

One thing you immediately notice is that .RTLink takes a long time to finish its work. A quick solution to this situation is to use pre-linked libraries. These libraries exist in the \CLIPPER5\PLL directory and their use will result in much quicker link times and smaller .EXE sizes. The reason for these improvements is that the unchanging portions of the main CA-Clipper libraries, CLIPPER.LIB and EXTEND.LIB, are placed in the pre-linked library so that when you begin a link, .RTLink does not relink the modules in the specified pre-linked library. To link in this manner you would enter:

```
rtlink fi <objList> /pll:base52
```

Another reason to use pre-linked libraries is if you perform Clipper development on a local area network with a group of other programmers. This way, all the programmers may refer to the same pre-linked library during program execution without the need for large executables. The use of pre-linked libraries is normally limited to development purposes only; before an application is distributed to end users or customers, you should create a complete and standalone .EXE.

RMAKE

Of interest to any new CA-Clipper developer is the "MAKE" (used in a generic sense as this term is used in many diverse development environments, most notably those involving the C language) utility that is included with the product. Clipper's "MAKE" utility is called RMAKE. The purpose of RMAKE is to provide a way to systematically build an application that is comprised of many pieces. More importantly, it allows for system builds without re-building pieces that have not changed since the last build.

Note

> The process of *building a system* involves compiling all program source-code modules, linking in all external object modules (possibly from third-party library products) and generating a standalone .EXE executable file for distribution purposes.

A special file used with RMAKE is called a *make file*. A make file is an ASCII file with a .RMK extension containing commands to RMAKE that define the steps required for the creation of an .EXE for the application. For example, an application might be composed of the modules, MMENU.PRG, ENTRY.PRG and REPORTS.PRG. To build the application, the .PRGs must first be compiled and then linked. But there is no reason to compile a module that has not changed since the last time the system was built. Hence, there is a need to establish relationships based on the date/time stamps of the files. These relationships are termed *dependency rules*. The format of a dependency rule is:

```
<targetFile>: <dependentFile list>
   [<action1>]
   .
   .
   .
   [<actionN>]
```

Consider the following sample MMENU.RMK file that contains four dependency rules:

```
mmenu.obj  :  mmenu.prg
   clipper main /m /w /a /p /n

entry.obj  :  entry.prg
   clipper entry /w /a /p /n

reports.obj  :  reports.prg
   clipper reports /w /a /p /n

mmenu.exe : mmenu.obj entry.obj reports.obj mmenu.lnk
   rtlink @mmenu
```

Here, the make file says to compile MMENU.PRG only if the date/time stamp of MMENU.PRG is later than MMENU.OBJ. This means that the .OBJ file is less current than the source code. We perform the same check for the other two modules of the system. The command(s) that actually build the object (in this case an .OBJ file) are listed immediately following the dependency rule. Now, in the case of MMENU.EXE, the linker will only be called if the date/time stamp of any of the files listed is later than that of MMENU.EXE, which would indicate that one or more of the object files is more current than the .EXE. Notice the list includes MMENU.LNK, the linker control file, which is referenced in the .RTLink command below the dependency rule.

RMAKE is located in the \CLIPPER5\BIN directory and to invoke it you would enter the following command at the DOS prompt:

```
rmake mmenu.rmk
```

In addition to dependency rules, you are able to define *inference rules*, which specify actions for dependency rules that have no associated operations. The format of an inference rule is:

```
.<dependentExt>.<targetExt>:
  [<action1>]
  .
  .
  .
  [<actionN>]
```

RMAKE scans the contents of the .RMK file and if it finds a dependency rule without any actions, then it applies any inference rules. For example:

```
.prg.obj:
clipper $** /w /a /p /n
```

will perform a compile for any .OBJ that has a dependency on a .PRG using the Clipper compiler command specified. The $** symbol is a predefined RMAKE macro causing the dependent filename to be substituted on the command line. To illustrate this concept, if the following dependency appeared in an .RMK file without any actions:

```
main.obj: main.prg
```

then the resulting action would be

```
clipper main.prg /w /a /p/ n
```

RMAKE contains many other commands and features to facilitate efficient application building. Thoughtful RMAKE programming takes some time but is well worth the trouble.

Program Execution

To begin the execution of your program, you simply enter the name of the .EXE file at the DOS prompt. If all goes well, your program will produce useful results. If, however, problems arise, it is best to control the execution of the program through use of the debugger which is described later in this chapter.

Note

> An undocumented feature available as you execute the program is the //INFO command line switch that you place after the name of the .EXE file as in:
>
> ```
> testprog //info
> ```
>
> Before the program executes, special debugging information is displayed on the screen. In addition, the current version of Clipper and the current build of the compiler are displayed.

Clipper Utilities

The CA-Clipper compiler comes with several ready to use utility programs that fill in the gap for functional areas that are inherently missing in a strictly compiled environment. Namely, since CA-Clipper does not come embedded in an interactive shell as found in dBASE IV or FoxPro, the developer may not utilize such features as the dBASE IV Control Center or the FoxPro menu system. In addition, certain commonly used interactive features such as a report/label designer or integrated programmer's editor, not to mention a screen designer are not part of a compiled environment.

The Clipper utilities that attempt to cover these functional areas are: **DBU** (the database utility), **RL** (the report and label designer) and **PE** (the programmer's editor). There is no equivalent of a screen designer in CA-Clipper although several are commercially available from the Clipper third-party market and shareware. Each of these utilities is written in Clipper and complete source code is provided. A full install of Clipper places the source code in the \CLIPPER5\SOURCE directory. In addition, a full install automatically compiles and links the utilities and deposits the resulting .EXE files also in the source code directory.

Note

> In order to gain access to the utilities from any development hard disk directory, you should copy their .EXE files to the \CLIPPER5\BIN directory which should become part of the DOS PATH.

Let's take a look at some of the basic features of these utilities.

DBU

The database utility enables you to perform the various commonly needed database file operations that arise during application development. The DBU main menu is shown in Figure 1.3 where the options to perform these functions are activated by function keys. The function keys and the menus they activate are listed in Table 1.2.

The normal uses the Clipper beginner may find helpful center around DBU's ability to create new database and index files. Without DBU, you would have to resort to using an interactive Xbase product like dBASE III Plus for creating databases. To create a Clipper .NTX index file however, a test program would be required to issue the required INDEX ON commands. DBU relieves these needs, since as an interactive utility, all such tasks may be done (using the F2 Open menu) and much more. DBU also provides a facility for viewing

Table 1.2 Activating Menus with Function Keys

Function Key	Menu
F1	**Help** (requires the file DBU.HLP)
F2	**Open**
	Database
	Index
	View
F3	**Create**
	Database
	Index
F4	**Save**
	View
	Structure
F5	**Browse**
	Database
	View
F6	**Utility**
	Copy
	Append
	Replace
	Pack
	Zap
	Run
F7	**Move**
	Seek
	Goto

Table 1.2 Activating Menus with Function Keys (Continued)

Function Key	Menu
	Locate
	Skip
F8	**Set**
	Relation
	Filter
	Fields
Esc	**Exit**

database contents through use of a browser. This ability is particularly useful during the debugging phase of the development in order to check the contents of the databases that your program writes. The software developer new to CA-Clipper should spend some time and experiment with each option. You should also have a prior knowledge of the Xbase file system (i.e. databases, records, fields, record pointers, end-of-file and beginning-of-file status, etc.).

RL

The report and label utility allows you to define and create both report and label forms using an interactive mechanism similar to (but not nearly as powerful as)

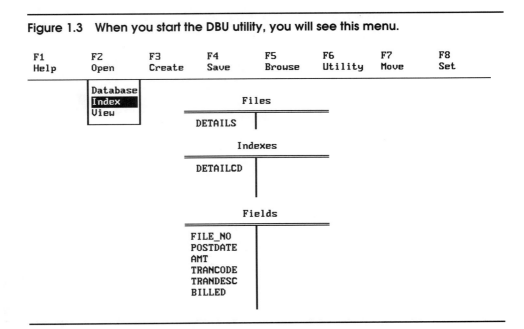

Figure 1.3 When you start the DBU utility, you will see this menu.

the report design surfaces in the leading interpretive Xbase products, such as dBASE IV and FoxPro. The main screen from RL is shown in Figure 1.4. The output of the RL utility is either a .FRM or .LBL file, which may be invoked by the REPORT FORM and/or LABEL FORM commands from a Clipper program.

PE

The programmer's editor represents a simple means by which you may enter or modify the contents of a .PRG program file. Figure 1.5 shows PE with a program loaded, ready for editing. Figure 1.6 shows the PE Help screen with the numerous editing commands.

Third-Party Utilities

Although the CA-Clipper utilities come with the program, many developers choose to go to third-party equivalents, which possess more powerful functionality. There are Clipper utilities that duplicate the functionality of the dBASE DOT prompt, there are feature rich report designers, and there are outstanding programmer's editors, as we mentioned in an earlier section. In addition, a plethora of third-party general- and special-purpose libraries allow for an abundance of added capabilities from within a Clipper program. Most developers

Figure 1.4 When you start the RL utility, you will see this menu.

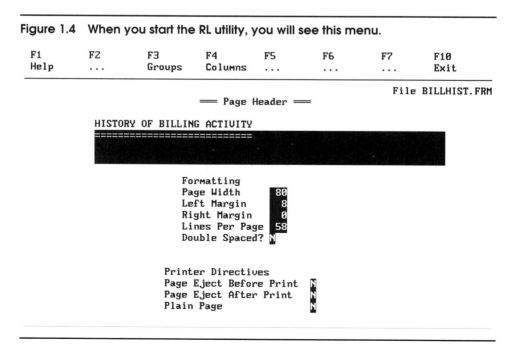

Figure 1.5 Use the programmer's editor to create and edit a .PRG file.

```
FUNCTION FPrompt( nTop, nLeft, nBottom, nRight, bFilter )

    MEMVAR getlist                              // Establish local get list array
    LOCAL cBuffer
    LOCAL cExitMsg := '(Leave blank to exit)'
    LOCAL cFileNo, cLoanNo, cName, cSaveColor, lRetVal:=TRUE
    LOCAL bFZold
    LOCAL bFZnew := {|cProc, nLine, cVar| FLookUp(cProc, nLine, cVar)}

        nTop    := IFNIL(nTop, 8)
        nLeft   := IFNIL(nLeft, 12)
        nBottom := IFNIL(nBottom, 17)
        nRight  := IFNIL(nRight, 60)

        bFZold  := SETKEY(K_F2, bFZnew)    // Save current K_F2 mapping

        SHADOWBOX BUFFER cBuffer TOP nTop LEFT nLeft BOTTOM nBottom RIGHT nRight ;
                TYPE BOX_DBLHOR_SINGVERT TITLE 'File Search' COLOR 'w+/rb'

        cSaveColor := SETCOLOR( 'w+/rb,n/w' )
        @ nTop+2, nLeft+2 SAY 'File Number:'
        @ nTop+4, nLeft+2 SAY 'Loan Number:'

File: amulib.prg                                              Line: 46    Col: 0
```

Figure 1.6 Use this screen to get help with the PE's commands.

```
PE Help

Uparrow/Ctrl-E          Line up              Alt-H, F1    Display Help screen
Dnarrow/Ctrl-X          Line down            Ctrl-W       Save and exit
Leftarrow/Ctrl-S        Char left            Alt-W        Save and continue
Rightarrow/Ctrl-D       Char right           Alt-O        New Output filename
Ctrl-Leftarrow/Ctrl-A   Word left            Alt-X, Esc   Exit
Ctrl-Rightarrow/Ctrl-F  Word right           Alt-F        Display Filename
Home                    Beginning of line    Alt-S        Search
End                     End of line          Alt-A        Search Again
Ctrl-Home               Top of window        Alt-I, Ins   Toggle Insert mode
Ctrl-End                End of window
PgUp                    Previous window
PgDn                    Next window
Ctrl-PgUp               Top of file
Ctrl-PgDn               End of file
Return                  Begin next line
Delete                  Delete char
Backspace               Delete char left
Tab                     Insert tab/spaces
Ctrl-Y                  Delete line
Ctrl-T                  Delete word right

Press any key to return to the edit screen...
```

have numerous tools at their disposal when creating new applications. Here is a brief list of common tools for routine Clipper development:

- General purpose function library
- Character graphics and/or GUI user interface builder
- Network access/control tools
- Presentation graphics
- Serial communication library
- Overlay linker
- DOS extender
- Class extender
- RDDs (Replaceable Database Drivers)
- Screen designer
- Application generator
- Memo field enhancer
- Laser printer library

The Debugger

Probably the most important utility program available with CA-Clipper is the debugger. The usefulness of a debugger has been proven over time and the concept is widely accepted in the Xbase community. Clipper has had a debugger for a long time, even before the Clipper 5 release. One of the important advantages of an interpretive over a compiled environment was supposed to be the ease of debugging due to the availability of the DOT prompt to do investigative work as the program is running. With the Clipper debugger, however, this ease and much more becomes available to the developer. In fact, through use of this robust debugger, Clipper's debugging capabilities now surpass those available from the dBASE DOT prompt. In this section, we'll supply the basics of using the debugger. Throughout the rest of the book, however, you should make a sincere attempt to use the debugger in testing and expanding on the numerous examples.

> **Note** A debugger is a program that controls the execution of another program in a controlled manner with the expectation of discovering and correcting inaccuracies, omissions, logic flaws, and general bugs.

The first step is to make sure that your .PRG files are compiled in a manner that is compatible with using the debugger. In order to use the debugger, you must always use the /b compiler switch, which embeds required debugging information in the resulting .OBJ file. Without this information, the debugger is unable to perform its task. Also, do not use the /l switch, which would take out all line number references in the .OBJ files. Line numbers are an important ingredient in debugger use. The link step in creating an executable remains the same.

After you have generated the .EXE file, the next step is to begin execution under control of the debugger. To do this you must enter:

```
CLD [[/43 | /50 | /s] [@<scriptFile>] <progname> [<argList>]]
```

at the DOS prompt, where <progname> is the name of your executable file. You may also choose the screen display mode by choosing *one* of these switches: /43, /50, or /S. The /43 switch requests 43 line display mode for EGA monitors only; the /50 switch requests 50 line mode for VGA monitors only; and the /S requests a split screen for either EGA or VGA monitors showing both the user screen and debugger screen at the same time.

Invoking the debugger will load your program and begin execution with the program "halted" on the first executable statement. All this means is that the program is loaded into RAM and remains waiting for your instructions to the debugger. The initial debugger screen that you see contains an image of your source code. It is at this point that you may begin to issue various debugger commands either by selecting them from menus or by entering them in command line form.

Debugger Features

There are actually two methods of directing the debugger: by selecting menu options or by entering commands at the command-prompt line. Which method you choose, depends on your experience level. As a Clipper beginner, you'll want to begin with the menus and then progress to commands. The various options selectable from the menus may also be accessed at the command prompt by first entering the menu name followed by the first word of the menu item desired (or a single letter abbreviation of both). For example, to turn on the preprocessor output display, you could either press Alt+O to pull down the Options menu and then select Preprocessor, or you could enter Option and then Preprocessor (or O and then P for short) at the command prompt to achieve the same function.

Rather than simply entering command-prompt equivalents of menu options, the debugger also has several special command prompt specific features. Table 1.3 summarizes the debugger commands available only from the command line.

Debugger Basics

In this section, we will not attempt to present an exhaustive survey of the Clipper debugger, but rather a beginner's introduction to the concept of shap-

Table 1.3 Debugger Command Line Features

Command	Description
`? <expr>`	Displays the value of a variable or expression
`?? <expr>`	Inspects the value of a variable or expression
`ANIMATE`	Executes application in Animate mode
`BP [[AT] [<lineNum>] [[IN] <programFile>]]`	Sets or removes a breakpoint
`BP <functionName>	<procedureName>`	Sets or removes a breakpoint
`CALLSTACK [on|OFF]`	Toggles display of CallStack window
`DELETE ALL [WP|TP|BP]`	Deletes all Watchpoints, Tracepoints, or Breakpoints
`DELETE WB|TP|BP <number>`	Deletes all or particular Watchpoint, Tracepoint, or Breakpoint
`FILE DOS`	Temporarily goes to the DOS prompt
`FILE EXIT`	Exits the Debugger and returns to DOS
`FILE OPEN <fileName>`	Examines a file during the current debugging session
`FILE RESUME`	Returns from viewing a file
`HELP`	Invokes the Help window
`LIST BP|WP|TP`	Lists Breakpoints, Watchpoints, or Tracepoints in the Command Window
`LOCATE CASE`	Turns on/off case sensitivity setting. This is a toggle
`LOCATE FIND <searchString>`	Searches the currently viewed program file for a specified character string
`LOCATE GOTO <lineNum>`	Moves the cursor to the specified line in currently viewed program file
`LOCATE NEXT`	Searches for the next occurrence of the FIND string
`LOCATE PREVIOUS`	Searches for previous occurrence of FIND string
`MONITOR ALL`	Toggles the display of all variables—regardless of storage class—in the Monitor window
`MONITOR LOCAL`	Toggles the display of LOCAL variables in the Monitor window
`MONITOR PRIVATE`	Toggles the display of PRIVATE variables in the Monitor window
`MONITOR PUBLIC`	Toggles display of PUBLIC variables in the Monitor window
`MONITOR SORT`	Sorts the variables displayed in the Monitor window by name regardless of storage class

Table 1.3 Debugger Command Line Features (Continued)

Command	Description
`MONITOR STATIC`	Toggles the display of STATIC variables in the Monitor window
`NUM ON|off`	Toggles the display of line numbers in Code window
`OPTIONS CODEBLOCK`	Controls whether or not the debugger traces code blocks in Single Step mode
`OPTIONS COLOR`	Activates the Set Colors window
`OPTIONS EXCHANGE`	Controls the display of program output while in Animate mode
`OPTIONS LINE`	Controls the display of line numbers at the beginning of each line in the Code Window
`OPTIONS MENU`	Toggles the display of the Debugger Menu Bar
`OPTIONS MONO`	Toggles the Debugger display mode between color and monochrome
`OPTIONS PATH <pathList>`	Defines the search path for source code files; <pathList> is one or more DOS pathnames separated by semicolons
`OPTIONS PREPROCESSED`	Toggles the display of preprocessed code in the Code window; the original source is still displayed
`OPTIONS RESTORE <scriptFile>`	Reads commands from the specified debugger Script File
`OPTIONS SAVE <scriptFile>`	Saves the current Debugger settings to a Script File
`OPTIONS SWAP`	Controls whether or not the application screen is displayed when input from the user is required
`OPTIONS TAB <tabSize>`	Sets the tab size for the Code window
`POINT BREAKPOINT`	Sets or removes a Breakpoint at the current line in the program
`POINT DELETE`	Deletes a Tracepoint or Watchpoint
`POINT TRACEPOINT <expression>`	Defines a variable or expression as a Tracepoint
`POINT WATCHPOINT <expression>`	Defines a variable or expression as a Watchpoint
`RUN ANIMATE`	Executes an application in Animate mode
`RUN GO`	Executes an application in Run mode
`RUN NEXT`	Executes an application in Run mode until the next call of a function, procedure, code block, or message send

Table 1.3 Debugger Command Line Features (Continued)

Command	Description
`RUN RESTART`	Restarts an application with the current debugger settings
`RUN SPEED <delay>`	Defines the step delay for Animate mode
`RUN STEP`	Executes one line of program code in Single Step mode
`RUN TO`	Executes the current program up to the cursor position and then halts
`RUN TRACE`	Executes the current program in Trace mode
`VIEW <fileName>`	Views the specified program file in the Code window
`VIEW APP`	Views the application screen; to return to the debugger, press any key
`VIEW CALLSTACK`	Toggles the Callstack window
`VIEW SETS`	Displays the View Sets window
`VIEW WORKSREAS`	Displays the View Workareas window
`WINDOW ICONIZE`	Toggles the currently active Debugger window between an icon and a window display
`WINDOW MOVE`	Repositions the active window on the Debugger screen
`WINDOW NEXT`	Selects the next Debugger window, making it active
`WINDOW PREV`	Selects the previous Debugger window, making it active
`WINDOW SIZE`	Resizes the currently active Debugger window
`WINDOW TILE`	Restores default size and position of Debugger windows
`WINDOW ZOOM`	Toggles the currently active Debugger window between window and full screen display

ing a program's correctness through use of a debugger. In this pursuit, we will now present you with a few common techniques to gain experience with the debugger. We assume that throughout the rest of the book, you will use the debugger as the basis for experimenting with the various code samples.

As for our discussion now, however, you must enter the following program into a program file named DTEST.PRG and compile and link it to produce an executable.

```
FUNCTION Main

LOCAL nCount, nSum := 0
FOR nCount := 1 TO 100
```

```
    nSum += nCount
    ? nCount, nSum
NEXT

RETURN NIL
```

Then, bring up the program under the debugger and you should see the screen shown in Figure 1.7.

In the Xbase days before debuggers, the methods by which developers would discover and eradicate bugs from their software included dropping down to the DOT prompt and using various interactive commands such as ?, DISPLAY MEMORY, and DISPLAY STATUS to obtain a "snapshot" of the dBASE environment at the time the program aborted with the hope that this knowledge would shed light on the problem area. In a compiled environment, the DOT prompt scenario is unavailable so early Xbase compiler users had to resort to embedded *implants* in their programs. Implants were strategically positioned commands (usually ? and @...SAY) that would display the contents of key memory variables. This method worked, but required a complete re-compile and re-link of the program, often a timely task.

Figure 1.7 You will see this screen when you begin debugging a program.

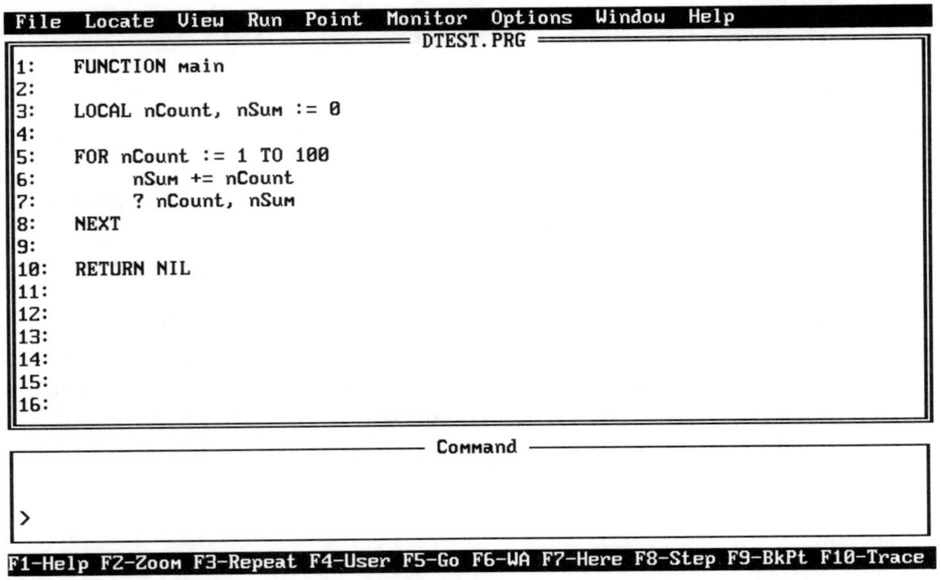

```
 File  Locate  View  Run  Point  Monitor  Options  Window  Help
═══════════════════════════════ DTEST.PRG ═══════════════════════════════
1:     FUNCTION main
2:
3:     LOCAL nCount, nSum := 0
4:
5:     FOR nCount := 1 TO 100
6:         nSum += nCount
7:         ? nCount, nSum
8:     NEXT
9:
10:    RETURN NIL
11:
12:
13:
14:
15:
16:
─────────────────────────────── Command ────────────────────────────────
>

F1-Help F2-Zoom F3-Repeat F4-User F5-Go F6-WA F7-Here F8-Step F9-BkPt F10-Trace
```

> **Note** The implant method may still find some utility in contemporary CA-Clipper development due to features of the Clipper preprocessor that allow for conditional compilation. This way, you can include debugging code in your program for use with the debugger and later easily "leave out" the code from the .EXE without physically removing it from the .PRG files. Chapter 3 explains this feature.

The features available in the CA-Clipper debugger offer this kind of simple variable monitoring and much more. Let's first itemize the different classes of debugging practices you can expect to perform with the debugger:

Monitor Variable Contents — The debugger allows you to specify that memory variables are to be monitored in a separate window. You may request that PRIVATE, PUBLIC, LOCAL, STATIC, or ALL variables be included.

Single Step the Program — This feature (using the F8 function key) provides for one of the oldest forms of debugging of computer programs. Often a program runs so quickly that a human has a difficult time discerning what is happening. By slowing down the execution process to one command at a time, the programmer is better able to grasp where things are going wrong. There is also a feature (using the F7 function key) where you may highlight a specific statement in your program and have the debugger execute until that statement is reached. In this way, you may execute quickly through code that you already know is working properly and go directly to the problem code.

Setting Breakpoints — As an expansion to the feature above, you may specify one or more breakpoints in a program (using the F9 function key). A *breakpoint* is a statement that when reached causes the program to halt so that you may "look around" to find any potential problems. Breakpoints are useful when you don't know exactly where a program is going astray and that by stopping it at key areas, may lead to some additional information. Once the program halts at a breakpoint, you may for example, check out the contents of specific variables by using the ? command at the Debugger command line:

```
? cEmpName
? EOF()
? txn->orderno
```

Also, you may need to check out which files, indexes, etc. are open at the time the breakpoint occurred.

Setting Watchpoints and Tracepoints

Both watchpoints and tracepoints are expansions of the concepts mentioned above. A *watchpoint* allows you to specify a variable whose value is to be constantly displayed in the special Watchpoint window. A *tracepoint* is similar to a watchpoint, with the added capability where each time the variable changes, the program halts for you to do some investigative work.

Monitor the Callstack

Since most programs you will write involve the interaction of multiple program modules (.PRG files, user defined functions, and procedures), it is useful to monitor which program has called which other program and in effect keep a history of this calling sequence of program modules. This is especially needed when the number of calling levels is large.

The Norton Guides

One particularly nice bonus that accompanies the CA-Clipper product is the Norton Guides online documentation. The Norton Guides product from Symantec is an interactive text retrieval and browsing tool included with many programming and non-programming software packages. The NG.EXE engine reads .NG online document files. Computer Associates, Inc. includes several .NG files for this purpose. After a full install of CA-Clipper, the /NG directory (off the root of your hard drive) contains these files along with the engine. To invoke the Norton Guides, simply enter NG at the DOS prompt. NG operates as a RAM resident utility, meaning that you may "pop-up" the guides over your text editor, over the debugger, or even over your running application. This feature is extremely useful for impromptu review of the CA-Clipper documentation (e.g. when you forget the parameter list of a built-in function).

You may think to yourself that if you have the manuals why do you need online documentation. The reason the Norton Guides for CA-Clipper are included is because they often contain more complete, more up-to-date, and often more detailed documentation than the manuals. The manuals and the Norton Guides should complement each other during the application development process.

Summary

In this chapter, we have set the stage for the beginning application developer to become productive with the CA-Clipper Xbase language compiler. We've looked at important topics in getting your PC's environment tuned up and illustrated all the components that accompany the product. The rest of the book focuses on the Clipper language and how to build applications.

Language Basics

> The Clipper Coding Style ➤ 32
> Data Types ➤ 35
> FIELD/MEMVAR Statements ➤ 37
> The Assignment Operator ➤ 38
> Other Operators ➤ 38
> Relational Operators ➤ 40
> The Fall of Macros ➤ 41
> Extended Expressions ➤ 41
> Alias Functions ➤ 42
> An Improved IF Statement ➤ 43
> The DO WHILE Looping Structure ➤ 44
> The FOR/NEXT Looping Structure ➤ 46
> The DO CASE/ENDCASE Control Structure ➤ 46
> The BEGIN/END SEQUENCE Control Structure ➤ 47
> Screen Input/Output ➤ 51
> Summary ➤ 60
> Exercise ➤ 60

In order to program in the Clipper language the way that was intended, its new and enhanced basic constructs should be used to the fullest extent. Once a developer has decided to make the move to Clipper, a second decision must also be made as to how much of the language will be used. At the low end, Clipper can be used as a glorified dBASE III Plus compiler, but if it is used in this manner, the end result will not perform up to expectations. Moreover, it would be a waste not to utilize all the enhanced constructs lurking in CA-Clipper that make programming easier, the resulting code easier to maintain, and the end result much more elegant. As stated earlier, in this book we promote writing *CA-Clipper optimized code*. This is code that takes advantage of the features that make Clipper stand out in terms of performance, extensibility, and maintainability.

The first place in which a first time CA-Clipper developer must focus is the area of basic language components such as overall coding philosophy, data types, operators, extended expressions, alias functions, and additional basic language constructs. In this chapter, we'll look at each of these issues in order to lay a framework for more comprehensive programming.

After completing this chapter we will have covered the following areas:

- The CA-Clipper *coding style*, which includes indenting, commenting, case usage in keywords, and user defined portions of a program
- Data types and the use of *Hungarian notation*, the self-imposed typing of memory variables
- How to apply the various new and enhanced language constructs available, including: revised operators, extended expressions, alias functions, limited use of macros, `IF/ELSE/ELSEIF/ENDIF`, `DO WHILE/ENDDO`, `FOR/NEXT`, `DO CASE/ENDCASE`, and `BEGIN/END SEQUENCE`
- Screen input and output including the traditional `@ SAY GET` command, screen saving and restoring, simple menuing, and keyboard stuffing

The Clipper Coding Style

Before we present any programs or code segments in this book, it is necessary to address the topic of comments and general coding style. Every effort should be taken to engage in *program beautification*, the process of making a computer program more aesthetically pleasing to both yourself and others. However, a pretty program does more than make the reviewer smile. There is also a technological basis for making programs nice to look at. Programs that are well commented, well indented, and interspersed with blank lines to identify related blocks of code inside a program module contain many benefits. For example, well-formed programs enable you to maintain a strong sense of direction when coding.

With the initial Clipper 5 release, commenting was made more attractive by allowing for the more "C-like" notation using // and /* */. The // comment syntax operates in the same manner and therefore replaces Xbase's && as in many of the examples shown in this book. The symbols /* */ lets you bracket off a group of text that shall be considered comments. The most common usage of this type of commenting is in surrounding major comment blocks such as those preceding subprogram code.

```
/***
*
* DispMsg( <cMsg>, <nTone>, <nDuration> ) -> NIL
*
* This function displays a message cMsg, sounds a tone
* described by nTone, for a duration of nDuration.
*
*/
```

The *comment block* in this example could have been written with an * as the first non-blank character of each line, but it is more easily done with /* */. This style of comment block was made popular in current the CA-Clipper community by the original developers of the Clipper 5 compiler.

Also illustrated here is a method of formally defining subprograms in CA-Clipper, namely using comments that self-document the program's calling sequence. We see in this example the prototype of the user defined function `DispMsg()`. The prototype includes all parameters in Hungarian notation plus the return value. You are encouraged to include a comment block and prototype in each subprogram of your future applications.

Indenting is another important concept that should be considered when speaking of coding style. I'm sure everyone has encountered Xbase and possibly older Clipper code like this:

```
CLEAR ALL
USE trans INDEX txncode
rec_cnt = 0
rejects = 0
DO WHILE .NOT. EOF()
IF trans->type = 'A'
? 'Found type A', trans->cust_name
rec_cnt = rec_cnt + 1
ELSE
rejects = rejects + 1
ENDIF
SKIP
ENDDO
CLOSE DATABASES
RETURN
```

The best one can say of this kind of code is that it is "un-inspired." In reality, programs without indents provide no sense of program structure and actually detract from an understanding of program flow. We highly recommend that indenting be placed in program code for each occurrence of any language construct that groups lines. Here is a list of these constructs:

```
DO WHILE/ENDDO
FOR/NEXT
IF/ELSE/ELSEIF/ENDIF
DO CASE/ENDCASE
BEGIN/END SEQUENCE
```

In addition, whenever a line continues on to one or more additional lines, indentation should be part of continuation lines. In Xbase, the norm is an indent level of three spaces, however, a deeper look—say, five spaces—is often preferable. Now consider the previous program module reformatted with indentations:

```
LOCAL nRecCnt := 0; nRejects := 0
CLEAR ALL
USE Trans INDEX TxnCode

WHILE !EOF()
   IF Trans->Type == 'A'
      ? 'Found type A', Trans->CustName
      nRecCnt++
   ELSE
      nRejects++
   ENDIF
   DBSKIP()
END
DBCLOSEAREA()

RETURN NIL
```

Another area of coding style that can drastically improve readability concerns multi-statements and continuation lines. Traditionally, the semicolon has provided a means to continue statements onto more than one line. Clipper continues to support this convention but adds another use of the semicolon, namely to allow for more than one complete statement on a single line. Many times it makes sense to group lines that together perform a single logical operation all on one program line. In Xbase, we might encounter:

```
* Update report counters
page_cnt = page_cnt + 1
line_cnt = 0
rec_cnt = 0
```

In CA-Clipper, we can rewrite this code all on a single line separated by semicolons as:

```
nPageCnt++ ; nLineCnt++; nRecCnt++
```

In the balance of the book, the many code samples represent a suggested coding style that will bring your code state-of-the-Clipper-art.

Data Types

CA-Clipper has all the Xbase data types plus a few new ones. The following is a complete list of all data types that a memory variable may assume:

- Character
- Numeric
- Date
- Logical
- Array
- Code Block
- Object
- NIL

As for database fields, only the standard Xbase Character, Numeric, Date, Logical, and Memo types are available. The type of a memory variable is determined by the type of the value it is first assigned. This is called *dynamic typing* and is considered a characteristic of a weakly typed language. The type of a memory variable may be changed dynamically by simply assigning it a value of a different type. Computer science purists have always considered this a shortcoming, if not a dangerous part of the Xbase standard. Xbase enthusiasts, on the other hand, have normally viewed dynamic typing as a programming plus, affording the flexibility to change types at will. Regardless of which camp you find yourself ascribing to, the use of Hungarian notation, along with a strict adherence to maintaining the initial type, type confusion can be avoided.

> **Note**
>
> Clipper recognizes memory variable names up to ten characters in length. This is not to say that you cannot use longer names, but only that the first ten characters are significant. Make sure that if you decide to use long names that there are no ties up to and including the tenth character. For example, the assignment statements:
>
> ```
> nSalaryRate := 25750
> nSalaryRateChange := 0.05
> ```

actually refer to the same variable because the names are the same up to the tenth character. This could obviously lead to dangerous situations and Clipper will not flag this as an error.

Also, it is customary in Clipper programming circles to abandon the Xbase usage of underscore characters to separate words in a variable name. Instead, the use of mixed case names is superior as it saves the use of one valuable significant character in the name. Consider the following Xbase name and its more contemporary Clipper counterpart:

```
HIRE_DATE = CTOD('12/08/63')      // Old Xbase style.
dHireDate := Employee->Hire       // New Clipper style.
```

The following declaration statement assigns a value of each available type to a memory variable:

```
LOCAL  cZIP      :='90024-4559',;
       nSalary   :=45675,;
       dHireDate :=CTOD('10/27/60'),;
       lFullTime :=.T.,;
       aTaxRate  :={8.25, 7.75, 6.5},;
       bMax      :={|a| maxwidth:=MAX(maxwidth, a) },;
       oBrowser  :=TBrowseNEW(10,10,20,70),;
       vTemp     := Unknown()
```

Among other things, this example demonstrates the Hungarian naming conventions, how to construct constant values for each data type, and the use of the inline assignment operator := (which we'll learn more about later). Notice that the last memory variable defined, `vTemp`, has a prefix of "v." This indicates that this memory variable can have a variable data type during program execution. In other words, this variable is expected to undergo dynamic retyping.

It is often convenient to be able to determine the type of a memory variable during execution. For example, a procedure or user-defined function may need to obtain the type of a parameter that is passed to it for proper processing. For this purpose, CA-Clipper has two built-in functions, `TYPE()` and `VALTYPE()`. The `VALTYPE()` function is generally considered more convenient. Both functions return a one or two character code indicating the type of the parameter.

The `TYPE()` function requires a single character expression parameter enclosed in quotes. For example, `TYPE("aMonth")` would return a character value "A" indicating an array type whereas `TYPE("aMonth[10]")` returns a "C" since the tenth element of the array holds a character string.

The following code to report the types of the memory variables assigned in the previous example will produce the output as indicated:

```
?  VALTYPE(cZIP), VALTYPE(nSalary), VALTYPE(dHireDate)
?? VALTYPE(lFullTime), VALTYPE(aTaxRate), VALTYPE(bMax)
?? VALTYPE(oBrowser), VALTYPE(vTemp)

* Results:   C  N  D  L  A  B  O  U
```

Notice that the type returned for `vTemp` is "U." This is because CA-Clipper assigns the value `NIL` to all declared, but uninitialized variables, so a type check of a variable whose value is `NIL` is "U" or undefined.

FIELD/MEMVAR Statements

As it is always favorable to explicitly declare all program data items, the `FIELD` and `MEMVAR` declaration statements allow you to tell CA-Clipper that certain identifiers are database fields using the `FIELD` statement. At the same time, the `MEMVAR` statement may be used to declare an identifier as being a memory variable.

Two common programming practices, however, make these two declaratives less needed. First, if you consistently prefix an alias before all database field references, then the `FIELD` statement is not needed. Here are a couple of examples without and with alias notation:

```
* First without alias
@ 10,25 SAY 'Enter customer name: GET Name
* Now with the alias
@ 10,25 SAY 'Enter customer name: GET   Customer->Name

* First without alias
ZipCode := '90278'              // Field or memory variable?
* Now with the alias
Customer->ZipCode := '90278'    // Now no conflict.
```

In both cases, the benefit should be obvious for including an alias, because without one, you cannot be sure if you are dealing with a database field or memory variable. Plus in programs manipulating more than one database, it is possible that the same field name exists in two or more database files. Specifying an alias cures both possible areas of conflict.

Second, if you consistently declare all memory variables in either a `LOCAL` or `STATIC` declarative statement (a topic for Chapter 5), then the `MEMVAR` declarative is not needed. We'll detail this a bit later during our discussion of the `@...GET` statement, which you will need to declare a special variable called `GETLIST` with a `MEMVAR` statement.

The Assignment Operator

As you saw in the previous section, the new := *assignment operator* is used to place a value in a memory variable or database field. This is in contrast to the use of =, which in Xbase is an *overloaded operator*, sometimes meaning assignment, sometimes meaning a test for equality, depending on context. In CA-Clipper, you can still use the = for assignment, but this use is discouraged in favor of the assignment operator. There are other reasons for using the assignment operator, namely because it may be more liberally placed in a program. Consider the following examples:

```
nSalary := 25000
IF (dDate := (DATE()-365)) > CTOD('10/27/60')
? SQRT(nValue := (nValue**2))
cCustNo := cSortSeq := Custfile->CustNo + DTOC(DATE())
CustFile->CustNo := Txn->TxnNo := cCustNo + DTOC(DATE())
```

First we see that := can be used as a substitute for = when assigning values to a memory variable. This has become quite fashionable in Clipper circles.

In the IF statement, the logical expression has two components, on the right side is a date constant, but the left side has an inline assignment. Here, the value (DATE()-365) is used for the comparison, but in addition it will be assigned to the memory variable dDate. Of course, the same could be done in Xbase, but two lines are needed. CA-Clipper, as will become evident, has many such shortcuts.

In the second example, the built-in SQRT() function is called, but its argument contains an inline assignment. The numeric expression nValue**2 is evaluated, passed to SQRT() and assigned to nValue. The third example shows a multiple assignment (which in Xbase can only be done with a STORE command). Finally, the assignment operator may be used instead of the REPLACE command to assign values to database fields.

Other Operators

CA-Clipper has many other operators to make the programming task more streamlined. First, we'll look at the increment ++ and decrement -- operators:

```
nValue++ ; nValue--
```

We see that in Clipper we no longer need to write:

```
nValue = nValue+1
```

since the increment operator achieves the same purpose. The decrement operator acts the same as nValue=nValue-1.

There are actually two forms of both the increment and decrement operators. The previous examples show the post-increment and post-decrement form. This means that the increment shall be performed *after* the original value is used in an expression. This is in contrast to the pre-increment and pre-decrement form, in which the operation is carried out *before* the value is used. Let's see some examples to clarify this concept:

```
LOCAL nValue:=0, nNewValue, nValue1, nValue2

* Prefix-increment operator
nValue := 0
nNewValue := ++nValue    // Change nValue BEFORE assignment.
? nValue                 // 1
? nNewValue              // 1

* Postfix-decrement operator
nValue := 1
nNewValue := nValue--    // Change nValue AFTER assignment.
? nValue                 // 0
? nNewValue              // 1

* Postfix-increment operator in an expression
nValue := 10
? nValue++ * nValue      // 110: use 10, incr, multiply by 11.
? nValue                 // 11

* Prefix-decrement operator in an expression
nValue := 10
? --nValue * nValue      // 81: decr, use 9, multiply by 9.
? nValue                 // 9

* Combined prefix and postfix operators
nValue := 10
? --nValue * nValue++    // 81: decr, use 9, mult by 9, incr.
? nValue                 // 10

* Combined prefix and postfix operators
nValue1 := 10
nValue2 := 10
? --nValue1 * nValue2++  // 90: decr, use 9, mult by 10, incr.
? nValue1                // 9
? nValue2                // 11
```

The comments associated with each usage detail how the expression is evaluated. If the answers don't make sense, just try to remember the difference between when a memory variable is *used* in an expression versus when it is *updated* with an increment or decrement operator.

There is also a set of operators that provide a shorthand notation when you want to update a variable's contents. Consider the following example that takes the place of `nValue := nValue + 365` and is used to make your code more concise:

```
nValue += 365   // Updates nValue.
                // also:  -=   *=   /=   %=   ^=
```

Relational Operators

As mentioned earlier, the = operator is overloaded in Xbase. CA-Clipper has created yet another operator to combat this situation. The *exactly equal* operator (==) is used in logical expressions to test equivalence. Although it can be used with any data type and it has become vogue to do so, == has special significance for character string comparisons. The basic difference between = and == lies in the way strings of unequal length are handled. The code sample shown next shall illustrate this. Moreover, = is affected by the current setting of SET EXACT whereas == is not. The following sample code illustrates how these two relational operators work:

```
SET EXACT OFF
? '123' = ''           // Always .T. if right string is null.
? '' = '123'           // Always .F. if right is longer.
? '123' = '123456'     // Same as above.
? '123456' = '123'     // Do comparison for each right string
                       // character. If all equal then .T.
```

Now with SET EXACT ON, all of the above logical expressions evaluate to .F. since strings with unequal lengths are automatically unequal. In addition, comparisons with = and SET EXACT OFF first begin by removing all trailing spaces (not physically, but just for the comparison). Under these conditions the following expression is evaluated as .T.:

```
SET EXACT ON
? '123' = '123'        // .T. since equal in length and equal
                       // in characters.
```

With the == operator, things are much simpler. First, the setting of SET EXACT does not matter; in fact it is a good idea to leave EXACT OFF, which is the default for the duration of the program. Consider the following:

```
? 'Fredi' == 'Fred'    // .F. since unequal in length.
? 'DDG' == 'DDG'       // .T. the only time equal is possible.
```

One other worthy mention at this point is the *not equal* operator (!=). For Xbase programmers testing for inequality has required the use of the obscure <> or # operators. Now, with CA-Clipper, we are able to use the more recognizable .NOT. operator (!) in conjunction with the equal sign. This operator also makes its way into the use of logical functions such as EOF() where testing for "not end-of-file" becomes !EOF().

The Fall of Macros

Most Xbase people, including developers coming from Clipper S'87, have all been educated to incorporate the use of the & macro operator. Indeed, in those dialects, & was an evil that most people convinced themselves was not only necessary but was also a good thing. CA-Clipper has taken the position that not only is & usually not necessary but is, in fact, a bad thing. It can easily be proved that programs with heavy use of & yield poorer performance than those that don't.

There are two specific applications (among others) of & that can now be avoided in CA-Clipper. One area is solved by extended expressions, the other by code blocks. We'll take a look at these areas in the next section.

Extended Expressions

A very useful CA-Clipper feature is *extended expressions*. Extended expressions represent a path away from a commonly used application of macros. Here is an example:

```
* Macro method
cDBFName := 'Orders'      // Variable DBF name becomes part of USE.
USE &cDBFName
```

can now be replaced with

```
* Extended expression method
USE (cDBFName)            // Clean alternative with no &.
```

thus eliminating a macro expansion. Another application of & is with variable database field names as in

```
* Macro method
cCodeField := 'CustNo'    // Variable field name becomes part of
                          // the REPLACE statement.
REPLACE &cCodeField WITH cTemp
```

which can be replaced in CA-Clipper with:

```
* Code block method
LOCAL cField:='SuppNo', bField
USE Supplier NEW
bField := FIELDBLOCK(cField)      // Create retrieval/assignment
                                  // code block for SuppNo.
EVAL(bField, 'DDG001')
```

In this example, the `FIELDBLOCK()` built-in function builds a code block (a topic that deserves a whole discussion itself in *Chapter 6*), which when evaluated, either gets or sets a database field's value. This example sets the field. If just the field's value is to be retrieved, `EVAL(bField)` would suffice. In this example, you can see that macros are no longer needed for variable field name situations.

Alias Functions

CA-Clipper has the big improvement over Xbase of enabling database-oriented functions to operate on a *non-selected work area*. Just as we prefixed a field name with an alias earlier, we can do the same to built-in and user-defined functions. The following example illustrates how this works:

```
? Customer->(EOF())       // Test end-of-file in CUSTOMER work area.
? Movie->(RECNO())        // Get current record number in MOVIE.
? Txn->(BOF())            // Test beginning-of-file in TXN work area.
? Txn->(DELETED())        // Return deleted flag of current record
                          // in TXN work area.
? Txn->(FCOUNT())         // Get number of fields in TXN work area.
? Txn->(LASTREC())        // Return last record number in TXN.
? Txn->(RECCOUNT())       // Display number of records in TXN.
? Txn->(RECSIZE())        // Record size in TXN work area.
```

In Xbase, you would have to use a `SELECT` statement in order to bring the desired work area into view and then perform the function. With CA-Clipper, you can even define your own `SEEK()` UDF (in Chapter 8, we'll see that the built-in `DBSEEK()` is also available) and use it in the following way:

```
Txn->(SEEK(Movie->ItemNo))
```

Aliased functions are extremely flexible, but you may prefer to have `ALIAS` clauses available for all related commands as in CA-Clipper's standard `SKIP` command:

```
SKIP 1 ALIAS Customer
```

SKIP is the only CA-Clipper command with an `ALIAS` clause, but using a feature of CA-Clipper's preprocessor (User-Defined Commands, which is the subject of Chapter 4) you can have

```
SEEK Movie->ItemNo   ALIAS Txn
```

even though this is not part of the CA-Clipper language definition.

An Improved IF Statement

One long lived Xbase *flow-of-control* statement that received a facelift in CA-Clipper is the `IF` statement. Clipper's improved `IF` statement allows for a structure more conducive to understandable code. The formal definition of the `IF` statement in CA-Clipper is:

```
IF <lExpr>
   .
   . <statements>
   .
[ELSEIF <lExpr>]
   .
   . <statements>
   .
[ELSE]
   .
   . <statements>
   .
ENDIF
```

When an `IF` statement is encountered as a program executes, the logical expression `<lexpr>` is evaluated. If the value is .T. then the statements immediately following the `IF` statement are executed until either an `ELSEIF`, `ELSE`, or `ENDIF` is encountered. If, on the other hand, the value is .F. then the statements following the `IF` statement are skipped and the next `ELSEIF`'s logical expression is evaluated (if there is an `ELSEIF`), or the code following the `ELSE` is executed (if there is an `ELSE`). In the simplest case, there is only an `IF` and `ENDIF` as in the following example:

```
* Simple IF/ENDIF
IF nSalary >= 25400
   nSenior++    // Skipped if nSalary < 25400.
ENDIF
```

The difference between Clipper's `IF` statement and the standard Xbase IF is in the addition of the optional `ELSEIF` component. In essence, `ELSEIF` is a shorthand way of embedding another `IF` statement inside the `ELSE` portion of an `IF` statement. For example, in Xbase you had to represent a long network of `IF` conditions in the following manner:

```
IF lFullTime              // If full time employee, then give
   nSalary *= 1.05        // 5% raise.
ELSE                      // Otherwise, calculate part time
   IF nPctTime > 0.4      // If better than 40% time, then
      nSalary * 1.1       // 10% raise.
   ELSE                   // No, <= 40% time
      IF nPctTime > 0.25  // If > 25%, then
         nSalary *= 1.15  // 15% raise
      ELSE                // No, <= 25% time
         nSalary *= 1.2   // 20% raise.
      ENDIF
   ENDIF
ENDIF
```

In this example, the logic requires that the `IF` be nested to three levels. As the logic becomes more complex, the nesting level increases and the code becomes unwieldy (not to mention excessively deep in indentation). Using Clipper's `ELSEIF` construct, we can simplify the situation somewhat:

```
IF lFullTime              // Full time gets smallest raise
   nSalary *= 1.05        // 5%.
ELSEIF nPctTime > 0.4     // Part time > 40% time gets
   nSalary * 1.1          // 10%.
ELSEIF nPctTime > 0.25    // Part time > 25% time gets
   nSalary *= 1.15        // 15%.
ELSE                      // Part time < 25% time gets
   nSalary *= 1.2         // 20%.
ENDIF
```

This version is easier to comprehend and illustrates how `ELSEIF` can aid in structuring a program. Notice also that `ELSEIF` helps keep the nesting depth a bit more under control. In fact, this `IF` organization is structured more like a `DO CASE/ENDCASE` statement as we'll see later in this chapter.

The DO WHILE Looping Structure

Now let's turn our attention to the standard Xbase looping construct `DO WHILE/ENDDO` and give it a CA-Clipper facelift. The formal definition of the `DO WHILE` statement in CA-Clipper is:

```
[DO] WHILE <lExpr>
   <statements>
   [EXIT]
```

```
   <statements>
   [LOOP]
   <statements>
END[DO]
```

As we can see in the definition, the keywords DO WHILE and ENDDO may be abbreviated to WHILE and END respectively. When a program encounters a WHILE statement, the logical expression <lexpr> is evaluated and if its value is .T., the statements immediately following the WHILE, up until the END statement, are executed. Then, control is passed back up (a looping effect) to WHILE where the logical expression is re-evaluated. This process continues until the logical expression evaluates to .F. A WHILE may not execute the statements in between the WHILE and END even one time, if the expression is .F. to start with.

There are two additional commands associated with looping in CA-Clipper. The first is LOOP, which is an unconditional transfer of control while inside a loop back up to the loop control statement (WHILE in our case now). The second statement is EXIT, which causes an unconditional premature exit of the loop to the line immediately after END. These statements have no effect outside of a looping structure.

Now for an example, consider the old style loop used to process all records in TRANS.DBF containing the given customer number:

```
* Xbase style looping
USE trans INDEX custno
xcustno = 'DDG001'
SEEK xcustno
DO WHILE custno=xcustno .AND. .NOT. EOF()
   ? itemno, qty, price
   SKIP
ENDDO
```

Now let's see the CA-Clipper version of this program:

```
LOCAL cCustNum := 'DDG001'
USE Trans INDEX CustNo
SEEK cCustNum
WHILE Trans->CustNo == cCustNum .AND. !EOF()
   ? Trans->ItemNo, Trans->Qty, Trans->Price
   DBSKIP()
END     // End of processing.
```

In this version of the loop, we have dropped the DO from the DO WHILE and have shortened ENDDO to just END. Notice also that even though the old Xbase practice of including *undelimited comments* at the tail end of the ENDDO (as is the case for ENDIF and ENDCASE) statement, Clipper programmers should resist and insert the // for consistency.

The FOR/NEXT Looping Structure

In addition to WHILE/END, CA-Clipper also has the FOR/NEXT looping construct. The formal definition of the FOR statement in CA-Clipper is:

```
FOR <counterVar> := <nStart> TO <nEnd> [STEP <nIncr>]
   <statements>
   [EXIT]
   <statements>
   [LOOP]
   <statements>
NEXT
```

When a program encounters a FOR loop, the loop control variable <counterVar> is initialized to the starting value <nStart>, a comparison is then made against the ending value <nEnd>. If <nStart> is *less than or equal to* <nEnd>, then the statements immediately following the FOR statement are executed until the NEXT statement is encountered. Control is then passed back up (a looping effect) to the FOR where the control variable is incremented by <nIncr> or the default value of 1 if <nIncr> is not specified.

The FOR statement is better suited for looping situations where the number of iterations is known, determined, and/or not connected to a database. Both the LOOP and EXIT statements also work with the FOR loop. Here is an example of using the FOR loop:

```
dEndDate := CTOD('08/15/94')
FOR nWeek := 1 TO 20
   dEndDate -= 7    // One week prior.
NEXT
? 'Date twenty weeks ago is: ', dEndDate
```

The DO CASE/ENDCASE Control Structure

One flow of control construct that is common in most contemporary programming disciplines is the CASE statement (used in a generic sense). CA-Clipper's equivalent is called DO CASE/ENDCASE. You may think of DO CASE/ENDCASE as an orderly sequence of IF statements and, in fact, we could represent any CASE statement as a network of IFs. The point is that a CASE is more suitable for situations where the series of conditions are related in some manner and an itemized list makes sense. The formal definition of the DO CASE/ENDCASE statement in CA-Clipper is:

```
DO CASE
   CASE <lExpr1>
      <statements>
   [CASE <lExpr2>]
```

```
      <statements>
   .
   .
   .
   [OTHERWISE]
      <statements>
END[CASE]
```

Next is an example of DO CASE/ENDCASE where we need to apply a different sales tax rate depending on a specific county code. Note that this code could have been implemented with a network of IF statements, but a CASE structure is more appropriate because it reads better:

```
.
. <statements>
.
DO CASE
   CASE Customer->County == '01'
      nTaxRate := .0825
   CASE Customer->County == '07'
      nTaxRate := .0775
   CASE Customer->County == '13'
      nTaxRate := .08
ENDCASE
nTaxAmount := Orders->Qty * nTaxRate
```

The BEGIN/END SEQUENCE Control Structure

Another language feature unique to CA-Clipper is the BEGIN/END SEQUENCE construct, along with the associated statements BREAK and RECOVER. These statements create a flow-of-control structure that may be used for *exception handling*. We use the term exception handling to mean the ability of a program to determine that an exceptional condition has arisen and then to process the condition appropriately (or even abort the program if necessary).

Let's now describe how this construct operates. Program control first passes through the BEGIN SEQUENCE statement. If the code following the BEGIN SEQUENCE (up until the corresponding RECOVER or END SEQUENCE statements) issues a BREAK statement, then control passes to the code *after* RECOVER. If no RECOVER is specified, then control passes to *after* the END SEQUENCE. The important feature to note is that BREAK may appear not only in the code, physically located after the BEGIN SEQUENCE, but in any procedure or user-defined function (at any depth) called by these statements.

The RECOVER statement may optionally receive a parameter expression passed by a BREAK statement. If a you include the optional expression as part of the BREAK, then this value is passed to the RECOVER USING statement.

The formal syntax definition of this control structure is:

```
BEGIN SEQUENCE
   <statements>
[BREAK [vExpr]]
   <statements>
[RECOVER [USING <memVar>]]
   <statements>
END [SEQUENCE]
```

The optional statement [BREAK [vExpr]] shows that the expression is also optional and of any data type (denoted with the "v" prefix). Correspondingly, the optional statement [RECOVER [USING <memVar>]] shows the optional <memVar> recipient of the passed value of <vExpr>.

As an example of how to use this structure consider the implementation of the Xbase language construct RETURN TO MASTER, which dBASE III Plus and dBASE IV programmers frequently use to return to a main program from a lower level (sometimes many levels lower) routine. This construct bypasses the calling modules in between.

Clipper does not offer this command for good reason: RETURN TO MASTER does not promote entirely structured programming, but you may need to simulate it when converting older programs to the CA-Clipper environment. In theory, RETURN TO MASTER enables the program to quickly run up the tree structure of options in an application, thus saving the user time in backward traversing that structure. Some program design philosophies maintain that this is bad programming, believing instead that once a module invokes another, it should eventually return to the point of invocation, yet some older dBASE applications use it extensively. The following CA-Clipper code uses BEGIN/END SEQUENCE to simulate RETURN TO MASTER:

```
FUNCTION Main()
LOCAL nOption := 0, nBreak

WHILE .T.
   CLEAR
   @ 10,10 SAY '(1) Level 1 Option A'
   @ 11,10 SAY '(2) Level 1 Option B'
   @ 12,10 SAY '(3) Level 1 Option C'
   @ 13,10 SAY '(4) Exit'
   @ 14,10 SAY 'Select: ' GET nOption PICT '9' RANGE 1,4
   READ
   BEGIN SEQUENCE
      DO CASE
         CASE nOption == 1
            Level1A()
         CASE nOption == 2
            Level1B()
```

```
            CASE nOption == 3
               Level1C()
            CASE nOption == 4
               BREAK 1         // Go back to DOS.
         ENDCASE
      RECOVER USING nBreak
         IF nBreak == 1        // BREAK 1 control passes here.
            EXIT
         ELSEIF nBreak == 2    // BREAK 2 control passes here.
            LOOP
         ENDIF
      END SEQUENCE
ENDDO
RETURN NIL                     // Return from Main().

FUNCTION Level1A()
? 'Level 1 Option A selected'
RETURN NIL                     // Return from Level1A().

FUNCTION Level1B()              // Second level menu structure.
LOCAL nOption := 0
WHILE .T.
   CLEAR
   @ 10,10 SAY '(1) Level 2 Option A'
   @ 11,10 SAY '(2) Level 2 Option B'
   @ 12,10 SAY '(3) Level 2 Option C'
   @ 13,10 SAY '(4) Return to Level 1 menu'
   @ 14,10 SAY 'Select: ' GET nOption PICT '9' RANGE 1,4
   READ
   DO CASE
      CASE nOption == 1
         Level2A()
      CASE nOption == 2
         Level2B()
      CASE nOption == 3
         Level2C()
      CASE nOption == 4
         RETURN NIL
   ENDCASE
ENDDO
RETURN NIL                     // Return from Level1B().

FUNCTION Level1C()
? 'Level 1 Option C selected'
RETURN NIL                     // Return from Level1C().

FUNCTION Level2A()
? 'Level 2 Option A selected'
RETURN NIL                     // Return from Level2A().
```

```
FUNCTION Level2B()          // Third level menu structure.
LOCAL nOption := 0

CLEAR
@ 10,10 SAY '(1) Level 3 Option A'
@ 11,10 SAY '(2) Level 3 Option B'
@ 12,10 SAY '(3) Level 3 Option C'
@ 13,10 SAY '(4) Return to Level 2 menu'
@ 14,10 SAY '(5) Return to MASTER'
@ 15,10 SAY 'Select: ' GET nOption PICT '9' RANGE 1,5
READ

DO CASE
   CASE nOption == 1
      Level3A()
   CASE nOption == 2
      Level3B()
   CASE nOption == 3
      Level3C()
   CASE nOption == 4
      RETURN NIL
   CASE nOption == 5
      BREAK 2                // Simulate RETURN TO MASTER.
ENDCASE
RETURN NIL                   // Return from Level2B().

FUNCTION Level2C()
? 'Level 2 Option C selected'
RETURN NIL                   // Return from Level2C().

FUNCTION Level3A()
? 'Level 3 Option A selected'
RETURN NIL                   // Return from Level3A().

FUNCTION Level3B()
? 'Level 3 Option B selected'
RETURN NIL                   // Return from Level3B().

FUNCTION Level3C()
? 'Level 3 Option C selected'
RETURN                       // Return from Level3C().
```

From this example, you can see that a selection by the user to "return to master" from the level 3 menu (function `Level2B()`) will jump directly to the level 1 menu without stopping at level 2. The enabling command is `BREAK`, which transfers control to the code in the `RECOVER USING` clause regardless of the module nesting level. In this example, the exception handling performed is the user selection of menu option 5, Return to Master.

Screen Input/Output

CA-Clipper has an abundance of commands and functions whose purpose is to direct output to the screen and retrieve input from the keyboard. In this section, we'll identify many of these features and show how they play an important role in most applications.

@ SAY GET

The mechanism in which full-screen data-entry processes can be implemented centers around the @ series of commands, specifically the @ SAY GET command. CA-Clipper contains a more refined form of the standard Xbase @ SAY GET command, which now includes color specifications for both the SAY and GET clauses, as well as *pre-validation* and *post-validation* features. The formal syntax of this command is:

```
@ <nRow>, <nCol>
  [SAY <vExpr>
   [PICTURE <cSayPicture>]
   [COLOR <cSayColorString>]]
  GET <variable>
   [PICTURE <cGetPicture>]
   [COLOR <cGetColorString>]
   [WHEN <lPreValidate>]
   [RANGE <lowerRange>, <upperRange>] | [VALID <lPostValidate>]
```

Many of the components of this command are equivalent to their Xbase counterparts, however, there are some differences. As in Xbase, you may define a @ SAY, @ GET, or @ SAY GET combination. As usual, a READ is required to initiate data entry after one or more GETs have been issued. Let's discuss how Clipper's @ SAY GET has been enhanced.

First, <variable> specifies the name of a memory variable or database field of type character, numeric, date, or logical associated with the GET. If <variable> contains an array reference, one or more subscripts must be supplied. The character expressions <cSayColorString> and <cGetColorString> define the color settings for the SAY output and the GET input, respectively. On a combined @ SAY GET command where colors settings are specified for both SAY and GET, two COLOR clauses are required.

The <lPreValidate> expression with the WHEN clause specifies an expression that must be satisfied before the cursor will be allowed to enter the GET during a READ. The <lPostCondition> expression with the VALID clause specifies an expression that must be satisfied before the cursor will be allowed to leave the GET during a READ.

The RANGE clause operates as in Xbase, specifying a range of allowable values for input to the GET. Only Numeric and Date data types are possible for

`<lowerRange>` and `<upperRange>`. RANGE is considered obsolete due to the availability of VALID.

Due to the manner in which CA-Clipper implements the GET system, an implicit array variable is referenced whenever GETs are used. We therefore recommend that you always include the following declaration in all program modules using GET:

```
MEMVAR GetList
```

This statement declares the public memory variable named GetList for use by the GET system. You'll find this eliminates many warning messages during compilation when using the /w compiler switch.

When the PICTURE clause is specified for a GET, `<cGetPicture>` is used to control formatting and edit validation. A picture string consists of two parts that may be specified together or alone: a *function string* and a *template string*.

- **Function string:** This portion of a picture string allows you to specify both formatting and validation rules that apply to an entire GET value (as opposed to particular character positions within it, something that PICTURE does). A picture function string begins with a @ character, followed by one or more additional characters, each of which has a particular meaning. Table 2.1 contains a complete list of these characters. You can specify a function string alone or with a picture template string. If both are present, the function string must precede the template string, and the two must be separated by a single space.
- **Template string:** This portion of a picture string allows you to specify both formatting and validation rules on a per character basis. The picture template string consists of a series of characters, some of which have special meanings. Table 2.2 contains a complete list of these characters.

The @ SAY GET command yields much power in developing sophisticated user data-entry processes. We'll see a complete application of CA-Clipper full-screen data-entry capabilities in Chapter 13.

@ BOX

We use the @ BOX command to draw boxes on the screen using a configurable border and color. You may choose to use the equivalent screen function DISPBOX(), which we'll describe in a later section of this chapter. The syntax for calling @ BOX is:

```
@ <nTop>, <nLeft>, <nBottom>, <nRight> BOX
   <cBoxString> [COLOR <cSayColorString>]
```

Table 2.1 GET PICTURE Functions

Function Character	Data Type	Purpose
A	Char	Allows only alphabetic characters
B	Num	Displays numerics left-justified
C	Num	Displays CR after positive numerics
D	Date/Num	Displays dates in format specified by SET DATE
E	Date/Num	Displays dates and numerics in European format—day and month reversed and commas and periods reversed respectively
K	All types	Deletes default text if first key is not a cursor key
R	Char	Tells Clipper to not store punctuation in GET variable
S<n>	Char	Allows horizontal scrolling within a GET; <n> is a numeric value that specifies the width of the data entry field
X	Num	Displays DB after negative numerics
Z	Num	Displays zero values as blanks
(	Num	Displays negative numerics in parentheses with leading spaces
)	Num	Display negative numerics in parentheses without leading spaces
!	Char	Converts alphabetic character to uppercase

Table 2.2 GET PICTURE Templates

Template Character	Purpose
A	Allows only alphabetic characters
N	Allows only alphabetic and numeric characters
X	Allows any character
9	Allows digits for any data type including sign for numerics
#	Allows digits, signs, and spaces for any data type
L	Allows only T, F, Y, or N (used for logical type)
Y	Allows only Y or N (used for logical type)
!	Converts an alphabetic character to uppercase
$	Displays a dollar sign in place of a leading space in a numeric
*	Displays an asterisk in place of a leading space in a numeric
.	Displays a decimal point
,	Displays a comma

Aside from the screen coordinate where the box is placed, you may also specify the standard or custom border string to use in generating the box. You will find several standard border strings in the Clipper header file named BOX.CH in the \INCLUDE directory. Using these as a model, you can create your own custom border strings.

The follow example displays several concurrent boxes to achieve an interesting graphic effect:

```
* Here is a sample program using the @ BOX command
#include 'box.ch'

LOCAL nTop:=1, nLeft:=0, nBottom:=22, nRight:=79
LOCAL nCount

CLEAR
FOR nCount := 1 TO 10
   @ nTop, nLeft, nBottom, nRight BOX S_SINGLE
   nTop++; nLeft += 3; nBottom—; nRight -= 3
NEXT

RETURN NIL
```

Simple Menuing with @ Prompt

CA-Clipper has a simple menuing command structure providing the means to put together functional, easy-to-use menus for user options selection. There are three commands in this group: @ PROMPT, MENU TO, and SET MESSAGE TO. Let's briefly state the purpose of each command. The @ PROMPT command displays the menu options on the screen, usually in stacked fashion, although you have complete control over where the options are placed on the screen. The MENU TO command gives control over to the user using the highlight bar selection approach; the user uses the cursor control keys to highlight the option desired and presses Enter. A numeric value is then deposited into a memory variable for later analysis. Finally, the SET MESSAGE TO command determines where on the screen the individual descriptions for each option will appear. Here are the formal syntax definitions for each command:

```
@ <nRow>, <nCol> PROMPT <cMenuItem> [MESSAGE <cMsg>]
MENU TO <variable>
SET MESSAGE TO [<nRow> [CENTER | CENTRE]]
```

Here is the sequence in which these commands are normally executed: SET MESSAGE TO, followed by several @ PROMPT commands, immediately followed by a MENU TO command.

> **Note**
>
> The SET WRAP command is another command used with @...PROMPT by enabling the highlight on the menu items to cycle from the last item to the first item (or vice versa) as the user presses the Up and Down (or Left and Right) arrow keys. The default is to not allow such wrapping. If the user highlights the last item and presses the Down (or Right) arrow again, there is no action taken. The syntax of SET WRAP is as follows:
>
> SET WRAP on | OFF | <lToggle>
>
> The status of menu item wrapping may also be determined through use of a logical expression <lToggle>. If the expression evaluates to .T. then wrapping is turned on.

Now, let's take a look at how the commands in the menuing group work together to generate simple menus.

```
LOCAL nChoice

SET MESSAGE TO 24    // Allow MESSAGE text to display.
SET WRAP ON          // Allow cursor to cycle from top to
                     // bottom in item list.
CLEAR SCREEN

@ 5,25 PROMPT 'Add records' ;
    MESSAGE 'Add a record to the Employee file'
@ 6,25 PROMPT 'Edit records' ;
    MESSAGE 'Edit a record in the Employee file'
@ 7,25 PROMPT 'Delete records' ;
    MESSAGE 'Delete a record in the Employee file'
MENU TO nChoice

DO CASE
   CASE nChoice == 1
      AddEmp()
   CASE nChoice == 2
      EditEmp()
   CASE nChoice == 3
      DelEmp()
   OTHERWISE
      * Do nothing
ENDCASE
```

Saving/Restoring Screen Contents

CA-Clipper accommodates the frequently required service of saving and restoring screen contents with two built-in functions, SAVESCREEN() and RESTSCREEN(). The prototypes for these functions are:

Prototype: SAVESCREEN([<nTop> ,[<nLeft>] ,[<nBottom>],

[<nRight>]) -> cScreen
Prototype: RESTSCREEN([<nTop>],[<nLeft>], [<nBottom>,
       [<nRight>], <cScreen>) -> NIL

The notion of the need for saving and restoring screen contents may be unclear until you try to develop an application that attempts to display several items on the screen at once. Developers of computer applications constantly battle the need for more screen real estate. One solution is to display overlapping, concurrent windows on the same screen. This is a common technique used in commercial software packages, and you may certainly achieve the same effect in your CA-Clipper applications. Let's see a simple example of saving and restoring a portion of the screen. In the code that follows, a function subprogram displays a message on the screen inside a box, but before it does, it first saves the screen portion to be occupied by the message box. Before continuing, the code erases the message box and returns the screen to its original state.

```
/***
*
* DispMsg(<nTop>, <nLeft>, <nBottom>, <nRight>, <cMsg>)
*      -> NIL
*
*/

FUNCTION DispMsg(nTop, nLeft, nBottom, nRight, cMsg)
LOCAL cSaveArea := SAVESCREEN(nTop, nLeft, nBottom, nRight)

@ nTop, nLeft, nBottom, nRight BOX B_DOUBLE_SINGLE

* Need to perform validity checking on parameters. For now
* just display in top/left corner.
@ nTop+1, nLeft+1 SAY cMsg

RESTSCREEN(nTop, nLeft, nBottom, nRight, cSaveArea)

RETURN NIL
```

> **Note** One way to clear the entire screen subsequent to saving the screen's contents is to use the CLEAR SCREEN command. The format of this command is:
>
> CLEAR [SCREEN] | CLS
>
> Actually, CLEAR SCREEN does several things at once. First, it erases the screen's contents. Second, it positions the cursor at row and column zero. Third, if SCREEN is specified, all pending GETs are flushed. You may also issue CLS which is synonymous with CLEAR SCREEN. You may find that some Clipper developers opt for the following code sequence in lieu of CLEAR:

```
Scroll()
SetPos(0,0)
```

Bear in mind that these functions yield the equivalent of CLEAR without the SCREEN clause, indicating that GETs will not be flushed.

Buffered Screen Output

In order to increase the appearance of performance for output directed to the screen, CA-Clipper provides two built-in functions, DISPBEGIN() and DISPEND(). To use these functions, place the targeted group of screen output commands in between calls to DISPBEGIN() and DISPEND(), respectively. This technique allows Clipper's display output system to accumulate the data in internal buffers. Once DISPEND() is encountered, the output is displayed all at once. This combats the problem of slow displays for complex output screens.

Before we present an example of buffered screen output, we need to present several other companion built-in screen oriented functions that you might wish to use with DISPBEGIN() and DISPEND().

DEVOUT()

Prototype: DEVOUT(<expr> [,<cColorString>]) -> NIL

This function writes a value to the current device (screen or printer) at the current cursor or printhead position. DEVOUT() is used in the STD.CH definition for the @...SAY command, so indirectly you use it each time you issue an @...SAY. You may also call the function directly.

DEVOUTPIC()

Prototype: DEVOUTPICT(<expr>, <cPictureString> [,<cColorString>]) -> NIL

This function operates identically to DEVOUT() with the addition of a picture string parameter <cPictureString> in which you may embed any valid picture (same as for @...SAY).

DEVPOS()

Prototype: DEVPOS(<nRow>, <nCol>) -> NIL

The DEVPOS() function moves the cursor or printhead to the specified row and column position on the current device.

If you first issue SET DEVICE TO SCREEN, DEVPOS() performs in the same manner as SETPOS(), positioning the screen cursor to the specified location (SETPOS() has the same parameters as DEVPOS()). If, however, you issue SET DEVICE TO PRINTER, DEVPOS() positions the printer's printhead. Think of DEVPOS() as a generic positioning function for both screen and printer output.

DISPBOX()

Prototype: DISPBOX(<nTop>, <nLeft>, <nBottom>, <nRight> [,<boxString>] [,<cColorString>]) —> NIL

DISPBOX() operates identically to the @...BOX and @...TO commands described earlier in the chapter.

DISPCOUNT()

Prototype: DISPCOUNT() —> nDispCount

This function returns a numeric value nDispCount, which indicates the number of pending DISPEND() requests. Because calling DISPBEGIN() defines a new display context and because these calls may be nested, DISPCOUNT() tells you how many DISPEND() calls are required to unravel all the contexts. Remember, for each DISPBEGIN() a matching DISPEND() is needed.

DISPOUT()

Prototype: DISPOUT(<expr> [,<cColorString>]) —> NIL

The DISPOUT() function writes a value to the screen at the current cursor position.

With these screen output functions now defined, let's illustrate their use through an example. Pay specific attention to the comments embedded in the code, as they provide a detailed explanation.

```
FUNCTION Main
DISPBEGIN()        // Request buffering of screen output.
SETPOS(5, 10)
DISPOUT('Context 1, update 1')
SETPOS(6, 10)
DISPOUT('Context 1, update 2')
MyUDF()            // Nothing displayed yet!
RETURN NIL
```

```
FUNCTION MyUDF()
DISPBEGIN()     // Create a new context.
SETPOS(10,40)
DISPOUT('Context 2, update 1')
DispAll()       // Still nothing displayed!
RETURN NIL

FUNCTION DispAll
WHILE DISPCOUNT() > 0// DISPCOUNT() begins with a 2.
   DISPEND()            // Display contexts.
END
RETURN NIL
```

Stuffing the Keyboard

Many times it is necessary to simulate the depression of keys on the keyboard as if the user has actually pressed the keys. When situations like this arise, we can use the KEYBOARD command. KEYBOARD first flushes any existing characters from the buffer. In the following short data entry example of KEYBOARD, we want the user to pick from a list of codes for the value of a GET, but the contents of the memory variable must be a character string associated with each code:

```
* Stuff the keyboard buffer based on user selection
LOCAL cLocation := SPACE(10)
MEMVAR GetList

@ 10,20 SAY 'Select location from list: ' GET cLocation ;
     WHEN ListLoc()
READ
? cLocation    // Contains the stuffed value.

RETURN NIL

/***
*
* ListLoc() -> .T.
*
* This UDF is called by the WHEN clause of the original GET
* and will present a mini-menu consisting of three numeric
* options. Upon selecting one, a corresponding word is
* KEYBOARDed into the KB buffer.
*
*/

FUNCTION ListLoc
* Define a local GetList array. This way we can have nested
```

```
* READs.
LOCAL GetList := {}, nChoice := 0

@ 24,0 SAY '1-Main 2-District 3-Regional' GET nChoice PICT '9' ;
   VALID nChoice >= 1 .AND. nChoice <= 3
READ

/* Depending on which numeric option was chosen by user,
   a word is stuffed into keyboard buffer and will
   appear in the data entry box of the original GET */
DO CASE
   CASE nChoice == 1
      KEYBOARD 'Main'
   CASE nChoice == 2
      KEYBOARD 'District'
   CASE nChoice == 3
      KEYBOARD 'Regional'
ENDCASE

RETURN .T.
```

If you need to key in characters from inside an expression (or as we'll see later a code block) we can define a simple user-defined function called KEYBOARD() that does the same work as the similarly named command. Here is the UDF:

```
/***
*
* KEYBOARD( <cString> ) —> NIL
*
*/

FUNCTION KeyBoard(cString)
KEYBOARD cString      // Now may be used as a function.
RETURN NIL
```

Summary

In this chapter, we have examined many Clipper language constructs that provide a framework for building complete applications. These commands are our building blocks and, in fact, there is not much we can do without them. A firm knowledge of the new commands presented here is essential to developing applications and exploring the topics later in this book. Take some time now to really understand this material.

Exercise

1. Write a small CA-Clipper application to convert temperatures from Fahrenheit to Celsius and vice versa. The program should present a simple menu with three options: Convert from F to C, Convert from C to F, and Exit. Use as many of the techniques presented in this chapter as you can in programming this exercise.

Answer

1. The solution code provided here uses numerous commands described in this chapter. Of course, for any one solution to a computer problem, there are ten more equally valid solutions. You should take this opportunity to run this program under the control of the Debugger to investigate its flow of controls and how it arrives at its results.

```
#include 'common.ch'
#include 'box.ch'

FUNCTION Main
LOCAL nChoice, nDegrees

MEMVAR GetList

SET MESSAGE TO 24 CENTRE
SET WRAP ON

WHILE TRUE
   nChoice := 0
   CLEAR SCREEN
   @ 3,18,9,35 BOX B_DOUBLE_SINGLE
   @ 5,20 PROMPT 'Convert F to C' ;
      MESSAGE 'Fahrenheit to Celsius'
   @ 6,20 PROMPT 'Convert C to F' ;
      MESSAGE 'Celsius to Fahrenheit'
   @ 7,20 PROMPT 'Exit' MESSAGE 'Return to DOS'
   MENU TO nChoice

   nDegrees := 0
   DO CASE
      CASE nChoice == 1
         @ 10,20 SAY 'Enter degrees in Fahrenheit: ' ;
            GET nDegrees ;
            PICTURE '999' ;
            VALID nDegrees >= -200 .AND. ;
               nDegrees <= 200
```

```
            READ
            @ 16,20 SAY 'Celsius: '
            @ 16,35 SAY (nDegrees - 32) * 5/9
            SETPOS(23,0)
            WAIT

        CASE nChoice == 2
            @ 10,20 SAY 'Enter degrees in Celsius: ' ;
              GET nDegrees ;
              PICTURE '999' ;
              VALID nDegrees >= -130 .AND. ;
                 nDegrees <= 100
            READ
            @ 16,20 SAY 'Fahrenheit: '
            @ 16,35 SAY nDegrees * 9/5 + 32
            SETPOS(23,0)
            WAIT

        CASE nChoice == 3
            EXIT
        ENDCASE
END

RETURN NIL
```

The Preprocessor

A Preprocessor Defined ➤ 64

Manifest Constants ➤ 68

Include Files ➤ 73

Conditional Compilation ➤ 76

Pseudo Functions ➤ 80

Other Features ➤ 82

Assertions ➤ 83

Summary ➤ 85

Exercises ➤ 85

One of the many exciting enhancements found in the CA-Clipper development environment is the preprocessor. It is the part of the compiler that provides for such features as *manifest constants, include files, conditional compilation, pseudo functions,* and *user-defined commands* (UDCs). In this chapter, we will focus on defining what a preprocessor is, what it does for you, and how to get the most out of using the preprocessor. We won't, however, tackle the portion of the preprocessor that enables the construction of user-defined commands and expressions until Chapter 4 because this concept is quite complex and powerful. For now, let's be content with exploring the first topic areas. The first order of business, and subject matter for the first section of this chapter, is to examine just what a preprocessor is.

After you've finished with this chapter, you will have learned:

- The purpose of the CA-Clipper preprocessor
- How to use the `#define` preprocessor directive for establishing manifest constants
- How to use the `#define` directive for defining pseudo functions
- How to use the `#undef` directive to un-define a name
- Instances where conditional compilation using the `#ifdef`, `#else`, and `#endif` directives come in useful
- How to read and comprehend the standard CA-Clipper *header files* and reasons to build your own

A Preprocessor Defined

CA-Clipper was the first Xbase derivative to contain a preprocessor. Previously, the most common language implementations to engage the use of a preprocessor were C compilers. C programmers have long since become accustomed to the ease of use and flexibility that this portion of a compiler provides. Now most of the other dialects, including dBASE IV and FoxPro have followed suit and now include a preprocessor but not to the extent that Clipper does. Basically, a preprocessor is the "front end" to a compiler, reading the input source, performing some manipulations, and then passing the resulting, modified code to the compiler itself. Think of a preprocessor as being a program that prepares your source code for the compiler. The concept of such a front end makes sense if you understand the result: the compiler must be able to handle less of a variety of possible source code combinations. The preprocessor standardizes the code before the compiler even sees it, thus making the compiler's job all that more tolerable.

Figure 3.1 illustrates the operation of the preprocessor. Everything begins with the source code you've written in .PRG files. Notice that there are external preprocessor files, Clipper header files, and alternate command sets that supple-

Figure 3.1 The preprocessor acts as the front end to the compiler.

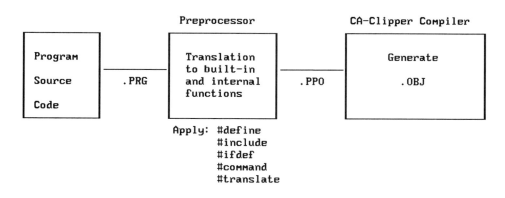

ment this source code. The preprocessor takes the source code and preprocessor files and produces a translation (that may be written to a disk file), which is then passed on to the actual compiler. This *preprocessed* version is actually a simpler version of your source code. If you examine the preprocessed code, you will find relatively few different commands. For example, there really is no ? command in the Clipper language, but instead all references to it are translated by the preprocessor to calls to the QOUT() internal function.

Much of what CA-Clipper actually does is by way of calls to various built-in and internal functions. You are generally discouraged from calling internal functions (those beginning with an underscore character) directly, because they may change from release to release, whereas the command syntax of the Clipper language will not. Many of the commands to which the preprocessor translates are those that you can call directly—DBEVAL(), SET(), ORDCREATE(), and so on—not the internal functions that you should avoid calling.

Notice from the figure that there is absolutely no way to avoid the preprocessor, which is good because without the actions of the preprocessor, you'd never successfully compile a program! CA-Clipper is now completely *table driven* in its command syntax, i.e. its commands are defined in STD.CH. This is, however, a topic for the next chapter.

In order for you to see the work of the preprocessor, include the /P switch whenever you compile a program. This will cause the preprocessed version of the program to be saved in a file with the same name as your program, but with a .PPO extension. When you view the contents of these files you will notice that they will contain blank lines throughout. This is due to the preprocessor's effort to preserve the line numbers in the .PPO file so that the correct line will be diagnosed in the event of a run-time error or during use of the Debugger.

To give you a glimpse of the preprocessor's handy work before we define the various directives it recognizes, let's look at a before (.PRG file) and after (.PPO file) picture of a Clipper program as it is read by the preprocessor. First, of course, is the before version:

```
   #include 'inkey.ch'
   #include 'set.ch'
1  #define DEMO
2  #define MAXRECS 50
3  #define CONCAT(s1, s2) s1+s2
4
5  FUNCTION Main
6  LOCAL nAns
7
8  SET(_SET_SCOREBOARD, .F.)
9  USE Customer INDEX Customer
10
11 #ifdef DEMO
12 DO WHILE .T.
13    IF LASTREC() > MAXRECS
14       CLS
15       @ 1,1 SAY CONCAT('Too many records in demo version', ;
16          STR(LASTREC(),5) )
17       nAns := INKEY(0)
18       IF nAns == K_ENTER
19          CLOSE DATABASES
20          QUIT
21       ENDIF
22    ELSE
23       EXIT
24    ENDIF
25 ENDDO
26 #endif
27
28 ? 'Demo program proceeds'
29
30 RETURN NIL
```

Now, let's take a look at the resulting .PPO file once the preprocessor finishes its job of applying the various directives. Note that we have supplied the line numbers for reference purposes only. Try and match them up with the original:

```
   #line 1 "c:\clipper5\include\inkey.ch"
   #line 2 "C:\CLIPPER5\BOOK\CHAP3_11.PRG"
   #line 1 "c:\clipper5\include\set.ch"
   #line 3 "C:\CLIPPER5\BOOK\CHAP3_11.PRG"
1
2
```

```
 3
 4
 5  FUNCTION Main
 6  LOCAL nAns
 7
 8  SET(32, .F.)
 9  dbUseArea( .F.,, "Customer",, if(.F. .OR. .F., !.F., NIL), (.F. );
            dbSetIndex( "Customer" )
10
11
12 while .T.
13    IF LASTREC() > 50
14       Scroll() ; SetPos(0,0)
15
16       DevPos( 1, 1 ) ;
         DevOut( "Too many records in demo version" ) ;
         STR(LASTREC(),5) )
17       nAns := INKEY(0)
18       IF nAns == 13
19          dbCloseAll()
20          __Quit()
21       ENDIF
22    ELSE
23       EXIT
24    ENDIF
25 ENDDO
26
27
28 QOut( "Demo program proceeds" )
29
30 RETURN NIL
```

One small but obvious benefit of the preprocessor is the ability to use mnemonics for otherwise hard to remember ASCII keyboard codes. In our example, note that the original program used the name K_ENTER to denote the keyboard's Enter key instead of the ASCII code 13. In the next several sections, we'll see many more benefits.

1. What is the primary benefit of the preprocessor in CA-Clipper?

1. Having a preprocessor allows the Clipper language to be entirely table driven. That is, all of the syntax of the commands, statements, and clauses recognized by CA-Clipper may be defined in a table that is used by the preprocessor. With this capability, Clipper is *extensible*, which means you may redefine the way Clipper interprets the syntax it is designed to recognize. Alternately, you could even make Clipper recognize other, diverse language constructs. There will be a more definitive glance at this topic in Chapter 4.

Manifest Constants

The first area of the preprocessor that we will examine is the *manifest constant*. Intelligent use of manifest constants can yield enhanced program readability and maintainability. A manifest constant is a definition to the compiler that assigns a string of text that may represent a constant, expression, part of a command, etc. to some identifier (similar to a memory variable). The difference between a manifest constant and a memory variable is that *all* manifest constants are resolved at compile-time whereas memory variables stay around for the duration of the program, i.e. during execution. What is meant by the term "resolved" here is simply that by the time the compiler gets hold of your source code, all the constant values you have equated to preprocessor names have been substituted in place of the names. Again, this process simplifies the job of the compiler considerably, since unlike memory variables, constants take up no space in the symbol table that is maintained by Clipper. Only the actual constant values are passed to the compiler.

One other difference between constants and memory variables is that constants are only known to the program module in which they are defined. If several modules need the constant then each module must include a definition for the constant. It's probably quite obvious to you what a tedious task it could be to include all such definitions in all the programs that need them. Fortunately, Clipper provides you with header files, which smooth over this problem. We will cover header files in the next section.

Another benefit to using manifest constants is in the event that a constant value may change in the future. If a certain constant is referenced in many program modules and that constant has to be changed, a memory variable approach would required you to change the value in each program that needs it. With manifest constants, on the other hand, only one change would be required (we'll see how to do this in the next section).

In order to define a manifest constant to the preprocessor the `#define` directive is needed. The general form of `#define` is:

```
#define <idConstant> [<resultText>]
```

Here, the directive name is `#define` and is usually written in lowercase (although uppercase is fine too). `<idConstant>` is the manifest constant name and `<resultText>` is the optional text string with which the preprocessor will replace the name. Think of the job of the preprocessor to handle manifest constants similar in nature to a global search and replace function in a word processor. The preprocessor scans the source code and makes replacements where appropriate for all names thus defined. Note that from the syntax definition, the `<resultText>` portion is optional. This is due to the usefulness of simply having a name being defined. Just how it becomes useful requires knowledge of another preprocessor directive, so we will discuss this optional form later in the chapter.

You can also use the /D switch to declare a manifest constant to a program. Use this switch to make a definition outside of the program. The syntax is:

```
/D<identifier>[=<text>]
```

Here, `<identifier>` is the name of the constant you wish to define. Notice that the `<text>` part is optional because the most frequent use of the /D switch is to define an empty value. This will become clear later on in the chapter when we discuss the `#ifdef`, `#else`, and `#endif` directives.

One very important consideration when coming up with names for manifest constants is that all substitutions are case sensitive. This is to say that if a directive such as

```
#define PageCnt "Page Number:"
```

is defined, then the following occurrence in the source code would *not* be replaced:

```
? PAGECNT+STR(nPage,3)
```

The characters found in the text of the source code must be identical in terms of case with the name in order for the replacement to occur. Manifest constants are the only place in which CA-Clipper cares about case (remember that case does not matter with memory variables). It is for this reason that the custom developed to make manifest constants uppercase only.

Alternately, you could define the manifest constant name on the Clipper command line using the /D compiler switch. Here is a simple example of this usage:

```
clipper foo.prg /P    /DRELEASE_NO=5.2D
```

Here a manifest constant named RELEASE_NO is defined and given a value of "5.2D". The preprocessor will use this name just as if it had appeared in a `#define` directive. As another example consider:

```
clipper foo.prg /P /DNAME=\"FREDIC\"
```

This time we define a manifest constant with the name NAME. The rest of the syntax may look strange because we wish the resulting text to contain quotation marks. To denote quotation marks you must precede each one by a backward slash character (\). In our example, NAME has associated with it the resulting text "FREDIC", including the quotation marks. Note also that you may not embed blank spaces in the value of a manifest constant defined on the command line.

There is no limit to the number of characters you can use in an identifier and all will be significant (as opposed to a maximum of 10 significant characters for memory variables).

In order to illustrate how a manifest constant might be used, consider the following code segment:

```
#define PAGELENGTH 60
.
. <statements>
.
IF nLineCnt == PAGELENGTH
   // End-of-page code goes here.
   nLineCnt := 1
ENDIF
```

Prior to the preprocessor, the IF statement's logical expression could have been nLineCnt == 60, or alternately, a memory variable could have been defined called nPageLength containing the value 60. Aside from taking up often precious symbol table space, using an unchanging memory variable instead of a manifest constant will tend to slow down your program ever so slightly. For example, this code

```
PRIVATE nConstant := 7      // PUBLIC yields same speed.
LOCAL nCount, nVal

FOR nCount := 1 TO 10000
   nVal := nConstant
NEXT
```

will yield slower execution speeds (approximately 29%) than the following code will:

```
#define CONSTANT 7
LOCAL nCount, nVal

FOR nCount := 1 TO 10000
   nVal := CONSTANT
NEXT
```

This slowing down is caused because the preprocessor automatically substitutes the references to CONSTANT and replaces it with a 7; that is, nVal := 7 is the resulting code that is executed 10,000 times. In the first example, repeated references to the memory location represented by the memory variable `nConstant` are required to supply the value to the assignment statement. Another benefit to using a manifest constant over a memory variable is that a memory variable may be changed inadvertently during the execution of the program whereas a constant is just that, it can never be altered unless another `#define` is embedded in the source code. Finally, a memory variable is also subject to the possibility that its type may change dynamically during the operation of the program. A program that changes the type of a memory variable is subject to the possibility of a runtime error in the future, but with manifest constants, its name, its value, and its type (implicitly speaking) remain the same at all times.

Another common example of using manifest constants is during the programming of applications that interact with the keyboard. Consider the following code:

```
#define K_ESC 27
IF nLastKey == K_ESC
   CLOSE DATABASES
   RETURN NIL
ENDIF
```

The logical expression will preprocess to `nLastKey == 27`; you can examine the resulting .PPO file for proof.

Note

> Be careful not to use Clipper keywords as manifest constant names. Under these circumstances, compiler errors may result. Consider the following example:
>
> `#define SKIP 5`
>
> In this case, each occurrence of the `SKIP` command will be replaced with the digit 5, which is not be very productive (nor valid!).

Constants are also good for defining standard error messages that may be referred to in various places in a program. If the following constant were defined in a program

```
#define MSG_NOCUST "Error: customer not found"
```

it may then appear in any one of several commands. For example:

```
@ 10,25 SAY MSG_NOCUST
@ 1,1 SAY "Severe "+MSG_NOCUST
```

You can also define a constant to contain an actual part of a Clipper command. For instance, in the following code, we store a whole `PICTURE` clause in a manifest constant for substitution into an `@...GET` command. The reason this works is clear once you remember that the preprocessor treats the program like one big chunk of text.

```
#define ALLUPPER PICTURE '@!'
@ 10,10 GET cCustName ALLUPPER
```

There is a general rule in CA-Clipper that states that a textual substitution will not occur on text inside the quotes of a string constant or in between a `TEXT/ENDTEXT` combination. Furthermore, the text must be separated by either whitespace (one or more blanks) or some delimiting characters.

Another usage of manifest constants is in the area of mapping locations in an array (a topic officially covered in Chapter 7). Many times, a programming methodology will use an array to act as a buffer to store a group of related information. For example, suppose an array has been established to hold all of an employee's data, e.g. Name, Department, Hire Date, Salary, etc. Let's say that each item is stored in a unique element of the array. This method, rather than using separate memory variables, will reduce memory consumption because the resulting symbol table will be smaller. Referencing the fields, however, becomes a problem because a statement like

```
@ 7,56 SAY "Enter current salary" GET aBuffer[8]
```

is difficult to read. The preferred approach is to use manifest constants:

```
#define nSalary aBuffer[8]
@ 7,56 SAY "Enter current salary" GET nSalary
```

Remember, at compile-time, the text "nSalary" will be replaced with the text "aBuffer[8]".

One additional preprocessor directive exists that pertains to manifest constants (and pseudo functions, which will be discussed a bit later). It is

```
#undef <identifier>
```

where `<identifier>` is either a manifest constant name or pseudo function name. The purpose of this directive is to *un-define* an identifier. This is needed since CA-Clipper does not allow the same identifier to be used more than once in a `#define` directive; a compiler warning results if the same identifier is redefined. If you wish to redefine an identifier, you must follow the original definition at some point with an `#undef` directive, followed at some point by another `#define`. For example:

```
#define MAXRECS 50
```

```
.<statements>
.
.
#undef MAXRECS
#define MAXRECS 100
```

You should now realize how important the use of manifest constants is to good coding practices. You should use them where appropriate and the effort will prove beneficial. In the next section, we'll go over some production examples, which have been supplied by Computer Associates, Inc.

1. Declare a constant that will represent the ASCII character to switch a dot matrix printer into condensed print mode and give an example of its use.
2. Will the preprocessor apply a substitution with the following example:

```
#define CRLF CHR(13)+CHR(10)
cRepLine := cCustNum+CRLF+cCustName+CRLF+REPLICATE('-',20)
nCredits := nCRLFREE * .98
```

1. The following directive will provide such a definition:

   ```
   #define CONDENSED CHR(15)
   ? CONDENSED + "Quarterly Earnings Report"
   ```

2. In the first statement, CRLF will be replaced because the plus signs act as delimiting characters, but the second statement does not yield a replacement because there is no whitespace surrounding the text.

Include Files

Once a group of manifest constants (and as we'll see in the next section, pseudo functions too) has been created for a particular application or part of an application, you will find it a timesaver to place them together in their own file instead of entering the `#define` directives in each program file. Once the constants are grouped, it is simple to reference them from a program module that would make use of them by using the `#INCLUDE` preprocessor directive. The general structure of this directive is:

```
#include "<headerFileSpec>"
```

Here, `<headerFileSpec>` may be any legal DOS filespec, i.e. a combination of drive letter, path name, and filename. Although not enforced by CA-Clipper, it has become somewhat of a standard convention to use a .CH file extension for Clipper header files (often called include files).

CA-Clipper uses header files extensively. In fact, the compiler comes with a collection of standard includes, shown in Table 3.1, that define manifest constants for specific purposes. For example, INKEY.CH is one of the most widely used standard header files because it contains names for each of the keys on the keyboard. Upon examining INKEY.CH, you can see that K_UP is defined to be 5. This corresponds to the fact that an ASCII character code of 5 represents the keyboard's Up Arrow key. So each time you need to refer to this key (possibly after calling the `LASTKEY()` function) you can use the manifest constant instead of "hard coding" the numeric ASCII value in your program.

You can also specify a header file for a compilation by using the /I compiler switch. Simply compile a program like:

```
Clipper foo /INETLIB.CH
```

This command would make available all definitions found in a user-defined include file named NETLIB.CH for use in the program being compiled.

Another technique is to use the special DOS environment variable IN-CLUDE which directs Clipper to a hard disk directory that contains include files. From the DOS prompt (or most likely from a batch file) you would enter:

```
SET INCLUDE c:\clipper5\include
```

Table 3.1 Standard Clipper Header Files

Header Filename	Constant Prefix	Usage Notes
ACHOICE.CH	AC_	Used with ACHOICE() user function
ASSERT.CH		Used for debugging programs
BOX.CH	B_	Used with box drawing commands
COLOR.CH	CLR_	Color indices for COLORSELECT() function
COMMON.CH		Commonly used definitions
DBEDIT.CH	DE_	Used with DBEDIT() user function
DBSTRUCT.CH	DBS_	Used with DBSTRUCT() function
DIRECTRY.CH	F_	Used with DIRECTORY() function
ERROR.CH	EG_	Error codes
FILIO.CH	F_,FC_,FO_,FS_	Used with direct file I/O functions
GETEXIT.CH	GE_	Contains get:exitState values
INKEY.CH	K_	Contains INKEY() return values
MEMOEDIT.CH	ME_	Used with MEMOEDIT() User function
RESERVED.CH		Identifies naming conflicts
SET.CH	_SET_	Used with SET() function
SETCURS.CH	SC_	Used with SETCURSOR() function
SIMPLEIO.CH		Simplified I/O commands
STD.CH		Contains standard command definitions

One benefit to using include files is that if a change is needed to a #define then that change must be made only once. Because all program files that depend on that include file have a #include directive, all references will automatically be resolved. This does require, however, that the program be recompiled for the new constant values to take effect.

There is one very special include file that CA-Clipper depends on heavily: STD.CH. We will focus our efforts on this file in Chapter 4, but for now let us just say that STD.CH contains the user-defined command definitions for all CA-Clipper commands. Unlike most header files, it contains exclusively #command, #xcommand, #translate, and #xtranslate directives. STD.CH is the only header file that has a compile-wide scope. All others are only seen by the current compile.

You may use the /U compiler switch to make an alternate header file's scope compiler-wide. The user-defined standard header file referenced by this switch will be used instead of STD.CH.

Note: A header file's definitions are only known in the current compile, therefore the file must be included in *each program* that makes reference to its contents.

If you wish, you may even nest include files, that is, one include file may contain a #include directive which refers to another include. This include then refers to another include and the process may continue up to 16 levels.

CA-Clipper include files possess a certain level of C language compatibility. This is to say that certain .CH files may be used in C programs, but only simple #define directives for manifest constants may be used. The reverse is not true, however, since there other items that a C header may include that CA-Clipper does not support. This simple level of compatibility does make certain cross environment development a bit more palatable.

One frequently used header file is COMMON.CH, which contains several commonly required manifest constant definitions and user-defined commands. The manifest constants found are:

```
#define TRUE  .T.
#define FALSE .F.
#define YES   .T.
#define NO    .F.
```

These constants are particularly useful in avoiding the terse logical constants found in all Xbase dialects. Using more readable constants like TRUE or FALSE make DO WHILE loops easier to read as in:

```
DO WHILE TRUE // Continue looping.
   .
```

```
   .  <statements>
   .
   .
ENDDO
```

Another useful header file is RESERVED.CH. This header file lets you check your older Clipper code against the current release to see if you've used function or procedure names that are the same as built-in CA-Clipper functions. This is a real problem especially when converting Summer '87 release programs to CA-Clipper. You should make using RESERVED.CH your priority when doing such a conversion. To test your existing code with this header file, you must compile in the following manner:

```
clipper progname /ureserved.ch
```

This statement causes RESERVED.CH to be used as an alternate standard command definition file (substituting STD.CH, which is the default). If any function or procedure found in your program conflicts with any listed in RESERVED.CH, the compilation halts with an `#error` directive and a C2074 compiler error. If your code has any such conflicts, you are faced with the task of changing the subprogram name and all references to it.

1. What is wrong with the following preprocessor directive?

   ```
   #include "testlib.prg"
   ```

1. You must only refer to a CA-Clipper header file inside an `#include` directive. In this case, a .PRG is shown, which may contain commands not suitable for a header file.

Conditional Compilation

The next preprocessor capability that needs to be addressed is *conditional compilation*. This feature provides a mechanism where certain statements or groups of statements may be selectively included or not included in the resulting compiled form of the program. Many times a program is developed in a general way, to provide functionality for a varied set of applications, but for a specific application, there may be sections of code that you don't wish to have compiled into the program. For example, let's say that you have developed a piece of software that targets two industries, but not at the same time. Believe for the moment that you've written a generic General Ledger program for normal for-profit businesses, but have also included Fund Accounting provisions for non-profit organizations. You only wish to maintain one set of source code, but depending on who you are selling the product to, the Fund Accounting portions may or may not be appropriate. Using the conditional compilation directives in CA-Clipper, you can compile the General Ledger program without the Fund Accounting features one time and then by changing only one line, compile a Fund Accounting version. As another example, conditional compilation gives you the ability to build *demonstration versions* of your software by compiling into the application, a certain group of code that may, for example, check for a maximum number of records in a database.

There are four directives in this area—`#ifdef`, `#ifndef`, `#else`, and `#endif`—that function identically like the standard Xbase IF statement. The difference between the preprocessor directives and the IF statement is that the former are all performed at compile-time as opposed to run-time. The precise syntax of these commands is

```
#ifdef <identifier>
   <statements>
[#else]
   <statements>
#endif
```

or alternately,

```
#ifndef <identifier>
   <statements>
[#else]
   <statements>
#endif
```

where `<identifier>` is a manifest constant name and `<statements>` represent any valid CA-Clipper statements or commands. In the case of `#ifdef`, the first set of `<statements>` will be included in the compilation if `<identifier>` was defined, whereas the second set will be compiled if it was not. The reverse is true when using `#ifndef`. It is here where the

```
#define <idConstant>
```

form of the `#define` directive comes into play. `<idconstant>` used in this way, does not need a `<resultText>`, as described earlier, when dealing with manifest constants. Instead, the mere fact that it is being defined is the information that is needed later on. Think of the preprocessor as managing a series of "existence markers" for manifest constants defined in this way. If a constant appears in such a `#define` then an "existence" or "true" marker is posted. For example, in both the `#ifdef` and `#ifndef` directives, `<identifier>` must contain the name of a manifest constant that may or may not have appeared in a #define directive. For the "true" <statements> to be executed, the identifier must only be defined. Consider the following example:

```
#define DEMOVERS

#ifdef DEMOVERS
   GO BOTTOM
   IF RECNO() > 50

      ? "Sorry, this is a demo version, too many records"

      QUIT

   ENDIF

#endif
```

Here, the preprocessor sees the definition of the DEMOVERS identifier. Notice that there is no value associated with it. Instead, the only piece of information that is needed is the fact that it is defined. Later, when the #ifdef directive is encountered, the preprocessor will check if DEMOVERS is defined and if so, the code that follows will be compiled into the program. In this case, the code to check for a maximum record count is compiled, but had the identifier *not* been defined then this code would *not* be compiled, and would be physically omitted from your program.

As we mentioned in the section about manifest constants, you may define a constant's value as a command-line switch when you invoke the Clipper compiler. Be careful however, to make sure that a #define does not exist for the same constant name. For example, if the program contains

```
#define MONTHS 12
LOCAL aPeriod[MONTHS], nCount
.
.<statements>
.
FOR nCount := 1 TO MONTHS
   aPeriod[nCount] := 100
NEXT
```

and you compile the program with this command line

```
Clipper foo /DMONTHS=12
```

then a compiler error will result, complaining that you've re-defined the same constant. Remember, only one or the other is necessary.

Conditional compilation is a very powerful feature and, as we mentioned earlier, one that has been present in C language preprocessors for a long time. All in all, this feature is quite welcome in the CA-Clipper environment. When you use this conditional compilation, make sure that if a certain group of statements are not included in the compilation, that the program will still function properly.

1. Propose at least two additional applications of the conditional compilation feature of the CA-Clipper preprocessor and state how you might go about implementing them.

1. Here are two possible applications for conditional compilation:
    a. Many reports are written with both detail and summary capabilities. You may choose to use the preprocessor to include or eliminate the code necessary to produce summary results. For example,

    ```
    #define DETAIL
    #ifndef DETAIL
        * Detail report was not requested so include summary
        * code here. Just include or remove the #define above
        * to get the desired type of report program.
    #endif
    ```

    b. It may be possible to maintain both single and multi-user versions of a program in one set of source code by using conditional compilation. The success of this approach depends on how sophisticated the multi-user provisions are required to be. Many times, only simple file locks are needed. Consider the following example:

    ```
    #define MULTIUSER
    .
    . <statements>
    .
    #ifdef MULTIUSER
        SET EXCLUSIVE OFF
    #endif
    USE Orders
    #ifdef MULTIUSER
        IF FLOCK()        // Obtain a file lock.
    #endif
    TOTAL qtyord TO nTotOrder
    @ 10,10 SAY 'Total ordered amount: '+STR(nTotOrder,7,2)
    #ifdef MULTIUSER
        ENDIF
    #endif
    ```

    You can see by this example that a program that supports both single and multi-user operation would have conditional compilation directives scattered throughout.

Pseudo Functions

The pseudo function capability of the CA-Clipper preprocessor provides a vehicle for defining functions that are resolved at compile-time instead of having the function evaluated as the program is running. Many times the use of a user-defined function (UDF) can be avoided by implementing the function as a pseudo function. There are several benefits to doing this. First of all, performance is enhanced because UDF calls can be expensive in terms of the added overhead required to issue a call to a function, pass parameters, and then return a value to the calling program. Even with pseudo functions, a function is still called and parameters are still passed, but the process occurs at compile-time, not run-time. Limited benchmark tests indicate that a UDF approach can be 2.5 times slower than using pseudo functions.

There is one caveat in using pseudo functions. Each time a pseudo function is recognized and translated by the preprocessor a duplicate set of code is inserted into your source code. Unlike regular user-defined functions, where you may repeatedly call the same function many times, the code for a pseudo function is simply duplicated in your code many times. If the pseudo function is large and is referenced a large number of times, this could result in bloated code. Therefore, the most appropriate applications for pseudo functions are situations where the pseudo function is small (a short expression) and is referenced only a few times.

> Whenever appropriate, use pseudo functions instead of UDFs to avoid overhead associated with calling a function.

The formal syntax of the pseudo function is:

```
#define <function name>([<parameter list>]) <expression>
```

`<function name>` is simply the name with which you may invoke the pseudo function and is case sensitive in its use in the calling program. `<paramater list>` is the optional list of parameters that need to be passed to the function. Lastly, `<expression>` is the function itself, or in other words, the expression that the function uses to determine a return value. Note that there should not be a space after `<function name>`.

Exactly what happens when a pseudo function is referenced in a program is really a matter of textual substitution. The preprocessor identifies a reference to a pseudo function with an optional parameter list, whose parameter count must match with that of the function's definition, and then substitutes the `<expression>` for the `<function name>`. In addition, each of the passed parameters is substituted in for its counterpart occurring somewhere in `<expression>`. Remember, all this occurs at compile-time, way before an .EXE file is even generated and no code is actually executed.

The parameters that appear in `<parameter list>` follow the same naming rules as manifest constants. Moreover, you may not skip any parameters found in the definition when a pseudo function is called (which, as we will see later, is possible with UDFs).

Sometimes pseudo functions are called *compiler macros*. This term is truly a misnomer and should be avoided. The term *macro* has special connotations in the Xbase world, normally indicating the process of performing textual substitution in the program using the & operator.

Note

> There is the possibility of misused operator precedence when using pseudo functions. For example,
>
> ```
> #define RAISE(SALARY, INCREASE) SALARY*INCREASE
> nExtra := RAISE(BASE+BONUS, PCT+PBONUS)
> ```
>
> Here, evaluating the pseudo function, the result of the preprocessor becomes BASE+BONUS*PCT+PBONUS, which is evaluated as BASE+(BONUS*PCT)+PBONUS because the * operator has precedence over the + operator. In order to avoid these problems, always include parentheses around each term in the function definition:
>
> ```
> #define RAISE(SALARY, INCREASE) (SALARY)*(INCREASE)
> ```
>
> In this way, the resulting text becomes (BASE+BONUS)*(PCT+PBONUS) which has the desired effect.

Pseudo functions can be used for many useful purposes. We'll provide a few examples to demonstrate this. First, suppose you need to convert a numeric memory variable to a string, and at the same time, strip off all leading blanks in the resulting string. Normally, the `STR()` function will pad out a converted numeric to a total of 10 characters, so we need a pseudo function, which we'll call `NTRIM()`, to get rid of the padded blanks. The following is a definition for `NTRIM()` that will perform this task:

```
#define NTRIM(n) (LTRIM(STR(n)))
```

A possible application of the `NTRIM()` pseudo function is:

```
LOCAL nSalary := 25000
? NTRIM(nSalary)          // No leading blanks.
```

Another example is to have a pseudo function call the `REPLICATE()` function, passing to it the number of times to replicate a graphics character. Consider the following definition:

```
#define SMOOTHLINE(n) REPLICATE(CHR(196),n)
```

This pseudo function accepts a numeric parameter and substitutes it in for the replication factor in `REPLICATE()`. Using `SMOOTHLINE()` would only make sense if the calling program requires numerous calls to `REPLICATE()` with the same replication string.

Note The implied scope of a pseudo function is *file-wide static* or until it is undefined with an `#undef`.

Pseudo functions have very far reaching capabilities, especially in their ability to replace certain UDFs. You should make every attempt to take advantage of their speed benefit whenever possible.

1. Suppose that a database named CUSTOMER contains two fields, LASTNAME and FIRSTNAME. Write a pseudo function definition that will yield a single string containing both LASTNAME and FIRSTNAME separated by a comma. Also, show a sample usage of the function.
2. Write a pseudo function that calculates the sales tax amount given two parameters are passed, AMOUNT and TAXRATE. Next, prepare a derivation of this function that will accept a memory variable as a third parameter that will be assigned the newly calculated tax amount.

1. The solution of this problem involves defining a pseudo function with the realization that database fields, complete with alias qualifiers, may be passed as parameters.

```
#define FULLNAME(FIRST, LAST) LAST+", "+FIRST
USE Customer
? FULLNAME(Customer->FirstName, Customer->LastName)
```

2. Consider the following solution with a sample usage:

```
#define EVALTAX(AMOUNT, TAXRATE) (AMOUNT * TAXRATE)
USE Orders
? EVALTAX(Orders->Amt, Orders->TaxRate)
```

Now consider a revised example using an inline assignment that performs an assignment of the resulting value to a passed memory variable:

```
#define ASSIGNTAX(AMOUNT, TAXRATE, TAX) ;
    (TAX := AMOUNT * TAXRATE)
USE Orders
? EVALTAX(Orders->Amt, Orders->TaxRate, nTaxAmount)
```

Other Features

Another preprocessor directive that we need to profile is `#error`. Basically, when `#error` is encountered during the compilation of a Clipper program, a compile-time error is generated, an optional user-defined error message is displayed, and the compilation stops. The primary use of this feature is to stop a compile from finishing if a crucial condition necessary for the successful completion of the compile does not exist. The command is specified as

```
#error [<messageText>]
```

where `<messageText>` is an optional, non-delimited (i.e. no quotation marks are needed unless they are to be displayed with the text) character string that will be displayed in the event that the `#error` directive is encountered. `#error` causes the compiler to generate error number C2074.

As an example of the `#error` directive, consider the following code segment:

```
#ifdef GRAPHICS
   #error Graphics are not currently supported
#endif
```

Here, if the `GRAPHICS` manifest constant was defined, that means that the developer wishes to produce a version of the software with graphics capabilities, but evidently the code does not yet exist for such a feature, hence, it makes no sense to go through with the compile.

One last preprocessor directive is `#stdout`. This directive sends a literal string of characters to the standard output device (STDOUT) during compilation. `#stdout` functions identically to `#error` except that the output is written to STDOUT and no compiler error is generated.

The command is specified as

```
#stdout [<messageText>]
```

where `<messageText>` is an optional, non-delimited (i.e. no quotation marks are needed unless they are to be displayed with the text) character string that will be displayed in the event that the `#error` directive is encountered. If `<messageText>` is not specified, a carriage return/line feed pair echoes to STDOUT.

```
#ifdef GRAPHICS
   #stdout Compiling GUI version
#endif
```

Assertions

We saw in Chapter 1 that CA-Clipper has quite a capable debugger with which you may undertake investigative work in finding program bugs. Another area that greatly aids in debugging and program verification chores are *assertions*. Assertions allow you to pose conditions that must be true in order to ensure the application executes properly. Often while coding a program module, you come across a logical condition that you are positive can never happen. Sure enough, however, after the program functions long enough in a production environment, the condition arises. The program may choose to ignore this possibility, proceeding along when it shouldn't.

CA-Clipper has a special header file, ASSERT.CH, that contains a facility to verify these conditions. Specifically, the header file contains a UDC definition for a new command ASSERT whose syntax is

```
ASSERT( <condition> [, <msg>])
```

where `<condition>` is any valid logical expression and `<msg>` is an optional character string.

ASSERT works like this: If the condition you specify evaluates to .T. then nothing happens to the program's execution. This means that the program is operating according to plan. If the value is .F., however, the message string is routed to STDOUT and execution halts. With ASSERT you are able to embed crucial error condition checking in your application, preventing it from proceeding under dangerous conditions. Consider the following examples:

```
ASSERT(nDivisor ==0, 'Division by zero about to occur')

ASSERT(RECCOUNT() != 0, 'Database must not be empty')

ASSERT(nParm1 != NIL, 'Important parameter not specified')
```

The first example evidently checks for a possible division by 0 problem before it happens and causes a run-time error. In this case, we cannot reliably continue since an important calculation cannot take place. In the second example, the program may have just done a database extract process. In this case, if the program didn't select any records, the program must not continue. The last example comes from a UDF or procedure that cannot proceed if the parameter nParm1 was not passed.

Bear in mind, ASSERT is to be used primarily during the debugging phase of development. The conditions that ASSERT looks out for should not happen in a fully debugged, production application. This is not to say that once you feel the program is completely debugged you should remove all ASSERTs. Instead, you can compile a program that uses ASSERT with a /DNDEBUG switch, for example. The manifest constant NDEBUG would cause a conditional compilation to remove all ASSERTs from the compile (without physically taking them out). If your application suddenly needs more debugging and you need your strategically positioned ASSERTs to assist again, you simply recompile the application *without* the /DNDEBUG switch.

Summary

In this chapter, we have examined most of the features of the CA-Clipper preprocessor. We've seen how the use of manifest constants can work to simplify and speed up your compiled programs and how collecting them in Clipper header files can aid the development process. The ability of the processor to conditionally compile sections of code was seen to enhance the way different versions of software can be maintained with only one set of source code. Finally, we pointed out that pseudo functions are an alternative to simple user-defined functions in order to remove some work from the compiler and have the preprocessor handle limited function evaluation. All in all, thoughtful and consistent use of the CA-Clipper preprocessor will yield more efficient and more manageable applications.

Exercises

1. Discuss how conditional compilation directives may be used to promote "debugging" versions of software. Also, how might the /D compiler switch aid in this pursuit?

2. Write a pseudo function called MAX3() that will take three numeric parameters and compute the maximum of the three.

3. What is potentially wrong with the following pseudo function definition and what can be done to repair it:

   ```
   #define DIVISION(x, y) x / y
   ```

4. Write a pseudo function that calculates the number of characters in a rectangular screen window whose coordinates are ur (upper row), uc (upper column), lr (lower row), lc (lower column).

Answers

1. During the process of debugging an application, you may choose to include various forms of aids that assist the process of gaining insight into how the software is functioning. This might include special forms of displayed and printed output and possibly temporary output files. Of course, once the system goes into production use, these items must be removed. In the future, however, you may need them again. Rather than take them out, you can utilize the conditional compilation feature of the CA-Clipper preprocessor to conditionally include the debugging code in the .EXE file. To do this, surround the debugging code with `#ifdef` and `#endif` directives. Then during compilation, use the /D switch to bring in or leave out the debugging code.

2. Here is the pseudo function MAX3() that determines the greater of three numeric parameters. To find the greatest value, we first compare the first two values, find the greatest, and then repeat the process against the third.

   ```
   #define MAX3(a, b, c) MAX(IIF(a > b, a, b), c)
   ```

3. The DIVISION pseudo function would be satisfactory for cases where single memory variables or constants are passed to it. If, however, expressions are passed there is the potential for confusion. Consider the following usage:

   ```
   ? DIVISION(nOrdQty * nPrice, nFactor * nUnits)
   ```

   The output from the preprocessor would be

   ```
   ? nOrdQty * nPrice / nFactor * nUnits
   ```

   which would yield an improper result because the operations would be performed from left to right. In order to cure this symptom, the pseudo function should be recoded as:

   ```
   #define DIVISION(x, y) (x) / (y)
   ```

4. The following pseudo function, SCREENDIM(), solves the screen real estate calculation problem. Remember to enclose each term in parentheses to avoid confusion in operator precedence.

   ```
   #define SCREENDIM(ur, uc, lr, lc) 
           (((lc) - (uc) + 1) * ((lr) - (ur) + 1) * 2)
   ```

User-Defined Commands

An Intelligent Search and Replace ➤ 89

Preprocessor Operations ➤ 89

Match Markers ➤ 91

Result Markers ➤ 101

Examples from COMMON.CH ➤ 106

Summary ➤ 108

Exercise ➤ 109

If there is one CA-Clipper feature that can be singled out to characterize the language, it must be *user-defined commands* (UDCs). The UDC concept is a very elegant philosophy that provides for *table driven syntax*. A special header file called STD.CH contains a collection of UDCs that define how to recognize valid Clipper commands and how to translate them into something the compiler actually understands. The CA-Clipper compiler really only knows a small subset of all the commands in the language. So, a library of internal functions is used to provide the functionality that programmers are accustomed to (e.g. the function DBUSEAREA() does the job of the USE command).

With all the commands defined in a table, this means that the table and therefore the commands themselves can be altered to suit specific needs. Even more important, UDCs allow you to define a new command syntax, giving Clipper a level of extensibility previously unknown in database languages. For compiler speed considerations, STD.CH is not used by Clipper during routine compiles, but if you decide to alter or enhance this header, you must tell the compiler. In order to specify an *alternate command set* (i.e. STD.CH or another you may construct), you must specify the /U compiler switch.

Prior to UDCs, Clipper and other development languages were extended through use of large libraries of UDFs with long parameter lists. Under the hood, this is also true of CA-Clipper, but the UDCs insulate the user from ugly function calls. Instead, you can define a pleasant Xbase style syntax and have the preprocessor translate it into obscure calls to internal functions. Currently, many third party products do just this.

You might ask why would a CA-Clipper beginner need to know about UDCs? The answer is that you really don't, but you'll be at a distinct advantage if you have a basic understanding at an early point. Any Clipper programmer should know of Clipper's extensibility. This knowledge will help when confronted with debugging sessions since the ability to read .PPO files and the knowledge of how the preprocessor went about translating your source code will greatly help your efforts. You may never write your own commands and structures, but it's still nice to know that you can.

After you've finished with this chapter, you will have learned:

- How to understand STD.CH, the Clipper syntax definition file
- The basic ingredients of the #command, #xcommand, #translate, and #xtranslate preprocessor directives so that you can modify or enhance the definitions found in STD.CH
- How to create new command set files containing completely new command structure definitions

An Intelligent Search and Replace

CA-Clipper's UDCs are really just a mechanism for doing very intelligent global search and replaces in program text. Think of your program as just a long sequence of characters that the preprocessor must read and manipulate. This source code is "intelligently" scanned for familiar—previously defined—constructs and translates them into equivalent command syntax and function calls (remember, the preprocessor does its job before the compiler even reads the program). Therefore, UDCs are nothing more than replacement rules, which are composed of *match markers* and *result markers*. The match markers are the character sequences that the preprocessor must "recognize." These sequences could be any command structure that the programmer might use in the source code. Result markers, on the other hand, represent the character sequences into which the match markers are translated. In our previous example, the USE command has components that are translated into parameters for the DBUSEAREA() function. Bear in mind that Clipper has many distinct syntax styles, many of which have their roots in the Xbase standard. Fortunately, the various styles of UDC markers are robust enough to handle all the classifications of CA-Clipper syntax:

- Regular command names and keywords
- Extended expressions
- Optional clauses
- Repeating clauses
- Lists
- Bulk text
- Code blocks
- Strings

In this chapter, we'll demonstrate how the various kinds of match and result markers are used by examining samples straight from STD.CH. In addition, we'll devise some custom examples that will further illustrate UDC concepts. But first, let's take a look at the preprocessor directives that make all this possible.

Preprocessor Operations

The basis of CA-Clipper's user-defined commands center around the following four preprocessor directives:

- `#command`
- `#translate`
- `#xcommand`
- `#xtranslate`

The first two in the list actually function the same as the last two. The exception is that `#command` and `#translate` require keyword matches on only the first four characters (in order to maintain dBASE compatibility). `#xcommand` and `#xtranslate`, however, need complete matches. For this reason, you'll see `#command` used throughout STD.CH, but for your own UDCs, we recommend that you use `#xcommand` and `#xtranslate`.

The difference between `#xcommand` and `#xtranslate` is that the former is used to recognize entire commands whereas the latter is for portions of commands. The use of `#xcommand` is much more common. One common question that arises: Why not just use the `#define` directive instead of `#xcommand` and `#xtranslate`? The answer is that `#define` cannot be used to recognize an entire command structure, but only parts of commands. Plus `#define` does not possess the power of UDC's intelligent replacement markers.

Here is the general structure of a UDC:

```
#command <text and match markers> => <text and result markers>
```

The text and match markers portion consists of the various familiar keywords found in CA-Clipper commands, such as PICTURE, INTO, USE, DO, etc. and match markers that will be defined in the sections that follow. The special symbol `=>` must separate the left side of the UDC definition from the right side. The text and result markers portion consists of the desired resulting structures, such as calls to internal functions. Note that UDC translations can be chained. This is to say that a UDC may recognize a structure that is translated into something that will in turn be recognized by another UDC that will translate it into yet something else.

The preprocessor will scan your programs, searching for text that matches the patterns found on the left side of the UDC definitions and then apply the translation rules that yield the resulting output text defined by the right side.

To see what the preprocessor has done to your program, compile with the /P option and then view the .PPO files that are generated. Consistent review of .PPO files is required for a firm grasp of how UDCs operate.

The UDC portion of the preprocessor is first a *recognizer* and then *translator*. It scans the input text, namely your program modules, recognizes various constructs, and translates them to alternate constructs, as dictated by the UDC definitions.

For this to come to light for a beginner, a simple example is required. Consider the ? Xbase command, which displays an expression value on the screen. The UDC definition in STD.CH for this command is:

```
#command ? [ <list,...> ] => QOut( <list> )
```

Much to our surprise, we see that the Clipper compiler does not actually have a ? command; only the QOut() function is understood. There is no reason to worry, UDCs handle the translation automatically so it appears that the CA-Clipper compiler does indeed have a ? command.

Probably the best way to become accustomed to UDCs is to see some practical examples. In the next several sections of this chapter, we'll break down UDCs by the different match and result markers that are possible and show examples that come straight out of STD.CH. It would be a good idea for you to print out a copy of this file, which is located in the \INCLUDE directory so you can see other examples and jot down notes. Later, we'll present some special situations through the use of some custom examples.

Note
You may place a UDC definition in any .CH file or even directly in a .PRG file (if the scope of the UDC is limited to only that program module). You should not make changes to STD.CH a common occurrence. Many developers choose to collect their favorite UDCs in special .CH files (think of these as UDC libraries) so that they may use them in many different applications. You might also consider building special UDC collections by building .CH files on a per application basis, since some UDCs could turn out to be very specialized. Although some Xbase developers have commented that extensive use of UDCs yield unmaintainable code, you should treat UDCs and .CH file collections of UDCs in the same light as function libraries. There really is no difference and, in fact, viewed in this way, UDCs offer a much more readable code solution.

1. CA-Clipper can be said to be a table driven syntax language. Briefly explain this notion and provide the benefits of this approach.

1. The STD.CH CA-Clipper header file contains the definitions for the Clipper language. You can direct the compiler to examine this file when translating your source code, giving you the ability to customize the constructs known to the compiler. The main benefit to this approach is that CA-Clipper command syntax is not static, but may be changed or enhanced to satisfy current needs.

Match Markers

This section illustrates several examples of each type of match marker: *word, regular, extended expression, option clause, list, restricted,* and *wild*. The examples show why each match marker is needed by examining the type of command structure that must be recognized. The general format for the code examples in the following sections will include the UDC definition, an example of its use, and then the preprocessed output (i.e. what would appear in the .PPO file).

Word Match Marker

In a UDC, you can create any new word to be a synonym for any other preprocessed command. This type of match marker is needed because the CA-Clipper compiler may not actually have a particular command, but instead rely on an internal function to do its work. For example, in STD.CH, there is a UDC that maps the EJECT command to a call to an internal function, __Eject(). The following examples define alternate words for existing Clipper commands whose definitions are already found in STD.CH:

```
// Define synonym for EJECT command.
#command NEWPAGE =>    __Eject()
NEWPAGE         // Use the new command.
// ppo: __Eject()
```

```
// Define synonym for USE: to close database.

#command CLOSEDB =>   dbCloseArea()

CLOSEDB         // Use the new command to close a database.

// ppo: dbCloseArea()
```

```
// Synonym for SET COLOR TO: to reset colors.

#command CLEARCOLOR => SetColor()

CLEARCOLOR      // Use the new command to reset colors.

// ppo: SetColor()
```

Through use of word match markers, you'll be able to create rather unique synonyms. If you were to create a custom .CH file containing these remappings, it would yield a custom flavor of Clipper that could be potentially quite unintelligible. Consider this:

```
// Take-off on SET PATH TO command definition in STD.CH.
#command NUKEPATH => Set(_SET_PATH, "")
```

Armed with a custom STD.CH, a whimsical developer could produce code that absolutely no one else could comprehend.

Regular Match Marker

Regular match markers are the most common type of match markers. They are used for simple textual replacement of variable components in a command structure. For example, in the SET DECIMALS TO command, you can specify an expression, though you would usually specify a numeric constant. The regular match marker recognizes this expression and maps it to something on the right side part of the definition. You begin by assigning a name to the text appearing in a recognized command. The name assigned to the text is of your choosing and must be of the form <idMarker>. Here are some examples found in STD.CH:

```
#command SET DECIMALS TO <x>   =>      ;
   Set( _SET_DECIMALS, <x> )
SET DECIMALS TO 3
// ppo: Set( _SET_DECIMALS, 3 )

// Remember: @ 10,4  will erase a line from col 40.
#command @ <row>, <col>                ;
   => Scroll( <row>, <col>, row> )  ;
   ; SetPos( <row>, <col> )
@ 10,40
// ppo: Scroll( 10, 40, 10 ) ; SetPos( 10, 40 )
```

In the first example, the match marker <x> marks the position of the text that is to be recognized after the keywords SET DECIMALS TO. <x> is then mapped to the second parameter passed to the SET() built-in Clipper function. Note that if <x> is not found, then the entire command structure will not be recognized. The <x> in this case is a required part of the command structure.

> **Note** The use of semicolons in UDCs may appear confusing. The key to understanding their use is to remember that there are two applications for semicolons: they can be used to continue UDC definitions onto more than one line, and they can be used to separate multiple program lines being output by the UDC translation process.

The second example is the first UDC we have seen containing multiple output lines. Here we see that a single semicolon is needed to separate the function calls Scroll() and SetPos() in order for the generated code to operate properly, so two semicolons appear one after the other in the input text (even though they are on different lines). Notice that only one semicolon appears in the output. The match markers <row> and <col> are mapped to parameters passed to the Scroll() and SetPos() functions.

As one last example of regular result markers, consider the definition of the Clipper Summer '87 style screen saving command SAVE SCREEN TO. In the following example, notice that this command is mapped to a call to the SAVESCREEN() built-in function where <var> is the regular result marker noting the name of the memory variable to hold the screen contents.

```
// The old SAVE SCREEN TO command as found in STD.CH.
#command SAVE SCREEN TO <var>     ;
   => <var> := SaveScreen (0, 0, Maxrow(), Maxcol() )
SAVE SCREEN TO z
// ppo: z := SaveScreen (0, 0, Maxrow(), Maxcol() )
```

Extended Expression Match Marker

The extended expression match marker is used to handle CA-Clipper syntax that includes extended filename expressions and is denoted as <(file)>. Extended expressions are very important because of CA-Clipper's emphasis on avoiding macro usage and also because they are part of many language constructs. Therefore, this match marker enables the preprocessor to recognize this syntax. Table 4.1 defines how this match marker recognizes extended expressions and what it maps them to.

It seems that from Table 4.1, the extended expression match marker only affects cases where actual filenames are specified; memory variables, character expressions, and character literals containing filenames are left unaltered. The examples that follow illustrate how this process works:

```
#command COPY FILE <(scr)> TO <(dest)> =>
        __CopyFile( <(src)>, <(dest)> )
COPY FILE TxnTemp TO ('Txn')
// ppo: __CopyFile( "TxnTemp" TO ("Txn") ).
COPY FILE TxnTemp TO (cFileName)
// ppo: __CopyFile( "TxnTemp" TO (cFileName) ).

// Special form of TEXT is TO FILE clause, echoes to text file.
#command TEXT TO FILE <(file)>
   => __TextSave( <(file)> )
   ; text QOut, __TextRestore

TEXT TO FILE ("amulet")
   line 1
   line 2
ENDTEXT
// ppo: __TextSave( ("amulet") ) ; QOUT(       line 1")
//         QOUT("      line 2").
```

Table 4.1 Extended Expression Translations

Source Code	Translation
customer	"customer"
("customer")	("customer")
(cFileName)	(cFileName)

In the first example, the definition of the COPY FILE command has two extended expression match markers, `<(src)>` and `<(dest)>`. The code sample illustrates what happens when both a database name and an extended expression with a character literal are used. The first, TxnTemp is changed to "TxnTemp" and the second, ('Txn') is unchanged. Then, (cFileName) is specified, indicating that the memory variable cFileName contains the name of a database, and also remains unchanged.

1. Look up the SET DEFAULT TO command in STD.CH to determine the preprocessed output of following Clipper command:

   SET DEFAULT TO c:\amulet\fredi

1. Upon reviewing STD.CH, we see that the UDC definition for SET DEFAULT TO is:

   ```
   #command SET DEFAULT TO <(path)>  =>      ;
       Set( _SET_DEFAULT, <(path)> )
   ```

   where it seems that an extended expression match marker `<(path)>` is used to recognize the path name. The preprocessed output would then be:

   ```
   // _SET_DEFAULT is a manifest constant defined in SET.CH as 7.
   // ppo: Set( 7, "c:\amulet\fredi")
   ```

Optional Clauses

Many CA-Clipper commands have optional clauses. For example, in the SET FUNCTION TO command, the TO portion is optional,— that is, the command is translated by the corresponding UDC successfully no matter if the TO keyword and its value is present or not. So there must be a device in UDCs to recognize these clauses if present. The method we need is called an optional clause and may be represented by square brackets as in [<matchPattern>]. These square brackets, which delimit optional clauses, may contain any kind of match marker. Following are some useful examples. Notice that the match marker appears without the brackets on the right side of the UDC definition.

```
// Notice we have a regular match marker inside brackets.
#command SET FUNCTION <n> [TO] [<c>]            ;
    => __SetFunction( <n>, <c> )
cEndPrompt := 'END'
SET FUNCTION 2 TO cEndPrompt
// ppo: __SetFunction( 2, cEndPrompt )
SET FUNCTION 2 TO
// Below, the missing optional clause ends up as a NIL parameter.
// ppo: __SetFunction( 2, )

#command COPY [STRUCTURE] [EXTENDED] [TO <(file)>]  ;
    => __dbCopyXStruct( <(file)> )
LOCAL cFileName := 'joyce.txt'
COPY STRUCTURE EXTENDED TO (cFileName)
// ppo: __dbCopyXStruct ( (cFileName) )
// Below, looking at STD.CH can show you shorthand notations.
COPY EXTENDED TO (cFileName)
// ppo: __dbCopyXStruct ( (cFileName) )
```

From these examples, it seems that there are actually two types of optional clauses. The first type is just a keyword enclosed in brackets, as in [TO] and the second type is a keyword followed by a match marker enclosed in brackets, as in [TO <(file)>]. If you are interested in learning the minimal construct required to represent a programming idea, a detailed trip through STD.CH could benefit you, since you would discover numerous shortcuts like the COPY command example.

Note In a command containing multiple optional clauses, you can specify the clauses in any order, but a required clause may not intercede between optional clauses when the optional clauses are out of order.

Note You can also nest optional clauses. In order for the preprocessor to recognize a nested optional clause, the outermost keyword must be specified in order for inner keywords to be recognized. For example, if a new PAINT command had an optional COORDS clause, which in turn had several optional clauses, COORDS must be specified first.

```
#xcommand PAINT [COORD [UPPER <u>] [LEFT <l>] [LOWER <w>] ;
    [RIGHT <r>]                                          ;
    =>                                                   ;
    __dbPaint( <u>, <l>, <w>, <r> )
```

1. Using the definition for the DIR command in STD.CH, determine the preprocessed output of the following CA-Clipper program segment:

```
LOCAL cFileSpec := '*.DBF'
DIR (cFileSpec)
```

2. Now repeat the process you performed in Exercise 1 for the SET DATE TO JAPANESE command and determine the output for:

   ```
   // The example below will be recognized properly.
   SET DATE TO TO TO TO TO JAPANESE
   ```

3. Considering the following UDC, determine the preprocessor output of the given code sample:

   ```
   #xcommand GRAPH [<r: RED>] [<g: GREEN, GRN]  ;
     [<b: BLUE>] DRAW <p>                        ;
     =>                                          ;
     f( <.r.>, <.g.>, <.b.>, <p> )

   // And now a usage:
   GRAPH DRAW "Box Title" BLUE RED
   ```

1. The UDC appearing in STD.CH for the DIR command is produced here for your reference:

   ```
   #command DIR [<(spec)>] => __Dir( <(spec)> )
   ```

   and the resulting .PPO output is:

   ```
   // ppo: __Dir( (cFileSpec) )
   ```

2. The UDC we need to consider is:

   ```
   // _DFSET is a pseudo function defined in STD.CH.
   #command SET DATE [TO] JAPANESE => ;
      _DFSET( "yyyy/mm/dd", "yy/mm/dd" )
   ```

   Notice that the TO clause is optional. Being an optional clause means that it may be repeated at often as necessary in the input text. Therefore, the numerous repetitions have no bearing in the resulting preprocessed output:

   ```
   // ppo: Set( 4, if(__SetCentury(), "yyyy/mm/dd", ;
   //       "yy/mm/dd") )
   ```

3. The code shown generates a compile-time error: "C2005 Statement not recognized" because the match fails at the character constant. This is because the optional clauses are out of order with an interceding required clause.

List Match Marker

The <list,...> notation handles the CA-Clipper command syntax that may contain a separated list of expressions. This UDC provision is required because many Clipper commands give the programmer the ability to list a series of items after a keyword (must be a mechanism to recognize such structures). When defining a UDC that must recognize a list, you must choose a name for the list and surround it by the necessary punctuation, for example: <parmlist,...>.

In the example that follows, notice that `<list,...>` becomes just `<list>` on the right side of the UDC definition.

```
#command DO <proc>.PRG [WITH <list,...>]          ;
  => do <proc> [ WITH <list>]
DO raise.prg WITH cEmpName, nPctIncr, dHireDate
// ppo: do fu WITH cEmpName, nPctIncr, dHireDate
```

Here, we remember the familiar Xbase style `DO...WITH` command, which accepts a variable number of parameters separated by commas after the keyword `WITH`. The STD.CH definition uses the list match marker `<list,...>` to recognize the list of parameters. Notice that this list is optional and therefore enclosed in square brackets. Note also that this UDC does not do much more than eliminate the .PRG extension.

1. With the help of a UDC, create a new command called PRINT, similar in function to the ? command, which accepts a series of expressions and displays them on the screen. For example, consider the sample code:

   ```
   PRINT
   PRINT "Entering Cyberspace", 123
   ```

1. The solution is easy once we look up the ? definition in STD.CH. We can alter it slightly to come up with similar results. This is often a logical technique when constructing new UDCs; begin with one that works and then tailor it to the current situation.

   ```
   // Notice that the list is optional.
   #xcommand PRINT [ <list,...> ] => QOut( <list> )
   // The preprocessed output for the above sample code:
   // ppo: QOut( )
   // ?   QOut( "Entering cyberspace", 123 )
   ```

Restricted Match Marker

This is a tricky type of match marker, but very necessary due to the nature of the internal functions referenced by many standard UDC definitions. The restricted match marker is used for the CA-Clipper commands in which the presence or absence of a keyword must be translated to either a .T. or .F. parameter or a call to a built-in or internal Clipper function. With a restricted match marker you specify that a logical flag must be set *only if* the clause in question was specified. The notation is `<lvarName: KEYWORD>`, where `lvarName` is the logical flag to be set if `KEYWORD` is recognized. Many CA-Clipper commands, such as the USE command, contain numerous optional keywords that affect the manner in which the command executes. But first, let us consider a simpler example:

```
// Allow alternate spellings this way:
#command SET MESSAGE TO <n> [<cent: CENTER, CENTRE>]   ;
  => Set(_SET_MESSAGE, <n>)                            ;
     Set(_SET_MCENTER, <.cent.>)
SET MESSAGE TO 22 CENTER
// ppo: Set( 36, 22 ) ; Set( 37, .T. )
```

Notice that the flag cent in the restricted match marker appears as <.cent.> on the right side of the UDC definition. This is called a *logify result marker*, which we'll see more of later. Notice also that this clause is optional.

```
// The __MRestore() function expects a logical value to
// determine if user requested ADDITIVE processing.
#command RESTORE [FROM <(file)>] [<add: ADDITIVE>] ;
  => __MRestore( <(file)>, <.add.> )

RESTORE FROM movie
// Since the ADDITIVE keyword was not include, a .F. is passed.
// ppo: __MRestore( "movie", .F. )
```

As stated earlier, some commands, like USE, have several keywords that require the restricted match marker. In the following example definition of USE from STD.CH, try to follow the restricted match markers.

```
#command USE <(db)>                                    ;
         [VIA <rdd>]                                   ;
         [ALIAS <a>]                                   ;
         [<new: NEW>]                                  ;
         [<ex: EXCLUSIVE>]                             ;
         [<sh: SHARED>]                                ;
         [<ro: READONLY>]                              ;
         [INDEX <(index1)> [, <(indexn)>]]             ;
                                                       ;
      => dbUseArea(                                    ;
            <.new.>, <rdd>, <(db)>, <(a)>,             ;
            if(<.sh.> .or. <.ex.>, !<.ex.>,            ;
            NIL), <.ro.>                               ;
            )                                          ;
                                                       ;
         [; dbSetIndex( <(index1)> )]
         [; dbSetIndex( <(indexn)> )]

USE Txn VIA 'DBFCDX' ALIAS pTxns NEW EXCLUSIVE READONLY
// ppo: dbUseArea( .T., "DBFCDX", "Txn", "pTxns",
//      if(.F. .OR. .T., !.T., NIL), .T. ).
// Note that VIA "DBFCDX" requires quotation marks, whereas ALIAS
// ptxns does not. This is due to: <rdd> is a regular
// result marker, but <(a)> is a smart stringify result marker.
// We shall see more of this later.
```

Wild Match Marker

Some CA-Clipper commands require a recognizer for miscellaneous groups of text. With the wild match marker, you can match bulk text appearing after a keyword or keywords to end of line or until some whitespace (blanks) is encountered. Use the notation <*marker*> to specify where the text may occur. Several commands should come to mind as an application of this match marker. Consider, for example, the following:

```
#command SET PATH TO <*path*> => ;
    Set(_SET_PATH, <(path)> )
SET PATH TO c:\amulet
// ppo: Set( 6, "c:\amulet" )
cPathName := "c:\amulet"
SET PATH TO (cPathName)
// ppo: Set( 6, (cPathName) )

// The old FIND command:
#command FIND <*text*> => dbSeek( <(text)> )
FIND William
// ppo: dbSeek( "William" ).
```

First, with the SET PATH TO command, the string of characters representing the DOS path name may be virtually any number of characters. The wild match marker is able to recognize this set of characters. Next, the outdated Xbase style of performing an indexed key search, using the FIND command, requires the literal text for which the database is searched to be placed immediately after the FIND keyword. Again, the wild match marker applies here.

As another example, remember the old Xbase ability to append uncommented text to the end of ENDIF, ENDCASE, and ENDDO; CA-Clipper brings you compatibility with this syntax by the following application of the wild match marker:

```
// You can also eliminate unwanted text after keyword.
#command ENDDO <*x*> => enddo
ENDDO    This is a comment
// ppo: ENDDO
```

One last example shows how CA-Clipper nullifies unsupported commands using the wild match marker:

```
#command SET SAFETY <*x*> =>
SET SAFETY ZONE TO SOMETHING REAL BIG
// ppo: nothing is copied to preprocessed output
```

This concludes our examination of match markers. Let's now turn to a discussion of the right-hand portion of a UDC definition: result match markers.

1. Create a UDC that defines a new command named COMMENT, which allows comment text to appear after the keyword as in:

```
COMMENT ***********************
COMMENT * TITLE BOX GOES HERE *
COMMENT ***********************
```

1. The solution is a variation of the ENDDO definition shown in the previous section. In this case, the keyword to be recognized is COMMENT.

```
#command COMMENT <*x*> =>
```

Result Markers

There are also replacement rules governing what may be specified on the right side of a UDC definition. In many cases, the result markers parallel their match marker counterparts, however, it is not always that simple. In the next several sections, we'll look at some examples of all the available types of result markers paired with several match markers. The available result markers are: *regular, dumb stringify, smart stringify, logify, blockify, normal stringify, and repeating clauses.*

Note

Actually, any type of match marker can be paired with any result marker. It is, however, true that certain combinations are much more common by their nature than others. Moreover, it is possible to construct a table defining the preprocessor output of each pair.

Regular Result Marker

We've already seen this type of result marker in our discussion of the regular match marker. Namely, whenever the notation `<idMarker>` appears on the right side of the definition it is called a regular result marker. This type of result marker is the most common type because it is used in such cases in which the recognized text by a regular match marker needs to appear unaltered in the resulting preprocessor output. In the following example, the match markers `<dividend>` and `<divisor>` are mapped into the like named result markers. This simply means that the recognized text on the left side maps into text positioned on the right side.

```
#xtranslate DIV (<dividend>, <divisor>) => ;
    (<dividend>) / (<divisor>)
// Here, right side markers are called "regular result
// markers".
? DIV( 10+20, 5 )
// ppo: QOut( (10+20) / (5) )
```

Dumb Stringify Result Marker

This result marker, denoted #<marker>, is used every time a match marker needs to be unconditionally surrounded by quotation marks (to create a string constant). There are several commands requiring this kind of operation as we will soon see. If no input text is matched, a null string ("") is written to the output text.

In the first example shown next, we see the STD.CH definition of the RELEASE ALL LIKE command. A regular match marker <skel> is mapped into a dumb stringify result maker using the same marker name, namely #<skel>. The situation requires a dumb stringify result marker because the RELEASE ALL LIKE command accepts a memory variable name pattern that must become a parameter to the __MRelease() internal function.

```
// Here, a regular match marker <skel> is used.
#command?  RELEASE ALL LIKE <skel> => ;
    __MRelease( #<skel>, .t. )
RELEASE ALL LIKE M*
// ppo: __MRelease( "M*", .T. )

// Here, a wild match marker <*cmd*> is used.
#command RUN <*cmd*> => __Run( #<cmd> )
RUN diskcopy a: a:
// ppo: __Run( "diskcopy a: a:" )
```

In the second example, a wild match marker is used to recognize some bulk text—a DOS command, for example—which is then mapped to a dumb stringify result marker. This causes a literal string containing the DOS command to be passed to the __Run() internal function.

Smart Stringify Result Marker

During our discussion of extended expression match markers earlier, we saw the form <(file)>. When this form appears on the right side of a UDC definition it is called a smart stringify result marker. This result marker adds a touch of intelligence to the process of adding quotation marks around a string of recognized text. If matched input text is enclosed in parentheses, smart stringify copies it unaltered to the output text, otherwise quotation marks are added.

Table 4.2 summarizes some rules that govern the operation of the smart stringify result marker.

The table indicates that the recognition of text or expressions results in quoted text in the output text whereas any text surrounded by parentheses is left alone. Here are some STD.CH examples that show these concepts:

Table 4.2 Rules for the Smart Stringify Result Marker

Text In	Text Out
chars	"chars"
(chars)	(chars)
cVar1+cVar2	"cVar1+cVar2"

```
#command CREATE <(file1)> [FROM <(file2)>          ;
  => __dbCreate( <(file1)>, <(file2)> )
CREATE temp FROM temp1
// ppo: __dbCreate( "temp", "temp1" )
CREATE (cFileName) FROM temp1
// ppo: __dbCreate( (cFileName), "temp1" )

#command SET PROCEDURE TO <f> => _ProcReq_( <(f)> )
SET PROCEDURE TO (cDrive+cPath+cProcName)
// ppo: _ProcReq( (cDrive+cPath+cProcName) )
```

In the first example, the `<(file1)>` on the left side is called an extended expression match marker, but the same symbol on the right side is called a smart stringify match marker. The utility of smart stringify comes into play with the second CREATE example. Notice here that `(cFileName)` is recognized but remains unaltered in the output text. The same is true for the character expression surrounded by parentheses in the second example.

Logify Result Marker

We have already seen the logify result marker during our discussion of restricted match markers, as they are often used together. Specifically, restricted match markers may be mapped to logify result markers by using the form: `<.lvarName.>`. As stated before, a logify result marker generates a logical constant in the output text whenever the optional clause in the restricted match marker is recognized.

Blockify Result Marker

The key to the success of many CA-Clipper commands is the ability to translate some clauses into code blocks. This is due to the fact that many Clipper clauses are implemented as code block parameters passed to internal functions. Although we won't officially cover code blocks until later in the book, for completeness on the topic of UDCs, we must introduce the concept now. The blockify result marker translates matched input text into a code block. This simply means that the text will be inserted as the body of a code block, namely

{||<text>}. In other words, the text is "blockified." The blockify result marker form: <{marker}> must be used on the right side of the definition. In the following example, we see the definition of the JOIN command, which includes a FOR clause:

```
#command JOIN [WITH <(alias)>] [TO <file>]            ;
  [FIELDS <fields,...>]                                ;
  [FOR <for>]                                          ;
                                                       ;
  => __dbJoin( <(alias)>, <(file)>, { <(fields)> },    ;
     <{for}> )
JOIN WITH (cFileName) TO (cOutFile) FOR inits == "DDG"
// The <for> regular result marker containing the logical
// expression required by the FOR clause is "blockified"
// and passed as a parameter to internal function
// __dbJoin().
// ppo: __dbJoin( (cFileName), (cOutFile), { },        ;
// {|| inits == "DDG"} )
```

In this code, the logical expression that constitutes the FOR clause is recognized and placed inside a code block, as in: {|| inits == 'DDG'}. Because code blocks can be passed as parameters to functions, the FOR expression can be handed over to the internal function __dbJoin().

Normal Stringify Result Marker

The normal stringify result marker functions in a manner similar to the dumb stringify result marker except that if no input text is matched, nothing is written to the output text. If the corresponding match marker is a list match marker, then all items recognized in the list are enclosed in quotaton marks. This result marker is denoted with <"marker">.

In the definition of the INDEX ON command, shown next, the normal stringify result marker <"key"> is used because of the possibility that no index key expression will be specified. If this is the case then a null parameter results as the second parameter of the dbCreateIndex() database function.

```
#command INDEX ON <key> TO <(file)> [<u: UNIQUE>]    ;
  => dbCreateIndex(                                   ;
        <(file)>, <"key">, <{key}>,                   ;
        if( <.u.>, .t., NIL )                         ;
     )
INDEX ON Last+First TO (FileName)
// ppo: dbCreateIndex( (cFileName), "Last+First",     ;
// {|| Last+First}, if( .F., .T., NIL ) ).
```

```
#command RELEASE <vars,...>  =>  __MXRelease( <"var"> )
RELEASE x,, z
// Since the list match marker <vars,...> is used, all of
// the items are stringified.
// ppo: __MXRelease( "x",, "z" )

#command SET FILTER TO <xpr>      => ;
    dbSetFilter( <{xpr}>, <"xpr"> )
SET FILTER TO !DELETED()
// Below example uses both blockify and normal stringify.
// ppo: dbSetFilter( {|| !DELETED()}, "!DELETED()" )
```

Repeating Clauses

To accommodate the recognition of CA-Clipper commands that accept repeated keyword clauses (e.g. REPLACE and its WITH clause), we use the square bracket notation again, but the structure is quite different from the optional clause we saw earlier. Here is the notation you would use for REPLACE.
On left side of definition:

```
<f1> WITH <v1> [,<fN> WITH <vN>]
```

On right side of definition:

```
_FIELD-><f1>:=<v1> [;_FIELD-><fN>:=<vN>]
```

You first define the appearance of the first item of the repeating clause and then the Nth item using the <f1>, <v1>, and <fN>, <vN> tuple (ordered pairs). Think of this as meaning "0 or more" occurrences. Take for example, the definition of the SET INDEX TO command, where a variable number of index files may be listed:

```
#command SET INDEX TO [ <(index1)> [, <(indexn)>]]   ;
        [<add: ADDITIVE>]                            ;
                                                     ;
    => if !<.add.> ; ordListClear() ; end            ;
                                                     ;
    [; ordListAdd( <(index1)> )]
    [; ordListAdd( <(indexn)> )]



SET INDEX TO ntx1, ntx2
// ppo: if !.F. ; ordListClear() ;
//    ordListAdd( "ntx1" ); ordListAdd( "ntx2" ).
```

In this case, many index files may appear in the command separated by commas. A list match marker would not suffice here because each item must be a separate parameter in a call to the `ordListAdd()` function. Therefore, we require the repeating clause.

1. Create a UDC that defines a new command named `INIT`, allowing multiple variable assignments of the following form:

```
INIT foo1 To 1 AND foo2 TO 2 AND foo3 TO 3
```

1. The solution we're looking for requires an application of repeating clauses that recognizes a number of memory variable name/value pairs and translates them into equivalent assignment statements. Here is how this is implemented:

```
#xcommand INIT <memvar1> TO <val1>            ;
         [AND <memvarN> TO <valN>]            ;
      =>                                      ;
      <memvar1> := <val1> [;<memvarN> := <valN>]
```

Examples from COMMON.CH

This section illustrates the use of UDCs by presenting some interesting examples found in the COMMON.CH header file, which is located in the \INCLUDE directory. This header contains several `#translate` definitions used to perform data type checking on a passed memory variable. You'll also find definitions for two useful commands: `DEFAULT` and `UPDATE`. Let's first examine the `#translate` commands:

```
#translate ISNIL( <v1>)        => ( <v1> == NIL )
#translate ISARRAY( <v1>)      => ( valtype( <v1> ) == "A" )
#translate ISBLOCK( <v1>)      => ( valtype( <v1> ) == "B" )
#translate ISCHARACTER( <v1>)  => ( valtype( <v1> ) == "C" )
#translate ISDATE( <v1> )      => ( valtype( <v1> ) == "D" )
#translate ISLOGICAL( <v1>)    => ( valtype( <v1> ) == "L" )
#translate ISMEMO( <v1> )      => ( valtype( <v1> ) == "M" )
#translate ISNUMBER( <v1> )    => ( valtype( <v1> ) == "N" )
#translate ISOBJECT( <v1> )    => ( valtype( <v1> ) == "O" )
```

As you can see, these new expressions will be recognized by the preprocessor and translated into the appropriate comparison using the `VALTYPE()` built-in function. If you remember from Chapter 2, `VALTYPE()` returns a single character value indicating the parameter's data type. Here are some applications:

```
// UDF has a parameter which should be a code block, as
// indicated by the 'b' prefix. However, to be safe we
```

```
// could explicitly check the data type before proceeding.

FUNCTION MyUDF(bParm1, cParm2)

IF ISBLOCK(bParm1)
   EVAL(bParm1)        // Evaluate the code block.
ELSE
   ? 'Parameter must be a code block'
ENDIF

// We use ISNIL() to check if a parameter was passed and if
// so then process it.

IF !ISNIL(cParm2)      // Check if a parm was passed.
   .
   . <statements>
   .
ENDIF
RETURN NIL
```

Now let's look at the two useful commands included in COMMON.CH. These commands were included because they both were already widely used by many CA-Clipper developers as unofficial commands, so in an attempt to standardize them, Computer Associates, Inc. placed them in this subsidiary header file instead of STD.CH. The first one, DEFAULT has the following definition:

```
#xcommand DEFAULT <v1> TO <x1> [, <vn> TO <xn> ]    ;
   =>                                               ;
   IF <v1> == NIL ; <v1> := <x1> ; END              ;
   [; IF <vn> == NIL ; <vn> := <xn> ; END ]
```

The DEFAULT command allows you to assign a default value to a memory variable *if it does not already have a value;* that is, it contains the value NIL. This ability comes in handy when you need to initialize a variable before using it. Here is an example:

```
/***
*
* DispMsg( <nRow>, <cMsg> )
*
* Purpose:    Display a message on the screen.
*
* Parameters: nRow (optional, defaults to 24)
*      cMsg
*
*/
```

```
FUNCTION DispMsg(nRow, cMsg)

// DEFAULT checks if nRow is NIL, if so it assigns
// default value.
DEFAULT nRow TO 24
@ nRow, 0 SAY cMsg

RETURN NIL
```

The `DEFAULT` command is ideal for cases like this where a parameter is to have a default value if none was specified. In addition, as you can tell from the UDC definition, multiple variables can receive default values.

The second new command is `UPDATE`, which has the following definition:

```
#command UPDATE <v1> IF <exp> TO <v2>      ;
    =>                                      ;
    IF <exp> ; <v1> := <v2> ; END
```

You use `UPDATE` to selectively modify a variable if the specified condition is true. Consider the following example:

```
LOCAL lTaxable

lTaxable := TRUE    // Item is taxable.
nExtendedPrice := Orders->Qty * Product->UnitPrice
UPDATE nExtendedPrice IF lTaxable TO 1.0825 * ;
    nExtendedPrice
```

In this example, `UPDATE` is used to decide whether to apply sales tax to the extended price amount. This determination is based on the logical value of the `lTaxable` memory variable. Of course, a logical expression of any complexity can appear in the `IF` clause.

Summary

In this chapter, we've examined CA-Clipper user-defined commands. With the numerous examples, we have seen each of the textual translation rules available in UDCs. UDCs may not be something a Clipper beginner deals with regularly, but a firm understanding definitely helps in the understanding of how Clipper really works. Just as a caution before you proceed, we'll be using UDCs in future chapters in order to demonstrate CA-Clipper's programming flexibility as it applies to other types of constructs, such as arrays, database access, memo fields, and others.

Exercise

1. Let's say that we wish to create a UDC that defines a new command named SERIAL and sends a block of text to a preconfigured serial communications port on your PC. We have previously created a function called SendSerial(), which performs the task of transmission (so you don't have to worry about the details of writing characters to the serial port). You invoke this command like this:

```
SERIAL Financial Report #104.G Beg
```

Answer

1. The answer depends on whether only raw text is to be passed to the SendSerial() function. If true, then an application of the wild match marker and dumb stringify result marker suffices:

```
#xcommand SERIAL <*commdata*>          ;
    =>                                  ;
    SendSerial( #<commdata> )
```

If however the data to send can come from a memory variable or expression, you should probably choose another stringify result marker.

5

Subprograms

Programs Units ➤ 112

Procedures ➤ 113

Functions ➤ 117

Scope and Lifetime ➤ 119

Static Functions and Procedures ➤ 129

Comparison of Scopes and Lifetimes ➤ 130

Announce and Request ➤ 131

INIT and EXIT Procedures ➤ 133

Summary ➤ 137

Exercise ➤ 138

The state-of-the-art with respect to modular programming took a significant step forward with CA-Clipper; moving away from the antiquated methodologies that persisted even in Summer '87, such as using the DO command to call a subprogram or placing common procedures in a procedure file (SET PROCEDURE TO, although supported, need not be used). Now, many CA-Clipper programmers maintain their logical program units in a *functionized* form, much like C and Pascal programmers have done for years. Also, allowing the linker to resolve references to subprograms alleviates the need for procedure files. In addition, there is a movement away from the cave-art-style PRIVATE and PUBLIC variables to the more contemporary and efficient LOCAL and STATIC scope and lifetime rules found in CA-Clipper.

In this chapter we'll look at all you need to know to get up to speed with Clipper's handling of *user-defined functions* (UDFs), *procedures, parameter passing techniques, variable scoping,* and *lifetime rules*. You'll find effective use of these areas in providing for the means to do CA-Clipper optimized programming. Moreover, for readers moving up to CA-Clipper from the Summer '87 release, you'll learn methods for giving your code a distinct facelift.

After completing this chapter, you will have learned:

- To move away from the older Xbase methods of program organization
- The means by which all program modules may be enclosed in a FUNCTION or PROCEDURE subprogram
- The basic ingredients of parameter passing for the various subprograms types in CA-Clipper, specifically *By Value* and *By Reference* parameter passing
- An understanding of variable scoping (visibility)
- An understanding of variable lifetime
- To avoid PUBLICs and still get an application-wide variable scope
- Methods for defining module identifiers and referencing external modules with ANNOUNCE and REQUEST
- To define both INIT and EXIT procedures

Programs Units

In CA-Clipper, there are two types of subprograms: *procedures* and *functions*. In past releases of Clipper, the two have had specific purposes in the language, but in the current version of Clipper, the differences are small. Many seasoned Clipper developers tend to write all code as a series of interrelated functions (UDFs).

> **Note** The official stance is, however, to use the *procedure* form of a subprogram when a *return value is not required* and the *function* form when a *return value is needed*.

The way this organization impacts .PRG files becomes important too. For example, in the past the norm was to write a separate .PRG file for each program unit. Each program, procedure, and function would reside in a .PRG, the exception being a procedure library containing miscellaneous, but frequently used, subprograms. Now, given the trend to *functionize* all program modules, it is better to place several subprograms together inside a single .PRG. For example, you might put several data entry screens together in one .PRG or a few similar report programs. All of this would tend to decrease the total number of .PRGs, and corresponding .OBJ files, that comprise your application (reducing the number of .OBJ files is also a stated goal of today's dynamic linker programs). Since Clipper is a compiled language and the end result is always a single .EXE file, the linker program gets responsibility for finding all compiled subprograms in order to construct the final .EXE.

Procedures

Let's start our investigation of CA-Clipper's subprogram capabilities with a discussion of the procedure-style subprogram and look at two ways to utilize them in CA-Clipper. First, we see that the Xbase-style procedure usage is still available, as shown in the following code sample (to further illustrate the point, we'll also use the Xbase commenting and naming conventions):

```
* Old Xbase method procedure definition and calling method
DO procname WITH ap1, ap2
RETURN

* Procedure definition
PROCEDURE procname
PARAMETERS fp1, fp2     && The old Xbase method
RETURN
```

Here, we use the `DO...WITH` command to invoke the procedure and pass it the required parameters. We call parameters in the calling program *actual parameters*. The CA-Clipper Reference Guide, however, lists the `DO` command as a "compatibility" command, indicating that its use is not recommended since there are better ways in Clipper to perform the same service. We'll see in a moment how you can avoid the `DO` command when you're calling procedures.

Notice that in the procedure definition we declare the parameters in a `PARAMETERS` statement. This statement is also not used in contemporary Clipper development. Inside a procedure (or any subprogram) we call the parameters *formal parameters*. Finally, note that a `RETURN` statement with no return value is the last statement of the procedure. This structure should be familiar to any programmer that has used an Xbase dialect.

Now let's look at the more contemporary CA-Clipper *function-style* procedure structure in the following code sample (along with the newer Clipper coding guidelines):

```
/* Main program */
ProcName(ap1, ap2)              // A function style call.
RETURN

/* Procedure */
PROCEDURE ProcName(fp1, fp2)    // A function style definition.
RETURN                          // Note, still no return value.
```

This time, the procedure is called in a manner normally associated with functions, namely without a `DO` command and with the parameters enclosed in parentheses. We don't need the `WITH` clause at all. The procedure definition also resembles that of a function.

> **Note** Note that we can also eliminate the `PARAMETERS` statement from the procedure body since the formal parameters are declared, in a sense, inside the `PROCEDURE` statement.

To further see the differences between Xbase and Clipper procedure definition and calling styles, here are some more examples of procedure usage:

```
* MAIN.PRG - Main program calls a procedure

* Xbase method using WITH to pass parameters:
DO CalcSal WITH nSalary, "Frederika", 5

* CA-Clipper method (preferred):
CalcSal(nSalary, 'Frederika', 5)



* CALCSAL.PRG - Xbase style procedure definition
PROCEDURE calcsal
PARAMETERS nBaseSal, cEmpName, nYears
* Above formal parameters will be declared as PRIVATE
* scope since they appear in a PARAMETERS statement
RETURN

/***
*
* CalcSal() - Function-style procedure definition
*
*/
```

```
PROCEDURE CalcSal(nBaseSal, cEmpName, nYears)
* Above formal parameters will be treated as LOCAL scope
RETURN
```

One important difference between procedures and functions is that we cannot depend on the value returned by procedures to the calling program. Officially, a procedure returns the value NIL, but in certain cases, other return values may result. This is not an important difference since functions that don't need to return a value may explicitly return NIL.

Of course, all parameters must be defined before they are passed to a either a procedure or function. So, in the following example, we see that if a variable vParm has no prior assignment, the program aborts, but if we assign a value, even a value of NIL, everything is fine.

```
DO TestProc WITH vParm      // Will crash with vParm undeclared.
*
vParm := NIL
DO TestProc WITH vParm      // Will not crash, since NIL is valid
                            // as a value for a parameter.
```

Another area of difference is how parameters are passed to procedures. When using Xbase-style procedures, parameters are passed *By Reference* to procedures, which means that the address in memory of the value, not the value itself, is passed. When using CA-Clipper function-style procedures, however, parameters are passed *By Value*. This notion is important when trying to determine if a parameter may be changed inside a procedure. We'll see later in this chapter that parameter passing for Clipper style procedures is identical to that of functions.

Note

Remember the difference between By Reference and By Value parameter passing this way: By Reference means you *may change the parameter's value* while inside the subprogram, and By Value means you *may not change the value.*

The following code examples demonstrate this important point. First, we'll consider Xbase-style procedures:

```
nDays := 100
DO IncDays WITH nDays       // nDays passed By Reference.
QOUT(nDays)                 // nDays now contains 101.
RETURN NIL

PROCEDURE IncDays
PARAMETERS nFormal
nFormal++                   // New value affects actual parameter.
RETURN
```

In this example, since we're using the `DO...WITH` method for calling a procedure, the actual parameter `nDays` is passed By Reference, hence its value is modified inside the procedure as indicated by the fact that upon return from `IncDays()`, `QOUT()` displays 101. Now let's see the function-style of the procedure:

```
/* Main program */
nDays := 100
IncDays(nDays) // nDays passed By Value.
QOUT(nDays)    // Shows same value for nDays: 100.
RETURN

PROCEDURE IncDays(nFormal)
nFormal++      // Does not affect nDays in calling program.
RETURN
```

This time we see that the value of `nDays` is unaffected by `IncDays()` since it is passed By Value. Notice also from the previous examples that the actual and formal parameters do not need to be named the same.

In the next example you'll see that you may instead pass parameters By Value with Xbase-style procedures by causing an evaluation using parentheses. Bear in mind, however, you need only remember this if you call a procedure with a `DO` command.

```
DO IncDays WITH (nDays)    // nDays is passed By Value.
```

Here, the procedure will make a copy of the value of the expression inside the parentheses. Therefore, when passing By Value, any change to the formal parameter is not reflected in the calling program.

Finally, we can pass parameters By Reference with Clipper-style procedures by preceding the actual parameter with an @ symbol. In the previous example, if the following line had been used, `nDays` would retain the new value as assigned inside the procedure:

```
IncDays(@nDays)            // nDays passed By Reference.
```

You may also pass entire expressions as parameters to a procedure. When you do, they are passed By Value. This makes sense if you consider:

```
nDays := 200
DO Plus10 WITH (nDays/10) // Pass expression By Value.
QOUT(nDays)               // nDays is still 200.

PROCEDURE Plus10
PARAMETERS nDiv
```

```
        nDiv := nDiv + 10      // nDiv is 30, inside the procedure.
RETURN
```

It is logical that expressions are passed By Value. What would it mean to change the formal parameter nDiv? The actual parameter is an expression based on nDays, and you would certainly not expect nDays to change.

Database fields must be passed By Value because the procedure doesn't necessarily know that its formal parameter has a database field for its corresponding actual parameter. In this situation, the procedure could not update the field's contents if its value were changed inside the procedure.

1. Write a Clipper function-style procedure EndPage() that provides end-of-page processing for a report program. The procedure accepts two formal parameters: nPage and nLine, the current page and line counters. If nLine exceeds the maximum lines per page, a new page is begun by printing "Page nnn" on the top of the new page. You must also update both counters.

1. Here is one possible solution for EndPage() along with a line in the calling program to invoke it:

```
#define REPORT_PAGE_LENGTH 55
FUNCTION Main
LOCAL nPage:= 0, nLine:= 99

EndPage(@nPage, @nLine)

RETURN NIL

PROCEDURE EndPage( nPage, nLine)
nLine++              // Increment line counter.
/* End of page processing */
IF nLine > REPORT_PAGE_LENGTH
   @ 0, 120 SAY 'Page: '+STR(nPage,3)
   nLine := 1
   nPage++
ENDIF
RETURN
```

We'll see later that another way to give access to the variables nLine and nPage from both the Main() and EndPage() subprograms is to declare the variables as file-wide statics instead of passing them By Reference as parameters.

Functions

UDFs are more commonly used as subprogram units in CA-Clipper than procedures. The main difference when using UDFs, as mentioned earlier, is that a

UDF always returns a value that appears as an expression after its RETURN statement. If you call a UDF on a line by itself as in

```
UpdRec(cTestVal)
lRetVal := UpdRec(cTestVal)  // Here, return value is saved.
```

any return value is lost since you have not indicated a place to put it.

A meaningless return value may be indicated by using NIL, e.g. RETURN NIL, to terminate the function. This is useful when using functions in a manner normally associated with procedures.

> The return value of a function may be of any data type, including array and codeblock.

You might even consider defining your main program as a function:

```
/* Compile with the /N switch if you choose this method */
FUNCTION Main
   * Code body goes here
RETURN NIL
```

With UDFs, parameters are passed By Value, which implies there is no problem passing database fields. If you wish to modify an actual parameter inside a function, you'll have to override the default and pass the parameters By Reference by using the special @ prefix:

```
PostTxn(@nCustBal)  // nCustBal passed "By Reference".
```

Table 5.1 summarizes our discussions of CA-Clipper's procedure and function parameter passing techniques.

Note that fields that are passed to procedures must be enclosed in parentheses unless they are declared in a FIELD statement, otherwise Clipper assumes they are variables.

Table 5.1 Parameter Passing Techniques

Technique	Expressions	Variables	Vars with @	Fields
UDF	By Value	By Value	By Reference	By Value
Procedure Xbase style	By Value	By Reference (By Value)	Not allowed	By Value
Procedure function style	By Value	By Value	By Reference	By Value

Notice also that the table illustrates a good reason for using function-style calling conventions when invoking a procedure, namely that the parameter passing mechanisms are the same for both functions and procedures when this style is used. Even better, just use functions all around.

One last characteristic of functions and procedures that are called like functions is that they may be called with an alias as in:

```
* Select ORDERS and then call function. Upon return
* reselect original work area.
Orders->(GenTxn(cCustId, cProdCode))
```

1. Determine the displayed output of the program modules:

```
FUNCTION Main
LOCAL nEeny := 1, nMoe

MyProc(nEeny)
nMoe := MyUDF(@nEeny)
? nEeny, nMoe    // What are the values?

RETURN NIL

PROCEDURE MyProc(nMeeny)
nMeeny += 10
RETURN

FUNCTION MyUDF(nMiny)
nMiny -= 10
RETURN (nMiny+10)
```

1. The program generates the output -9 and 1. Let's analyze the program to see why. First, nEeny is initialized to 1 and nMoe has no initial value. We then call MyProc(), passing nEeny By Value, which means that any changes to the formal parameter will not affect nEeny (the actual parameter). So, upon returning, nEeny remains 1. Next we call the UDF MyUDF(), this time passing nEeny By Reference. Inside MyUDF(), the formal parameter nMiny is decremented by 10, leaving a -9 in nMiny (formal parameter) and in nEeny (actual parameter). Finally, the return value 1 (-9 + 10) of the function is given to nMoe.

Scope and Lifetime

The concepts of *scope* and *lifetime* are not new in the Xbase world. They have been around a long time, but were so simple that no one paid much attention. CA-Clipper complicated things to a small degree by advancing the technology to align itself with more contemporary compilers and in doing so introduced *lexical scoping* (determining the scope of a variable at compile-time) to the Xbase world. An understanding of the concepts of scope and lifetime is crucial to writing CA-Clipper optimized code.

In the following discussions, think of *scope* as referring to where the variable is known, its *visibility*, as it applies to variables, UDFs, and procedures. In Clipper, there are four kinds of scope: *private, public, local,* and *static.*

The other term we need to clarify, *lifetime*, refers to how long the variable stays around before being released. Lifetime applies only to variables, not subprograms.

Xbase has only private and public variables that remain in CA-Clipper. The concepts of scope and lifetime, when applied to privates and publics, are simple, and we'll discuss them momentarily. Privates and publics are based around the use of a *symbol table* to manage their names and values. Each private or public variable uses 18 bytes in the symbol table. The use of a table lookup mechanism for referencing variables means that programs run slower; they must search the table to determine the variable's value.

The original release of the Clipper 5 language introduced the additional scoping and lifetime facilities, local and static. Locals and statics use lexical scoping to manage their properties. You'll find the developer industry consensus to be that you should opt to use LOCAL and STATIC scope over PRIVATE and PUBLIC scope.

There are, however, some things that can't be done with locals and statics. The commands CLEAR ALL and CLEAR MEMORY have no effect on locals and statics so if publics and privates are avoided, issuing a CLEAR ALL does no more than a CLOSE ALL.

Private Scope

A private variable, once the most frequently used in Xbase programs, is visible in the program module that declared it (i.e., the module that assigned a value to it first) and any module(s) called from it. The process of passing the scope of a variable to a lower-level module is called *inheritance*. Private is the only Clipper variable scoping method in which inheritance occurs. You may declare a private, although it is not required, by using the PRIVATE statement. If you simply assign a value to a variable that has not previously been used, its scope automatically becomes private. There is a maximum 2048 private and public variables.

Private variables remain in lifetime until you return from the module in which the variable was declared or use a CLEAR ALL, CLEAR MEMORY, or RELEASE command, all of which free up its space in the symbol table. The following code sample describes a situation where a firm understanding of privates avoids problems.

```
FUNCTION EndLess
PRIVATE nCnt

FOR nCnt:= TO 10    // Endless loop.
   Counter()        // After return nCnt is always 4.
NEXT

RETURN NIL

FUNCTION Counter    // Note that nCnt IS NOT PASSED!
FOR nCnt:=1 TO 3    // Same nCnt as in EndLess() since private.
   * <statements>
NEXT
RETURN NIL
```

We see here that during the call to Counter(), nCnt is inherited from EndLess(). The programmer obviously did not understand the concept of inheritance of privates because upon return to EndLess(), nCnt will have already been re-assigned, thus causing the FOR loop control variable to change. Now let's see a new version of Counter() that addresses this problem.

```
/* Replacing above Counter() with the following will fix the
problem since the private nCnt will not be affected. */

FUNCTION Counter

FOR nCnt2:=1 TO 3
   * <statements>
NEXT

RETURN NIL
```

In this version of Counter(), we use the variable nCnt2, thus creating a new private. The inheritance problem with nCnt no longer exists. Remembering the simple law of inheritance, you may circumvent many potential debugging problems.

Note The horrors of unbridled inheritance of private scope variables make a strong case in favor of locals. Too often is the case where a program refers to a memory variable "out of nowhere." You later discover that it was previously defined many program modules up the calling hierarchy. Searching for such a variable and determining each possible place it may have been assigned wastes time and effort during debugging and program maintenance. A good policy to adopt is to pass variables as parameters to lower-level modules that need them or use *file-wide statics* or *globals* if a broader scope is required.

Next, we have an example illustrating a private variable's lifetime:

```
FUNCTION Caller
Called()
nVar:=1             // Different private nVar than
                    // inside Called().
RETURN NIL

FUNCTION Called
FOR nVar:=1 TO 3    // nVar is a private whose lifetime is
                    // limited to Called().
   * <statements>
NEXT
RETURN NIL
```

The call to Called() creates a private variable nVar. Upon returning to Caller() however, nVar goes out-of-lifetime. Consequently, the assignment statement that follows creates an entirely new private nVar. This example shows that a private's lifetime only lasts until the defining module terminates (returns to its caller).

Another case against undeclared and unmonitored private variables presents a particularly onerous problem area for Xbase programs. As mentioned in the previous note, this new problem is due to inheritance of private variables by lower-level modules that may change them and affect higher-level modules. Again, to combat these side effects, variables should be passed as parameters to lower-level modules so that there is a clear path of assignment.

1. Determine the displayed output of the following code segments:

```
* Segment 1

nCount := 1
Func1()
? nCount

FUNCTION Func1
nCount := 2
RETURN NIL

* Segment 2

Func1()
? nCount

FUNCTION Func1
nCount := 2
RETURN NIL
```

1. The first code segment displays the value 2. The calling program declares a private `nCount` and assigns it a value of 1. Later, inside `Func1()`, `nCount` is inherited so the change in value is reflected back in the calling program.

In the second code segment the code calls `Func1()` first. The private variable `nCount` defined in the subprogram, however, becomes out-of-lifetime upon returning to the calling program. The program crashes at the ? command because the variable is unknown.

Local Scope

A local variable is only visible in the procedure or function that declared it and *not* in any lower-level modules. *You cannot inherit local variables.* This limited scope directly solves problems due to inheritance. A local variable must be declared with a LOCAL statement, which must appear before the first executable statement in the module, even before any PRIVATE or PUBLIC statements. You may use multiple LOCAL statements to improve clarity. There is no limit to the number of LOCALs and STATICs that you can define since no symbol table is involved.

A local variable's lifetime is the same as that for private. Once the defining routine terminates, the local goes out-of-lifetime.

One potentially important difference between local/static variables and private/public variables is that the former cannot be saved to .MEM files due to their lack of symbol table entries. As it turns out, due to the decreasing use of .MEM files in the Clipper community in favor of small database files, this limitation is no longer problematic. The following code illustrates the use of local variables.

```
FUNCTION Main
LOCAL nLocal := 102755

MyFunc1()
? nLocal            // Still 102755, original value.
MyFunc2()
? nLocal            // Crash before this.

RETURN NIL

FUNCTION MyFunc1
LOCAL nLocal
nLocal := 120863    // This is one different than Main()'s.
RETURN NIL

FUNCTION MyFunc2
nLocal++            // Variable unknown, but a
                    // PRIVATE would have worked.
RETURN NIL
```

Here, `Main()` declares a local `nLocal` and assigns it a value of 102755. Then, inside the call to `MyFunc1()` another `nLocal` is defined and assigned, but upon return to `Main()` this new local quickly goes out-of-lifetime and the previous local comes back into scope. Finally, inside the call to `MyFun2()`, we refer to `nLocal`. The program crashes since `nLocal` is out of scope and no inheritance occurs. Things would be much different had `nLocal` been a private.

Before we move on, we should say one more thing about locals and their relationship to parameters. If you use function or function-style procedure parameter passing, the formal parameters inside the subprogram possess a local scope.

1. Determine the displayed output of the following code segments:

   ```
   * Segment 1

   LOCAL nCount := 1
   Func1()
   ? nCount

   FUNCTION Func1
   nCount := 2
   RETURN NIL

   * Segment 2

   nCount := 1
   Func1()
   ? nCount


   FUNCTION Func1
   LOCAL nCount := 2
   Func2()
   ? nCount
   RETURN NIL

   FUNCTION Func2
   nCount := 3
   RETURN NIL

   * Segment 3

   LOCAL nCount := 1
   nCount := Func1()
   ? nCount
   nCount := Func2()
   ? nCount
   ```

```
FUNCTION Func1
LOCAL nCount := 1
nCount++
RETURN (nCount)
```

 1. The first code segment displays a 1. Since nCount has a local scope in the calling program, it is not in scope inside Func1(). The variable declared in the function is therefore a private and goes out-of-lifetime upon return. The local nCount never changes.

The second code segment is more challenging. The initial variable nCount is a private assigned a value of 1. Once inside Func1() another nCount is declared, this one is a local with a value of 2. The private nCount is masked out by the local and is out of scope. Now, when Func2() is called, the private comes back in scope, so it is the private nCount being assigned in Func2().

The last segment shows a function—Func1()—that contains the declaration of a local variable that is assigned twice in succession. Even though the function increments the variable and passes back the value, two 2s are displayed. This is due to the local variable inside Func1() being re-initialized for each call.

Public Scope

Once a public variable is declared it immediately has application-wide visibility. Even if a public is declared in a lower-level module, it is instantly known in every other module above or below it. You must declare a public variable with a PUBLIC command.

Public variables remain in lifetime forever unless they are included in a RELEASE command or until a CLEAR ALL or CLEAR MEMORY is issued. Privates, remember, are released when the defining routine exits.

The public variable scoping and lifetime are powerful but maintain the capacity to be misused. One point of frustration surfaces when you are performing maintenance programming chores on an application only to come across a variable that seemingly appears out of nowhere. Later, you'll probably discover that the variable was declared as PUBLIC in a lower-level module.

 Note For the sake of program clarity and ease of future maintenance, you should declare all PUBLIC variables (if you decide to use them at all) in the main program module only!

The PUBLIC declaration is considered an executable statement and therefore must follow any LOCAL or STATIC declarations. Here is an example of the public scope that shouldn't be a surprise to anyone:

```
FUNCTION Main
MyFunc()
```

```
    ? cPublic    // cPublic has a global scope.  This
                 // would not work if cPublic was a
                 // PRIVATE in MyFunc().
RETURN NIL

FUNCTION MyFunc
* Dangerous to declare a public anywhere but main.
PUBLIC cPublic := 'hello world'
RETURN NIL
```

1. Determine the displayed output of the following code segments:

```
/* — Segment 1 — */
PUBLIC nCount := 1
Func1()
? nCount

FUNCTION Func1
PRIVATE nCount := 2
? nCount
RETURN NIL

/* — Segment 2 — */
Func1()
? nCount

FUNCTION Func1
PUBLIC nCount := 2
RETURN NIL

/* — Segment 3 — */
PRIVATE nCount := 1
Func1()
? nCount

FUNCTION Func1
PUBLIC nCount := 2
? nCount
RETURN NIL
```

1. The first code segment displays a 1 and then a 2. Although the public nCount is declared and initialized in the main program, the private nCount in Func1() "hides" the public until the private goes out of scope (namely upon returning to the main).
   The second code segment demonstrates an unfortunate use of the public scope. Here, the main program refers to nCount out of nowhere. We see that a lower-level subprogram defines a public nCount. Bear in mind that this is bad coding practice, although it is allowed in Clipper (and all other Xbase dialects).

The third code segment shows a private variable that is quickly doomed as the function `Func1()` immediately declares a public of the same name. This action masks the private forever since the public has infinite lifetime.

Static Scope

Many developers new to the Clipper language liken the static scope to public. This is, however an inaccurate comparison. It is true that both static and public lifetimes are unbounded, but in terms of scope, they are very different. As with locals, a static is in scope only while the defining routine is active. The difference lies in that once the defining routine returns, a local goes out-of-lifetime whereas a static remains in-lifetime. This is to say that a static's variable name and value remain intact even when the routine is not active.

In many cases, statics are used to hide variables from subprograms. Consider the case where two program modules have a similarly named variable. Statics have no problem with this as each occurrence of the variable may be hidden from the other. Data hiding is an important characteristic of the static scope.

There are actually two types of static variables: *regular static* and *file-wide static*. Which one you get depends solely on where you place the STATIC declaration. If the static variable is defined inside a UDF or procedure (before a PARAMETERS statement or any executable code), then it is considered a regular static. If, however, the definition is positioned outside any UDF or procedure it is a file-wide static. Let's look at an example of using statics.

```
* Main program
FUNCTION Main
STATIC cTitle := 'Let us count'
LOCAL nCount

QOUT( cTitle )           // Only known in Main().
FOR nCount := 1 TO 10
  QOUT( Incr() )
NEXT

RETURN NIL

/* Subprogram */
FUNCTION Incr
STATIC nCountUp := 1     // Only initialized once.
RETURN (nCountUp++)      // Previous value remains alive.
```

Here we see two static variables, each in scope only when the defining routine is running; that is, `cTitle` is unknown during a call to `Incr()` and `nCountUp` is unknown when inside `Main()`. During the first call to `Incr()`, `nCountUp` is set to 1 and during subsequent calls, it is incremented. Consider single-stepping this code in the debugger to get a feeling for what is happening.

File-wide statics are declared with a STATIC statement positioned at the beginning of the .PRG file, outside of any procedure or function definition. You must use ("a" or "the" or "switches" /N compiler switch) to be able to use file-wide statics. File-wide statics are visible to routines only in same .PRG file. This implies that file-wide statics can be considered *limited-scope* publics because unlike true publics, which have a global scope, file-wide statics are only global to all subprograms within the defining .PRG file.

1. Determine the displayed output of the following code segments:

```
/* — Segment 1 — */

LOCAL nCount := 1
nCount := Func1()
? nCount
nCount := 1
nCount := Func1()
? nCount

FUNCTION Func1
STATIC nCount := 1
nCount++
RETURN (nCount)

/* — Segment 2 — */

* Source1.PRG
LOCAL nCount := 1
nCount := Func1()
? nCount

* Source2.PRG
FUNCTION Func1
STATIC nCount := 2
nCount := Func2()
? nCount
RETURN NIL

FUNCTION Func2
nCount++
RETURN (nCount)
```

1. In the first code segment, a 2 and then a 3 is displayed. In the Func1() procedure, a static is defined and initialized. The initialization is done once at compile-time. Consequently, any change to the static nCount is remembered from one call to the next.

In the second code segment we see two .PRG files linked together. The main program calls `Func1()`, which declares a static variable. `Func1()` in turn calls `Func2()`, which references the out-of-scope static, so the program crashes at that reference. We could correct the problem by making the static into a file-wide static.

Global Scope

At first glance, it may seem strange to see a section in this chapter describing a global scope, after all there is no GLOBAL declaration statement in the language. However, even though CA-Clipper does not officially provide a global variable declaration, we can implement one using a combination of file-wide statics (regular statics will work also) and GET/SET functions. Using these simulated globals, one can completely rid their code of PUBLICs. There is a somewhat sneaky technique to obtain the effect of a true public variable without actually using the PUBLIC declaration:

```
/* Main program module: MAIN.PRG */
STATIC nGlobal1 := 0    // A file-wide static acting like a public.

FUNCTION Global1(nValue)
RETURN (nGlobal1 := ;
   IIF(VALTYPE(nValue) == 'U', nGlobal1, nValue))

/* Other program module: OTHER.PRG
This would not be possible using only a file-wide static */
? Global1()             // GET "global" variable.
Global1(99)             // SET "global" to 99.
```

Here, the `Global1()` UDF is responsible for accessing and assigning values for the `nGlobal1` global variable. The only problem is that a separate UDF is needed to manage each global. You could use a regular static or file-wide static array to hold multiple global variables for a entire application and utilize manifest constants to act as an index into the array in order to access the correct variable.

There is one penalty related to the use of globals in a Clipper program. In order to either GET (retrieve the value) or SET (assign a value) the contents of a global you must issue a function call. As it turns out, the overhead of a function call may out-weigh the overhead in accessing the symbol table for a public variable.

Static Functions and Procedures

You may also prefix a function or procedure declaration with the STATIC keyword. Whereas local and static variables allowed *data hiding*, the use of the

STATIC keyword with functions and procedures enables you to engage in *code hiding*. Specifically, the code of a subprogram may be hidden from other program modules not in the same .PRG file. This ability is useful when trying to deal with duplicate subprogram names. For example, if two or more programs (i.e. .PRG files) have a UDF named Update(), then giving them the STATIC attribute will resolve the conflict. The Update() function in program A is hidden from the Update() function in program B. The following code sequence illustrates these points:

```
* SOURCE1.PRG

LOCAL nCount := 1
nCount := Func1()
? nCount              // Displays: 3
nCount := Func2()
? nCount              // Displays: 2

FUNCTION Func2        // Non-static Func2().
LOCAL nCount := 2
RETURN (nCount)

* SOURCE2.PRG - A separate .PRG file

STATIC nCount := 2    // File-wide static.

FUNCTION Func1
nCount := Func2()     // Func1() calls static Func2().
RETURN (nCount)

STATIC FUNCTION Func2 // Only known inside SOURCE2.PRG.
nCount := 3
RETURN (nCount)
```

In this example, we have two .PRG files, both with a Func2() function. The Func2() in SOURCE1.PRG is not static and may be called from any other program module, except those located inside SOURCE2.PRG because it has a static Func2() function. The first ? displays a 3 since we call Func1() in SOURCE1.PRG which in turn calls the static Func2().

Comparison of Scopes and Lifetimes

Table 5.2 summarizes the rules governing scope and lifetime in CA-Clipper:

Table 5.2 Scope and Lifetime Rules

Declared as	Scope (visibility)	Lifetime
LOCAL	Local scope	Creating routine
PRIVATE	Private scope	Creating routine
PUBLIC	Global scope	Lives forever
STATIC	Local scope	Lives forever
file-wide STATIC	Only in same .PRG	Lives forever
GLOBAL	Global scope	Lives forever
none	Private scope	Creating routine

Announce and Request

CA-Clipper has two statements used to manage program modules in an application. ANNOUNCE enables you to assign a module identifier name to a specific program unit. REQUEST is used to list all the external names that an application may need during execution.

The ANNOUNCE statement defines a module identifier for a .PRG. The statement must be placed before any executable commands. There can be only one ANNOUNCE in a source program (.PRG). All module identifiers should be unique within the application. The identifier used with ANNOUNCE may be later used to satisfy a REQUEST. When using module identifiers, you should always compile with the /N switch. You may consider using ANNOUNCE when you need to assign a module identifier to a module that has no public symbols; that is, a module that is not surrounded by a FUNCTION or PROCEDURE declaration. For example, if you had a .PRG file containing a series of INDEX ON commands you may wish to say:

```
ANNOUNCE BldIndex
INDEX ON Customer->CustNum TO CustNum
INDEX ON Customer->Zip TO CustZip
```

Later, another program module may issue a REQUEST BldIndex in order to ensure that this module gets into the .EXE file.

In prior versions of Clipper, the EXTERNAL statement was used to identify a program module that needed to be included in the .EXE by the linker. Now, we should use the REQUEST statement to achieve the same purpose. The syntax of the REQUEST statement is

```
REQUEST <modulelist>
```

where `<modulelist>` is a sequence of module names that need to be linked into the .EXE file.

EXTERNAL should be used for compatibility purposes only and may not be present in the language in future releases. For now, simply think of REQUEST as having the same purpose as EXTERNAL. It is interesting to note that the UDC definition for REQUEST in STD.CH is:

```
#command REQUEST <vars,...> ;
   => EXTERNAL <vars>
```

There are several instances where use of REQUEST is necessary; all relate to the situation where references to user-defined functions and procedures and built-in functions are hidden to the linker and thus result in an .EXE file not containing the code required for successful execution at run-time. Here is a list of these circumstances:

- When the expansion of a macro expression results in the reference of a UDF or procedure, you would need to include a REQUEST statement. There is no way to know at compile- or link-time that such a reference will arise, so at run-time the subprogram's code will not be available (i.e. linked into the .EXE) and the program aborts. Here is an example of how this might happen:

```
cProcName := 'PrtInv()'
&cProcName
```

In this case, you would need to include a REQUEST statement that would tell the linker to include the procedure PrtInv() in the .EXE file:

```
REQUEST PrtInv
```

- If you reference a subprogram inside of a report or label form, and nowhere else in the source code, its name would have to appear in a REQUEST statement.
- If you reference a subprogram inside of a index key expression, and nowhere else in the source code, its name would have to appear in a REQUEST statement.
- Any UDFs used in the ACHOICE(), DBEDIT(), or MEMOEDIT() functions should appear in a REQUEST statement.
- When you declare initialization or exit procedures with INIT PROCEDURE or EXIT PROCEDURE their names should appear in a REQUEST statement.

The ANNOUNCE statement is used to declare a module identifier that can be used by the linker to resolve any outstanding REQUESTs. The ANNOUNCE statement should be placed in a program above any executable statements and, as we mentioned earlier, a .PRG file can have only one ANNOUNCE. Any other

.PRG requiring this module must then issue a REQUEST for the module identifier. The module identifier appearing in an ANNOUNCE statement must be unique within the application in that it must not conflict with any other function or procedure name.

The syntax of the ANNOUNCE statement is:

ANNOUNCE <modulename>

As an example of the use of ANNOUNCE and REQUEST consider the following program module that contains a call to MEMOEDIT(). The MEMOEDIT() user function parameter refers to a function, ExtUDF(), that is defined in a separate .PRG file. Since the user function name is passed to MEMOEDIT() as a character string, the linker would normally not see it is required, thus a runtime error occurs due to the fact that the .EXE file doesn't contain the UDF. Announcing and requesting this module cures the problem.

```
REQUEST ME_UDFs

FUNCTION Main
USE Employee NEW

Employee->Resume := MEMOEDIT(Employee->Resume, ;
    5, 10, 15, 70,, 'ExtUDF')

DBCLOSEAREA()
RETURN NIL

/***
*
* This is a separate .PRG containing the ExtUDF() required
* by the program above
*
*/

ANNOUNCE ME_UDFs

FUNCTION ExtUDF
.
. <statements>
.
RETURN NIL
```

INIT and EXIT Procedures

CA-Clipper's INIT and EXIT procedures provide a way to automatically call one or more subprograms at startup and/or termination of the application without explicitly calling the routines. `INIT` procedures are automatically called before the first executable command in an application. They are used to perform required initialization tasks such as establishing a configuration environment, checking files, or completing network administration functions. These commands are best used with third-party libraries and black-box subsystems that need to perform their own setup and/or shutdown processes. For normal developers, the use of standard functions and procedures to perform these tasks is acceptable. For example, to directly call such functions without the service of `INIT` and `EXIT` procedures, the following code could arise:

```
FUNCTION Main

InitProc1()      // Call initialization procedure 1.
InitProc2()      // Call initialization procedure 2.
.
. <statements>
.
ExitProc1()      // Call exit procedure 1.
ExitProc2()      // Call exit procedure 2.

RETURN NIL
```

The equivalent code using `INIT` and `EXIT` procedures would be something like the code that follows. We see that all the `INIT` and `EXIT` procedures are collected together in a single .PRG and then *announced* with a specified module identifier. Now all the main program must do is issue the command `REQUEST IEProcs` and then each `INIT` and `EXIT` procedure will be executed automatically at the appropriate time; that is, when you start up the program, `InitProc1()` and `InitProc2()` are performed and when the program ends, `ExitProc1()` and `ExitProc2()` are performed.

```
/***
*
* IELib.PRG - Library of INIT and EXIT procedure
*
*/

ANNOUNCE IEProcs

INIT PROCEDURE InitProc1
.
. <statements>
.
RETURN

INIT PROCEDURE InitProc2
```

```
     .
     . <statements>
     .
     RETURN

EXIT PROCEDURE ExitProc1
     .
     . <statements>
     .
     RETURN

EXIT PROCEDURE ExitProc2
     .
     . <statements>
     .
     RETURN
```

Here is the syntax of the INIT PROCEDURE statement:

```
INIT PROCEDURE <procedurename> [(parmlist)]
   [FIELD <fieldlist> [IN <aliasname>]]
   [LOCAL <identifier> [:= <expr>]]
   [MEMVAR <identifierlist>]
     .
     . <statements>
     .
   [RETURN]
```

INIT procedures have a visibility limited to the system (the CA-Clipper runtime system), therefore you may not directly call an INIT procedure from another subprogram module. However, you can define more than one INIT procedure. In this case, control is passed from one procedure in the *initialization list* (the series of defined INIT procedures) to the next. There is, however, no set sequence in which multiple INIT procedures are executed, although the special procedure, CLIPINIT (which installs the default error recovery system ERRORSYS), is always executed first. After all INIT procedures have been visited, control is passed to the first executable statement in the application. The parameter passed to each INIT procedure is a copy of the DOS command line parameters specified when the application was started. For example if the user entered the command

```
MYAPP STARTUP
```

at the DOS prompt, the following INIT procedure would display "STARTUP."

```
INIT PROCEDURE BeginProc(cParm)
  ? QOUT('Passed from DOS command line', cParm)
RETURN
```

Let's move on to EXIT PROCEDURE. Here is this statement's syntax:

```
EXIT PROCEDURE <procedurename>
   [FIELD <fieldlist> [IN <aliasname>]]
   [LOCAL <identifier> [:= <expr>]]
   [MEMVAR <identifierlist>]
   .
   . <statements>
   .
   [RETURN]
```

EXIT procedures have a visibility limited to the system (the CA-Clipper runtime system), therefore you may not directly call an EXIT procedure from another subprogram module. However, you can define more than one EXIT procedure. In this case, control is passed from one procedure in the *exit list* (the series of defined EXIT procedures) to the next. There is, however, no set sequence in which multiple EXIT procedures are executed. After each EXIT procedure has been visited, control is passed back to DOS.

Note There are four ways in which a Clipper program may terminate: issuing a RETURN from the main program module, thus returning to DOS; issuing a QUIT command; issuing a BREAK command not enclosed within a BEGIN/END SEQUENCE structure; and aborting due to an unrecoverable error.

One handy application of an EXIT PROCEDURE is to define a procedure that searches for and deletes any unwanted temporary files before control is returned to DOS. Another possibility would be to display a trailing credits banner to the user upon exiting the application.

1. Write an INIT procedure to generate an application usage logging mechanism where an entry is written each time a user starts the application. Each log entry should contain a date and time stamp. A database LOG.DBF should store the log entries. The structure of this database should have two fields: DateIn and TimeIn.

1. The solution shown here defines an INIT procedure and saves the current date and time in two file-wide statics. Once the INIT procedure passes control to the application, we open the LOG database and write a new entry.

```
/***
*
```

```
 * Application with usage logging mechanism.
 *
 */

STATIC dDateIn, cTimeIn

FUNCTION Main

   USE Log NEW
   DBAPPEND()            // Write new log IN entry.
   Log->DateIn := dDateIn
   Log->TimeIn := cTimeIn
   DBCLOSEAREA()
   .
   . <statements>
   .
   RETURN NIL

INIT PROCEDURE UserIn

   dDateIn := DATE()     // Save date/time stamp info.
   cTimeIn := TIME()

   RETURN
```

> **Note**
>
> In the previous exercise, you may have come up with a solution that involved accessing the LOG database from within the INIT procedure as in:
>
> ```
> INIT PROCEDURE UserIn
>
>    USE Log NEW
>    DBAPPEND()
>    Log->DateIn := DATE()
>    Log->TimeIn := TIME()
>    DBCLOSEAREA()
>    RETURN
> ```
>
> This would be an elegant solution, however it will not work since the default RDD DBFNTX (a topic for Chapter 8) is not yet registered. Since RDDs are activated themselves inside an INIT procedure and since the order of execution for INIT procedures cannot be guaranteed, database access commands such as USE may not work. The bottom line is, don't attempt to do database access from within an INIT procedure.

Summary

As we've seen in this chapter, CA-Clipper has taken a bold step forward in providing a more sensible methodology of organizing subprograms. Placing functions and procedures called like functions together in logical groupings inside a single .PRG yields a more cohesive and maintainable application. It may take a bit of effort to get comfortable with CA-Clipper's methods of handling functions, procedures, parameters, scope, and lifetime, but after a few good debugger sessions, things will start to fall into place.

Exercise

1. Write a Clipper function subprogram that accepts two formal parameters: cCustNum and nBOTotal, opens a database ORDERS, calculates the total number of product units not yet shipped, and places this value in nBOTotal. Assume ORDERS has the fields CustNum and BOUnits and an index file, CustNum.NTX, which has a key value of CustNum.

Answer

1. The solution centers around the fact that the actual parameter nBOUnits in Main() is passed to the TotUnits() By Reference. In TotUnits() we see a standard database traversal loop that calculates the sum of all the customer's backorder quantities. Notice however, that the UDF doesn't have a return value, but instead accumulates the required value in the formal parameter nBOTotal. Since we have a By Reference parameter, this value flows back to the calling program.

```
FUNCTION Main
LOCAL nBOUnits := 0

TotUnits('DDG01', @nBOUnits)
? nBOUnits

RETURN NIL

FUNCTION TotUnits(cCustNum, nBOTotal)

USE Orders INDEX OrdCust NEW
SEEK cCustNum // Position to 1st
DO WHILE Orders->CustNum == cCustNum .AND. !EOF()
   nBOTotal += Orders->BOUnits
   SKIP
ENDDO
DBCLOSEAREA()

RETURN NIL
```

6

Code Blocks

> **What Is a Code Block?** ➤ 140
>
> **Definition** ➤ 141
>
> **Evaluation** ➤ 141
>
> **Programming Applications** ➤ 143
>
> **Code Block Parameter Passing** ➤ 146
>
> **Get/Set Block Functions** ➤ 147
>
> **Summary** ➤ 150
>
> **Exercise** ➤ 150

The CA-Clipper feature that receives the most blank stares from Xbase and Summer '87 programmers who are climbing aboard the CA-Clipper bandwagon has got to be code blocks. The problem lies not in definition. Staunch Xbase developers, to be sure, are able to learn new tricks and after an introduction to code blocks the consensus is that the concept is very elegant. The problem is, instead, one of application. Even after a programmer learns the ins and outs of code blocks, it remains difficult to apply them in everyday coding chores. Once mastered, some developers go overboard and stick code blocks everywhere; in effect, forcing the issue. The secret is to get to the point where you can introduce a code block and have it help you represent a programming problem and allow the program to run efficiently.

After completing this chapter, you will have learned:

- How code blocks are the basis for CA-Clipper optimized coding practices
- What a code block is and how to define one
- The method of evaluating the contents of a code block
- Several programming applications where code blocks are appropriate
- Parameter passing techniques involving code blocks
- How to use the built-in Get/Set block functions

What Is a Code Block?

A code block is simply a way to store one or more precompiled CA-Clipper expressions in a memory variable. The code block is a distinct Clipper data type (as we saw in Chapter 2, VALTYPE() returns a "B" for a variable holding a code block). Once these expressions are stored, the code block must then be evaluated in order for it to be useful. There are several ways to evaluate a code block. We'll cover one method in this chapter and save some others for future explorations.

A simple analogy is appropriate here. Think of a code block as a function; it has code, you can pass it parameters, it returns a value, and it has a name—the name of the memory variable you assign it to. (In order to "call" this facsimile of a function, you execute the code within.) So why not just use functions and forget about code blocks? The answer lies in the ways in which code blocks are embedded in various CA-Clipper constructs. Rest assured, this will become obvious as we explore code blocks here and in future chapters.

Here's the bottom line: you've got to be good at applying code blocks because CA-Clipper relies upon them everywhere. Nowhere is this more true than in STD.CH, the preprocessor file containing UDC definitions that define Clipper's syntax. Upon close examination, you'll see that many UDCs map various statements and clauses into code blocks that are then passed as parameters to the low-level functions that make up CA-Clipper. Moreover, in order to do optimized CA-Clipper programming, you'll need to use code blocks for processing arrays, database contents, browse screens, and much more. Remember this: code blocks are an integral part of CA-Clipper and to ignore them is to ignore much of the power of the language.

Definition

The structure of a code block definition is formally defined as:

```
<variable> := {|[<parmList>]| <expressionList>}
```

In this definition <variable> is any valid variable name that (will) possess the *code block data type*. <parmList> is an optional list of formal parameters, separated by commas, to be passed to the expressions contained in the code block (in much the same manner as those passed to UDFs). If there are no parameters to be passed, the || characters must still be included. <expressionList> is a series of one or more expressions, separated by commas, that are compiled and stored in the block. These expressions can be of any kind allowed in Clipper, for example nPageCnt+1, or nRecCnt++, or cCustName := LEFT(Customer->Last,10), which shows that the inline assignment operator := is perfectly fine in a code block. Likewise, even a simple UDF call, such as CalcAvg(), is acceptable. Also, the IIF() function is particularly well suited for code blocks since it provides the ability to represent logic in the code (remember statements like IF/ELSE/ENDIF are not allowed in code blocks). The value returned by the code block once evaluated becomes the value of the last expression in the list.

As an example, consider the following code block:

```
bSample := { |x, y| x + y }
```

In this example, a code block is defined with two parameters and assigned to the variable bSample. The operation of the code block will apply the + operator to the passed parameters. The block will succeed with any two parameters on which + is defined, for example, "A one" + "and a two", 1 + 2, CTOD('01/01/80') + 7.

Evaluation

Unlike regular expressions that are compiled and then executed as they are encountered in the program, code blocks must be explicitly evaluated. CA-Clipper has the EVAL() built-in function for this purpose. The calling sequence for EVAL() is

```
EVAL(<bBlock>, [<blockParmList>]) --> vlastBlockValue
```

where `<bBlock>` is the name of the memory variable containing the code block and `<blockParmList>` is an optional list of actual parameters, separated by commas, that are passed to the expressions in the block. The return value of `EVAL()`, `vlastBlockValue`, is the *value of the last expression of the block*. Many times when evaluating a code block, a return value is not needed. We can call `EVAL()` without it appearing on the right of an assignment operator. In this case, the return value, whatever it happens to be, is simply lost.

Before we look at evaluating code blocks, let's first consider the following program that assigns a sequence of CA-Clipper expressions to a memory variable:

```
#define ANNIV 5

FUNCTION Main
LOCAL nNewSal, nYears, dHireDate, nCurSal

nNewSal := ( dHireDate := CTOD('01/01/84'), ;
    nCurSal    := 22500, ;
    nYears     := Seniority(dHireDate), ;
    IIF(nYears > ANNIV, nCurSal*1.1, nCurSal*1.05) )
    * 8 and 24750.0 shall be displayed

? 'Years in service: ',nYears, 'New Salary: ', nNewSal

RETURN NIL

FUNCTION Seniority(dBegin)
RETURN (INT((DATE()-dBegin)/365))
```

Here, the assignment statement involving `nNewSal` shows how a series of expressions may be grouped using a surrounding set of parentheses. The value returned from this extended set of expressions is simply the value of the last expression, in this case the `IIF()`. Of course, in reality, one would code this process without embedding the expressions and the `IIF()` call would be an `IF` statement. Nevertheless, to prove a point, we see that the embedded expressions are compiled and when executed they yield the proper results. Note that the expressions are executed immediately when the `nNewSal` assignment statement is encountered.

Now that we feel in tune to expression groups, let's look at the code block equivalent. But first, we must learn how to evaluate a code block. We can take the expressions, separate them by commas, and wrap them inside a code block casing. Then we take the block and assign it to a memory variable. The `EVAL()` function evaluates the expressions found in a code block variable and returns a value. As usual with any built-in function, `EVAL()` may be invoked on a line by itself or embedded in any expression.

```
#define ANNIV 5

FUNCTION Main
LOCAL nNewSal, nYears, dHireDate, nCurSal, bNewSal

bNewSal := { || dHireDate := CTOD('01/01/84'), ;
    nCurSal    := 22500, ;
    nYears     := Seniority(dHireDate), ;
    IIF(nYears > ANNIV, nCurSal*1.1, nCurSal*1.05) }
nNewSal := EVAL(bNewSal)

? 'Years in service: ',nYears, 'New Salary: ', nNewSal

RETURN NIL
```

The results are identical for both examples, but one uses a code block while the other does not. The second example is preferable, however, since the expressions as a group may appear anywhere a code block is permitted.

1. What is the displayed output of the following code segments involving code blocks?

   ```
   LOCAL bOne   := {|a| QOUT(a)}
   LOCAL bTwo   := {|a, b| b:= a--, QOUT(a, b)}
   LOCAL bThree := {|a| a*a}

   ? EVAL(b1, 9)
   ? EVAL(b2, 7)
   ? EVAL(b3, 6)
   ```

1. The displayed output is:

   ```
   9
   NIL
   6  7
   NIL
   36
   ```

Programming Applications

This section of the chapter will seem somewhat light in terms of real life examples. There is a good reason for this. Most of the places where code blocks may be applied have not been covered yet by this series. For this reason, you'll have to stayed tuned for more insight into where you might use a code block.

Suffice it to say right now, we'll see more of code blocks when we cover arrays, the browse system, database manipulation, and other topics. For now, let's take a look at a series of simple code block examples given the tools we now have:

```
* Evaluating a simple code block
LOCAL bBlock := { || nValue }      // "nValue" is not yet defined.
LOCAL nValue := 123
LOCAL nResult


nResult := EVAL(bBlock)

? nResult                          // 123.
```

Note that the local variable nValue is not yet known when the code block that depends on it is defined. This is fine since by the time the code block is evaluated, a value for nValue is assigned.

```
* More on evaluation

LOCAL bBlock := { || QOUT(cChar1), QQOUT(cChar2), 123 }
LOCAL cChar1 := 'Hello ', cChar2 := 'world'
LOCAL nResult

nResult := EVAL(bBlock)    // "Hello world" is displayed by code block.
? nResult                  // 123 since last expression.
```

In this example, the code block displays a message to the screen. Since the ? command cannot appear inside a code block (it is not an expression), we use the QOUT() and QQOUT() functions instead.

```
* One final example of calling a code block w/no parameters
FUNCTION Main
LOCAL bBlock := { || bFunc() }

EVAL(bBlock)

RETURN NIL

FUNCTION bFunc
? "Hello world"
RETURN NIL
```

This example shows that there is more than one way to do the same thing. Much of the power of code blocks lies in their ability to call UDFs.

Next, we see that some simple UDFs can be written in the form of a code block. The following example arrives at both a code block solution and a UDF solution.

```
FUNCTION Main
LOCAL bMaxBlock := { |p1,p2,p3| MAX(p1, MAX(p2,p3)) }

? MaxFunc(3, 10, 7.5)          // UDF yields: 10.
* Note below, parm list follows code block name
? EVAL(bMaxBlock, 3, 10, 7.5)  // Code block yields: 10.

RETURN NIL

FUNCTION MaxFunc( p1, p2, p3 )
RETURN MAX(p1, MAX(p2, p3))
```

Code blocks, like UDFs, can accept a variable number of parameters as shown in the following example:

```
LOCAL bBlock := {|x, y, z| QOUT(x, y, z)}
LOCAL vRetVal

* First pass full parameter list and get: 'Hello there world'
EVAL(bBlock, 'Hello', 'there', 'world')

* Now leave off one of the passed parameters
* and get: 'Hello there NIL'
vRetVal := EVAL(bBlock, 'Hello', 'there')
? vRetVal   // NIL, since QOUT() always RETURNS a NIL.
```

1. Write a CA-Clipper code segment that uses a code block to control the operation of a WHILE/END loop. Let's say that just prior to the loop, we issue the command SEEK 'Victoria', which uses an index based on a database field called Employee->Name. Have the loop process the rest of the occurrences of this value.

1. To solve this problem, we'll utilize a code block that returns a *logical value* in the condition portion of the WHILE/END construct. All we have to do is to remember to EVAL() the block for each loop iteration. See the following code:

    ```
    LOCAL bCondition

    SEEK 'Victoria' // Position to first.
    bCondition := {|| Employee->Name == 'Victoria'}
    WHILE EVAL(bCondition)
    ```

```
    .
    . <statements>
    .
    SKIP   // Next record please.
END
```

Code Block Parameter Passing

As with UDFs, parameters are passed to code blocks By Value which means that they cannot be changed by the block's expressions. Consider the following:

```
LOCAL cActual := 'foo'
LOCAL bBlock := { |cFormal| QOUT(cFormal), cFormal := 'fu' }

EVAL(bBlock, cActual)     // Pass By Value.
? cActual                 // "foo" unchanged.

EVAL(bBlock, @cActual)    // Pass By Reference.
? cActual                 // "fu" changed.
```

In this case, when `bBlock` is evaluated, a new variable `cFormal`, which is local to the block, is created. The `QOUT()` displays the passed value "foo," but then the formal parameter `cFormal` is changed to "fu." Upon return however, `cActual` retains its original value "foo," unaltered by the evaluation of the code block.

In the second `EVAL()`, the actual parameter is passed By Reference using the `@` prefix, which allows the value to be changed inside the code block.

Note

> As with functions and procedures, the formal parameters of a code block have a local scope.

In addition to what we've covered so far, you also need a solid understanding of scope when defining and evaluating code blocks. Consider the following example:

```
LOCAL bBlock1 := {|| QOUT(nParm) }
LOCAL bBlock2 := {|nParm| nParm++, QOUT(nParm), EVAL(bBlock1) }

EVAL(bBlock2,1)
```

The main program passes a 1 to `bBlock2` during evaluation. This actual parameter is mapped to `nParm`, which is a variable local to `bBlock2`. Next, `bBlock1` is evaluated without any parameters, but inside of `bBlock1` is a reference to `nParm`. But, of course, `nParm` is only known inside of `bBlock2` and is therefore out of scope in `bBlock1`. The program aborts because `nParm` is not known inside of `bBlock1`.

Code Blocks ▲ 147

You may also find it necessary to pass the code blocks themselves as parameters to user-defined functions or procedures, or to return a code block as a return value from a function. CA-Clipper allows both of these situations.

1. Determine the output of the following code segment:

```
FUNCTION Main
LOCAL bParm := {|a| QOUT(a)}

? MyUDF(bParm, 10)

RETURN NIL

FUNCTION MyUDF(bFormal, nValue)
RETURN (EVAL(bFormal, nValue * 10))
```

1. The answer is 100 NIL since the return value of MyUDF() is simply the evaluation of the code block passed to it as a parameter.

Get/Set Block Functions

Before we finish our discussion of code blocks, CA-Clipper has three new functions designed for use with code blocks, FIELDBLOCK(), FIELDWBLOCK(), and MEMVARBLOCK(). We will discuss all three in standard function declaration notation where the parameters and return value are defined in Hungarian notation.

FIELDBLOCK()

The FIELDBLOCK() function is used to construct a code block that may be used in conjunction with EVAL() to either get (return) or set (update) the contents of a database field. Here we see the prototype for the function:

```
FIELDBLOCK(<cFieldName>) -> bFieldBlock
```

This function accepts a character parameter that contains the name of a database field opened in the current work area whose value you wish to retrieve (get) or update (set). These functions are thus called Get/Set functions. For example,

```
FIELD zip
LOCAL bZipAgain := {|| zip}
LOCAL cField := 'ZIP', bZipBlock

USE Customer NEW                    // Open CUSTOMER.DBF containing ZIP.
bZipBlock := FIELDBLOCK(cField)     // Create GET/SET block.
? EVAL(bZipBlock)                   // '90024', using GET block.
```

```
? EVAL(bZipAgain)                    // '90024', using code block.

EVAL(bZipBlock, '99999-9999')        // Replace using SET block.
```

Prior to code blocks, you would have to resort to a much less efficient method, using macro expansions as in:

```
cField := 'ZIP'
? &cField                            // Display contents of CUSTOMER->ZIP.
REPLACE &cField WITH '99999-9999'    // Replace contents.
```

FIELDWBLOCK()

The `FIELDWBLOCK()` function operates identically to `FIELDBLOCK()` in that it returns a Get/Set code block for a database field. The one exception is the function's second parameter, a work area number. The added capability allows you to specify in which work area the database containing the field referenced in the code block is opened. In contrast, `FIELDBLOCK()` assumes that the field is in the current work area.

Here is the prototype for the function:

```
FIELDWBLOCK(<cFieldName>, <nWorkArea>) —> bFieldBlock
```

Note

> The specified database field in `FIELDBLOCK()` and `FIELDWBLOCK()` does not have to exist or be accessible when the code block is created. It must be accessible as the code block is evaluated.

Let's take a look at an example where these points concerning `FIELDWBLOCK()` come into play:

```
LOCAL bCustName := FIELDWBLOCK('Company', SELECT('Customer'))
LOCAL bSuppName := FIELDWBLOCK('Company', SELECT('Supplier'))

USE Customer NEW
USE Supplier NEW
USE Movie NEW

SELECT Movie
? EVAL(bCustName)
? EVAL(bSuppName)

EVAL(bCustName, 'Erwin')
```

Notice how the code blocks were assigned their values in the LOCAL statements, even before the databases were opened. Notice also, how the databases are opened before the blocks are evaluated. The first two EVAL() functions return the code block's value. The third, however, actually replaces a field's contents. In essence, this evaluation is the same as using the command:

```
REPLACE Customer->Company WITH 'Erwin'
```

MEMVARBLOCK()

The MEMVARBLOCK() function operates identically to FIELDBLOCK() with the exception that the set/get code block returned operates on a memory variable instead of a database field. Here is the prototype for the function:

```
MEMVARBLOCK(<cMemVar>) -> bMemVarBlock
```

As with the two previous functions, MEMVARBLOCK() returns a code block. This time however, the block is based on the name of a memory variable passed in cMemVar. One thing to note about MEMVARBLOCK() is that it is only able to use private or public variables; locals and statics may not be referenced.

In the next example, many of you may remember the old Xbase method of using macros to simulate arrays. Here, this method is replaced with code blocks:

```
* First, the macro method
LOCAL i
PRIVATE c

FOR i:=1 TO 3    // Create 3 privates and assign values.
  c := STR(i,1) // Convert to char for macro.
  cMonth&c := i
NEXT

* Now, with code blocks
PRIVATE cMonth1, cMonth2, cMonth3

FOR i:=1 TO 3
  * Remember, MEMVARBLOCK() returns a code block EVAL()
  * Will use it to assign a value to the new private
  EVAL(MEMVARBLOCK('cMonth'+STR(i,1)),i)
NEXT
```

The second method may appear more involved, but it does run much more efficiently since we're avoiding macros.

CA-Clipper is the first Xbase derivative to institute a philosophy of trying to break the mystique of the macro. It has long been agreed that the use of macros is an evil that should be avoided whenever possible! Clipper, with the aid of code blocks, makes this a reality. Code blocks are faster because they contain precompiled code, whereas macros must interpret the code on-the-fly. In addition, code blocks may be passed as parameters to procedures and functions.

Summary

In this chapter, we've examined the basics of code block theory. Now, the discussion of the blockify result marker from Chapter 4 may make more sense. In the chapters that follow, we'll see some more applications of code blocks. Specifically, in Chapter 7, we'll look at CA-Clipper style arrays. In doing so, we'll see that arrays are a prime example of where code blocks can be useful.

Exercise

1. Prepare a code block that opens a database file whose name is passed to it as a character parameter. Remember, you can't place CA-Clipper commands (e.g. USE) in a block, only expressions are allowed. Before you attempt to open any database file, it's always a good idea to check whether it exists.

Answer

1. Even though you cannot include CA-Clipper commands in a code block, you can always call a UDF that contains these commands. Our solution revolves around this realization. The code block bOpenFile references OpenFile() so when evaluated, the code block calls the function, passing to it the filename.

```
FUNCTION Main

LOCAL bOpenFile := {|filename| OpenFile(filename)}

IF !EVAL(bOpenFile, 'Orders.DBF')
   ? 'File not found'
ENDIF

CLOSE DATABASES

RETURN NIL

FUNCTION OpenFile(cFile)
LOCAL lRetVal := .F.

IF FILE(cFile)        // Check for existence.
   USE (cFile) NEW    // Open using extended expression.
   lRetVal := .T.
ENDIF

RETURN lRetVal
```

Arrays

Why Are Clipper's Arrays So Special ➤ 152

Declaring and Using Arrays ➤ 153

Applying Arrays in Everyday Coding ➤ 158

Array Functions ➤ 159

Array Manipulation ➤ 160

User Interface ➤ 165

Database Related ➤ 167

Code Block Related ➤ 169

Environment ➤ 169

Passing Arrays as Parameters ➤ 172

Recursion ➤ 174

Global Variables ➤ 175

Summary ➤ 176

Exercises ➤ 176

For many years, Xbase aficionados lived without the means for collecting and manipulating groups of data under a single, subscripted name. Arrays, as these groups are usually called, were not part of the dBASE language until the dBASE IV release. Early on however, other vendors were quick to include this sorely missing feature in their products, yielding a powerful selling point. The original Clipper 5 language took even greater strides in giving developers tremendous flexibility with its new array capabilities. In this chapter, we'll examine CA-Clipper's so-called *ragged arrays*. Specifically, we'll see how to define an array, how to assign it values, how to manipulate it using standard operators and special built-in functions, ways to incorporate code blocks with arrays, and most importantly, how arrays can be introduced into normal coding tasks.

After completing this chapter, you will have learned:

- Why the CA-Clipper array implementation is quite different from any other Xbase dialect
- To define an array and assign values to its elements
- To identify the numerous built-in array functions in CA-Clipper and how to pass entire arrays and array elements as parameters
- To manipulate array structures using code blocks

Why Are Clipper's Arrays So Special

The overwhelming difference between CA-Clipper arrays and those of other Xbase languages, is the ultimate flexibility that Clipper's arrays afford the developer. Clipper arrays may assume any *topology* that makes sense for the problem being solved. This is to say that, in Clipper, more than just the standard n-dimensional array may be represented. Indeed, arrays with all sorts of structures become possible. For example, consider the case where customer order summary information is extracted from a database (or databases) and needs to be represented in memory for easy manipulation. CA-Clipper arrays can handle this easily. Pictorially it may appear as shown in Figure 7.1

With CA-Clipper, representing this complex, roughly textured structure is no problem because each element of an array may itself be an array of multiple dimensions. CA-Clipper does not officially have the ability to declare data structures as in C, but with such a flexible array capability, such structures can be easily represented.

Unlike its Xbase brethren, CA-Clipper array structures can be of virtually any size, although each individual array has a maximum of 4,096 elements. There is no limit to the number of subarrays that can be attached. There is, however, an underlying limit to the size of a Clipper array and that is dictated by the maximum capacity of the Segment Virtual Object Store (SVOS), Clipper's

Figure 7.1 Using CA-Clipper arrays to store data.

```
Customer base information
         Name: character
         Contact: character
         Address: character
         Phone: character

    Credit history: array of 3 elements
         Invoice totals for 30-60-90 days

    Current detail: array, unbounded dimension
         Product Code: Character
         Quantity Ordered: Numeric
         On Backorder: Logical
         Ship Date: Date
```

place to store arrays and other items. If you declare very large arrays, you may eventually run out of array memory. Because of the dynamic nature of SVOS, it is difficult to determine exactly when this might occur. The stated worst case is when slightly over 1Mb of strings and arrays are in use and best case is in excess of 16Mb. Remember that if you declare a large array as in

```
LOCAL aBigOne[500, 300]
```

a total of 150,500 elements is defined. Each array element in CA-Clipper occupies 14 bytes, therefore this array requires over 2Mb and is consequently of a dangerous size.

Declaring and Using Arrays

CA-Clipper arrays are easy to define and, in fact, there are several ways of doing so. For declarative purposes, there is still the Summer '87 flavor DECLARE statement that can be used with the current Clipper language. The trend, however, is now to declare an array's name and dimension in a LOCAL, STATIC, PUBLIC, or PRIVATE declarative statement. When using these four statements, the scope of the array is explicit. When using DECLARE, the scope is the same as using PRIVATE.

Whenever you declare a new memory variable to contain an array, always make sure that the Hungarian notation prefix "a" for an array is used. The next three sections define the primary ways in which you can declare an array.

Literal Declarations

The first method of declaring an array that usually comes to mind is the *literal declaration* method. With this method, you achieve three things: you declare the array, determine its initial size, and assign its elements initial values. The following is a typical example of this method:

```
LOCAL aMonths := { 'Jan', 'Feb', 'Mar', 'Apr', 'May', 'Jun', 'Jul',
                   'Aug', 'Sep', 'Oct', 'Nov', 'Dec' }
```

Here we see that the array aMonths has been declared. Its size is 12 elements and the initial values are the names of the months. Note the special use of the curly brackets to signify a literal array declaration. A literal declaration may appear anywhere an array data type is expected, including parameters for built-in functions and UDFs and code blocks. As we'll see later, an array declared in this manner can be dynamically resized (either smaller or larger) and its values can be changed.

In CA-Clipper, an array can have elements that contain values of different data types. For example, the following declaration is perfectly valid:

```
LOCAL aVariety := {0, 'Michael Joseph', .T.}
```

The next example declares a null array. The concept of a null array is this: it is an array-type variable, but it has no elements. The elements can be added dynamically later, as we'll see.

```
LOCAL aStates := {}    // Null array, no elements.
```

Much of the power behind CA-Clipper's arrays is derived from the fact that a subarray is a valid value for an array element. Structures called *ragged arrays* become possible. If you wish to define the dimensions of a ragged array using the literal declaration method, use a definition like this :

```
LOCAL aRagged := {1027.55, .T., {'a', 'b', {1, 2}}}
```

This array has three elements, aRagged[1] is a Numeric, aRagged[2] is a Logical, and aRagged[3] is a Subarray. When we apply the LEN() function to the definition, which may be used with arrays as well as strings, we get a rather interesting result:

```
? LEN(aRagged)         // Length is 3!
```

The length of aRagged is 3 because the elements in the subarray are not counted. You can extrapolate from this discussion that CA-Clipper arrays are completely flexible in the shapes they can assume. Moreover, the type of information that you can store in an array is flexible too:

```
? VALTYPE(aRagged)        // 'A'
? VALTYPE(aRagged[3])     // 'A'
? VALTYPE(aRagged[3,1])   // 'C'
? VALTYPE(aRagged[3][3])  // 'A'
? VALTYPE(aRagged[2])     // 'L'
```

Fixed-Size Declarations

The next technique for declaring arrays is called the *fixed-size declaration* method. You would use this technique if the array you need to declare has constant dimensions. The examples shown here illustrate situations where you might define an array of fixed dimensions if you know how many elements you need, but are not sure what to put in them. Bear in mind that an array's size can be altered at run-time.

```
LOCAL aQtr[4]         // Empty array with four elements.
LOCAL aMatrix[2][2]   // Two-dimensional array.
STATIC aPrices[5,5,5] // Three-dimensional array.
aStates := ARRAY(50)  // Another empty array.
```

The first example simply declares an array with four elements, all of which are set to the value NIL. The second and third example define arrays with subarrays. CA-Clipper handles multi-dimensional arrays differently than the traditional sense. Consider this: aMatrix has two elements, aMatrix[1] and aMatrix[2], each of which is a subarray, itself containing two elements. The last example uses the built-in ARRAY() function to return an array of the specified dimension.

Dynamic Declarations

The final way to declare an array structure involves the *dynamic declaration* method. With this method, you always begin with the null array and then expand outward by adding elements or groups of elements as required. This is possible through use of the AADD() and ASIZE() built-in functions. The following example demonstrates how this happens:

```
LOCAL aDynamic := {}            // Null array to start.
ASIZE(aDynamic, 3)              // Result: {NIL, NIL, NIL}
AADD(aDynamic, 'Hello world')   // Now four elements.
AADD(aDynamic, {1,2,3})         // Now five elements.
```

The topology of the array after the sequence illustrated here results in an array with five elements with the fifth element as a subarray (itself containing three elements). So you can see that an array that began with nothing can easily become something rather involved.

Assigning Values to Array Elements

Once an array has been declared, you can assign initial values or change current values of array elements in several ways. Here are some examples. Be sure to read the comments associated with each for additional information.

```
aStates[1] := 'Alaska'      // Single subscript, element
                            // assigned a character value.

aCommission[6][2] := 0.85   // A "C" style multiple subscript.

aPrices[2,3,4] := 25.67     // Comma subscripting: [2,3,4]
                            // is equivalent to
                            // bracket subscripting: [2][3][4].

aGrades[nCount] := 'A'      // Memory variable for subscript.
```

Many times in routine coding chores, arrays are assigned values in some sort of iteration. We'll see later, when we introduce arrays to our programming repertoire, exactly how this notion is of prime importance.

Array references can be generalized through use of a subscript variable as in the next example:

```
* Save integers 1..10 in aCount
LOCAL i, aCount[10]
FOR i:=1 TO 10 ; aCount[i]:=i ; NEXT
```

Array References

One interesting aspect of CA-Clipper arrays is the way they are referenced. Consider the following example, where it seems that we are creating a duplicate array:

```
LOCAL aFirst := {1,2,3}
LOCAL aSecond := {}

aSecond := aFirst    // Will not result in two arrays
```

At first glance, it may appear that another copy of `aFirst` is generated and named `aSecond`. This is not the case because in Clipper, an array's reference can be viewed separately from its value. In this case, `aSecond` actually *points* to the same memory locations as `aFirst`. So:

```
aFirst[2] := 'Hello world'
? aSecond[2]   // "Hello world" is displayed.
```

To create a completely unique copy of aFirst, you must utilize a special built-in function called ACLONE().

Comparing Arrays

As a direct relation to our previous comments about array references, we can use the comparison operator == to test whether two memory variable names refer to the same array (i.e., they point to the same place in memory). As an example of this concept, consider the following code segment:

```
LOCAL aOne := { NIL, NIL, NIL }, aTwo, aThree
aTwo := aOne        // Duplicate reference to array.
? aOne == aTwo      // Result: .T. since arrays are equivalent.

aThree := ACLONE(aOne)
? aOne == aThree    // Result: .F. not equivalent.
```

Many times, however, we need to determine the *equality* of an entire ragged array. In this case, the comparison operator does not help. Instead, we need a special function to traverse the arrays' structures, determining along the way whether the arrays are equal in both topology and content.

1. Declare and initialize a two-dimensional array named aStudent, with each row containing a student's name and student number, followed by three numeric test scores. The maximum number of students in class is 25.
2. Define and initialize a CA-Clipper ragged array that represents the screen coordinates of the corner points of a rectangular region on the screen.

1. The following code segment is one possible way to create and initialize this array structure. Later in this chapter, we'll learn about more automated means using various array functions.

```
#define ST_NAME_LEN 32
#define ST_NUM_LEN 5
#define ST_NAME 1
#define ST_NUM 2
#define ST_TEST_1
#define ST_TEST_2
#define ST_TEST_3

LOCAL aStudent[25, 5]
FOR nIndex := 1 TO 25
```

```
            aStudent[nIndex,ST_NAME]        := SPACE(LEN(ST_NAME_LEN))
            aStudent[nIndex,ST_NUM]         := SPACE(LEN(ST_NUM_LEN))
            aStudent[nIndex,ST_TEST_1]      := 0
            aStudent[nIndex,ST_TEST_2]      := 0
            aStudent[nIndex,ST_TEST_3]      := 0
         NEXT
```

2. We'll see that the solution to this question is actually quite needed when saving generic kinds of screen objects.

```
/* Define screen object with specific end points,
   aCoords[1] == array containing top/left coord
   aCoords[2] == array containing bottom/right coord
*/
LOCAL aCoords := {{5,5}, {20,75}}
```

Applying Arrays in Everyday Coding

One of the most difficult characteristics associated with arrays is when to use them. For software developers coming to Clipper from other languages like C or Pascal, arrays may already be second nature. For others, coming from Xbase, a flexible array structure such as CA-Clipper's was not available. Let's therefore discuss some implementation topics that will help you to see when arrays might come in handy. First, you should use arrays whenever a data structure seems necessary. This includes situations where reasonably sized, temporary tables are required to support some kind of processing. For example, a payroll program might need a tax rate table for use when generating checks. Or an order entry program might need a place to store detailed order information for editing purposes.

Another good area to apply arrays is in code that is becoming too specialized, or code that has become a series of special cases. Arrays force you to *generalize* the code, making the solution smaller, more compact, and certainly more elegant. Consider the following code that is not generalized:

```
IF nCounty == 1        // Los Angeles county.
   nSalesTax := nTaxRate1 * Orders->Amount
ELSEIF nCounty == 2    // Kern county.
   nSalesTax := nTaxRate2 * Orders->Amount
ELSEIF nCounty == 3    // Orange county.
   nSalesTax := nTaxRate3 * Orders->Amount
.
. <statements>
.
```

As you can see, the code continues on without generalizing. Now consider another version, this time using arrays. The array aCountyTax has a tax rate for each county in California. Now we can generalize:

```
LOCAL aCountyTax[26]

nSalesTax := aCountyTax[nCounty] * Orders->Amount
```

Not only is this version smaller and easier to understand, but it is less prone to errors and performs better.

Array Functions

CA-Clipper also has quite a complement of built-in functions to support the use of arrays. This section contains a description of these functions, a function prototype, and sample use. We will group the array functions in terms of functionality: array manipulation, user interface, database, code block, and environment. As noted in the calling sequence descriptions, some functions accept arrays and some return them.

A Brief Tour

Before we examine the specifics of each array function, let's take a brief tour of several important array functions in the form of a detailed example. Take some time and trace the flow of the following program to see how the array values evolve. Be sure to verify your results with the comments in the code. This is a good time to begin experimenting with the Clipper Debugger, which allows you to control the execution of the code and check out intermediate results.

```
LOCAL aSimple := {}, aNIL := { {NIL,NIL,NIL}, {NIL,NIL,NIL} }
LOCAL aSame
* Think of aNIL as a traditional 2-by-3 matrix

? LEN(aSimple)           // 0 length
? LEN(aNIL)              // 2: since two subarray elements.
ASIZE(aSimple,5)         // Dynamically dimension array
? LEN(aSimple)           // five empty elements.
? aSimple[1]             // NIL: value of empty elements.

AADD(aSimple, '6th')     // Now {NIL,NIL,NIL,NIL,NIL,'6th'}
? LEN(aSimple)           // of length six.
aSimple[2]:=.T.          // Now {NIL,.T.,NIL,NIL,NIL,'6th'}
ADEL(aSimple,1)          // Now {.T.,NIL,NIL,NIL,'6th',NIL}
                         // still with six elements!  ADEL()
                         // gets rid of first element and
                         // brings in a NIL element from
                         // the right.  Length preserved.

ASIZE(aSimple,5)         // This gets rid of dangling NIL element
                         // and re-dimension array.
```

```
        AADD(aSimple,ARRAY(3))    // ARRAY() returns: {NIL,NIL,NIL}
                                  // and it is added at the sixth
                                  // element of aSimple, producing an
                                  // "L" shaped topology.
        ? LEN(aSimple)            // Still six.

        aSame:=ACLONE(aSimple)    // Duplicates aSimple's topology,
                                  // i.e. aSame has the same "L"
                                  // shape as aSimple.

        AADD(aNIL, ARRAY(3))      // Now aNIL is 3-by-3, but empty.
        AFILL(aNIL, 'Foo')        // An attempt to fill all nine elements
                                  // produces unexpected results:
                                  // { 'Foo', 'Foo', 'Foo' }, remember
                                  // aNIL is an array with three elements!

        aSimple[6] := {1, 2, 3}
        ? ATAIL(aSimple)[2]       // Displays 2, note that since
                                  // ATAIL() returns an array in this
                                  // case, it may be subscripted.
        AINS(aNIL,2)              // {'Foo', NIL, 'Foo'}. Here length
                                  // preserved, new second element NIL is
                                  // inserted, rightmost element is
                                  // lost.
```

In general, you should take care when using array functions on multi-dimensional arrays because the results may not always be as expected. Remember that multi-dimensional arrays are just arrays of subarrays.

That's all we have space for here. We highly recommend that you continue experimenting with the other functions by writing some test code and then doing a bit of investigation in the Debugger. Now, let's look at each function individually.

Array Manipulation

This section contains the bulk of the array functions. The functions described here are used for general array manipulation. As CA-Clipper arrays may grow dynamically, many of these functions deal with sizing considerations.

AADD()
Prototype: AADD(<aArray>, <vValue>) —> vValue

The purpose of AADD() is to add a new element to the end of an array, thus expanding the size of the array by one element. <aArray> is the array to expand and <vValue> is an expression whose value shall be added as a new element. If <vValue> is not specified, a NIL element is added to the array. The return value of AADD() is the value of the expression. You might want to think of `AADD()` as a special case of `ASIZE()` in that `AADD()` can only add one element at a time.

Example:

```
LOCAL aSample := {}     // NULL array to start with.
AADD(aSample, 1)        // One-element array {1}
AADD(aSample, 2)        // Two-element array {1,2}
AADD(aSample, {3,4})    // Three-element array {1,2,{3,4}}
```

ACLONE()

Prototype: `ACLONE(<aSource>) -> aDuplicate`

`ACLONE()` duplicates a ragged array by creating a physically unique copy of the original array. This process is entirely different from simply assigning one array to another (which only duplicates its reference). The topology of the new array matches the original completely. You might want to think of `ACLONE()` as a general case of `ACOPY()`, the difference being that `ACOPY()` does not duplicate arrays with subarrays.

Example:

```
LOCAL aBefore := {9, 9, 9}, aAfter
aAfter := ACLONE(aBefore)  // Result: aAfter has {9,9,9}
aAfter[3] := 8             // Result: aBefore has {9,9,9}
                           // aAfter has {9,9,8}
```

ACOPY()

Prototype: `ACOPY(<aSource>, <aTarget>, [<nStart>], [<nCount>], [<nTargetPos>]) -> aTarget`

The purpose of `ACOPY()` is to copy elements from one array into another. The process proceeds as elements are copied from the `<aSource>` array to the `<aTarget>` array. Note that the target array must already exist and must be big enough to accommodate the copied elements. `ACOPY()` is even more flexible in the sense that `<nStart>` gives you control over where the copying begins and `<nCount>` allows you to specify how many elements are to be copied. `ACOPY()` returns a reference to the target array.

Elements of any data type may be copied using `ACOPY()`, however, if subarrays are copied, only a reference to the subarrays is copied to the target array, thus true copying of ragged arrays is not possible with `ACOPY()`. `ACLONE()` should be used for this purpose.

Example:

```
LOCAL aFrom := {99, 99, 99, 99, 99}
LOCAL aTo := {0, 0, 0, 0, 0}
ACOPY(aFrom, aTo)              // Result: aTo now has {99,99,99,99,99}
ACOPY({1,2,3}, aTo, 2, 2, 4)   // Result: aTo now has {99,99,99,2,3}
```

ADEL()
Prototype: ADEL(<aArray>, <nPosition>) —> aArray

Use `ADEL()` to delete an array element at a specified position in the passed array. All elements are promoted upward after the deletion operation. The number of elements in the array, however, remains unchanged and a NIL element enters at the end. This means that if the element deleted is a subarray, the resulting array could possess a topology quite different than the original. The return value of `ADEL()` is a reference to the modified array.

Example:

```
LOCAL aTemporary := {1, 2, {3, 4}, 5}
ADEL(aTemporary, 3)    // Result: {1, 2, 5, NIL}
```

AFILL()
Prototype: AFILL(<aArray>, <vValue>, [<nStart>], [<nCount>]) —> aArray

The purpose of the `AFILL()` function is to fill an array with a specified value. The array passed in <aArray> is filled with the value of <vValue>. <vValue> can be an expression that evaluates to a value of any data type. You can, optionally, specify the element position in the array to begin filling (<nStart>), as well as the number of elements to fill (<nCount>).

Example:

```
LOCAL aBase := ARRAY(5)
AFILL(aBase, NIL)          // Result: aBase has all NIL elements.
AFILL(aBase, 'foo', 3, 1)  // Result: {NIL,NIL,'foo',NIL,NIL}
```

AINS()
Prototype: AINS(<aArray>, <nPosition>) —> aArray

`AINS()` is a useful function that allows you to insert a NIL element into an existing array. The new element is placed at the position indicated by <nPosition> inside of the array <aArray>. The number of elements contained in the array, however, remains unchanged. In order for the size of the array to be constant, the last element is discarded. If the last element is a subarray, this means the topology of the resulting array may have quite a different structure than the original. `AINS()` returns a reference to the modified array.

Example:

```
LOCAL aTier := {{1}, {2,2}, {3,3,3}}, nPlace := 2
AINS(aTier,nPlace) // Result: {{1}, NIL, {2,2}}
```

ARRAY()
Prototype: ARRAY(<nElements>, [, <nElements> ...]) —> aArray

This array function creates an uninitialized array of specified dimensions. The variable number of <nElements> parameters indicates that you may define multi-dimensional arrays with ARRAY(). Remember that a CA-Clipper array may not have more than 4,096 elements, hence, this is the upper limit for these parameters. There are several ways to create an array, but using ARRAY() gives you the advantage of being a function and may consequently appear in an expression or code block.

Example:

```
#define ARRAY_SIZE 3

LOCAL bArrayGen := {|numelems| ARRAY(numelems)}
LOCAL aNew

aNew := EVAL(bArrayGen, ARRAY_SIZE) // Result: {NIL, NIL, NIL}
```

ASCAN()
Prototype: ASCAN(<aArray>, <vSearch>, [<nStart>], [<nCount>]) —> nStoppedAt

ASCAN() represents an efficient and compact way to search an array for a given value or condition. In the simplest case, ASCAN() searches through <aArray> for the value of the expression specified in <vSearch>. The data type for the search value can be Character, Numeric, Date, or Logical. The return value is the position of the element that matches the search value. Note that during the search process, comparisons between the array elements and the search value are done with the = operator, not ==. This means that the comparisons are affected by the status of SET EXACT.

A more advanced form of ASCAN() accepts a code block for the search value parameter. In this case, ASCAN() evaluates the code block for each element. The process stops when the code block returns a value of .T. or the last element is reached.

Example:

```
LOCAL aScanMe := {'10078', '90024', '90278', '45060'}
LOCAL bScanBlock := {|elem| '4' $ elem}

? ASCAN(aScanMe, '90024')      // Result: 2
? ASCAN(aScanMe, bScanBlock}   // Result: 4
```

ASIZE()
Prototype: ASIZE(<aArray>, <nSize>) —> aArray

A perfect example of the dynamic nature of CA-Clipper arrays is the ASIZE() function. Use ASIZE() to expand or contract an array's size. If the size of <aArray> is less than the new size specified by <nSize> then new NIL elements are added to the end of the array. If the size of the array is greater than the new size then existing elements are truncated. ASIZE() returns a reference to the modified array.

Example:

```
LOCAL aStorage := {3, 1, 4, 1, 5, 9}, nNumElements

nNumElements := LEN(aStorage)
ASIZE(aStorage, 3)                  // Result: {3, 1, 4}
ASIZE(aStorage, nNumElements)       // Result: {3,1,4,NIL,NIL,NIL}
```

ASORT()
Prototype: ASORT(<aArray>, [<nStart>], [<nCount>] , [<bOrder>]) —> aArray

The ASORT() function provides a mechanism where the elements of an array may be physically ordered according to a user-definable sequence (the default being ascending order). <aTarget> is the array to be sorted, <nStart> is the first element to sort (the default is 1), <nCount> is the number of elements to sort (the default is LEN(aArray)-nStart+1), and <bOrder> is an optional code block used to control the sorting process. All elements considered in the sort should be of the same data type. The return value is the sorted equivalent of the <aArray> array.

When specified, the code block controls the sorting process by comparing two array elements at a time. The code block should return either a .T. value, meaning the values are in the correct order, or .F., indicating they are not.

> The ASORT() code block always requires two parameters. The expressions contained within the block define what it means for one element to sort before another. When the code block is used, ASORT() rearranges the array by passing two elements at a time through the code block. Do not become concerned about the specific algorithm being used by CA-Clipper to traverse the array's elements. Suffice it to say, all elements will be visited and the array will be sorted according to the rules you've specified inside the code block.

Example:

```
/* Example 1 */
LOCAL aTestArray := {'AA', 'CC', 'BB'}
ASORT(aTestArray)      // Results: {'AA','BB','CC'}
```

```
/* Example 2: with code block */
aTestArray := { 'Jason', 'Eduard', 'Alexander', ; 'Alexa', 'Jennafer' }
ASORT(aTestArray,,,{ |x,y| x < y })
```

In the second example, we see a code block controls the sorting process, placing the elements in *descending order*.

ATAIL()
Prototype: ATAIL(<aArray>) -> vElement

This array function returns the highest numbered element of an array. <aArray> is the target array from which the last element is extracted and vElement is the last element return value. Due to the flexibility of CA-Clipper arrays, the data type of the last element cannot be guaranteed. It could be of any type, including Array.

Example:

```
LOCAL aSimple  := {'one', 'two', 'three'}
LOCAL aStrange := {1, {2, 3, {4, 5, 6}}}

? ATAIL(aSimple)              // Result: 'three'
? aSimple[LEN(aSimple)]       // Result: 'three', same as ATAIL()
? LEN(ATAIL(aStrange))        // Result: 3 since {4,5,6} has 3 elements.
```

LEN()
Prototype: LEN(<aArray>) -> nCount

The LEN() function, which we normally associate with character strings, may also be used with arrays. <aArray> is the array for which the length is determined. When you pass an array to LEN(), the numeric value returned is the number of elements in the array. If the array has a single dimension, the result is simply the number of elements, however, if the array has more than one dimension, the result is the number of subarrays.

Example:

```
LOCAL aTemp[5]
? LEN(aTemp)     // Result: 5, even though no values.
aTemp := { {1}, {1,2}, {3,5,8}, {13,21,34,55} }
? LEN(aTemp)     // Result: 4, since four subarrays.
```

User Interface

Next we'll take a look at an array function whose primary purpose serves to act as a simple building block for giving developers a means for producing picklist windows and pop-up menus.

ACHOICE()

Prototype: ACHOICE(<nTop>,<nLeft>, <nBottom>, <nRight>, <aOptions>, [<aSelectable> | <lSelectable>], [<cUserFunction>], [<nInitialOption>], [<nWindowRow>]) —> nPosition

As a means to implement portions of a user interface, ACHOICE() allows for the creation of a pop-up menu and/or picklist. Although this function provides for default reactions to user keystrokes while inside the window, through use of the user-function capability, these reactions are entirely programmable.

The coordinates <nTop>, <nLeft>, <nBottom>, and <nRight> specify the location of the window on the screen. ACHOICE() does not save the screen contents prior to displaying the pop-up. <aOptions> is an array containing the options selectable from the pop-up. The next parameter is optional, but when specified determines which menu options may be selected by the user. If this parameter is an array <aSelectable>, its elements parallel the elements in <aOptions>. For example, if the third element of <aSelectable> has a value of .F., then the third menu option of <aOptions> will not be selectable. If this parameter is specified as .T., then all options are selectable; if its value is .F., then none of the options is selectable. The optional <cUserFunction> parameter is the name of a UDF that handles keystroke processing while the user is in the pop-up.

Example:

```
#include 'box.ch'

FUNCTION Main
LOCAL aList := { 'Santa Monica'  , ;
        'Redondo Beach',          ;
        'Northridge',             ;
        'La Puente'     ,         ;
        'Mill Valley' }
LOCAL nItem := 0, cScrSave
LOCAL aSel[LEN(aList)]

cScrSave := SAVESCREEN( 5, 15, 11, 35 )
@ 5, 15, 11, 35 BOX B_SINGLE// Draw a smooth line border.

AFILL( aSel, .T. )
aSel[4] := .F.   // Make one non-selectable.

WHILE nItem == 0
   nItem := ACHOICE(6, 16, 10, 34, aList, aSel)
END

RESTSCREEN( 5, 15, 11, 35, cScrSave )
RETURN NIL
```

Database Related

We have in this category two array functions that provide an interface between arrays and database file structures. DBCREATE() allows for the creation of self-contained applications that are able to build necessary databases on-the-fly. While, DBSTRUCT(), on the other hand, allows you insight into the structure of a .DBF file.

DBCREATE()
Prototype: DBCREATE(<cDatabase>, <aStruct>, <cDriver>) -> NIL

DBCREATE() creates a database file from a database structure array. When you use this function, CA-Clipper allows an application to test the existence of a required database and, if not present, build a structure according to specifications. <cDatabase> is the name of the database file and <aStruct> is a multi-dimensional array containing subarrays, each of which describes a field in the new database. The structure of each subarray is shown in Table 7.1.

The special Clipper header file, DBSTRUCT.CH, found in \CLIPPER5\INCLUDE contains the manifest constants, shown in Table 7.1, for the use of indexing the subarrays required by DBCREATE().

The <cDriver> parameter specifies a replaceable database driver (RDD) to use to process the current work area.

> **Note**
> When you deliver a production Clipper application, every attempt should be made to make it as self reliant as possible. For example, your application should not assume that critical database files are present. Instead, at start-up time, the application should perform a series of checks for existence on the various files that comprise the system using the built-in FILE() function. If the files don't exist, the application should presume that this is the first time the program is executing and consequently have DBCREATE() create the databases automatically.

Table 7.1 The Structure for each Subarray for the <aStruct> Parameter in DBCREATE()

Position	Data Type	Manifest Constant
1	Character	DBS_NAME
2	Character	DBS_TYPE
3	Numeric	DBS_LEN
4	Numeric	DBS_DEC

Example:

```
LOCAL aStudent := {}
AADD(aStudent, { 'Name',    'C', 30 }
AADD(aStudent, { 'Address', 'C', 45 }
AADD(aStudent, { 'City',    'C', 20 }
AADD(aStudent, { 'State',   'C', 2 }
AADD(aStudent, { 'Zip',     'C', 5 }
AADD(aStudent, { 'Score',   'N', 3 }
AADD(aStudent, { 'FullTime','L', 1}
AADD(aStudent, { 'Enroll',  'D', 8 }

/* Now build a .DBF using aStudent */
DBCREATE('Student', aStudent)
```

DBSTRUCT()
Prototype: `DBSTRUCT() -> aStruct`

In a process opposite to DBCREATE(), DBSTRUCT() builds an array containing the structure of a database file stored in a series of subarrays. By default, the structure of the database file opened in the current work area is built.

Note

> DBSTRUCT() is very useful when used in conjunction with ACHOICE() to provide the user with a picklist of database field names. For example, if you wish to allow the user to decide which fields are to appear on an impromptu report, you could use these functions to let the user choose from a complete or partial list of available fields.

Another function, AFIELDS() provides essentially the same service as DBSTRUCT() and is still available in the current version of CA-Clipper. The primary difference between the two functions is that AFIELDS() populates a series of parallel single-dimension arrays, while DBSTRUCT() simply uses a single, multi-dimensional array, making for easier handling of the information. In addition, with DBSTRUCT(), the array does not have to previously exist.

Example:

```
#include 'dbstruct.ch'

LOCAL aDBFStruct, aFieldList := {}

USE Customer NEW
USE Orders NEW

aDBFStruct := Orders->(DBSTRUCT())

/* Populate aFieldList with field names of Orders.DBF */
AEVAL(aDBFStruct, {|elem| AADD(aFieldList, elem[DBS_NAME])})
```

Code Block Related

As the single entry in this category, we have probably the most important array function, AEVAL(), which provides for the conduit between arrays and code blocks. You will frequently witness the marriage of arrays and code blocks in CA-Clipper optimized coding styles. Programs developed with these techniques tend to be highly compact and portable.

AEVAL()

Prototype: AEVAL(<aArray>, <bBlock>, [<nStart>], [<nCount>]) —> aArray

This function evaluates a code block for each element in an array. The array to be traversed is passed as <aArray> and the code block to be evaluated is <bBlock>. In the case of a single-dimension array, each element of the array is given to the code block for processing. You might want to think of AEVAL() as an automated looping structure. In fact, you may choose to use the FOR/NEXT control structure instead of AEVAL(). You can also process multi-dimensional arrays with AEVAL(), but remember that in CA-Clipper such arrays are nothing more than arrays of subarrays. This means that instead of passing simple elements to the code block, you are passing entire subarrays.

Example:

```
/* Sum an array using AEVAL() */
aValues := {1, 1, 2, 3, 5, 8, 13}
nSum := 0
AEVAL(aValues, {|elem| nSum += elem}

/* FOR/NEXT method */
FOR nCount := 1 TO LEN(aValues)
   nSum += aValues[nCount]
NEXT
```

In the above example, AEVAL() is able to sum the numeric elements of the aValue array because each element of an array passed to the function is selected one at a time and given to the code block. The code block, in this case, receives each element through the elem formal parameter. AEVAL() continues this iterative process until all elements have been processed by the code block.

Environment

This final category contains a single built-in function (with a reference to a second, obsolete function), that provides a CA-Clipper application an interface to the DOS directory and file system.

DIRECTORY()

Prototype: `DIRECTORY(<cDirSpec>, [<cAttributes>]) -> aDirectory`

This built-in function creates a multi-dimensional array of DOS directory and file information. You may specify the files selected with the `<cDirSpec>` parameter. For example, specifying *.TXT selects all files with the .TXT file extension.

The function returns an array of subarrays. Each subarray contains the information, shown in Table 7.2, about a single selected file.

The special Clipper header file, DIRECTRY.CH, found in \CLIPPER5\INCLUDE contains the manifest constants, shown in Table 7.2, for the use of indexing the subarrays returned by DIRECTORY().

Note

> One rather useful area in which `DIRECTORY()` might come in handy is in the situation where `ACHOICE()` is used to allow the user to choose a disk file in a DOS disk directory.

Another function, `ADIR()`, which provides essentially the same service, is still available in the current version of CA-Clipper. The primary difference between the two functions is that `ADIR()` populates a series of parallel single-dimension arrays, while `DIRECTORY()` simply uses a single, multi-dimensional array, making for easier handling of the information.

Example:

```
#include 'directry.ch'

LOCAL aTextFiles := DIRECTORY('*.TXT')
/* aTextFiles contains a number of subarrays equal to
   the number of disk files with the .TXT extension.
   For our example, let's assume three files were found. */
? aTextFiles[1, F_NAME]   // Display name of first file.
? aTextFiles[3, F_DATE]   // Display file data of third file.
```

Table 7.2 The Structure of Each Subarray for the aDirectory Array Returned by DIRECTORY()

Position	Data Type	Manifest Constant
1	Character	F_NAME
2	Numeric	F_SIZE
3	Date	F_DATE
4	Character	F_TIME
5	Character	F_ATT

Jump Tables

One very useful technique I picked up as a mainframe assembler-language programmer was the use of a "jump table." With a jump table, you store the "addresses" of the routines you want to call depending on some event, such as a menu choice. In CA-Clipper, we can implement a jump table by storing a series of code blocks in an array where each code block simply contains a function call. In this way, we can call a function by EVAL()ing an indexed array element.

Here is an example of how code blocks can be stored in arrays. This ability can result in some curious applications:

```
LOCAL i, aJumpTable := { { || gl() } , ;
         { || ar() } ,                  ;
         { || ap() } ,                  ;
         { || so() } }

FOR i := 1 TO 4
   EVAL(aJumpTable[i])    // Visit each UDF.
NEXT
```

In this example, a series of code blocks is stored in an array. The EVAL() function is used to evaluate each array element in sequence, thus calling the named UDF.

1. Write a function to display a picklist of all .NTX files found in the current directory whenever the F3 function key is pressed in a "wait state," such as what exists when processing a GET. Please also provide a brief main program that establishes this capability. (Hint: use ACHOICE(), and make sure the prior screen content is saved and restored).

1. This is the typical file list picklist problem. In our solution, we use the SETKEY() built-in function to evaluate a code block when the user presses F3 in a wait state. The block simply calls the IPick() UDF, which uses the DIRECTORY(), ACHOICE(), and AEVAL() array functions to do the work.

```
#include 'inkey.ch'
#include 'box.ch'
#include 'directry.ch'

FUNCTION Main

MEMVAR getlist
LOCAL cTest:=SPACE(10)
/* Whenever the user presses F3, evaluate code block */
SETKEY(K_F3, {|| IPick()})
```

```
CLS
@ 10,5 SAY 'Enter index file name' GET cTest
READ

RETURN NIL

FUNCTION IPick

LOCAL cScrSave := SAVESCREEN(10,30,20,45)
LOCAL cCurSave := SETCURSOR(0)
LOCAL aDir := DIRECTORY('*.NTX')
LOCAL aFiles:={}, nChoice:=0

IF LEN(aDir) == 0
   @ 24,0 SAY 'No index files were found in the ' +;
      current directory'
   INKEY(0)
   @ 24,0
   RETURN NIL
ENDIF

AEVAL(aDir, {|ifile| AADD(aFiles, ifile[F_NAME]) } )
@ 10,30,20,45 BOX B_SINGLE+" "

KEYBOARD aFiles[ ACHOICE(11,31,19,44,aFiles) ]

RESTSCREEN(10,30,20,45,cScrSave)
SETCURSOR(cCurSave)

RETURN NIL
```

Passing Arrays as Parameters

At times, you may need to pass an array to a function and/or return an array from a function. CA-Clipper handles this situation without a problem. The only difference between passing arrays as parameters to functions versus regular memory variables is that arrays are passed *By Reference*, unlike memory variables which are normally passed *By Value*. This means that arrays may be altered inside the UDF by default. Single array elements, on the other hand, are passed By Value. There is no way to pass a single array element By Reference.

Note

There is normally no way to pass a whole array element By Value. As a work-around, however, you may use the ACLONE() built-in array function in the following manner:

```
LOCAL aArray := {1, 2, 3}
MyUDF(ACLONE(aArray))
```

> What happens here is that ACLONE() makes a copy of the original array, sending this "value" to the function. Since the function is working on the return value of a built-in function, it is not possible to modify it.

Note
> There is no way to pass a single array element By Reference. An attempt to do so, as illustrated in the following code segment, results in an error:
>
> ```
> LOCAL aArray := {1, 2, 3}
> MyUDF(@aArray[2])
> ```
>
> To get around this limitation, you would pass the entire array instead and then reference the single element inside the UDF.

Let's now summarize the various ways to pass arrays and memory variables to a function by considering the following code extract:

```
FUNCTION Main
LOCAL aArray := {1,2,3}
LOCAL nNum := 7

* MyFunc(aArray)        // Pass array By Reference.
MyFunc(nNum)            // Pass memory variable By Value.
MyFunc(@nNum)           // Pass memory variable By Reference.
MyFunc(aArray[1])       // Pass array element By Value.
*MyFunc(@aArray[1])     // Illegal, compile-time error.
RETURN NIL

FUNCTION MyFunc(a)
   a++                  // Modify formal parameter.
RETURN NIL
```

Note that we commented out two lines in the sample code. This was necessary to indicate a line that would yield a compile-time error (we don't wish to imply bug ridden code would compile!).

Array Return Values

Arrays may also be returned as parameters from functions. In fact, as seen in the *Array Functions* section earlier, this is quite common for the built-in functions. User-defined functions, however, can also return arrays. Consider the following:

```
#include 'directry.ch'
GetFiles('*.dbf')

/***
*
```

```
*  GetFiles( <cFileSpec> ) -> aFileList
*
*/

FUNCTION GetFiles( cFileSpec )
LOCAL aDir := DIRECTORY(cFileSpec)
LOCAL aFileList := {}

AEVAL(aDir, {|elem| AADD(aFileList, elem[F_NAME])})
RETURN (aFileList)
```

Recursion

As another, somewhat esoteric, example of array access, suppose we needed a way to print each element of an array no matter what the topology. This is not a problem for the flexible CA-Clipper array structures! The solution involves a *recursive function call* (where a function calls itself) inside a code block evaluation.

```
FUNCTION Main
LOCAL aRagged := {1,1,1, {2,2, {3, {4,4} } } }

PrintRagged(aRagged)

RETURN NIL

FUNCTION PrintRagged( aArray )
/* If a subarray is encountered, dive deeper into the
   recursion, otherwise, just display the element's value */
AEVAL( aArray, {|elem| IIF(VALTYPE(elem) == 'A' ,;
    PrintRagged(elem) ,;
    QOUT(elem) ) } )
RETURN NIL
```

The output of this program is simply a list of numerics: 1, 1, 1, 2, 2, 3, 4, 4. `PrintRagged()` visits each element of each subarray in `aRagged` and displays its value. Notice the call to `PrintRagged()` from within the body of `PrintRagged()`. It is this action that makes the function recursive. At first, recursion is difficult to conceptualize. It's kind of like believing in infinity. But recursion is the only way to traverse a completely flexible array structure.

One way to get recursion to come alive for you is to single step through the above code inside the Clipper Debugger. Make sure you activate the *Call Stack* so that you'll get an appreciation of the calling depth that recursion produces.

Global Variables

Another useful programming technique involving arrays centers around setting up an array to implement a group of *globally* scoped variables. We saw a simple version of this technique in Chapter 5, but now we'll go a step further with the help of arrays. Using these new globals, we may virtually eliminate the PUBLIC scope altogether. There are many reasons to avoid publics. For example, accessing variables that possess a global scope through a controlled mechanism, such as an access function, is very desirable. We also avoid using the symbol table. The technique goes like this:

- Establish a special Get/Set function in the main program of your application. We call this routine Global(). The purpose of this UDF is to allow access, both read and write, to the globals. Global() must *not* be a STATIC function since it must have an application-wide scope.
- Inside of Global(), we may define a STATIC array with enough elements for each global scope variable you wish to accommodate. An alternative, as shown in the following code , is to set up a file-wide STATIC in the .PRG file in which Global() resides. In either case, the array must be static as it must retain its value from one access to the next.
- Create a Clipper header file that contains symbolic names, one defined for each subscript in the array. This will be the name with which you refer to the global variable.

```
#define MAX_GLOBALS 10
#define G_PATHNAME 1
#define G_PRINT_DEST 2
#define G_TITLE 3

/* Main program module: MAIN.PRG */
STATIC aGlobal[MAX_GLOBALS]    // A file-wide STATIC.
                               // acting like a PUBLIC.

/***
*
* Global( <nGlobal>, <vValue> ) -> vValue
*
*/

FUNCTION Global(nGlobal, vValue)
RETURN (aGlobal[nGlobal] := ;
IIF(VALTYPE(vValue) == 'U', aGlobal[nGlobal], vValue))

/* Other program module: OTHER.PRG
This would not be possible using only a file-wide STATIC */
```

```
Global(G_PATHNAME, 'f:\data')    // SET "global" variable.
? Global(G_PATHNAME)             // GET "global" variable.
```

Here, the `Global()` UDF is responsible for accessing and assigning values for the globals stored in the `aGlobal` array. There is one penalty related to the use of globals in a Clipper program. In order to either *get* (retrieve the value) or *set* (assign a value) the contents of a global, you must issue a function call, and a function call always involves some overhead.

Summary

In this chapter, we've seen that CA-Clipper's arrays are quite generous in the features provided to the developer. They are truly a pleasure to use. After you feel comfortable with the various methods to define, assign, and manipulate arrays, the challenging part becomes learning how to solve problems with them and recognize when an array solution is appropriate.

Exercises

1. Write a CA-Clipper function `ADIM()` that accepts a two-dimensional array as a parameter. The function returns a single-dimension array containing two elements, which describe the dimensions of the passed array. For example:

   ```
   LOCAL aRect := { {1,0}, {0,0}, {1,1} }
   ADIM(aRect)    // Result: {3,2}
   ```

2. Write a CA-Clipper function ATRUE() using only to take a two-dimensional array containing only integers and change all elements having a value of 0 to .T. You may use the following array for your test data:

   ```
   LOCAL aMatrix := { {0, 1, 0, 2}, ;
                      {7, 0, 0, 0}, ;
                      {8, 3, 4, 0} }

   aTemp := ATRUE(aMatrix)

   /* The desired output array should be:

      {.T., 1, .T., 2}
      {7, .T., .T., .T.}
      {8, 3, 4, .T. }          */
   ```

Answers

1. As it turns out, the ADIM() can be rather simple. In fact, the only code needed is embedded in the function's RETURN statement. Since the array being passed is guaranteed to be precisely two dimensions, taking the length of the array gives us the number of rows and taking the length of one of its elements gives us the number of columns. We passed back an array of two elements.

   ```
   FUNCTION Main

   LOCAL aRect := { {1,0}, {0,0}, {1,1} }, aReturn

   aReturn := ADIM(aRect)
   ? aReturn[1], aReturn[2]

   RETURN NIL

   FUNCTION ADIM(aArray)
   RETURN ({LEN(aArray), LEN(aArray[1])})
   ```

2. One solution involves nested code block evaluations using the AEVAL() function. Notice that AEVAL()ing bBlock1 causes an AEVAL() of bBlock2. You should definitely sit through a debugger session to fully understand how this works.

   ```
   STATIC nRow := 0, nCol := 0

   FUNCTION Main

   LOCAL aInt := { {0, 1, 0, 2},              ;
           {7, 0, 0, 0},                      ;
           {8, 3, 4, 0} }

   LOCAL bBlock1 := {|elem_r| nRow++, nCol := 0,  ;
           AEVAL(elem_r, bBlock2)}
   LOCAL bBlock2 := {|elem_c| nCol++,                ;
           IF(elem_c == 0, aInt[nRow, nCol] := .T. ,; NIL)}

   AEVAL(aInt, bBlock1)

   RETURN NIL
   ```

Database Access

Accessing Databases with CA-Clipper ➤ 180

RDD Technology ➤ 182

Database Commands ➤ 192

Database Functions ➤ 199

RDD Commands ➤ 214

RDD Functions ➤ 215

The Importance of Code Blocks ➤ 226

Database Traversal and DBEVAL() ➤ 226

Setting Relations ➤ 228

The Many-to-Many Relation ➤ 231

Summary ➤ 238

Exercise ➤ 238

From the early beginnings of the Xbase language, there has been a standard set of commands whose job it was to access information in database files. The various means of access include the following classes of operations: opening and closing database files, activating and using index files, searching for data, establishing filter conditions, setting relationships between databases, etc. The CA-Clipper language covers all the standard Xbase mechanisms supporting these forms of database access, plus many more. The main difference is with their implementation. Any current Xbase programmer wishing to rise to the task with CA-Clipper should be aware of language differences. In this chapter, we'll cover the CA-Clipper flavor of database access techniques using code blocks, arrays, and various built-in functions.

After completing this chapter, you will have learned:

- How CA-Clipper commands used for database access are implemented as calls to special "database functions"
- How to invoke database oriented commands
- How to directly call database functions
- The basics of the CA-Clipper Order Management System
- Methods of using replaceable database drivers (RDDs) through special commands and functions to access foreign data
- How code blocks play an important role in database access
- Traversing databases using DBEVAL()
- Methods for relational access to Clipper databases including the 1:M and M:M relationships

Accessing Databases with CA-Clipper

All of the basic Xbase commands used to manipulate databases, plus many unique to Clipper, are implemented by UDC definitions that call special built-in database functions that actually do the work. These functions, along with code examples, are outlined in the section *Database Functions*. Although you can continue to use the Xbase and Clipper command syntax, it is also possible to call these functions directly. Which direction you take could depend on how unwieldy direct function usage becomes. For example, the USE command is mapped into a call to the DBUSEAREA() function (and optionally the DBSETINDEX() function) that has six parameters. In this case, the normal USE command syntax is easier to understand. For example, consider the two alternate approaches:

```
* Using the standard Xbase USE command. You should review
* the UDC definition in STD.CH for USE.
```

```
USE Orders INDEX OrderNo NEW
* Now, open ORDERS.DBF with the Clipper database functions.
DBUSEAREA(.T.,,'Orders')   // Same as: USE Orders NEW.
DBSETINDEX('OrderNo')      // Activate ORDERNO.NTX.
```

It is pretty clear that the first way is easier to comprehend, at least for Clipper beginners. The choice is, however, not always that clear cut. If you are issuing USE alone (i.e. to close the database file opened in the current work area) it may be more clear to do a DBCLOSEAREA() function call. Upon reviewing STD.CH, we see that the USE and CLOSE commands actually map to the same function calls:

```
#command CLOSE => DBCLOSEAREA()
#command USE   => DBCLOSEAREA()
```

Regardless of the rationale, it has become acceptable (if not trendy) to call these functions directly in lieu of using Xbase command structures.

Consider now, the UDC for the CLOSE <alias> command:

```
#command CLOSE <alias>  => <alias>->( DBCLOSEAREA() )
```

We see here that this command is simply mapped into an alias prefixed call to the DBCLOSEAREA() function. This is the same way the SKIP ALIAS command is implemented, which leads to another point. For a command, such as SKIP ALIAS, that has an alias clause, you should probably just use it as it stands. But with commands where specifying an alias is not supported in the command syntax, calling the equivalent built-in database function is convenient, since you can use alias notation (see numerous examples of this in the sections to come). Otherwise, you'd have to issue a SELECT command in order to do the operation.

Other database commands of note are defined as follows:

```
#command CLOSE DATABASES   => DBCLOSEALL()

#command CLOSE INDEXES     => DBCLEARINDEX()

#command CLOSE ALL              ;
   => CLOSE DATABASES           ;
    ; SELECT 1                  ;
    ; CLOSE FORMAT

#command CLEAR ALL              ;
   => CLOSE DATABASES           ;
    ; CLOSE FORMAT              ;
    ; CLEAR MEMORY              ;
```

```
;   CLEAR GETS                      ;
;   SET ALTERNATE OFF               ;
;   SET ALTERNATE TO
```

Notice that these UDCs are chained in the sense that `CLOSE ALL` maps to `CLOSE DATABASES`, which in turn is mapped to `DBCLOSEALL()`.

RDD Technology

Much of our discussion involving database access concerns RDD technology and the Order Management System that is based on this technology. In this section, we'll define various terminology and constructs that we can then use throughout the rest of this chapter. Most of the technology that utilizes the inherent RDD capabilities arrived in the CA-Clipper language with the 5.2 release.

Replaceable Database Driver Architecture Overview

A very unique feature of CA-Clipper centers around its support for the architecture that allows applications to use replaceable database drivers (RDDs). In essence, RDDs make CA-Clipper applications data format independent, allowing direct access to foreign data formats of other database systems, including Xbase/dBASE III Plus (.NDX), dBASE IV (.MDX), FoxPro (.CDX), and Paradox (.DB).

Replaceable database drivers are not new to CA-Clipper. In fact, since the introduction of Clipper 5, the use of the default database driver (DBFNTX.LIB) was present but hidden by the fact that it was automatically linked into an application. This is actually still the case, but now there are additional choices of RDDs, a situation we'll explore in some detail in this chapter.

Usage of the RDD system begins at the work area level. All CA-Clipper database commands and functions operate in a work area through a database driver that actually performs the access to the stored database information. The layering of this approach to database access looks like this:

- Database commands and functions
- RDD API (application program interface)
- Database driver
- Data

In this scheme, each work area is associated with a specific database driver. Each database driver, in turn, is supplied as a separate library file (.LIB) that you link in with your application programs. Inside the application, you specify the name of the database driver when you open or access a database file with the `USE` command or `DBUSEAREA()` function. (The default driver is used if you do not specify a database driver at the time a file is opened.) There is also a way to select which driver will be used as the default driver.

Table 8.1 RDD Characteristics

Description	NTX	NDX	MDX	CDX	DBPX
Multiple Record Locks	Yes	Yes	Yes	Yes	No
Order Management Support	Yes	Yes	Yes	Yes	No
Orders per Order Bag	1	1	47	50	N/A
Number of Order Bags per Work Area	15	15	15	15	N/A
Conditional Indexes	Yes	No	Yes	Yes	No
Temporary Indexes	Yes	No	No	Yes	No
Descending	Yes	No	Yes	Yes	No
Unique	Yes	Yes	Yes	Yes	No
EVAL and EVERY Clause Support	Yes	No	No	Yes	No
Production/Structural Indexes	No	No	Yes	Yes	No
Max Key Expression length (bytes)	256	256	220	255	N/A
Maximum FOR Condition length (bytes)	256	N/A	261	255	N/A

Once you open a database in a work area and request that a particular RDD be used, it will automatically be used for all operations on that database. For commands or functions that create a new table (e.g., CREATE FROM and DBCREATE()) the default RDD is used. Most of the new commands and functions let you specify a driver other than the default driver.

Take some time to review Table 8.1, which summarizes the vital characteristics of all currently available RDDs.

Using the RDD technology embedded in CA-Clipper is easy. For example, the normal default database driver, DBFNTX, which supports the traditional .DBF, .NTX, and .DBT files is automatically linked into each program. To use any of the other supplied drivers, you must issue the REQUEST command to ensure that the driver will be linked in. We'll see examples of how to link with RDDs in the section *Linking with RDDs* later in the chapter.

A program called RDDSYS.PRG, which is located in the \CLIPPER5\SOURCE\SYS subdirectory, relates to how CA-Clipper programs access RDDs. By default, all CA-Clipper applications will automatically include code found in RDDSYS.PRG. If you wish to automatically load another RDD, you must modify and compile RDDSYS.PRG and link the resulting object file into your application. Here is the content of RDDSYS.PRG:

```
// RDDSYS.PRG
#include 'rddsys.ch'

ANNOUNCE RDDSYS
INIT PROCEDURE RDDInit
REQUEST DBFNTX                  // Force link for DBFNTX RDD.
RDDSETDEFAULT('DBFNTX')         // Set up DBFNTX as default driver.
RETURN
```

To change the default to a different driver that will be automatically loaded, you must modify the lines shown in bold to include the name of the new driver. In this way, all CA-Clipper applications in which the revised RDDSYS.PRG is linked will automatically include the new RDD. The following example will install the DBFMDX driver as the default:

```
// Modified RDDSYS.PRG
#include 'rddsys.ch'

ANNOUNCE RDDSYS
INIT PROCEDURE RDDInit
REQUEST DBFMDX                  // Force link for DBFMDX RDD.
RDDSETDEFAULT('DBFMDX')         // Set up DBFMDX as default driver.
RETURN
```

To disable the automatic loading of a default RDD, use the following version of RDDSYS.PRG:

```
// Modified RDDSYS.PRG that disables loading default RDD
#include 'rddsys.ch'

ANNOUNCE RDDSYS
INIT PROCEDURE RDDInit
RETURN
```

RDD Terminology

The RDD architecture introduces several new terms and concepts that are important to the design and usage of RDDs. You should familiarize yourself with these concepts and terms as you begin to use the RDD functionality inherent in CA-Clipper. We'll also expand the meaning of some earlier terminology to better suit CA-Clipper's widened view of ordering technology. Here are the definitions of the RDD terms:

Key Expression refers to any valid CA-Clipper expression that generates a *key value* from a single record.

Key Value is a value that is based on database field contents of a specific record in a database.

Identity is a unique value that must refer to a specific record in a database. In the Xbase .DBF file structure, the identity is a *record number*.

Keyed-Pair is a tuple consisting of a *key value* and an *identity*.

Identity Order describes the order in which the records were physically added to the database (natural order). In Xbase, identity Order indicates record number order.

Order provides a named ordering mechanism that yields logical access to a database according to the keyed-pairs. Orders are logical entities, not disk files. Orders provide access to data that gives the appearance that the data is physically sorted in a specific way but in fact does not change the physical (natural order) sequence of data in a database. The ordering can also be modified to be in ascending or descending sequence.

Tag is another term used to denote an Order. It is usually associated with Orders in multiple-Order indexes. The term began with dBASE IV's .MDX indexing technology.

Controlling Order is the name given to the active Order for a specified work area. There can be only one controlling Order for a work area at any given time.

Order List is a list of all active Orders in a specified work area. Each work area has one Order list. An Order List is created when a new work area is opened and exists only as long as that work area is active. The SET INDEX TO command acts to empty the contents of an *Order Bag* into the Order List. Once in the Order List, the Orders will be updated as the data associated with the work area is modified. An Order in the list may be accessed by its *Order Number* or by its *Order Name*. It is generally advisable to access an Order by its name rather than its number—its position in the Order List may change, but its name will not. Any Order in the Order List can be made the controlling Order by giving it *focus*.

Order List Focus refers to a pointer to the Order that is used to change the view of the data. This term is synonymous with *controlling Order*. The SET ORDER TO command changes the Order List focus but does not modify the Order List in any way. Order Bag denotes a container (a disk file) that holds zero or more Orders. Each Order contains two elements: *Order Name* and *Order Expression*. In prior versions of Clipper, the traditional .NTX index is an Order Bag that holds at most one Order. Now CA-Clipper supports multiple-Order Bags that can hold zero or more Orders. The maximum number of Orders is determined by the RDD being used. Within an Order Bag, you can access specific Orders by referencing a particular Order Name.

Order Number is an integer value representing the position of an Order in the Order List. In general, referencing Orders by name is preferable to Order Numbers.

Order Name is a symbolic name that may be used to manipulate an Order. It is similar in nature to a file's alias. One difference between an Order Name and an Order Number, is that the former is stored in the index file. The Order Number, however, is generated each time the Order is added to an Order List and may change from one program execution to another. For this reason, Order Names are the preferred means of referencing Orders.

Order Expression is a valid CA-Clipper expression used to produce an ordered view of the data. The values derived from this expression based on database field contents are sorted, and it is the relationship of these values to one another that provides the actual ordering.

Record of a database is traditionally thought of in relational theory as a row in a table. A row in turn consists of one or more related columns (fields) of data. CA-Clipper views the concept of a row in a somewhat different and broader light. In this expanded view, a record is data associated with an identity. In the normal Xbase sense, this orientation corresponds to a record (several fields tied to a record number). In foreign data formats, this definition may not be the case. We will therefore use the term *record* in the Xbase tradition. Just remember that CA-Clipper possesses an expanded meaning of record.

Single-Order Bag is an Order Bag (a disk file) that can contain only one Order. Index files such as .NTX and .NDX files are examples of single-Order Bags.

Multiple-Order Bag is an Order Bag (a disk file) that can contain one or more Orders. Index files such as .CDX and .MDX files are examples of multiple-Order Bags.

Maintainable Scoped Orders identifies conditional Orders created using the FOR clause. The logical expression specified in the FOR clause is stored in the index header. This means Orders of this type are updated to reflect record updates, deletions, and additions.

Non-Maintainable/Temporary Orders refers to Orders created with the WHILE or NEXT clauses. A point of distinction is that the logical expressions specified in these clauses are not stored in the index header, so consequently Orders of this type are not updated to reflect record updates, deletions, and additions. They are intended for temporary use only. The benefit of this kind of Order is that they can be created quickly.

Lock List is a list of the Records that are locked in the current work area.

Order Management System

CA-Clipper contains an abstract Order Management system, which provides for an effective and flexible way of ordering (indexing) data in a database. The main advantage of CA-Clipper's order scheme over the standard Xbase methodology is that it functions from a higher level of abstraction. In Xbase (and prior versions of Clipper) the ordering abstraction was rather low, completely connected to the database and index file architecture (field names and sizes, methods of handling controlling indexes, etc.). A higher level of abstraction, on the other hand, conceptualizes general elements in a data source. This allows you to set a controlling Order without explicitly knowing the characteristics of the file structure.

As we'll see later in this chapter, there exists a whole set of built-in Order Management functions, which begin with the letters *ORD* for *Order*. The generic feel of these functions' names is such that they do not connote a specific file structure. Sticking to the purpose of abstraction, this naming was by design.

Let's talk for a moment about how the components of CA-Clipper's Order Management scheme fit together. An Order is a set of keyed-pairs that provides a logical ordering of the records in an associated database file. Each key in an Order (index) is associated with a particular identity (record number) in the data table (database file). The records can be processed sequentially in key value order, and any record can be located by performing a SEEK (an index key search) operation with a specified key value. An Order never physically changes the data it describes, but instead only changes the sequence in which the data is viewed. You can also use an Order to limit the visibility of data according to specified bounds conditions. This involves a scoping construct such as the WHILE clause. Finally, you can use an Order to restrict the visibility of data by subjecting it to conditional evaluation using a filter construct such as the FOR clause.

In the next several sections, we'll examine how to use each of the available RDDs: DBFNTX, DBFNDX, DBFMDX, DBFCDX, and DBPX.

Using the DBFNTX RDD

DBFNTX (Clipper style indexes) is the default database driver and is linked into and used automatically by your application unless you compile using the /R option. This RDD includes the following features:

- Specifies record scoping and conditional filtering using the standard ALL, FOR, WHILE, NEXT, REST, and RECORD clauses
- Monitors the indexing process on a per record or interval using the EVAL and EVERY clauses
- Provides for descending Order keys using the DESCENDING clause

Using the DBFNDX RDD

The DBFNDX database driver allows creation, access, and updating of dBASE III and dBASE III PLUS compatible index .NDX files. All operations that can be performed on standard CA-Clipper index .NTX files can be performed on .NDX files using this database driver.

To use .NDX files in a CA-Clipper program, follow these guidelines:

1. Issue a `REQUEST DBFNDX` in your main program module or at the top of the first program module that opens a database file using the DBFNDX driver.
2. Specify the `VIA 'DBFNDX'` clause in the `USE` command used to open the database file. If you use the `DBUSEAREA()` database function to open the file, you should specify `'DBFNDX'` for the `<cDriver>` parameter.
3. Issue the RDD function call `RDDSETDEFAULT('DBFNDX')` to set the default driver to DBFNDX.

Consider the following program code segments that illustrate the use of DBFNDX:

```
/* First let's not change the default driver, requiring the VIA clause */
REQUEST DBFNDX
.
. <statements>
.
USE Employee INDEX EmpName, EmpDept NEW VIA 'DBFNDX'

/* The next sample uses RDDSETDEFAULT() to change the
   default driver so VIA is no longer needed */
REQUEST DBFNDX
RDDSETDEFAULT('DBFNDX')
.
. <statements>
.
USE Employee INDEX EmpName, EmpDept NEW
```

In some situations, both .NDX and .NTX files might be needed concurrently. The following code segment illustrates how this can be achieved:

```
REQUEST DBFNDX
// Note that DBFNTX is still the default driver, so the
// index on the next line is assumed .NTX
USE Temp1 INDEX Temp1 NEW

// Now we can explicitly use the DBFNDX driver using VIA
USE Temp2 INDEX Temp2 NEW VIA 'DBFNDX'
```

Using the DBFMDX RDD

The DBFMDX database driver allows you to create, access, and update dBASE IV compatible .DBF database files, .MDX multiple index files, and .DBT memo field files. The driver also supports dBASE IV compatible file and record locking schemes, allowing shared access between CA-Clipper and dBASE IV programs.

To use the .MDX driver in a CA-Clipper program, follow these guidelines:

1. Issue a `REQUEST DBFMDX` in your main program module or at the top of the first program module that opens a database file using the DBFMDX driver.
2. Specify the `VIA 'DBFMDX'` clause in the `USE` command used to open the database file. If you use the `DBUSEAREA()` database function to open the file, you should specify `'DBFMDX'` for the `<cDriver>` parameter.
3. Issue the RDD function call `RDDSETDEFAULT('DBFMDX')` to set the default driver to DBFMDX.

Using the DBFCDX RDD

The DBFCDX driver enables you to create and maintain FoxPro 2 compatible .CDX and .IDX index files. This RDD includes the following features:

- Creates indexes smaller than those created with the DBFNTX driver. This is due to the key data being stored in a compressed format that substantially reduces the size of the index file.
- Creates a compound index file that contains multiple Orders. A single .CDX file may contain up to 99 index keys (the practical limit is 50). Once you open a compound index, all the Orders are automatically updated as the database records are changed. The first tag in Order of creation in the compound index is the controlling index.
- Creates conditional indexes with `FOR`, `WHILE`, `REST`, and `NEXT`. The logical expressions used to create a conditional index can include built-in or user-defined functions. As the database is updated, only records that match the index condition are added to the index, and records that satisfied the condition previously, but do not any longer, are automatically removed.

In a manner like FoxPro 2, the DBFCDX driver creates *compact indexes* that store key data in a compressed format. Compact indexes store only the actual data for the index keys. Trailing blanks and duplicate bytes between keys are compressed out. This allows considerable space savings in indexes containing a high percentage of empty space and similar keys. Since the amount of compression is dependent on many variables, including the number of unique keys in an index, the exact amount of compression cannot be predetermined.

To use the .CDX driver in a CA-Clipper program, follow these guidelines:

1. Issue a `REQUEST DBFCDX` in your main program module or at the top of the first program module that opens a database file using the DBFCDX driver.
2. Specify the `VIA 'DBFCDX'` clause in the `USE` command used to open the database file. If you use the `DBUSEAREA()` database function to open the file, you should specify `'DBFCDX'` for the `<cDriver>` parameter.

3. Issue the RDD function call `RDDSETDEFAULT('DBFCDX')` to set the default driver to DBFCDX.

Consider the following program code segments that illustrate the use of DBFCDX:

```
/* First let's not change the default driver, requiring
   the VIA clause */
REQUEST DBFCDX
.
. <statements>
.
USE Employee INDEX EmpName, EmpDept NEW VIA 'DBFCDX'

/* The next sample uses RDDSETDEFAULT() to change the
   default driver so VIA is no longer needed */
REQUEST DBFCDX
RDDSETDEFAULT('DBFCDX')
.
. <statements>
.
USE Employee INDEX EmpName, EmpDept NEW
```

Using the DBPX RDD

The DBPX driver allows you to create and maintain Paradox 3.5 compatible .DB (table file), .PX (primary index), .X?derivative, and .Y?? (both secondary indexes) files. The DBPX driver provides a simple, seamless interface to the Paradox database file system. This RDD contains the following features:

- Creates tables that recognize the standard CA-Clipper data types as well as Currency ($) and Short (S) numbers between -32,767 to +32,767
- Creates keyed and unkeyed tables
- Creates, selects, and activates secondary indexes on Paradox tables

When using the DBPX driver you must observe the following field naming restrictions:

- The Paradox file structure allows field names to be up to 25 characters long. Since Xbase (and CA-Clipper) names can only be 10 characters, the DBPX driver truncates long Paradox names to 10 characters.
- The Paradox file structure allows embedded spaces in field names. This practice is not allowed in Xbase (and CA-Clipper). The DBPX driver consequently converts spaces into underscore characters.

As with any interface between two diverse database systems, some differences do exist between Paradox data types and those in standard Xbase. Here is a summary of these differences:

- You can store all ASCII characters except null characters (an ASCII 0) in the Alphanumeric field type. Otherwise, the Alphanumeric type is identical to the Xbase Character (C) data type. The Paradox limit for this field type is 255 characters.
- Paradox tables support two forms of numeric data: the Numeric (N) data type and the Currency ($) data type. Both the N and $ data types can have as many as 15 significant digits. The DBPX driver also supports the Short (S) data type to represent integers in the range -32,767 and +32,767.
- Paradox supports a Date (D) field type, which is stored as a long integer. The valid range of values is between January 1, 100 A.D. and December 31, 9999.

To use the DBPX driver in a CA-Clipper program, follow these guidelines:

1. Issue a REQUEST DBPX in your main program module or at the top of the first program module that opens a database file using the DBPX driver.
2. Specify the VIA 'DBPX' clause in the USE command used to open the database file. If you use the DBUSEAREA() database function to open the file, you should specify 'DBPX' for the <cDriver> parameter.
3. Issue the RDD function call RDDSETDEFAULT('DBPX') to set the default driver to DBPX.

Consider the following program code segments that illustrate the use of DBPX:

```
/* First let's not change the default driver, requiring
   the VIA clause */
REQUEST DBPX
.
. <statements>
.
USE Supplier INDEX SuppName, SuppZip NEW VIA 'DBPX'

/* The next sample uses RDDSETDEFAULT() to change the
   default driver so VIA is no longer needed */
REQUEST DBPX
RDDSETDEFAULT('DBPX')
.
. <statements>
.
USE Supplier INDEX SuppName, SuppZip NEW
```

Installing RDD Files

All CA-Clipper RDDs are supplied as files with an .LIB extension. Table 8.2 summarizes the RDD files. The CA-Clipper installation program installs all drivers in the \CLIPPER5\LIB subdirectory, so you need not install the drivers manually.

Linking with RDDs

To link any of the replaceable database drivers into an application program, you must specify the correct .LIB file to the linker in addition to your application object files (.OBJ).

Here are some `RTLink` command-line examples for each driver:

```
RTLINK FI <ObjectList> LIB DBFCDX
RTLINK FI <ObjectList> LIB DBFMDX
RTLINK FI <ObjectList> LIB DBFNDX
RTLINK FI <ObjectList> LIB DBPX
```

Note: These link commands all assume the `LIB`, `OBJ`, and `PLL` environment variables are set to the standard locations. They also assume that the CA-Clipper programs were compiled without the /R option.

Since DBFNTX is the default database driver for CA-Clipper, there are no special instructions for linking. Unless you specify the /R option when you compile, the new driver will be linked into each program automatically if you specify a `USE` command or `DBUSEAREA()` function without an explicit request for another database driver. The driver is also linked if you specify an `INDEX` or `REINDEX` command with any of the new features.

Database Commands

In this section, we'll review all the CA-Clipper commands dealing specifically with database access. Most of these commands have been in the Xbase lan-

Table 8.2   RDD Files

Data Format	RDD	.LIB File
CA-Clipper	DBFNTX	DBFNTX.LIB
dBASE III Plus	DBFNDX	DBFNDX.LIB
dBASE IV	DBFMDX	DBFMDX.LIB
FoxPro	DBFCDX	DBFCDX.LIB
Paradox	DBPX	DBPX.LIB

guage, as well as the Clipper dialect for a long time. With the version 5.2 release, as stated earlier, numerous existing Clipper commands were affected by the inclusion of built-in RDD technology in the language. In most cases, the commands were enhanced to include the ability to specify a replaceable device driver to tailor its operation to the source or target data.

For each database access command, we will provide a *syntax definition*. The syntax definition shows the command's name and its formal list of clauses. We'll go on to describe each command in detail and also present a simple example of its use. As mentioned, in the previous section, various UDCs found in STD.CH ultimately map these commands to equivalent database functions. You might find it helpful to compare these command definitions with the database functions presented in the next section.

APPEND FROM

Syntax: `APPEND FROM <cFile>`
`[FIELDS <FieldList>]`
`[<Scope>] [WHILE <lCondition>] [FOR <lCondition>]`
`[SDF | DELIMITED [WITH BLANK | <cDelimiter>] |`
`[VIA <cDriver>]]`

The `APPEND FROM` command adds records to the database opened in the currently selected work area from another database file or ASCII text file named in `<cFile>`. This is the primary import facility in the CA-Clipper language. Only certain fields of the database can be affected by specifying a `<FieldList>`.

Here we see that the keyword `VIA <cDriver>` specifies the replaceable database driver (RDD) to use to import the desired data from a foreign source. `<cDriver>` is the *literal name* enclosed in quotation marks or the *extended expression* enclosed in parentheses of the RDD.

If the `VIA` clause is omitted, `APPEND FROM` uses the `RDD` of the current work area. If you specify the `VIA` clause, you must issue a `REQUEST` that the appropriate `RDD` be linked into the application.

Example:

```
USE Employee NEW
* Add new employee records for full timers. Obviously,
* the field FullTime must be a logical type.
APPEND FROM NewHires FOR FullTime VIA 'DBFMDX'
```

COPY TO

Syntax: `COPY [FIELDS <Field list>] TO <cFile>`
`[<scope>] [WHILE <lCondition>] [FOR <lCondition>]`
`[SDF | DELIMITED [WITH BLANK | <cDelimiter>] |`
`[VIA <cDriver>]]`

The COPY TO command exports records from the database opened in the currently selected work area to the new database or ASCII file specified in <cFile>. COPY TO is the primary export facility in the CA-Clipper language. Only certain fields of the database can be affected by specifying a <FieldList>.

The VIA clause specifies the replaceable database driver (RDD) to use during the creation of the resulting copy. <cDriver> is the name of the RDD specified either as a *literal name* enclosed in quotation marks or as an *extended expression* enclosed in parentheses. If the VIA clause is omitted, COPY TO uses the driver of the current work area. If you specify the VIA clause, you must issue a REQUEST that the appropriate RDD be linked into the application.

Example:

```
USE Employee NEW
* Write an ASCII text file containing the first and
* last names of each employee who is not full time
COPY TO EmpOut FIELDS First, Last FOR !FullTime SDF
```

GO

Syntax: GO[TO] <Identity>

The GO command positions the record pointer of the database opened in the currently selected work area to the specified identity <Identity>. The identity is a unique value offered by the structure of the data source to reference a specific item in the database. In a standard .DBF database the identity is a record number. In other data source formats, identity is the unique primary key value. This distinction is needed since CA-Clipper is able to directly access foreign data sources.

Example:

```
FUNCTION Main

USE Employee NEW

* Data entry portion of program.  A common requirement is
* is to not allow duplicate key values.
@ 10, 10 SAY 'Employee #: ' GET Employee->EmpNo ;
     VALID !DupKey(Employee->EmpNo)
READ

RETURN NIL
/***
*
* DupKey( <cKeyValue> ) -> lDuplicate
*
* Purpose: This function searches for duplicate key values
```

```
*
*/

FUNCTION DupKey(cKeyValue)
LOCAL nSaveRec := RECNO()    // Save the current record pointer position.
LOCAL lDup
SEEK cKeyValue
IF ( lDup := FOUND() )
   * Display message here
ENDIF
GOTO nSavRec                 // Restore the record pointer position
                             // before returning.
RETURN ( lDup )
```

INDEX

Syntax: INDEX ON <KeyExpression> TAG <cOrderName> | TO
<cOrderBagName> [FOR <lCondition>] [ALL]
[WHILE <lCondition>] [NEXT <nNumber>]
[RECORD <nRecord>] [REST]
[EVAL <bBlock>] [EVERY <nInterval>]
[UNIQUE] [ASCENDING|DESCENDING]

The INDEX command creates an index file that is used to order the database file it describes. <KeyExpression> is a Character, Date, Numeric, or Logical type expression that defines the key value to place in the index for each record in the currently selected work area. The maximum length of the index key expression is determined by the RDD driver.

Either the TAG or TO clause must be specified. TAG <cOrderName> is the name of the Order to be created. With .NTX and .NDX index files, the filename (without the extension or path name) is the Order Name if none is specified.

TO <cOrderBagName> is the name of a disk file containing one or more Orders. The active RDD determines the order capacity of an Order Bag. The default DBFNTX driver only supports single-Order Bags, while other RDDs may support multiple-Order Bags (e.g., the DBFCDX and DBFMDX drivers). You may specify <cOrderBagName> as the filename with or without a path name or extension (in which case the default extension of the current RDD will be used). The FOR clause condition is stored as part of the Order Bag and used when updating or recreating the index using the REINDEX command. ALL, the default scope of INDEX ON, specifies all Orders in the current work area.

EVAL <bBlock> evaluates the specified code block every <nInterval> as defined in the EVERY clause. The default interval is 1. The interval feature and code block is useful in producing a status indicator that monitors the indexing progress. You should take care to make this process as simple as possible as the potential exists for degraded indexing performance. Note that the return value of <bBlock> must be a Logical data type and indexing halts if <bBlock> returns a logical false.

UNIQUE specifies that the key value of each record inserted into the Order be unique. When UNIQUE is specified, duplicate key values are not added to the Order.

ASCENDING (the default) specifies that the key values be sorted in increasing order of value whereas DESCENDING specifies that the key values be sorted in decreasing order of value. In prior versions of Clipper, the DESCEND() built-in function was used in the index key expression. Now DESCENDING can be used instead without the performance penalty during Order updates.

Examples:

```
/* The following example creates a simple Order based on a single field */
USE Customer NEW
INDEX ON Customer->CustNo TO CustNo

/* This example creates a conditional Order using the FOR clause.
   This index will contain only records whose Balance field contains
   a value less than 25000. */
USE Customer NEW
INDEX ON Customer->Name TO CustName ;
   FOR Customer->Balance < 25000

/* This example creates an Order that calls the Odometer() UDF every
   10 records. This routine could display a graphic completion
   indicator to the user. */
USE Parts NEW
INDEX ON Parts->PartNo TO PartNo EVAL {|| Odometer() } EVERY 10

/* The following example creates an Order in a multiple Order Bag */
USE Customer NEW VIA 'DBFMDX'
INDEX ON Customer->CustNo TAG CustNo TO Customer
```

SEEK

Syntax: SEEK <SearchExpression> [SOFTSEEK]

The SEEK command searches an Order for a specified key value <SearchExpression>. Searching proceeds with the controlling Order from the first key value and continues until a match is found or there is a key value greater than <SearchExpression>. If there is a match, the record pointer is positioned to the identity found in the Order. In the event of a failed Order search, SOFTSEEK causes the record pointer to be moved to the next record with a higher key value. Without SOFTSEEK, the record pointer moves to EOF() after a failed Order search. The SET SOFTSEEK command is still available, although the SOFTSEEK clause is often more convenient when a global setting is not desired.

Examples:

```
/* First we'll see an example that does a soft-seek search for
   "Jackson" using the SOFTSEEK clause of the SEEK command */
USE Employee NEW
SET ORDER TO EmpName
SEEK "Jackson" SOFTSEEK
IF !FOUND()
   * Even if not found, we will not be at EOF()
   ? Employee->Name      // Display next name in sequence after "Jackson".
ENDIF
/* The next example does a softseek using SET SOFTSEEK */
#include 'set.ch'
USE Employee INDEX EmpName NEW
SET SOFTSEEK ON             // Turn on global SOFTSEEK.
SEEK 'Beatrice'
IF FOUND()
   .
   . < statements >
   .
ENDIF
SET(_SET_SOFTSEEK, .F. )   // Reset global SOFTSEEK setting
                           // using SET() built-in function.
```

SET INDEX TO

Syntax: SET INDEX TO [<cOrderBagNameList>] [ADDITIVE]

The SET INDEX TO command opens one or more Order Bags in the current work area. <cOrderBagNameList> specifies Order Bags to be emptied into the Order List of the current work area. The ADDITIVE clause lets additional Order Bags be added to an existing Order List. Without the ADDITIVE clause, SET INDEX TO clears the currently active Order List, then builds a new Order List from the Orders in the specified Order Bags. When several Order Bags are opened at once, the first Order in the first Order Bag becomes the controlling Order. The database record pointer is initially positioned at the first identity in this Order.

During regular database processing, all open Orders are normally updated whenever a key value is added or changed. To change the controlling Order without issuing another SET INDEX command (performance will suffer if you do), use SET ORDER TO or ORDSETFOCUS().

Examples:

```
/* Here is simple example that opens a database and two indexes */
USE Employee NEW
SET INDEX TO EmpNo, EmpName
/* Later, if we wish to open a 3rd index, you should not do:
   SET INDEX TO EmpNo, EmpName, EmpDept
SET INDEX TO EmpDept ADDITIVE    // Much better performance.
```

SET ORDER TO

Syntax: SET ORDER TO [<nOrder> | [TAG <cOrderName>] [IN <cOrderBagName>]]

The SET ORDER TO command allows you to select the controlling Order. The optional TAG clause provides compatibility with RDDs that provide access to multiple-Order Bags. <cOrderName> is the name of an Order that will become the controlling Order in the Order List. Unlike dBASE IV and FoxPro, the TAG keyword is required. <nOrder> is the number of the target Order in the Order List and is only provided for compatibility with earlier versions of CA-Clipper. Using <cOrderName> is a more expressive way of accessing the correct Order in the Order List. To determine which Order is the controlling Order use the ORDSETFOCUS() function.

The IN <cOrderBagName> clause specifies the name of a disk file containing one or more Orders. If you do not include the extension as part of <cOrderBagName>, CA-Clipper uses the default extension of the current RDD.

When you SET ORDER TO a new controlling Order, all Orders are properly updated when you add or edit records. Upon issuing SET ORDER TO 0, the database access is reset to *natural order* but leaves all Orders open. Using SET ORDER TO alone closes all Orders and empties the Order List.

Examples:

```
FUNCTION Main
REQUEST DBFMDX              // Must request RDD
RDDSETDEFAULT('DBFMDX')     // and make it default.

USE Part NEW VIA 'DBFMDX'

* Create two tags in a new .MDX file
INDEX ON Part->PartNo TAG 'Tag1' TO TagBag
INDEX ON Part->Desc TAG 'Tag2' TO TagBag

SET ORDER TO 'TAG2'

LIST Part->PartNo, Part->Desc
DBCLOSEAREA()
RETURN NIL

/* Now another simple example using the default DBFNTX RDD */

FUNCTION Main

USE Part NEW

* Create two new .NTX files
INDEX ON Part->PartNo TO PartNo
INDEX ON Part->Desc TO PartDesc
```

```
SET ORDER TO 2    // Specify 2nd ordering, PartDesc.NTX

LIST Part->PartNo, Part->Desc
DBCLOSEAREA()
RETURN NIL
```

Database Functions

In this section, we'll define each database function available in CA-CLIPPER. For each function, we will provide a *function prototype*. A prototype shows the function's name, its formal parameter list, and its return value. Note that a function prototype is not real code and is used for documentation purposes only. When you code your own UDF, you should create a prototype and place it as a comment in the function's comment block. We'll go on to describe each function in detail and also present a simple example of its use. As mentioned, in the previous section, various UDCs found in STD.CH ultimately call these functions in order to implement CA-Clipper's standard database access command set.

There are many reasons why you may want to use a database function instead of a command. One important motivation is that you can prefix an alias to the function thus enabling the operation on a database not currently selected. We'll present numerous examples of this technique. Another reason to use database functions is that they are accessible from within code blocks. Remember from Chapter 6 that commands are not allowed in code blocks.

ALIAS()

Prototype: ALIAS([<nWorkArea>]) —> cAlias

The ALIAS() function returns the specified work area's alias name. If no parameter is specified, the current work area is assumed. The DBF() function also performs the same service but is officially classified as a compatibility function and should not be used.

Example:

```
USE Supplier NEW
USE Movie NEW
? ALIAS(1), ALIAS(2) // Displays: Supplier Movie
```

DBAPPEND()

Prototype: DBAPPEND([<lReleaseRecLocks>]) —> NIL

The DBAPPEND() function provides the ability to append a blank record frame to the database open in the currently selected work area. DBAPPEND() is functionally equivalent to the APPEND BLANK command.

The single parameter, <lReleaseRecLocks> has a Logical data type. If a true (.T.) value is used, which is the default, all pending record locks are cleared and a new record is appended. If <lReleaseRecLocks> is false (.F.), all pending record locks are maintained and the new record is added to the end of the *Lock List*. Passing no parameter to DBAPPEND() is equivalent to passing .T. This function lets you maintain multiple record locks during an append operation.

Example:

```
/* First example */
USE Txn INDEX CustNo NEW
.
. <statements>
.
/* Append blank record without releasing the record locks in the
   current Lock List */
DBAPPEND(.F.)
/* Example 2 */
USE Txn INDEX TxnNo NEW
USE Customer INDEX CustNo NEW
SELECT Customer
WHILE !EOF()
   IF Customer->Status == '01'
     Txn->( DBAPPEND() )   // Add new record to TXN alias.
     Txn->CustNo := Customer->CustNo
   ENDIF
END
```

DBCLEARFILTER()

Prototype: DBCLEARFILTER() -> NIL

This database function provides a mechanism to clear the active filter condition for the database opened in the currently selected work area. DBCLEARFILTER() is functionally equivalent to the SET FILTER TO command.

Example:

```
Movie->( DBCLEARFILTER() )   // Clear filter condition in the
                             // work area containing MOVIE.
```

DBCLEARINDEX()

Prototype: DBCLEARINDEX() -> NIL

The DBCLEARINDEX() function serves as a way to close all indexes opened in the current work area. DBCLEARINDEX() is functionally equivalent to the SET

INDEX TO command. Bear in mind that DBCLEARINDEX() is a compatibility (with prior Clipper 5 versions) function. The ORDLISTCLEAR() Order Management function (see the *RDD Functions* section) should now be used instead.

Example:

```
USE Txn INDEX CustNo, MovieNo  // Open the CUSTONO.NTX and
                               // MOVIENO.NTX index files.
DBCLEARINDEX()                 // Now close them.
```

DBCLEARRELATION()

Prototype: DBCLEARRELATION() -> NIL

The DBCLEARRELATION() function provides a way to clear any active relations in the current work area. DBCLEARRELATION() is functionally equivalent to the SET RELATION TO command.

Example:

```
/* Establish a relation, M:1 Txn to Customer */
USE Customer INDEX CustNo NEW
USE Txn NEW
SELECT Txn
SET RELATION TO Txn->CustNo INTO Customer
.
. <statements>
.
DBCLEARRELATION()    // Now clear the relation.
```

DBCLOSEALL()

Prototype: DBCLOSEALL() -> NIL

This database function releases all work areas from use. DBCLOSEALL() is functionally equivalent to the CLOSE DATABASES command or issuing a DBCLOSEAREA() database function for each work area containing an open database.

Example:

```
USE Orders INDEX OrderNo NEW
USE Product INDEX ProdNo NEW
.
. <statements>
.
DBCLOSEALL()         // Close both databases at once.
* SELECT Orders      // Here is another method.
* DBCLOSEAREA()
* SELECT Product
* DBCLOSEAREA()
```

DBCLOSEAREA()

Prototype: `DBCLOSEAREA() -> NIL`

This database function clears the currently selected work area from use. Any resources associated with the work area, such as indexes, relations, filters, etc., are also released. `DBCLOSEAREA()` is functionally equivalent to issuing the `USE` command without a database name or the `CLOSE` command.

Example:

```
SELECT Customer              // Select previously opened database.
* USE                        // Xbase style close.
* CLOSE                      // This would work too.
Customer->( DBCLOSEAREA() )  // No need to SELECT first.
```

DBCOMMIT()

Prototype: `DBCOMMIT() -> NIL`

`DBCOMMIT()` causes all pending updates in the current work area to be written to disk, including all updated database and index buffers. `DBCOMMIT()` is functionally equivalent to the `COMMIT` command, except that it causes updates for only the current work area. There is no equivalent command in CA-Clipper to commit a single work area.

Example:

```
Txn->( DBCOMMIT() )   // Commit updates to work area for TXN.
```

DBCOMMITALL()

Prototype: `DBCOMMITALL() -> NIL`

The `DBCOMMITALL()` database function causes all pending updates in all work areas to be written to disk. `DBCOMMITALL()` is functionally equivalent to the `COMMIT` command.

Example:

```
/* Complete processing by writing updates to disk and close */
DBCOMMITALL()      // Same as COMMIT.
DBCLOSEALL()
```

DBCREATE()

Prototype: `DBCREATE( <cDatabaseName>, <aStructure> ) -> NIL`

This is the primary CA-Clipper built-in function that allows you to dynamically create a new database file. `<cDatabaseName>` is a character expression containing the name of the database to create. You must also pass a special array <aStructure> containing the structure elements of the new file. As you will see when you review the following example, the array must have the field name, data type, length, and number of decimals in the case of a Numeric. In order to index this array symbolically, you should routinely include the DBSTRUCT.CH header file with all programs that use DBCREATE().

Example:

```
#include 'dbstruct.ch'
LOCAL aDatabase[1][4]
/* Define first element using brute force method */
aDatabase[1][ DBS_NAME ]   := 'CustNo'
aDatabase[1][ DBS_TYPE ]   := 'C'
aDatabase[1][ DBS_LEN  ]   := 7
aDatabase[1][ DBS_DEC  ]   := 0
/* Now for the rest, an easier method */
AADD(aDatabase, { 'Name'    , 'C', 30 , 0 })
AADD(aDatabase, { 'Address' , 'C', 35 , 0 })
AADD(aDatabase, { 'City'    , 'C', 15 , 0 })
AADD(aDatabase, { 'State'   , 'C', 2  , 0 })
AADD(aDatabase, { 'Zip'     , 'C', 10 , 0 })
AADD(aDatabase, { 'Balance' , 'N', 7  , 2 })
/* Finally create the .DBF */
DBCREATE('Customer', aDatabase)
```

DBCREATEINDEX()

Prototype: DBCREATEINDEX(<cIndexFileName>, <cIndexKeyExpr>, [<bIndexKeyExpr>], [<lUnique>]) –> NIL

You can use the DBCREATEINDEX() function in conjunction with DBCREATE() to create an .NTX index file associated with the database open in the currently selected work area. Calling DBCREATEINDEX() directly is equivalent to issuing the INDEX ON...TO command. Bear in mind that DBCREATENDEX() is a compatibility (with prior Clipper 5 versions) function. The ORDCREATE() Order Management function (see the *RDD Functions* section) should now be used instead.

Example:

```
USE Txn NEW
* Below is same as: INDEX ON Txn->ItemNo TO TxnItem
* Note: <cIndexKeyExpr> is required even though we specify
* the code block parameter
DBCREATEINDEX( 'TxnItem', 'Txn->ItemNo', {|| Txn->ItemNo} )

* From STD.CH we have the definition of the syntax for the
* INDEX ON...TO command
```

```
* Note the regular match marker <key> is mapped to both
* a normal stringify result marker <"key"> AND a blockify
* match marker <{key}>
#command INDEX ON <key> TO <(file)> [<u: UNIQUE>]  ;
   => dbCreateIndex(                                ;
     <(file)>, <"key">, <{key}>,                    ;
     if( <.u.>, .t., NIL )                          ;
     )
```

DBDELETE()

Prototype: DBDELETE() -> NIL

This function serves as the vehicle with which you may mark a database record for deletion. DBDELETE() is functionally equivalent to the DELETE command.

Example:

```
Customer->( DBDELETE() )  // Mark current record in
                          // Customer work area.
```

DBEVAL()

Prototype: DBEVAL(<bBlock>, [<bForCondition>], [<bWhileCondition>],
         [<nNextRecords>], [<nRecord>], [<lRest>]) -> NIL

DBEVAL() is a very important function used for traversing a database. You may choose to use DBEVAL() instead of the standard Xbase WHILE/END method of looping through records. Because of DBEVAL()'s importance, we devote an entire section of this chapter to its use and application.

DBFILTER()

Prototype: DBFILTER() -> cFilterExpr

DBFILTER() is a database function that returns the current filter expression as a character string. Since any work area can have a filter, providing an alias prefix for this function enables you to obtain the condition for any active filter. Many times you need to temporarily disable a filter condition. To do this, you may use DBFILTER() to save the condition in a memory variable. Later, you may use the DBSETFILTER() function to re-establish the filter.

Example:

```
USE Txn INDEX TxnCust NEW
SET FILTER TO Txn->Type == 'I'
USE Customer INDEX CustName NEW
SET FILTER TO Customer->Zip > '90000'
SELECT Txn
```

```
* Following will display respective filter conditions:
* Txn->type == "I"    customer->zip > "90000"
? DBFILTER(), Customer->( DBFILTER() )
```

DBGOBOTTOM()

Prototype: DBGOBOTTOM() -> NIL

This function causes the record pointer in the current work area to move to the last logical (according to an active Order) record. If there is no active Order, the record pointer will land on the last record added to the database.

Example:

```
Orders->( DBGOBOTTOM() )    // Go to bottom of ORDERS.DBF
```

DBGOTO()

Prototype: DBGOTO(<Identity>) -> NIL

The DBGOTO() function positions the record pointer to a specific identity <Identity>. In a .DBF file <Identity> is a record number, consequently, DBGOTO() causes the record pointer in the current work area to move to a specified record number. In other data formats, <Identity> is the unique primary key value.

Example:

```
LOCAL nRecSave
  .
  .<statements>
  .
nRecSave := RECNO()     // Save current record pointer.
SEEK 'Dale'             // Record pointer somewhere else.
  .
  .<statements>
  .
DBGOTO(nRecSave)        // Restore the record pointer position.
```

DBGOTOP()

Prototype: DBGOTOP() -> NIL

This function causes the record pointer in the current work area to move to the first logical (according to an active Order) record. If there is no active Order, the record pointer will land on the first record added to the database.

Example:

```
USE Movie INDEX MovieNo
 .
 . <statements>
 .
DBGOTOP()        // Position to first record.
WHILE !EOF()
   ? Movie->Title
   DBSKIP()
END
```

DBRECALL()

Prototype: DBRECALL() -> NIL

The DBRECALL() function provides for a way to undelete a record previously marked for deletion. This function is equivalent to the RECALL command. This is possible since in Xbase languages records are only physically removed from a database as a result of a PACK operation.

Example:

```
Txn->(DBRECALL())    // Undelete current TXN record.
```

DBREINDEX()

Prototype: DBREINDEX() -> NIL

You can use this function to recreate all indexes active in the current or aliased work area. DBREINDEX() is functionally equivalent to the REINDEX command. The Order Management function ORDLISTREBUILD() is a more contemporary equivalent to DBREINDEX() in that it rebuilds all Orders in the Order List.

Example:

```
USE Orders INDEX OrderNo, OrdDate, Status
DBREINDEX()      // Rebuild index files: ORDERNO.NTX, ORDDATE.NTX
                 // and STATUS.NTX
```

DBRELATION()

Prototype: DBRELATION(<nRelation>) -> cLinkExpr

When working with databases that are linked together using the SET RELATION TO command, you may encounter the need to obtain the linking expression of a specified relation in the current or aliased work area. DBRELATION() is a database function that accepts a single parameter, <nRelation>, that indicates which relation expression (in the case of multiple-child relationships) to access.

Example:

```
#define CHILD1 1
#define CHILD2 2
* Define a multiple-child relation
USE Customer INDEX CustNo NEW
USE Movie INDEX ItemNo NEW
USE Txn NEW
SET RELATION TO Txn->cust_no INTO Customer,
Txn->item_no INTO Movie ? DBRELATION(CHILD2)    // Display: Txn->item_no
USE Supplier INDEX SuppNo NEW
SELECT Supplier
? Txn->(DBRELATION(CHILD1))                     // Display: Txn->cust_no
```

DBRSELECT()

Prototype: DBRSELECT(<nRelation>) —> nWorkArea

DBRSELECT() is a database function that returns the work area number of the child component of a relation. This is the database specified after the INTO clause of the SET RELATION TO command.

Example:

```
* Using the above relations, you may do the following from
* any work area
? Txn->(DBRELATION(CHILD1)), Txn->(DBRSELECT(CHILD1))
?? ALIAS(Txn->(DBRSELECT(CHILD1)))
* Display: Txn->custno    1    customer
```

DBSEEK()

Prototype: DBSEEK(<KeyExpr>, [<lSoftSeek>]) —> lFound

The DBSEEK() database function is the functional equivalent of the SEEK command. This function positions the record pointer to the record containing a specified key value. If the key value is found, the function returns a .T. value. In order for a successful search of the database, an Order must be active in the current or aliased work area. Be careful to supply a <KeyExpr> value possessing a data type that matches that of the index key expression of the Order. The optional parameter <lSoftSeek> allows for a local soft-seek search, which causes the record pointer to go to the record with a key value closest to the one specified (in the case that the key is not found).

Example:

```
STATIC FUNCTION CustSeek(cCustNo)
LOCAL lRetVal := .T.
IF !Customer->(DBSEEK(cCustNo))
```

```
   ? 'Error: customer not found'
   lRetVal := .F.
ENDIF
RETURN (lRetVal)
```

DBSELECTAREA()

Prototype: `DBSELECTAREA( <nWorkArea> | <cAlias> ) -> NIL`

DBSELECTAREA() is a database function that changes the current work area to the one specified. You may specify the new work area either by number or alias name. DBSELECTAREA() is the functional equivalent of the SELECT command.

Example:

```
DBSELECTAREA('Txn')     // Same as: SELECT Txn
```

DBSETDRIVER()

Prototype: `DBSETDRIVER([<cDriver>]) -> cCurrentDriver`

The DBSETDRIVER() database functions provides a way to get/set the name of the default database driver. The RDD function RDDSETDEFAULT() replaces this function which, although still available, should now be used for compatibility purposes only.

Example:

```
DBSETDRIVER('DBFMDX')   // Process dBASE IV .MDX files.
IF DBSETDRIVER() != 'DBFMDX'
   QOUT('Error: DBFMDX driver not available')
ENDIF
```

DBSETFILTER()

Prototype: `DBSETFILTER( <bFilterCondition>, [<cFilterCondition>] ) -> NIL`

DBSETFILTER() is the database function equivalent to the SET FILTER TO command. The purpose of this function is to establish a filter condition for the current or aliased work area. The logical expression that constitutes the filter condition may be represented as a character string in <cFilterCondition> or as a code block in <bFilterCondition>. You may use either or both parameters. If you expect to use DBFILTER() then you must specify the character expression for the condition. Filtering a database in an Xbase language is like producing a subset database containing only qualifying records.

Example:

```
USE Movie INDEX ItemNo NEW
* Specify the filter condition as a code block
DBSETFILTER({|| Movie->RentPrice > 1.99})
LIST Movie->Descr, Movie->RentPrice // Display subset records.
```

DBSETINDEX()

Prototype: DBSETINDEX(<cOrderBagName>) -> NIL

DBSETINDEX() is an Order Management function that adds Orders to the Order List. This function allows for the extension of the Order List without issuing a SET INDEX TO command that begins by clearing all the active Orders from the Order List. With ORDLISTADD(), any Orders already associated with the work area continue to be active. The parameter <cOrderBagName> is the name of an Order Bag (a disk file) containing one or more Orders. The default filename extension of the current RDD will be assumed if none is included with <cOrderBagName>.

The ORDLISTADD() RDD function supersedes the DBSETINDEX() function, which should now be used for compatibility purposes only.

Example:

```
USE Customer NEW
DBSETINDEX('Cust01')    // Open the index Cust01 in the current work area.
DBSETINDEX('Cust02')    // Open the index Cust02 leaving Cust01 open.
/* Example 2 */
USE Orders NEW
DBSETINDEX('OrderNo')   // Activate ORDERNO.NTX
                        // Same as: SET INDEX TO OrderNo
```

DBSETORDER()

Prototype: DBSETORDER(<nOrderNumber>) -> NIL

DBSETORDER() sets the focus to a new order. This function is equivalent to the SET ORDER TO command. Values of the parameter <nOrderNumber> must be greater than or equal to 1. The RDD function ORDSETFOCUS() replaces the DBSETORDER() function which, although still available, should now be used for compatibility purposes only.

Example:

```
#define ORDER1 1
#define ORDER2 2
```

```
USE Orders NEW         // Place two Orders in the Order List, OrderNo is
                       // Order 1 and OrdCust is Order 2.
SET INDEX TO OrderNo, OrdCust
DBSETORDER(ORDER2)     // Set focus to OrdCust
```

DBSETRELATION()

Prototype: DBSETRELATION(<nWorkArea> | <cAlias>, <bLinkExpr>, [<cLinkExpr>]) —> NIL

The DBSETRELATION() database function is functionally equivalent to the SET RELATION TO command. Its purpose is to relate two work areas via a common link field.

Example:

```
* Establish a M:1 relation between TXN (parent) and
* CUSTOMER (child)
USE Txn INDEX TxnCust NEW
USE Customer INDEX CustNo NEW
Txn->(DBSETRELATION('Customer', {|| Txn->CustNo}, ; 'Txn->CustNo'))
SELECT Txn
LIST Txn->CustNo, Customer->Name
```

DBSKIP()

Prototype: DBSKIP([<nRecords>]) —> NIL

DBSKIP() is a database function that moves the record pointer either forward or backward relative to its current position. The value of the parameter <nRecords> may be both positive (forward movement) and negative (backward movement). DBSKIP() is functionally equivalent to the SKIP command. Skipping through database records is a logical process—that is, active Orders and filter conditions are honored. If <nRecords> is omitted, the value 1 is assumed.

Example:

```
LOCAL nIncr := 2
Invoice->(DBSKIP(nIncr))    // Skip in INVOICE.DBF by nIncr
```

DBUNLOCK()

Prototype: DBUNLOCK() —> NIL

The DBUNLOCK() database function releases all file and record locks for the current or aliased work area. DBUNLOCK() is functionally equivalent to the UNLOCK command. This function is *only* useful in a network environment.

Example:

```
DBUNLOCK()    // Unlock file lock for current work area.
```

DBUNLOCKALL()

Prototype: DBUNLOCKALL() –> NIL

The DBUNLOCKALL() database function releases all file and record locks for all work areas. DBUNLOCKALL() is functionally equivalent to the UNLOCKALL command. This function is only useful in a network environment.

Example:

```
DBUNLOCKALL()  // Unlock all work areas.
```

DBUSEAREA()

Prototype: DBUSEAREA([<lNewArea>], [<cDriver>], <cName>, [<cAlias>], [<lShared>], [<lReadonly>]) –> NIL

The DBUSEAREA() database function opens a database file in the current work area. DBUSEAREA() is functionally equivalent to the USE command. Whether you use the function or command depends on the application. If you must open a file, for example, inside a code block, DBUSEAREA() serves this purpose. A .T. value for <lNewArea> requests that the database be opened in an unused work area. <cDriver> is the RDD name. <cName> is the name of the database file to open.

Example:

```
// Open the Sales database using the DBFMDX driver
DBUSEAREA(.T., 'DBFMDX', 'Sales')
```

HEADER()

Prototype: HEADER() –> nLength

HEADER() is a database function that returns a numeric value that is header length of the database file open in the current or aliased work area.

Example:

```
USE Movie NEW
? HEADER()     // Displays: 258
```

INDEXEXT()

Prototype: INDEXEXT() –> cFileExt

The INDEXEXT() database function returns the default index file extension defined by the current database driver.

Example:

```
USE Customer NEW
* If CUSTOMER.??? doesn't exist then create it, where the
* .??? extension is determined by the database driver
IIF(FILE('customer'+INDEXEXT()), NIL, ;
   DBCREATEINDEX('customer',              ;
     'customer->cust_no',                 ;
     {||customer->cust_no}) )
```

INDEXKEY()

Prototype: `INDEXKEY(<nOrder>) -> cKeyExpr`

This database function returns the key expression of a specified index opened in the current or aliased work area. `<nOrder>` is the position of the Order in the Order List. The RDD function ORDKEY() replaces the INDEXKEY() function which, although still available, should now be used for compatibility purposes only.

Example:

```
#define CONTROLLING 0
#define ORDER1      1
#define ORDER2      2
USE Customer INDEX CustNo, CustZip NEW
USE Txn INDEX Movie NEW
?  INDEXKEY(CONTROLLING)
?? Customer->( INDEXKEY(CONTROLLING) )
* Display: Txn->ItemNo   Customer->CustNo
```

INDEXORD()

Prototype: `INDEXORD() -> nOrder`

This database function returns the position in the Order List of the controlling Order. The RDD function ORDSETFOCUS() replaces the INDEXORD() function which, although still available, should now be used for compatibility purposes only.

Example:

```
#define ORDER1 1
#define ORDER2 2
LOCAL nOrdSave
USE Orders INDEX OrderNo, ProdNo NEW
nOrdSave := INDEXORD()    // Save: 1
```

```
DBSETORDER(ORDER2)        // Now activate ProdNo.NTX
? INDEXORD()              // Display: 2
DBSETORDER(nOrdSave)      // Restore previous order.
? INDEXORD()              // Display: 1
```

LASTREC()

Prototype: `LASTREC() -> nRecords`

The `LASTREC()` database function returns a numeric value representing the number of physical records in the database opened in the current or aliased work area. `LASTREC()` supersedes the `RECCOUNT()` function, which should no longer be used.

Example:

```
LOCAL nRecords:=0
USE Customer NEW
? LASTREC()         // Display: number of physical records.
DBSETFILTER({|| Customer->Zip > '90000'})
DBEVAL({|| nRecords++})
? nRecords          // Display: number of filtered records.
? LASTREC()         // Display: number of physical records.
```

RECNO()

Prototype: `RECNO() -> Identity`

This database function returns the identity located at the current position of the record pointer. The return value identity is a unique value referencing a specific record in the data file. In an Xbase .DBF database this value is a record number.

Example:

```
USE Employee NEW VIA 'DBFNDX'
DBGOBOTTOM()     // Position to last record.
RECNO()          // Returns record number.
```

RECSIZE()

Prototype: `RECSIZE() -> nLength`

The `RECSIZE()` database function returns the record length of the database file opened in the current or aliased work area. The integer value returned is equal to the sum of the lengths of each field in the database, plus one for the deletion flag. This function, combined with `LASTREC()` and `HEADER()` provide a means in which the size of the file in bytes can be determined.

Example:

```
#define FILESIZE() (RECSIZE() * LASTREC()) + HEADER() + 1

USE Employee NEW
? FILESIZE()      // Display number of bytes in Employee.DBF.
```

RDD Commands

In this section, we have one CA-Clipper command used exclusively with RDD technology. As mentioned before, several other commands were enhanced with the introduction of RDDs. These commands are listed in the section *Database Commands*, earlier in the chapter.

DELETE TAG

Syntax: DELETE TAG <cOrderName> [IN <cOrderBagName>] [, <cOrderName> [IN cOrderBagName]]

This command deletes an Order from an Order Bag (a disk file) in the current work area. <cOrderBagName> is the name of a disk file containing one or more Orders. If you do not specify an <cOrderBagName>, all Orders Bags are searched in the current work area. <cOrderName> is a character expression that represents the Order Name. The first occurrence of the Order named in <cOrderName> is deleted.

You can use DELETE TAG to list a series of Order and Order Bag Name pairs, separated by commas.

Example:

```
/* Open a file using the DBFMDX driver that supports
   multiple-Order Bags. */
USE Orders NEW VIA 'DBFMDX'
SET INDEX TO Orders              // Order Bag has: OrdDate, OrdCust
DELETE TAG OrdDate IN Orders     // Delete the tag: OrdDate
```

RDD Functions

With the introduction of expanded RDDs in the 5.2 release of CA-Clipper, many new database functions were included in the language. This section describes the functions specifically designed for use with RDDs. This section presents all these functions, including a prototype and sample usage.

DBRLOCK()

Prototype: DBRLOCK([<Identity>]) --> lSuccess

The DBRLOCK() is a database function that locks the record at the specified identity, or if no identity is specified, the current record. <Identity> is a unique value guaranteed by the structure of the data file to reference a specific item in a data source (database file). In a .DBF database, <Identity> refers to the record number. In other data formats, <Identity> is a unique primary key value. If <Identity> is specified, DBRLOCK() attempts to lock it and, if successful, adds it to the locked record list. If <Identity> is not specified, all record locks are released and the current record is locked.

DBRLOCK() returns a logical value lSuccess whose value is true (.T.) if the lock was successful and false (.F.) otherwise.

This example shows two different methods for locking multiple records:

Example:

```
/***
*
* GroupLock( <nFirstRec>, <nLastRec> )
*
* Purpose: UDF to lock a series of records
*
*/

FUNCTION GroupLock(nFirstRec, nLastRec)
LOCAL nRecPtr
FOR nRecPtr := nFirstRec TO nLastRec
   * If any lock in the group is unsuccessful, then
   * unlock all records
   IF !DBRLOCK(nRecPtr)
     DBRUNLOCK()
   ENDIF
ENDFOR
RETURN DBRLOCKLIST() // Return array of actual locks.
```

DBRLOCKLIST()

Protoype: DBRLOCKLIST() -> aRecordLocks

The DBRLOCKLIST() database function returns a single-dimension array containing the current Lock List. aRecordLocks is an array of the identities of locked records active in the current or aliased work area.

Example:

```
/***
*
* DispUnLock() -> NIL
*
* Purpose: Unlock each item in the current Lock List and
```

```
*      display the identity
*
*/

FUNCTION DispUnLock()
LOCAL aLockList := DBRLOCKLIST()
LOCAL nCount

? 'Lock list being unlocked: '
FOR nCount := 1 TO LEN(aLockList)
   ? aLockList[nCount]
   ?? ' ... unlocked'
   DBRUNLOCK(aLockList[nCount])
ENDFOR
RETURN NIL
```

DBRUNLOCK()

Protoype: DBRUNLOCK([<Identity>]) -> NIL

The DBRUNLOCK() database function releases the lock specified for <Identity> and removes it from the Lock List. <Identity> is a unique value guaranteed by the structure of the data file to reference a specific item in a data source (database file). In a .DBF database, <Identity> is a record number. In other data formats, <Identity> is a unique primary key value. If <Identity> is not specified, all record locks are released.

Example:

```
DBRUNLOCK()    // Unlock entire Lock List.
               // Also see DBRLOCKLIST() example.
```

ORDBAGEXT()

Protoype: ORDBAGEXT() -> cBagExt

ORDBAGEXT() is an order management function that returns the default Order Bag RDD extension of the current or aliased work area as a character expression. The return value, cBagExt is determined by the RDD active in the current work area. ORDBAGEXT() supersedes the INDEXEXT(), which should now be used for compatibility purposes only.

Example:

```
USE Movie VIA 'DBFMDX' NEW
? ORDBAGEXT()  // Displays: .MDX
```

ORDBAGNAME()

Protoype: ORDBAGNAME(<nOrder> | <cOrderName>) -> cOrderBagName

ORDBAGNAME() is an Order Management function that returns a character string containing the Order Bag name of a specified Order. There are two ways to specify the Order. First, <nOrder> is an integer that identifies the position in the Order List of the desired Order whose Order Bag name we wish to know. Second, <cOrderName> is a character string that represents the name of the desired Order whose Order Bag name we wish to know.

If the active RDD is able to hold more than one Order in an Order Bag (such as the DBFMDX and the DBFCDX drivers), then calls to ORDBAGNAME() with different Orders specified return the same return value.

Example:

```
/* Use ORDBAGNAME() with the default DBFNTX driver */
USE Orders VIA 'DBFNTX' NEW
SET INDEX TO ORDate, ORCust, ORProd
ORDBAGNAME(3)       // Returns: ORProd
ORDBAGNAME(2)       // Returns: ORCust
ORDBAGNAME(1)       // Returns: ORDate
```

ORDCREATE()

Protoype: ORDCREATE([<cOrderBagName>], [<cOrderName>], <cExpKey>,
            [<bKeyExpr>], [<lUnique>]) -> NIL

ORDCREATE() is an Order Management function that creates an Order in an Order Bag. The parameter <cOrderBagName> is the name of an Order Bag (a disk file) containing one or more Orders. The default filename extension of the current RDD is assumed if none is included with <cOrderBagName>. <cOrderName> is the name of the Order to be created. One or both of the parameters <cOrderBagName> and <cOrderName> must be specified.

If <cOrderBagName> does not exist, it is created in the current or aliased work area. If <cOrderBagName> exists, but the current RDD only supports Order Bags that can contain a single Order, <cOrderBagName> is erased and the new Order is added to the Order List. If <cOrderBagName> exists, and the current RDD supports Order Bags that can contain multiple tags, <cOrderName> is created if it does not already exist. Then <cOrderName> is replaced in <cOrderBagName> and the Order is added to the Order List.

<cKeyExpr> is a key expression that determines the value to place in the Order for each record. Only Character, Numeric, Date, and Logical data types are valid for <cKeyExpr>. <bKeyExpr> is a code block that when evaluated, determines the value that is placed in the Order for each record. If <bExpKey> is not specified, it is automatically created from a macro based on <cExpKey>.

The <lUnique> parameter allows you to request a unique Order. If its value is .T., then a unique Order is created; an .F. value will create a non-unique Order. If this parameter is not specified, the global status setting _SET_UNIQUE is used.

ORDCREATE() functions in a similar manner as DBCREATEINDEX() except that it allows the creation of Orders in RDDs that provide for multiple-Order Bags. ORDCREATE() supersedes the DBCREATEINDEX() function, which should now be used for compatibility purposes only. The currently active RDD determines how many Orders are possible for an Order Bag. The DBFNTX and the DBFNDX drivers only support single-Order Bags, while DBFCDX and DBFMDX support multiple-Order Bags.

When using RDDs that support multiple-Order Bags, you must explicitly use the SET ORDER TO command or call the ORDSETFOCUS() Order Management function to specify the desired controlling Order; otherwise, the data is processed in its natural Order.

Examples:

```
* Use the DBFNTX driver. Single-Order Bag
USE Supplier VIA 'DBFNTX' NEW
ORDCREATE('SuppName', 'SuppName', 'Supplier->Company', ;
   {|| Supplier->Company})

* Use the DBFMDX driver. Multiple-Order Bag
USE Supplier VIA 'DBFMDX' NEW
ORDCREATE('Supplier', 'SuppName', 'Supplier->Company')
```

ORDDESTROY()

Protoype: ORDDESTROY(<cOrderName> [, <cOrderBagName>]) –> NIL

The ORDDESTROY() Order Management function removes a specified Order from an Order Bag. The parameter <cOrderName> is the name of the Order to be removed from the current or aliased work area. The <cOrderBagName> parameter is the name of a multiple-Order Bag (a disk file) containing one or more Orders. The default filename extension of the current RDD is used if none is included with <cOrderBagName>. The currently active RDD determines how many Orders are possible for an Order Bag. ORDDESTROY() is not supported for DBFNDX and DBFNTX since these RDDs support only single-Order Bags.

Example:

```
* Delete an order in a DBFMDX Order Bag
USE Dept VIA 'DBFMDX' NEW
SET INDEX TO Dept
ORDDESTROY('DeptName', 'Dept') // Delete DeptName order.
```

ORDFOR()

Protoype: ORDFOR(<cOrderName> | <nOrder> [, <cOrderBagName>])
              -> cForExpr

The ORDFOR() Order Management function returns the FOR expression of an Order. You may specify the Order by name or with a number that represents its position in the Order List, although using the Order name is preferred. The <cOrderName> parameter is the name of the Order for which the FOR expression is needed. <nOrder> is an integer indicating the position of the desired Order in the Order List. <cOrderBagName> is the name of the Order Bag (a disk file) in which the Order resides. The default filename extension of the current RDD is assumed if none is included with <cOrderBagName>.

ORDFOR() returns the character expression cForExpr which represents the FOR condition of the specified Order. If a FOR clause was not created for the specified Order, the return value will be the null string ("").

Example:

```
* Get the FOR condition for an Order
USE Supplier NEW
INDEX ON Supplier->SuppZip TO Supplier ;
   FOR Supplier->SuppZip > '90000'
? ORDFOR('Supplier') // Displays: Supplier->SuppZip > '90000'
```

ORDKEY()

Protoype: ORDKEY(<cOrderName> | <nOrder> [, <cOrderBagName>])
              -> cKeyExpr

The ORDKEY() order management function returns the key expression of an Order. You can specify the Order by name or with a number that represents its position in the Order List, although using the Order name is preferred. The <cOrderName> parameter is the name of the Order for which the key expression is needed. <nOrder> is an integer indicating the position of the desired Order in the Order List. <cOrderBagName> is the name of the Order Bag (a disk file) in which the Order resides. The default filename extension of the current RDD is assumed if none is included with <cOrderBagName>.

ORDKEY() returns the character expression cKeyExpr, which represents the key expression of the specified Order.

Example:

```
* Get the key expression for an Order
USE Customer NEW
INDEX ON Customer->State + Customer->City ;
   TO Customer
? ORDKEY('Customer') // Displays: Customer->State+Customer->City
```

ORDLISTADD()

Prototype: ORDLISTADD(<cOrderBagName> [, <cOrderName>]) -> NIL

ORDLISTADD() is an Order Management function that adds Orders to the Order List. This function allows for the extension of the Order List without issuing a SET INDEX TO command that begins by clearing all the active Orders from the Order List. With ORDLISTADD(), any Orders already associated with the work area continue to be active. The parameter <cOrderBagName> is the name of an Order Bag (a disk file) containing one or more Orders. The default filename extension of the current RDD is assumed if none is included with <cOrderBagName>.

<cOrderName> is the name of the specific Order from the Order Bag to be added to the Order List of the current work area. If <cOrderName> is not specified then all orders in the Order Bag are added to the Order List.

ORDLISTADD() supersedes the DBSETINDEX() function, which should now be used for compatibility purposes only.

Example:

```
USE Employee VIA 'DBFMDX' NEW      // Note: Employee.MDX contains
                                   // two orders: EmpNo, EmpName
ORDLISTADD('Employee', 'EmpName')  // Put EmpName on Order List.
```

ORDLISTCLEAR()

Prototype: ORDLISTCLEAR() -> NIL

The ORDLISTCLEAR() Order Management function removes all Order from the current Order List for the current or aliased work area. After calling this function, the Order List is empty. This function supersedes the DBCLEARINDEX() function, which should now be used for compatibility purposes only.

Example:

```
USE Customer NEW
* Add three Orders to the Order List
SET INDEX TO CustNo, CustName, CustZip
.
. <statements>
.
ORDLISTCLEAR()    // Remove all Order from Order List, in
                  // effect, all index files are closed.
```

ORDLISTREBUILD()

Prototype: ORDLISTREBUILD() -> NIL

ORDLISTREBUILD() is an Order Management function that rebuilds all Orders in the Order List of the current or aliased work area. In order to rebuild a single Order the function ORDCREATE() must be used. ORDLISTREBUILD() is equivalent to the REINDEX command in that it rebuilds all Orders in the Order List.

Example:

```
USE Customer NEW
SET INDEX TO CustNo, CustName, CustZip
ORDLISTREBUILD()    // Rebuild: CustNo, CustName, CustZip
```

ORDNAME()

Prototype: ORDNAME(<nOrder>[,<cOrderBagName>]) –> cOrderName

The ORDNAME() Order Management function returns the name of the specified Order in the Order List or the specified Order Bag if opened in the current Order List. <nOrder> is an integer that identifies the position in the Order List of the target Order whose name is needed. The parameter <cOrderBagName> is the name of an Order Bag (a disk file) containing one or more Orders. The default filename extension of the current RDD is assumed if none is included with <cOrderBagName>.

cOrderName is the return value containing the name of the specified Order in the current Order List.

Example:

```
/* This example retrieves the name of an Order using its position in
   the Order List */
USE Supplier NEW
SET INDEX TO SuppNo, SuppName, SuppZip
ORDNAME(3)     // Returns: SuppZip
```

ORDNUMBER()

Protoype: ORDNUMBER(<cOrderName> [, <cOrderBagName>]) –> nOrderNo

The ORDNUMBER() Order Management function determines the position of an Order in the current Order List. The <cOrderName> parameter is the name of the Order whose position in the Order List is needed. <cOrderBagName> is the name of an Order Bag (a disk file) containing one or more Orders. The default filename extension of the current RDD is assumed if none is included with <cOrderBagName>. ORDNUMBER() searches the current work area's Order List and returns the position of the first Order that matches the Order name passed in <cOrderName>. If <cOrderBagName> is the name of an Order Bag newly emptied into the current Order List, only those orders in the Order List that have been emptied from <cOrderBagName> are searched.

The return value nOrderNo, is an integer that represents the position of the specified Order in the Order List.

Example:

```
USE WareHse VIA 'DBFNDX' NEW
SET INDEX TO WHid, WHName, WHLoc
* Order List now has 3 different orders
? ORDNUMBER('WHid')      // Displays: 1
```

ORDSETFOCUS()

Protoype: ORDSETFOCUS([<cOrderName> | <nOrder>] [,<cOrderBagName>])
               -> cPrevOrderName

ORDSETFOCUS() is an Order Management function that returns the Order Name of the *previous* controlling Order and optionally *establishes the focus* to a new Order. <cOrderName> is an existing Order name. <nOrder> is an integer representing the position in the Order List of the specified Order. If you do not specify <cOrderName> or <nOrder>, the name of the currently controlling Order is returned and the controlling Order remains unchanged. <cOrderBagName> is the name of an Order Bag (a disk file) containing one or more Orders. The default filename extension of the current RDD is assumed if none is included with <cOrderBagName>.

ORDSETFOCUS() returns a character expression containing the Order Name of the previous controlling Order. ORDSETFOCUS() replaces the INDEXORD() function which, although still available, should now be used for compatibility purposes only.

Example:

```
USE Movie NEW
SET INDEX TO MovieNo, MovieTtl, MovieSup
* Note: the MovieNo Order is in focus now
? ORDSETFOCUS('MovieSup') // Displays: MovieNo
? ORDSETFOCUS()            // Displays: MovieSup
```

RDDLIST()

Protoype: RDDLIST([<nRDDType>]) -> aRDDList

The RDDLIST() RDD function returns an array consisting of the names of available RDDs. The <nRDDType> parameter is an integer that represents the type of the RDD desired to list. There are only two type of RDDs currently available, and they are represented by the manifest constants RDT_FULL and RDT_TRANSFER shown in Table 8.3.

Table 8.3 RDD Type Summary

Constant Name	Value	Definition
RDT_FULL	1	Full implementation
RDT_TRANSFER	2	Import/Export only driver

RDT_FULL identifies full-featured RDDs that have all the features and capabilities normally associated with an RDD, whereas RDT_TRANSFER identifies RDDs of limited capability. These limited capacity RDDs can only transfer records between files and they cannot be used to open a file in a work area. The SDF and DELIM drivers are examples of this type of RDD, which are used in the implementation of the APPEND FROM and COPY TO commands with the SDF or DELIMITED keywords. If <nRDDType> is not specified, the names of all available RDDs, no matter what their type, are returned in the array.

RDDLIST() returns a one-dimension array, aRDDList, containing the names of RDDs known to the application as <nRDDType>.

Example:

```
REQUEST DBFMDX         // Pull in the MDX driver.

aRDD := RDDLIST()      // Get all RDD names. aRDD contains the
                       // following: {'DBF', 'SDF', 'DELIM', 'DBFMDX',
                       // 'DBFNTX'}
```

RDDNAME()

Protoype: RDDNAME() -> cRDDName

RDDNAME() is an RDD function that returns a character string containing the name of the RDD active in the current or aliased work area. The function returns cRDDName, the name of the active RDD.

Example:

```
USE Orders VIA 'DBFNDX' NEW
USE Customer VIA 'DBFCDX' NEW
* Current table is Customer, current RDD is DBFCDX
? RDDNAME()                  // Displays: DBFCDX
? Customer->(RDDNAME())      // Displays: DBFCDX
? Orders->(RDDNAME())        // Displays: DBFNDX
```

RDDSETDEFAULT()

Protoype: RDDSETDEFAULT([<cNewDefaultRDD>]) -> cPreviousDefaultRDD

The RDDSETDEFAULT() RDD function sets/gets the name of the previous default RDD and, optionally sets the current driver to a new driver for the application. The parameter <cNewDefaultRDD> is a character expression containing the name of the RDD that is to be made the new default RDD. The default driver is the driver that CA-Clipper uses if an RDD is not explicitly specified with the VIA clause of the USE command. If <cNewDefaultDriver> is not specified, the current default driver name is returned and continues to be the current default driver.

The return value is a character string, cPreviousDefaultRDD, which is the name of the previous default driver. This function replaces the DBSETDRIVER() function which, although still available, should now be used for compatibility purposes only.

Example:

```
/***
*
* MDXDef() -> cPrevDefRDD
*
* Purpose: Determine whether DBFMDX is current default RDD and
*   if not, then make it so
*
* Returns: Current default RDD name or NIL if already current
*
*/

FUNCTION MDXDef()
RETURN (IIF(RDDSETDEFAULT()!='DBFMDX',
RDDSETDEFAULT('DBFMDX'), NIL))
```

1. Write a UDF called GroupLock() that locks multiple records whose identities are stored in an array that is passed to the function.

2. Assume we wish to open a database called Employee using the DBFCDX driver. Write a code segment to open the database, empty the Employee Order Bag onto the Order List, and display the Order Number of the Order EmpName in the multiple-Order Bag associated with the file. The Employee Order Bag contains three Orders: EmpNo, EmpName, and EmpDept.

1. The code segment shown here simply passes array elements containing identities to the DBRLOCK() database function and then returns an array containing the current lock list.

```
/***
*
* GroupLock( <aIdentityList> )  -> aLockList
*
```

```
* Purpose: UDF to lock a series of records
*
*/

FUNCTION GroupLock(aIdentityList)
LOCAL nIdentity
FOR nIdentity := 1 TO LEN(aIdentityList)
   IF !DBRLOCK(aIdentityList[nIdentity])
      DBRUNLOCK()
   ENDIF
NEXT
RETURN DBRLOCKLIST()
```

2. Note that in the code, the `SET INDEX TO` command populates the Order List.

```
USE Employee VIA 'DBFCDX' NEW
SET INDEX TO Customer
? ORDNAME(2, 'Employee')   // Displays: EmpName
```

The Importance of Code Blocks

After looking at some of the examples in the previous section, the further importance of code blocks becomes evident. The examples show that code blocks do the work needed to support command clauses such as `FOR` and `WHILE`. They also demonstrate how to pass code blocks as parameters to UDFs.

Take the case of `DBCREATEINDEX()`, the function that implements `SET INDEX TO`. We see that the third parameter is a code block used to define the index key expression. Specifying a code block here is superior to using the second parameter, a textual form of the expression, since a macro expansion would otherwise be needed inside the function. Another example of the usefulness of code blocks is the first parameter of `DBSETFILTER()`, the filter condition, which controls the visibility of records during database processing.

Database Traversal and DBEVAL()

Another area of importance with respect to database access, is database traversal (the visitation of records in an orderly fashion). This importance is best described via an example. Have you ever encountered Xbase code like this:

```
USE orders
STORE 0 TO sum_oqty, no_recs, avg_units
SUM orders->ord_qty TO sum_oqty FOR orders->ord_date > DATE()-7
COUNT TO no_recs FOR orders->ord_date > DATE()-7
AVERAGE orders->units TO avg_units FOR orders->ord_date > DATE()-7
```

If you have, you probably have also heard the users complaining about the slowness of the process (of course, the performance depends on the size of

ORDERS.DBF). The poor performance can be attributed to the multiple passes required to collect the information. Of course, you could eliminate the SUM, COUNT, and AVERAGE commands entirely and replace them all with the equivalent WHILE/END loop structure, but we'll see now there is even an easier method.

The powerful CA-Clipper function DBEVAL() solves this problem by using code blocks to do the work. Consider the Clipper equivalent of the previous Xbase code:

```
LOCAL nSumOQty:=0, nNoRecs:=0 , nAvgUnits:=0, nSumUnits:=0
USE Orders NEW
DBEVAL({|| nSumOQty += Orders->OrdQty , ;
    nNoRecs++ ,                          ;
    nSumUnits += Orders->Units },        ;
    {|| Orders->OrdDate > DATE()-7} )
nAvgUnits := nSumUnits / nNoRecs
```

This version performs much better because all the required data is collected in a single pass of the database. This is possible through use of the code block specified as the first parameter of DBEVAL(). This code block contains several expressions that collect the individual pieces of data. The second parameter is also a code block, performing the function of a FOR clause.

Let's look at STD.CH to see how a database traversal command is actually implemented using DBEVAL(). We'll use COUNT as our example, but other CA-Clipper commands implemented in the manner are: AVERAGE, DELETE, RECALL, REPLACE, and SUM.

```
#command COUNT [TO <var>]                               ;
    [FOR <for>]                                         ;
    [WHILE <while>]                                     ;
    [NEXT <next>]                                       ;
    [RECORD <rec>]                                      ;
    [<rest:REST>]                                       ;
    [ALL]                                               ;
                                                        ;
    => <var> := 0                                       ;
    ; DBEval(                                           ;
      {|| <var> := <var> + 1},                          ;
      <{for}>, <{while}>, <next>, <rec>, <.rest.>       ;
      )
```

See how COUNT is nothing more than a call to DBEVAL(). The code block as the first parameter of DBEVAL() is the key, namely {|| <var> := <var> + 1}. This block is evaluated each time a record is processed by DBEVAL(), thus counting the number of records. The database traversal process is controlled by the second and third parameters, `<{for}>` and `<{while}>`, which are blockify result markers in the UDC definition.

As a real life example, here is a technique to generalize the database traversal process by providing a mechanism to build a set of DBEVAL() scope parameters and save them for future use:

```
#xcommand BUILD SCOPE TO <aScope>           ;
    [FOR <for>]                             ;
    [WHILE <while>]                         ;
    [NEXT <next>]                           ;
    [RECORD <rec>]                          ;
    [<rest:REST>]                           ;
    [ALL]                                   ;
                                            ;
    =>                                      ;
    <aScope> := { <{for}>, <{while}>,       ;
       <next>, <rec>, <.rest.> }
#define DBEVAL_FOR      1
#define DBEVAL_WHILE    2
#define DBEVAL_NEXT     3
#define DBEVAL_RECORD   4
#define DBEVAL_REST     5

LOCAL aNewScope:={}, nTotal:=0, dSearchKey:=CTOD('09/21/92')

USE Txn INDEX DateOut NEW // Open Txn.DBF indexed by the
                          // Txn->RentDate field.
* Build a reusable scope-set, creating aNewScope
BUILD SCOPE TO aNewScope FOR Txn->Type == 'I';
    WHILE  Txn->DateOut >= dSearchKey
DBSEEK(dSearchKey, .T.)        // Position record pointer with local SOFTSEEK.
* Sum up all qualifying Txn->TotalAmt fields
DBEVAL( {|| nTotal += Txn->TotalAmt}, ;
    aNewScope[DBEVAL_FOR],              ;
    aNewScope[DBEVAL_WHILE],            ;
    aNewScope[DBEVAL_NEXT],             ;
    aNewScope[DBEVAL_RECORD],           ;
    aNewScope[DBEVAL_REST]              ;
  )
```

In this example, we first build a new set of scope parameters using a newly defined command called BUILD SCOPE TO. The result of this command is an array containing one element for each DBEVAL() parameter. We then call DBEVAL() to do the work with aNewScope element to drive the process. The nice thing about the dynamically built scope-set is that it is completely reusable for future DBEVAL() calls.

Setting Relations

Although CA-Clipper cannot be considered a true relational database management system (the creator of relational database theory E. F. Codd has very strict guidelines for a database software package to qualify), the language does however include facilities to establish links between multiple database files. The primary command used for linking databases is SET RELATION TO. As noted during our discussion of database functions earlier in this chapter, the DBSETRELATION() built-in function also provides this functionality and may be a more convenient method in certain circumstances, such as code blocks.

Here is the syntax of the SET RELATION TO command:

```
SET RELATION TO [<KeyExpr> | <nRecord> INTO <Child>]
    [, [TO] <KeyExpr2> | <nRecord2> INTO <Child2>...]
    [ADDITIVE]
```

The purpose of SET RELATION TO is to establish a link between a parent database and one or more child databases. You should remember three important tips for a successful relation:

- The item that comes after the TO keyword is usually a database field in the parent database, and the item that follows the INTO keyword is the name of the child database.
- The parent and child database must have a common field in terms of data type (and usually length) to use as the linkage field. These fields do not have to have the same name however.
- The child database must be indexed on the common field. The parent database, however, does not require an index for the relation to function properly (although in normal use, an index on the parent is typical).

Consider the following example, which links up an orders database (ORDERS.DBF) with a parts database (PARTS.DBF):

```
USE Parts NEW                     // Open the parent.
USE Orders INDEX OrdPart NEW      // Open the child indexed on PartNo.
SELECT Parts
SET RELATION TO Parts->PartNo INTO Orders
```

According to the last two rules identified previously, the parent database has a field Parts->PartNo and the child database has a field Orders->PartNo to be used as the link field. Moreover, the ORDERS database must be indexed by Orders->PartNo. The relation is set, specifying the Parts->PartNo field in the parent is to be tied to the ORDPART.NTX index or the child.

Here is the whole point of a relation: now that the relation is set, a record pointer movement in the parent database causes an automatic record pointer movement in the child. In our example, the child will be positioned to the first (of possibly many) occurrence of the current part number of the parent. You can think of the child's record pointer as being dragged around by the parent. If there is no key match in the child, then the child's record pointer is positioned at end-of-file.

Another way to visualize the operation of SET RELATION TO is as an automated SEEK. Instead of using the current part number field value for a SEEK in the child database, the relation will automatically position to that point in the child for you. The ability to link databases together in CA-Clipper is a convenience, but the same result can be achieved using a SEEK.

The order-linked-to-part example described previously is an example of a *one-to-many* (*1:M*) relationship, meaning for every unique parent key value, there may be many child records with that same key value. In our example, the part numbers are unique in the PARTS (parent) database, but there may be many of the same part number in the ORDERS (child) database. Consider the code to process a 1:M relationship:

```
SELECT Parts
WHILE !EOF()   // Loop through all parent records.
   ? Parts->Descript
   SELECT Orders
   WHILE Orders->PartNo == Parts->PartNo .AND. !EOF()
     ? SPACE(5),Orders->Qty, Orders->OrdDate
     DBSKIP()
   END
   SELECT Parts
   DBSKIP()
END
```

In this code, we are looping through each part record and displaying data from each order record for that part. This is a very typical piece of code for processing data in a 1:M relationship.

> **Note**
>
> There are two important forms of database relations that frequently appear in CA-Clipper coding. The first is a *chained relationship* between three or more databases. Consider the following example that establishes a chained relationship:
>
> ```
> USE Parts NEW                   // Open the parent.
> USE Orders INDEX OrdPart NEW    // Open the child indexed on
>                                 // Orders->PartNo
> USE SalePers INDEX SPNo NEW     // Open the grandchild indexed
>                                 // SalePers->SPNo
> ```

```
SELECT Parts
SET RELATION TO Parts->PartNo INTO Orders
SELECT Orders
SET RELATION TO Orders->SPNo INTO SalesPers
```

The result of a chained relationship is that a record pointer movement in the parent will trickle down to the child and then to the grandchild, all automatically.

The second important variation of SET RELATION TO involves the situation with *multiple children*. Consider the following code:

```
USE Parts NEW                   // Open the parent.
USE Orders INDEX OrdPart NEW    // Open the child indexed on
                                // Orders->PartNo
USE WareHse INDEX WHNo NEW      // Open the second child indexed
                                // WareHse->WHNo
SELECT Parts
SET RELATION TO Parts->PartNo INTO Orders, ;
   TO Parts->WHNo INTO WareHse
```

The result of a multiple child relationship is that a record pointer movement in the parent will cause a corresponding record pointer movement in all the children. In this case, going from record to record in PARTS causes the record pointers to move in both the ORDERS and WAREHSE databases, all automatically.

The Many-to-Many Relation

For most applications, the well known 1:M relationship between tables yields enough power to build reasonably complex queries and reports. Often however, we need a bit more horsepower to represent certain real-life situations. For these times, we may turn to the often misunderstood *many-to-many (M:M)* relationship.

In this section, we'll examine methods for accessing data in an M:M relationship. Specifically, we'll see how to set up a M:M relationship and then introduce some CA-Clipper code to manipulate the relationship.

Most relationships between tables involve a master record/multiple detail records scenario typical in many business applications. Take the classic order entry problem for example. Here, you have an order record, containing order specific data and one or more transaction records, each describing an item that was ordered. A query or report based on this 1:M relationship between the orders and detail transactions table, would simply rely on a relation set from the order table to the detail transaction table in order to process the data.

With a M:M relationship, the situation is somewhat more involved. Consider another example where a company maintains supplier and part information.

Perhaps a certain supplier is able to supply many different parts, but any given part can be obtained from only a single supplier. This is a 1:M relationship. But what happens if a part can be obtained by several suppliers *and* each supplier can supply several different parts. This is a M:M relationship and such relationships are often needed in the solution of real-life business problems.

Let's now turn to an explanation of an implementation methodology for M:M relationships using CA-Clipper. For our discussion, consider the database structures shown in Figure 8.1. The way in which you may implement an M:M in CA-Clipper involves the introduction of a *linkage database*, which contains the key field from both of the databases to be related. In the example outlined earlier, we would use `Parts->PartNo` and `Supplier->SuppNo` as the fields of the linkage database, which we'll call PSLINK.DBF. By encountering a record in this database, such as (PRT001, DDG001) you're in essence using a tuple, which says that part number PRT001 is obtained from supplier DDG001. PSLINK would have a record defining each occurrence of a part being obtained from a supplier. We can go a small step forward by inserting another field into PSLINK such as `PSLink->Price`. In this way you may specify a unique price for a part coming from a particular supplier. Other such fields could of course be added to PSLINK.

When dealing with an M:M relationship you will always have two orientations to consider. In our example, we have intimated that there is both the *Part-by-Supplier* and the *Supplier-by-Part* orientations. Both are useful and which one you choose depends entirely on your requirements. We'll see a code example later that is based on the latter orientation.

Figure 8.1 These are the database structures for an M:M relationship.

```
PART.DBF
Field Name        Type       Length       Decimals
PARTNO            C          6
DESC              C          25
WAREHSE           C          15
QTYOH             N          4            0

SUPPLIER.DBF
Field Name        Type       Length       Decimals
SUPPNO            C          6
NAME              C          25
PHONE             C          12
CONTACT           C          30

PSLINK.DBF
Field Name        Type       Length       Decimals
PARTNO            C          6
SUPPNO            C          6
PRICE             N          9            2
```

Index file support for an M:M is crucial. For our example, we need the following:

```
USE Part NEW
INDEX ON Part->PartNo TO PartNo
USE Supplier NEW
INDEX ON Supplier->SuppNo TO SuppNo
USE PSLink NEW
* Create index for "Part-by-Supplier" orientation
INDEX ON PSLink->SuppNo + PSLink->PartNo TO PSSupp
* Create index for "Supplier-by-Part" orientation
INDEX ON PSLink->PartNo + PSLink->SuppNo TO PSPart
```

All four index files should be activated during a data entry or update process since they must be kept current for future flexibility in generating queries and/or reports. Rebuilding them on-the-fly would be a time consuming operation. PARTNO.NDX and SUPPNO.NDX are used for either linking the databases they describe to the linkage database or for ordering purposes if they describe the controlling database in the M:M relationship. The code required to establish an M:M relationship in CA-Clipper requires several tables, indexes, and relations. The command sequence provided in the Listing 8.1 code segment yields an M:M. Although the amount of code is not too great, later on we'll introduce a streamlined method to build an M:M relationship.

Listing 8.1 Establishing a "Supplier-by-Part" M:M Relationship

```
/* SUPPLIER BY PART orientation */

* Open "child" database indexed by its key
USE Supplier INDEX SuppNo NEW

* Open "parent" database indexed by its key
USE Part INDEX PartNo NEW

* Open the M:M linkage database indexed by
* PSLink->PartNo + PSLink->SuppNo
USE PSLink INDEX PSPart NEW

* Relate Part (parent) to PSLink (child)
SELECT Part
SET RELATION TO Part->PartNo INTO PSLink

* Relate PSLink (parent) to Supplier (child)
SELECT PSLink
SET RELATION TO PSLink->SuppNo INTO Supplier

SELECT Part     // Select parent.
```

One difficulty in using an M:M relationship in CA-Clipper is populating the linkage database. Normally, the two existing databases already contain data, but the linkage database is new and doesn't contain the tuples that map the records to each other.

Generating linkage database records requires some thought. A simple "intersection" of parts and suppliers will not suffice because obviously there are some parts not supplied by some suppliers. So how does the data get entered? The most common method requires you to create a very simple data entry screen, prompting for the two key fields and any data unique to the tuple (Price in our example). This requires a problem domain expert (AKA the user) to sit down and define who supplies what. For many M:M situations this is the only alternative because no authoritative machine readable source exists that can be interrogated to get the information.

Now that we have set the stage for utilizing an M:M, it's time to see some code. The code that we are about to examine could be used as part of a query, update, report, etc. Remember, however, the two orientations of any M:M. One typical programming requirement might entail the need for a list of all suppliers who supply a particular part. To satisfy this request, we can pop in the code from Listing 8.1. After establishing the database environment, we can write some code to manipulate the relationship. So, for each part found in the PART.DBF database, we display all associated suppliers.

In this orientation, PART.DBF is the controlling table, SUPPLIER.DBF is the table dragged around, and PSLINK.DBF is in the middle. Notice the index used for PSLINK.DBF has to be PSPART.NTX where the key is PartNo+SuppNo. With the relation from PART to PSLINK in effect, namely with the link field being Part->PartNo, the record pointer for PSLINK is automatically positioned to the first occurrence of the current part, thereby enabling the program to simply loop through the rest of the tuple records in PSLINK (if there are anymore).

Before we take a look at the code to traverse the M:M, we'll first describe a new command called M:M, which is defined as a UDC. The purpose of the M:M command is to enable the programmer to establish a many-to-many relationship without the hassle of writing all the code as in Listing 8.1. Here is the syntax definition for the M:M command:

```
M:M PARENT <ParentDatabase>
   [PARENTINDEX <ParentIndex>]
   CHILD <(ChildDatabase)>
   CHILDINDEX <(ChildIndex)>
   LINKAGE <(LinkageDatabase)>
   LINKAGEINDEX <(LinkageIndex)>
   PARENTKEY <ParentKey>
   LINKAGEKEY <LinkageKey>
```

The various clauses of the command specify the required components of a many-to-many relationship. The only optional clause is the index file for the parent table. The precise UDC definition is shown in Listing 8.2. As an example of how you can use the new `M:M` command, let us define a *Part-by-Supplier* orientation:

```
M:M PARENT Supplier PARENTINDEX SuppNo       ;
    CHILD Part CHILDINDEX PartNo             ;
    LINKAGE PSLink LINKAGEINDEX PSSupp       ;
    PARENTKEY Supplier->SuppNo LINKAGEKEY PSLink->PartNo
```

Upon executing this command, the entire many-to-many relationship is ready with the parent database selected. Now we are prepared to consider the code seen in Listing 8.2. This code begins by using the `M:M` command to set up the *Supplier-by-Part* orientation. Next, a WHILE/WEND (the WEND command is a new creation and should be considered synonymous with ENDDO) is used to loop through all the part records. For each part, another WHILE/WEND loop goes through all its suppliers with the help of the many-to-many relationship and displays both the part header and supplier detail information. Notice that once the relationship is established, the code to manipulate it is not very involved. The displayed output of the query is shown in Figure 8.2.

Figure 8.2   This is the query output of our M:M relationship.

```
DDG001 486/66 Motherboard          NORTH          45
  AEI111 Assoc. Electronic Inc.    212-555-9099   Mr. Cary C. Harwin
  GCD222 General Computer Design   213-555-6856   Ms. Frederika Gutierrez

DDG004 1.2 Meg Floppy Drive        WEST           18
  ACM333 Advanced Computer Memory  415-555-1234   Mr. William Claproth
  EEE444 Triple Elec.              214-555-6978   Ms. Tyron Scholaces
  GCD222 General Computer Design   213-555-6856   Ms. Frederika Gutierrez

DDG005 9600 Baud Modem             NORTH          19
  EEE444 Triple Elec.              214-555-6978   Ms. Tyron Scholaces

DDG006 360 K Floppy Drive          EAST           54
  ACM333 Advanced Computer Memory  415-555-1234   Mr. William Claproth
  GCD222 General Computer Design   213-555-6856   Ms. Frederika Gutierrez

DDG008 Multi-Media Kit             EAST           4
  GCD222 General Computer Design   213-555-6856   Ms. Frederika Gutierrez

DDG009 220 Watt Power Supply       NORTH          3
  ACM333 Advanced Computer Memory  415-555-1234   Mr. William Claproth
  AEI111 Assoc. Electronic Inc.    212-555-9099   Mr. Cary C. Harwin
  EEE444 Triple Elec.              214-555-6978   Ms. Tyron Scholaces
  GCD222 General Computer Design   213-555-6856   Ms. Frederika Gutierrez
```

Listing 8.2 Program using "Suppliers-by-Part" M:M Orientation

```
/***
 *
 * SuppPart() -This query displays "Suppliers-by-Part",
 *      i.e. it displays information for all
 *      suppliers who supply a specific part.
 */

#xcommand M:M  PARENT <(ParentDatabase)>         ;
        [PARENTINDEX <(ParentIndex)>]            ;
        CHILD <(ChildDatabase)>                  ;
        CHILDINDEX <(ChildIndex)>                ;
        LINKAGE <(LinkageDatabase)>              ;
        LINKAGEINDEX <(LinkageIndex)>            ;
        PARENTKEY <ParentKey>                    ;
        LINKAGEKEY <LinkageKey>                  ;
                                                 ;
    =>                                           ;
                                                 ;
    DBUSEAREA(.T.,, <(ChildDatabase)> )          ;
    ; DBSETINDEX( <(ChildIndex)> )               ;
    ; DBUSEAREA(.T.,, <(LinkageDatabase)> )      ;
    ; DBSETINDEX( <(LinkageIndex)> )             ;
    ; DBUSEAREA(.T.,, <(ParentDatabase)> )       ;
    [;DBSETINDEX( <(ParentIndex)> )]             ;
                                                 ;
    ; DBSETRELATION( <(LinkageDatabase)> ,       ;
            <{ParentKey}>,                       ;
            <"ParentKey"> )                      ;
    ; DBSELECTAREA( <(LinkageDatabase)> )        ;
    ; DBSETRELATION( <(ChildDatabase)>,          ;
            <{LinkageKey}>,                      ;
            <"LinkageKey"> )                     ;
      ; DBSELECTAREA( <(ParentDatabase)> )

#command WEND => enddo

FUNCTION SuppPart

Scroll(); SetPos(0,0)

/* Use the new M:M command to define the many-to-many
   relationship which establishes a "chained" linkage
   between PART to PSLINK to SUPPLIER and where the
   controlling index for PSLINK is PSPART (PartNo+SuppNo) */

M:M PARENT Part PARENTINDEX PartNo CHILD Supplier        ;
    CHILDINDEX SuppNo LINKAGE PSLink LINKAGEINDEX PSPart ;
```

```
              PARENTKEY Part->PartNo LINKAGEKEY PSLink->SuppNo

   WHILE !EOF()        // Loop through all parts.
      * Display the part group information
      QOUT()
      ? Part->PartNo, Part->Desc, Part->WareHse, Part->QtyOH
      SELECT PSLink    // Select M:M linkage database

      /* Loop through all (if any) suppliers who supply
         current part and display supplier information */

      WHILE PSLink->PartNo == Part->PartNo .AND. !EOF()
         ?  SPACE(2) + Supplier->SuppNo
         ?? SPACE(1) + Supplier->Name
         ?? SPACE(1) + Supplier->Phone
         ?? SPACE(1) + Supplier->Contact
         DBSKIP()        // Next M:M link record
      WEND
      SELECT Part       // Back to controlling database
      DBSKIP()           // Next part record
   WEND

   DBCLOSEALL()
   RETURN NIL
```

In summary, the many-to-many relationship offers an enhancement to the usual 1:M. Whether or not you utilize the power of the M:M relationship is a matter of need. As we've seen in this section, CA-Clipper is well equipped to handle it. When that real-life situation arises and an M:M seems to make sense, then you'll have the capability to represent it efficiently.

1. Modify the code in SuppPart() (shown earlier) to traverse the M:M relationship in an equivalent manner using only the DBEVAL() database function.

1. The code segment shown here produces the same displayed output as the code in Listing 8.2 but does so using a pair of nested DBEVAL()s.

```
         DBEVAL({|| QOUT(), QOUT(Part->PartNo),                    ;
            QQOUT(Part->Desc), QQOUT(Part->WareHse),               ;
            QQOUT(Part->QtyOH),                                    ;
            PSLink->(DBEVAL({|| QOUT(SPACE(2)+Supplier->SuppNo)   ,;
               QQOUT(SPACE(1)+Supplier->Name)                    ,;
               QQOUT(SPACE(1)+Supplier->Phone)                   ,;
               QQOUT(SPACE(1)+Supplier->Contact)}                ,;
               {|| PSLink->PartNo == Part->PartNo }))})
```

Summary

In this chapter, we've illustrated the CA-Clipper specific methods of manipulating database files. We've seen how the extensive set of database and RDD access functions Clipper contains yield unique power. We also have more evidence that code blocks, and the part they play in database access techniques, should be part of the optimized Clipper coding style.

Exercise

1. Write a general purpose CA-Clipper function called `DispRDD()` that when called will display all RDDs currently available to the program. Write a test program that first requests the DBFNDX and DBFMDX drivers.

Answer

1. The solution to this exercise is simple if you remembered the `RDDLIST()` RDD function! Here, we REQUEST DBFNDX and DBFMDX in the main program module and call our new UDF `DispRDD()`. We complete our task of displaying all available RDDs by passing `RDDLIST()`'s array return value over to `AEVAL()`.

```
/***
*
* Main() -> NIL
*
*/

REQUEST DBFNDX
REQUEST DBFMDX

FUNCTION Main

DispRDD()                   // Display all available RDDs.

RETURN NIL

FUNCTION DispRDD
   AEVAL(RDDLIST(), {|rdd| QOUT(rdd)})
RETURN NIL
```

Memo Fields

Memo Technology Revisited ➤ 240

Memo Field Basics ➤ 242

Memo Field/Character String Functions ➤ 243

MEMOEDIT() ➤ 250

Converting Summer '87 Memo Fields ➤ 260

Summary ➤ 262

Exercise ➤ 263

The memo field capability in CA-Clipper offers a suite of components that enable the handling of free format groups of text that are stored in a subsidiary file outside the .DBF file. Memo fields, however, a feature of the Xbase standard often viewed as the great panacea in the past, have suffered from shaky historical roots. Their renowned inefficient file handling in various dialects including Clipper, has caused many developers to look the other way. Not much is new in CA-Clipper from the Summer '87 release with regard to memos. Unlike replacing the aged DBEDIT() function with two new predefined classes, TBrowse and TBcolumn (which are the subject of Chapters 10 and 11), the MEMOEDIT() function remains as it was in earlier Clipper releases.

CA-Clipper beginners coming from other Xbase products may view the memo handling techniques somewhat different from what they're used to, whereas beginners migrating from Summer '87 will find much is still the same.

In this chapter, we'll apply the powerful new features of the Clipper language to memo field technology in order to yield some interesting results by examining memo field basics from the CA-Clipper perspective.

After completing this chapter, you will have learned:

- The basics of CA-Clipper's memo field technology
- How to utilize the various built-in functions that support memo field (as well as character string) manipulation
- The intricacies of the MEMOEDIT() functions, which provide for a user-interface mechanism for accessing customizable memo field data that is entirely customizable via its *user function* feature

Memo Technology Revisited

To start off, let's review the memo field technology found in the Clipper language. As in Xbase, CA-Clipper has a memo database field data type, but unlike other database field types, there is no parallel memory variable (there is no memo variable type). The lack of this memory variable type is not a problem since the entire contents of a memo field may be assigned to a character memory variable. A database can have more than one memo field. The amount of space used in each record for each memo field is 10 bytes. If you create or view a database structure in DBU (the CA-Clipper utility program described in Chapter 1) you'll see an "M" field type.

Note | The actual value stored in this field is a Numeric that points to a position (the beginning block) in the associated .DBT file where the memo data is actually located.

Note that this organization is a *one-way link* between the .DBF and .DBT files, which means that if the pointer in the .DBF becomes corrupt, the memo data becomes lost. This is a frequent problem with Xbase memo fields. One possible cure would be to implement a *backward pointer* from the .DBT to the record/field in the .DBF file. Unfortunately, this requires a change in the .DBT file format and no vendor has officially taken this direction.

The .DBT file has the same DOS filename as the .DBF file and contains all the text entered into the memo fields. Think of these two files as dependent on one another. A .DBT without its .DBF is useless and a .DBF without its .DBT cannot even be opened. If you attempt to do so, an OPEN error occurs during the call to `DBUSEAREA()`.

Memo field data is stored in the .DBT file in contiguous 512-byte blocks. Space for memos is allocated in 512-byte increments. The minimum size of a memo is 512 bytes. This is to say if the data to be stored in a memo field is 520 bytes, two blocks are allocated, one full block and another partial block. The excess bytes in the second block go unused. This is one area of inefficiency.

At first thought, memo fields may seem to cure the lack of variable length records in the Xbase .DBF file structure since you don't have to define their size in advance. A closer examination, however, shows that memo fields could waste more space than long character fields depending on the data stored due to the 512-byte block scheme. Here are some considerations you should weigh when deciding which to use:

- How many records will have any data in the memo field? If there will be only a few, then a memo field could save space over a character field, since blocks are added only for records that have memo field data.

- How long is the data going to be? If every record will have short length strings, then a memo field could waste much more than a character field (remember the 512-byte block, memo field minimum).

Another area of inefficiency lies in the fact that whenever you modify the contents of a memo and the new data exceeds the previous number of blocks it required, the data is copied to the end of the .DBT so that it can still be contiguous. This leaves the old version of the data remaining in the .DBT file. Using the `PACK` command on the .DBF file only physically deletes records marked for deletion and does not touch the contents of the .DBT file.

Currently in CA-Clipper, there are three ways to eliminate old memo data from a .DBT file:

- Use the `DBT50.EXE` utility program that comes with the product. You can either execute this program from the DOS prompt or directly from within a Clipper program via the `RUN` command.

- Use the `COPY TO` command to copy the .DBF/.DBT files to a temporary location, delete the original files, and then `COPY TO` back to the original filename. The copy operation causes the .DBT file to be packed and the .DBF pointers to be adjusted.
- Use the low-level file functions (the topic of Chapter 12) to directly access and pack the .DBT file.

Without performing a regular .DBT pack process and assuming that your application modifies memo field contents (if your memos are static in size there is no problem), the .DBT file will grow disproportionately to the .DBF. Most developers in the Xbase community agree that a better storage management scheme is needed.

Memo Field Basics

Remember that Clipper character strings can be up to 64K bytes in length. A memo field is nothing more than a long string, so this is also the maximum length of a memo. This being the case, you can use the usual string functions, `LEN()`, `SUBSTR()`, `AT()`, `$`, and so on, on memo fields too.

When the content of a memo field is accessed—a reference to a memo field is made as in `EMPLOYEE->RESUME`—one or more 512-byte blocks are read from the .DBT file. To assign a value to a memo field, you can place its name on the left side of an assignment operator as in:

```
<cAlias> -> <cMemoField> := <cCharExpression>
```

or, you can include it in a `REPLACE` command. To assign a memo field's value to a character memory variable you would use this form:

```
<cMemVar> := <cAlias> -> <cMemoField>
```

Clipper knows to translate this request into a .DBT file access.

As a guide, take a look at the following `MemoCount()` example. This UDF uses the flexible CA-Clipper memo field access capabilities to search through each record's memo field contents for a specified string and tallies the number of occurrences.

```
FUNCTION Main

USE Customer NEW
* Parm1: string to count, Parm2: memo field name
? MemoCount('Alexandra', 'Notes')

RETURN NIL
```

```
FUNCTION MemoCount(cSearch, cMemo)
LOCAL nCount:=0

DBGOTOP()
DBEVAL({|| IIF(cSearch $ FIELDGET(FIELDPOS(cMemo)), ;
   nCount++, NIL)})

RETURN (nCount)
```

Here, a main program calls the `MemoCount()` UDF with the CUSTOMER database active. Two parameters are passed: the string to search for and the memo field name in which to search. The function uses `DBEVAL()` to perform the tabulation. `DBEVAL()`'s code block is evaluated for each record. `FIELDPOS()` is a built-in Clipper function that returns the field number of the current work area for the field name passed to it, which in turn is passed to `FIELDGET()` in order to access the memo data. Put all together, the code block tests for an occurrence of the search string `cSearch` inside the memo or character field referenced and updates `nCount` accordingly. The tally result, stored in `nCount`, is then returned to the calling program.

Memo Field/Character String Functions

CA-Clipper has the same complement of *memo field/character string* functions available in the Summer '87 release with the exception of two new additions, `LCTOPOS()` and `MPOSTOLC()`. These functions operate on either memo fields or character string (normally long strings) memory variables. We use the term "memo function" to indicate functions specifically designed for memo fields, but which may also be used with character memory variables. In this section, we'll take a look at how these functions can be applied with respect to CA-Clipper through use of some simple code examples. The functions and their parameter lists are shown in Table 9.1.

First, we'll consider the `HARDCR()` function.

```
USE Customer NEW

? Customer->Notes            // Messy display results.
? HARDCR(Customer->Notes)    // Now with proper line breaks.

DBCLOSEALL()
```

Here, we're using `HARDCR()` to replace all soft carriage return characters (represented in Xbase using the built-in `CHR()` function as: `CHR(141)`) with hard carriage return characters `CHR(13)`. Otherwise, if the memo field contents were displayed "as-is," then the ? command would not handle the line breaks

Table 9.1 Memo Functions

Function	Description
HARDCR(<cString>) -> cConvertedString	Replaces all soft carriage returns CHR(141) in a memo field or character string with hard carriage returns CHR(13)

MEMOLINE(<cString>,
   [<nLineLength>],
   [<nLineNumber>],
   [<nTabSize>],
   [<lWrap>]) -> cLine
	Extracts "a line" or "lines" of text from a memo field or character string according to the specified line length

MEMOREAD(<cFile>) -> cString	Returns the contents of the specified DOS disk file as a contiguous long character string

MEMOTRAN(<cString>,
   [<cReplaceHardCR>],
   [<cReplaceSoftCR>])
   -> cNewString
	Replaces carriage return/line feeds in a memo field or character string with the specified characters

MEMOWRIT(<cFile>, <cString>) -> lSuccess	Writes the contents of a memo field or character string to the specified DOS disk file

MLCOUNT(<cString>,
   [<nLineLength>],
   [<nTabSize>],
   [<lWrap>]) -> nLines
	Counts the number of lines in a memo field or character string according to the specified line length

MLCTOPOS(<cString>,
   <nLineLength>,
   <nLine>,
   <nCol>,
   [<nTabSize>],
   [<lWrap>]) -> nPosition
	Returns the byte position of a formatted string (i.e. justified into a series of individual lines) based on the specified line and column position

MLPOS(<cString>,
   <nLineLength>,
   <nLine>,
   [<nTabSize>],
   [<lWrap>]) -> nPosition
	Determines the position of a line in a memo field or character string according to the specified line length

MPOSTOLC(<cString>,
   <nLineLength>,
   <nPos>,
   [<nTabSize>],
   [<lWrap>]) -> aLineColumn
	Returns an array containing the line and column position of a formatted string based on a specified byte position

Table 9.1 Memo Functions (Continued)

Function	Description

STRTRAN(<cString>,
   <cSearch>,
   [<cReplace>],
   [<nStart>],
   [<nCount>]) —> cNewString
	Searches and replaces multiple occurrences of characters within a memo field or character string

STUFF(<cString>, <nStart>, <nDelete>, <cInsert>) —> cNewString	Replaces, deletes, and inserts characters in a memo field or character string

properly because the soft carriage returns would not be recognized. Using HARDCR() instead will yield the same line breaks as seen in MEMOEDIT(), which is the culprit here since it automatically generates soft carriage returns with its word wrap feature.

Next, we see a code segment illustrating a general method of how to display memo fields and character strings using the MLCOUNT() and MEMOLINE() functions. In this case, we'll display the contents of each Notes memo field in CUSTOMER.DBF.

```
#define TRUE .T.
#define HARDCRLF CHR(13) + CHR(10)
#define SOFTCRLF CHR(141) + CHR(10)

LOCAL nLineLength := 60, nTabSize := 5, lWrap := TRUE
LOCAL nNumLines, nLine

USE Customer NEW
WHILE !EOF()
   * Determine the number of lines in current memo field
   nNumLines := MLCOUNT(Customer->Notes, nLineLength, nTabSize, lWrap)
   FOR nLine := 1 TO nNumLines
      * Now pull out one line of the memo at a time
      * for display
      ? MEMOLINE(Customer->Notes, nLineLength, nLine, nTabSize, lWrap)
   NEXT
   DBSKIP()    // Next record please.
   QOUT()      // For space in between complete memos.
END
DBCLOSEAREA()
```

Here, `MLCOUNT()` is called first in order to determine the number of text lines that result given the user-specified line length, in this case specified in `nLineLength`. This value then controls the `FOR` loop, which uses `MEMOLINE()` to extract each line of data for display purposes.

In the following code segment, we use the `MEMOREAD()` function to load the ASCII text data from a disk file named NOTEFILE.TXT into the `Notes` memo field of record 5 in the CUSTOMER database. Then, the memo field contents are written out to another ASCII text file, XMIT.TXT using the `MEMOWRIT()` function. Note that if the writing operation is not successful, an error message is displayed.

```
USE Customer NEW
GOTO 5

* REPLACE not needed in CA-Clipper
Customer->Notes := MEMOREAD('NOTEFILE.TXT')
IF !MEMOWRIT('XMIT.TXT', Customer->Notes)
   QOUT('Error: writing XMIT.TXT')
ENDIF
DBCLOSEALL()
```

Note that in this example, `MEMOWRIT()` is called from inside an `IF` statement (a common technique used with built-in Clipper functions or UDFs that return a logical value) and the return value is then used as the logical value tested to determine flow of control.

The next example uses `MEMOTRAN()` to eliminate both hard and soft carriage returns from a memo field. Although `MEMOTRAN()`'s true purpose is to replace carriage returns with some other character, we'll just replace them with blank spaces.

```
 #define REPLACECR ' '
USE Customer NEW
GOTO 5    // Go to arbitrary record.

Customer->Notes := MEMOTRAN(Customer->Notes, REPLACECR, REPLACECR)
DBCLOSEAREA()
```

The manifest constant `REPLACECR` provides for the means of substituting a blank space for both hard (`CHR(13)`) and soft (`CHR(141)`)carriage return characters. We'll have a more in-depth discussion about carriage return characters after we examine the `MEMOEDIT()` function more closely later in this chapter.

In the next several examples, we'll investigate several functions—`MLPOS()`, `MLCTOPOS()`, and `MPOSTOLC()`—that all pertain to determining character positions inside a memo field or long character string. These functions reinforce the notion that the text inside a memo field can be viewed as being just one long string of characters. Moreover, these characters can be "formatted" according to a variable line length.

First, we see how `MLPOS()` is used to find the character position at which a certain line begins, given a specific line length. Note that we're using a character string `cString`, but a memo field would work fine here too.

```
* Ten 1's, ten 2's, etc.
LOCAL cString := '1111111111222222222233333333334444444444'
LOCAL nLineLength := 10, nLine := 3, nCol := 5, nPosition

* Find the character starting position of the 3rd line given
* a line length of 10.
nPosition := MLPOS(cString, nLineLength, nLine)
? nPosition                                   // 21
? SUBSTR(cString, nPosition, nLineLength)     // '3333333333'
```

New in CA-Clipper are the `MLCTOPOS()` and `MPOSTOLC()` functions shown next. The first is used as an extension to `MLPOS()` in allowing not only the character position of a line, but also an offset within that line.

```
* Find the character position of the fifth character of the
* third line
nPosition := MLCTOPOS(cString, nLineLength, nLine, nCol)
? nPosition     // Displays: 26
```

In the following example, we use `MPOSTOLC()` to determine, for `cString`, the line and column corresponding to the sixteenth character of the text, given a line length of 10 characters. A line length of 10 would cause the first word, *Josephine*, to be on a line by itself. The second line would contain the next two words, *is a*. Then, on the third line *helpful* would be placed again alone. Therefore the line of the sixteenth character, *h* in *helpful*, is 3 and the column is 0 (the first column). These values are returned in a two element array, in which the first element contains the line number and the second element contains the column number. In our example, the function yields the array {3,0}.

```
LOCAL aLineColumn := {}             // Array returned by MPOSTOLC()
LOCAL cString := 'Josephine is a helpful person.'
LOCAL nPos, nLineLength := 10

nPos := 16                          // Point to 'h' in 'helpful'
aLineColumn := MPOSTOLC(cString, nLineLength, nPos)
? aLineColumn[1], aLineColumn[2]    // Displays: 3  0
```

Another very useful function, `STRTRAN()`, replaces multiple occurrences of a search string with a replacement string in a memo field or long character string.

```
  LOCAL cString := 'row, row, row your boat ...'
* Displays: sink, sink, sink your boat
? STRTRAN(cString, 'row', 'sink')
```

The last function in the long string category, STUFF(), can be used to do some very creative stuff. Have you ever wished you could put a SUBSTR() on the left hand side of the assignment operator := so that you could assign a new value to the set of characters it defines? Well, STUFF() allows you to do exactly this type of operation and several others relating to intra-string manipulations. Specifically, STUFF() has the following capabilities: replace, insert, delete, replace/insert, and replace/delete.

Here is an example showing the various features of STUFF(). Make sure you review STUFF()'s parameter list in Table 9.1 before proceeding.

```
#define SOURCE  'Hello world'
#define SOURCE1 'Billy and Jolande'

* Replace
* Five characters are deleted beginning at position 7, at
* which point a new string of same length is inserted
? STUFF(SOURCE, 7, 5, 'Billy')    // Displays: 'Hello Billy'

* Insert
* No characters are deleted, but a new string is inserted
* beginning at position 6
? STUFF(SOURCE, 6, 0, ' there')
* Above displays: 'Hello there world'

* Delete
* FOur characters are deleted beginning at position 6, and
* no new string is inserted
? STUFF(SOURCE1, 6, 4, '')      // Displays: 'Billy Jolande'

* Replace/Insert
* Three characters are deleted beginning at position 7, and
* a new, longer string is inserted
? STUFF(SOURCE1, 7, 3, 'with')
* Above displays: 'Billy with Jolande'

* Replace/Delete
* Five characters are deleted beginning at position 7, and
* a new, shorter string is inserted
? STUFF(SOURCE, 7, 5, 'me')      // Displays: 'Hello me'
```

1. Consider the following file structure for the database EMPLOYEE.DBF:

Field Name	Field Type	Field Length
EmpNo	Character	6
Name	Character	30
Resume	Memo	10

Write a UDF that will search through the contents of the Resume memo field of each record in the database for a character value passed as a parameter. You must return an array value back to the calling program that contains both the EmpNo and Name fields for each match found.

2. Write a program that will operate on the contents of a character memory variable by displaying the first five characters of each justified line, given a line length of 20.

1. The solution to this problem requires the understanding that all the usual string functions and operators also work for memo fields. With this, the $ operator is the key here. Consider the following UDF code that implements the desired functionality:

```
FUNCTION SearchMemo(cString)
LOCAL aMatchArray := {}     // Declare null array.

GO TOP                       // Start looking at beginning.
WHILE !EOF()                 // Consider all records.
   IF cString $ Employee->Resume
     * If match, add a subarray with employee
     * number and name.
     AADD(aMatchArray, {Employee->EmpNo, ;
         Employee->Name})
   ENDIF
   SKIP                      // Go on to next memo field.
END

RETURN aMatchArray           // Return collection of matches.
```

2. One possible solution to this problem involves both the MLCOUNT() and MLCTOPOS() functions. In our solution, we use MLCOUNT() to determine the number of lines of length 20 that the input text fits into. We can then use MLCTOPOS() to point to the first position of each of the lines and from there, the standard SUBSTR() extracts the required five characters.

```
#define TAB_SIZE 5
#define WRAP .T.

FUNCTION Main
LOCAL nCnt, nPos, nLen := 20
LOCAL cText := 'Joyce, Tony and Alexander were last ' +;
   'seen fishing in a pond'
```

```
FOR nCnt := 1 TO MLCOUNT(cText, nLen, TAB_SIZE, WRAP)
   nPos := MLCTOPOS(cText, nLen, nCnt, 0)
   ? SUBSTR(cText, nPos, 5)
NEXT

RETURN NIL
```

MEMOEDIT()

The one particular built-in function in CA-Clipper that is the focal point of memo use is MEMOEDIT(). For programmers entering the Clipper arena from the Summer '87 release, the mechanisms remain the same, and for those readers in this category, this chapter provides for a sense of giving this aging technology a new and updated look. For those of you moving to CA-Clipper from other Xbase products, MEMOEDIT() may seem quite strange in the way it provides for memo field access. If you're in this group, we'll start by spelling out the basics for becoming productive with MEMOEDIT().

Before we begin, let's summarize the various uses of MEMOEDIT():

- This function allows for interactive entry and editing of data stored in .DBT files, or in other words, memo field data.
- This function allows for interactive entry and editing of data stored in character strings (normally strings of reasonably long length).
- This function allows for interactive entry and editing of data stored in ASCII text disk files by first loading the contents of the file into a character string and then using MEMOEDIT() for editing purposes.

Let's now turn our attention to a brief introduction to the mechanisms underlying MEMOEDIT().

An Introduction to MEMOEDIT()

MEMOEDIT() is the function used to enter and edit data stored in memo fields or character strings. Remember, Clipper does not distinguish between memo fields and character strings when it comes to its built-in memo functions. In its raw form, MEMOEDIT() gives you a *full screen editor* that you use to type in or change free form text.

Here is the formal definition of MEMOEDIT():

```
MEMOEDIT( [<cString>],
    [<nTop>],
    [<nLeft>],
    [<nBottom>],
    [<nRight>],
    [<lEditMode>],
```

```
            [<cUserFunction>],
            [<nLineLength>],
            [<nTabSize>],
            [<nTextBufferRow>],
            [<nTextBufferColumn>],
            [<nWindowRow>],
            [<nWindowColumn>] ) -> cTextBuffer
```

With 13 parameters, `MEMOEDIT()` is one of Clipper's most complex built-in functions, but when you view each parameter on its own, the complexity isn't really too bad. Before we move to an example, let's first define each parameter in Table 9.2.

We see that most of the parameters deal with how the memo window appears on the screen and cursor positioning. `<lEditMode>` provides for display-only text, a useful feature when presenting static text, such as a procedures manual, to the user.

Table 9.2 MEMOEDIT() Parameters

Parameter	Definition
`<cString>`	Name of memo field or character string to edit
`<nTop>`	Top screen row of the memo window (default is 0)
`<nLeft>`	Left screen column of the memo window (default is 0)
`<nBottom>`	Bottom screen row of the memo window (default is `MaxRow()`)
`<nRight>`	Right screen column of the memo window (default is `MaxCol()`)
`<lEditMode>`	Logical parameter that determines whether text can be edited inside the memo window; a .T. value means the text is editable and an .F. value means non-editable (the default is .T.)
`<cUserFunction>`	Character expression containing the name of the UDF to call as an exception handler
`<nLineLength>`	Number of characters in a line before word wrap occurs (the default is `<nRight>` - `<nLeft>`)
`<nTabSize>`	Number of spaces to skip when Tab key is pressed
`<nTextBufferRow>`	Line number of formatted text on which to begin editing (the default is 0)
`<nTextBufferColumn>`	Column number to begin editing (the default is 0)
`<nWindowRow>`	Row in window on which to position cursor (default is 0)
`<nWindowColumn>`	Column in window on which to position cursor (the default is 0)

> **Note:** Note that `MEMOEDIT()` does not save the contents of the screen prior to displaying its window, nor does it draw a box around the window. These chores are up to you.

The default line length for `MEMOEDIT()` is the number of column positions in the memo window. As new text is entered, the cursor automatically advances (wraps) to the next line if a word won't fit on the current line (in addition, a soft carriage return is inserted in the text at that point). When presented in the memo window, existing text is automatically justified (divided up in equal length lines) to appear in the window according to the current line length. You can change the line length by using the `<nLineLength>` parameter. If, however, you specify a line length longer than the window width, the line scrolls horizontally during editing.

The User Function

The `<cUserFunction>` parameter is of particular concern because it is the one that facilitates programming of the manner in which `MEMOEDIT()` operates. Namely, it handles the interpretation of keystrokes generated by the user and carries out either default or custom implementations of these keystrokes. The `MEMOEDIT()` user function, as it is called, listens to each keystroke and takes appropriate actions depending on what you've said to do in each case. When it is specified (as this feature is optional), the user function is called repeatedly as the user enters text and presses control keys while inside the memo window. At the same time, `MEMOEDIT()` enters into various *modes* (see Figure 9.1 for a list) and the user function interprets them accordingly. This modal activity constitutes flexibility of design with regards to custom processing user keyboard entry.

Since the `MEMOEDIT()` UDF is keystroke dependent, the INKEY.CH header file is of prime importance since each keystroke that can be recognized has a corresponding manifest constant in INKEY.CH. Another header file, MEMOEDIT.CH, is specifically designed for use with `MEMOEDIT()`. MEMOEDIT.CH contains manifest constants for user function entry modes and return codes. See Figure 9.1 for the contents of this header file.

Once you begin editing data through a `MEMOEDIT()` window, several editing keys are available. The keys operate in a Wordstar-like fashion (such as Ctrl+Y to delete a line, Ctrl+N to insert a line, and Ctrl+B to rejustify the text). Note that through the use of the user function UDF, these keys are configurable, meaning that you may assign an action different than the default one, or recognize entirely new control keys.

Upon calling the user function, `MEMOEDIT()` passes three numeric parameters: *mode*, *row*, and *column*, which represent `MEMOEDIT()`'s current mode and the screen row and column position of the cursor inside the memo window. The user function can use these parameters in carrying out its purpose.

Memo Fields

Figure 9.1 The MEMOEDIT.CH header file is specifically designed for use with MEMOEDIT().

```
// User function entry modes

#define ME_IDLE          0    // idle, all keys processed.
#define ME_UNKEY         1    // unknown key, memo unaltered.
#define ME_UNKEYX        2    // unknown key, memo altered.
#define ME_INIT          3    // initialization mode.

// User function return codes

#define ME_DEFAULT       0    // perform default action.
#define ME_IGNORE        32   // ignore unknown key.
#define ME_DATA          33   // treat unknown key as data.
#define ME_TOGGLEWRAP    34   // toggle word-wrap mode.
#define ME_TOGGLESCROLL  35   // toggle scrolling mode.
#define ME_WORDRIGHT     100  // perform word-right operation.
#define ME_BOTTOMRIGHT   101  // perform bottom-right operation.

// NOTE:  Return codes 1 - 31 cause MEMOEDIT() to perform the
// edit action corresponding to the key whose value is returned.

#define _MEMOEDIT_CH
```

Simple Memo Field Access

Before all the details surrounding MEMOEDIT() become overwhelming, we need to provide you with a couple of basic examples. As mentioned before, MEMOEDIT() is a powerful function with many possibilities. Our purpose is, however, to learn the basics. Therefore, the following examples show the basic setup for using MEMOEDIT(). In both examples, all the default options are accepted and MEMOEDIT() is used straight "out-of-the-box" with no user function specified.

```
FUNCTION Main

USE Customer NEW
Customer->Notes := MEMOEDIT(Customer->Notes, 5, 10, 15, 70)
DBCLOSEAREA()

RETURN NIL
```

Here, a memo field is retrieved, the user edits its contents within a memo window, which is located at the specified coordinates, and the new value replaces the old. In this simple example, the prior screen contents are lost and no window border appears. A little bit more sophistication is generally required, which leads us to the next example:

```
FUNCTION Main

USE Customer NEW
* Edit memo of first record
Customer->Notes := ReadNotes(Customer->Notes, 5, 10, 15, 70)
DBCLOSEAREA()

RETURN NIL

/***
*   ReadNotes() - Function that uses MEMOEDIT() to allow
*                 interactive editing of character data
*
*   (1) Save screen contents based on passed screen coordinates
*   (2) Call MEMOEDIT() for editing
*   (3) Restore screen contents
*   (4) Return new character data
*/

FUNCTION ReadNotes(cCharData, nTop, nLeft, nBottom, nRight)
LOCAL cScreenSave := SAVESCREEN(nTop, nLeft, nBottom, nRight)

@ nTop, nLeft TO nBottom, nRight DOUBLE
cCharData := MEMOEDIT(cCharData, nTop+1, nLeft+1, nBottom-1, nRight-1)
RESTSCREEN(nTop, nLeft, nBottom, nRight, cScreenSave)

RETURN (cCharData)
```

In the second example, we define, `ReadNotes()`, a general purpose UDF whose purpose is to utilize `MEMOEDIT()` as the vehicle to provide for interactive editing of character text (either memo field or character memory variable data), which is passed as the first parameter. The other four parameters are simply screen coordinates defining the dimensions of the editing window. `ReadNotes()` also saves and restores the prior screen contents (using the built-in `SAVESCREEN()` and `RESTSCREEN()` functions) and draws a double line border.

In the main program, the memo field `Customer->Notes` is passed to `ReadNotes()` By Value. Its value is mapped to the function's formal parameter `cCharData`, whose value after editing is passed through the `RETURN` statement back for assignment to the memo field.

Implemented in this manner, `ReadNotes()` may be used to edit character text coming from a character memory variable or database field, memo field, or text disk file (which had previously been loaded in a character memory variable).

Getting Memo Fields

For Xbase developers moving to Clipper, you'll find the process of issuing GETs on memo fields to be much less automatic. In dBASE IV, for example, if you use the command

```
@ 10,10 GET Customer->Notes  // Read memo field.
```

where `Notes` is a memo field, a data entry box appears with the word "MEMO" inside. To move inside a memo editing window, you press Ctrl+Home. Clipper does not work this way. With Clipper, the above @...GET statement would display a long data entry box stretching across the screen (not very appealing). Instead, you must perform some special handling on the field for proper editing. The next example illustrates one possible solution to this situation:

```
#include 'inkey.ch'

FUNCTION Main
LOCAL cMemoMarker1 := 'NOTES'     // Give GET something to display.

USE Customer NEW
CLEAR
SET KEY K_CTRL_HOME TO ReadMemo   // Map key to UDF call.
@ 10, 10 GET Customer->Name       // Regular character field.
@ 12, 10 GET cMemoMarker1         // Display memo marker only.
@ 14, 10 GET Customer->Phone      // Regular character field.
READ
DBCLOSEAREA()

RETURN NIL

/***
*   ReadMemo() - Function that uses MEMOEDIT() to provide
*       GET support for memo fields.
*/

FUNCTION ReadMemo( cProgName, nLine, cVarName )
LOCAL cSaveScreen

IF cVarName == 'CMEMOMARKER1'
   cSaveScreen := SAVESCREEN( 5, 10, 15, 60 )
   @ 5, 10 TO 15, 60
   Customer->Notes := MEMOEDIT(Customer->Notes, 6, 11, 14, 59)
   RESTSCREEN(5, 10, 15, 60, cSaveScreen)
ELSEIF
   // Additional memo fields added here.
ENDIF

RETURN NIL
```

In this example, the desire is to issue `GET`s for several database fields including one memo field, Notes. Instead of issuing the command `@ 10,10 GET Customer->Notes` directly, we set up a memory variable containing a simulated marker value 'NOTES'. The `GET` is issued for the memory variable, *not* the memo field. To make this useful, we also establish a `SET KEY TO` mapping for the Ctrl+Home key combination. Ctrl+Home was chosen arbitrarily, any other key or combination could also be used. `SET KEY TO` causes a UDF or procedure to be called if the specified key is pressed during a wait state (in this case a pending `GET`).

When the user positions to the second `GET` during data entry, Ctrl+Home must then be pressed in order to enter the memo window. See Figure 9.2, which illustrates the data entry screen immediately prior to pressing the Ctrl+Home key. Using the `SET KEY TO` mapping, the `ReadMemo()` function is called. Three parameters are automatically passed: the name of the calling program, the line number in the calling program, and the memory variable name of the `GET` that is active when the `SET KEY TO` command was invoked.

Once inside `ReadMemo()`, we examine the contents of the third parameter to determine which `GET` was active. In this way, `ReadMemo()` could handle multiple memo field `GET`s by adding another `ELSEIF` and additional program code to call `MEMOEDIT()`.

Editing Text Disk Files

The next example demonstrates a somewhat more ambitious effort using `MEMOEDIT()`. This time we'll use the function to edit the text in any ASCII disk file. The program is structured in the following way: a main program prompts the user for a disk filename, while using a `VALID` clause UDF to check its existence. If the file exists, `MEMOEDIT()` is called for the user to edit its contents.

In preparation for `MEMOEDIT()`, however, we do two things. First, we turn insert mode on with the built-in `READINSERT()` function. When in a memo window, insert mode works the same as in any word processor, pushing existing text to the right instead of overwriting it. Next, we change the shape of

---

Figure 9.2 Issuing a GET on a Memo Field.

```
Mr. Paul Klose

NOTES

310-798-3985
```

the cursor to a block (the norm for insert mode in most text editors) using the built-in SETCURSOR() function. Notice we're using a manifest constant defined in SETCURS.CH here. This Clipper header file is specifically designed for the SETCURSOR() function.

Finally, MEMOEDIT() is called. Notice how we're using the return value from MEMOREAD() as the <cString> to edit. Remember that MEMOREAD() reads the contents of a disk file into a character string. It is this character string that we'll be editing in the memo window. After we're done, the new content is written back out to disk, using MEMOWRIT().

The interesting part of this example lies in the MemoUDF() user function attached to the call to MEMOEDIT(). MemoUDF() handles two keystroke exceptions. First, if the user presses Ins, the key is trapped, the insert toggle is interrogated, the cursor is changed, and some new, custom screen indicators are updated. Notice that K_INS is passed back to MEMOEDIT() to toggle insert mode. It is this *two-way communication* from MEMOEDIT() and the user function that makes memo processing powerful in CA-Clipper.

Second, F2 is trapped and the KEYBOARD command is used to stuff a text string into the keyboard buffer. Thus, when the user presses F2, the copyright text is inserted wherever the cursor is currently positioned. Figure 9.3 depicts how the screen might appear when using this sample program to edit its own source code.

Figure 9.3   Here MEMOEDIT() is used as a programmer's editor.

```
                                              <insert>
FUNCTION MemoUDF( nMode, nRow, nCol )

    LOCAL nKey := LASTKEY()             // Save last user keystroke

    IF nMode == ME_INIT                 // Initialization mode
        RETURN (ME_DEFAULT)
    ELSEIF nMode == ME_IDLE             // User inactive, so ME_IDLE
                                        // is passed to UDF
        EditStat( nRow, nCol )          // Just update status
    ELSE
```

Row: 69 Col: 0 REPLACE

Note Use the KEYBOARD command whenever you need to automatically enter text into the keyboard buffer instead of having the user type it. The effect is the same.

Using this example as a model, you may think of ideas to expand on the editor's operation by adding other special purpose functionality. To fully understand how this program works and how MEMOEDIT() and the user function communicate, I would highly recommend that you to curl up in front of the fireplace with this program running under the debugger using the single step option.

```
#include 'inkey.ch'
#include 'memoedit.ch'
#include 'box.ch'
#include 'set.ch'
#include 'setcurs.ch'
#define INSERTMODE .T.

FUNCTION Main
LOCAL GetList := {}   // Initialize a fresh getlist array.
LOCAL cText, cFileName := SPACE(11)

Scroll(); SetPos(0,0)// CLEAR SCREEN.
@ 1,1 SAY 'Enter filename to edit: ' ;
   GET cFileName ;
   VALID FileChk( cFileName )
READ

IF LASTKEY() != K_ESC
   @ 0,0
   * Draw half screen box using BOX.CH
   @ 1,0,MAXROW()/2,MAXCOL() BOX B_SINGLE
   * Now make the call to MEMOEDIT(), notice the
   * reference to MemoUDF().
   READINSERT(INSERTMODE) // Initial INS mode.
   SETCURSOR(SC_SPECIAL1) // Block cursor for INS.
   cText := MEMOEDIT(MEMOREAD(cFileName), 2, 1, MAXROW()/2-1,
         MAXCOL()-1,, 'MemoUDF')
   * Write edited text back out to disk file
   MEMOWRIT(cFileName, cText)
ENDIF
Scroll(); SetPos(0,0)

RETURN NIL
```

```
/***
*
*   FileChk() - Function to check existence of a disk file
*
*/

STATIC FUNCTION FileChk ( cFile )
LOCAL lRetVal := .T.

IF !FILE(TRIM(cFile))
   @ 0,0 SAY 'Error: file does not exist'
   lRetVal := .F.
ENDIF

RETURN (lRetVal)

/***
*
*   MemoUDF() - User function for MEMOEDIT() that implements
*       the following features normally not available
*       with MEMOEDIT()
*
*   (1) Changes cursor type depending on Ins key status
*   (2) Keeps Row/Col/Ins indicators at bottom of screen
*   (3) Maps F2 to special text
*
*/

STATIC FUNCTION MemoUDF( nMode, nRow, nCol )
LOCAL nKey := LASTKEY()    // Save last user keystroke.

IF nMode == ME_INIT        // Initialization mode.
   RETURN (ME_DEFAULT)
ELSEIF nMode == ME_IDLE    // User inactive, so ME_IDLE
                           // is passed to UDF.
   EditStat( nRow, nCol )  // Just update status.
ELSE
   DO CASE
      CASE nKey == K_INS   // Ins key was pressed.
         IF READINSERT()   // Read insert mode indicator.
            * "Overwrite" cursor
            SETCURSOR(SC_NORMAL)
         ELSE
            * "Insert" cursor
            SETCURSOR(SC_SPECIAL1)
         ENDIF
```

```
            EditStat( nRow, nCol )  // Update screen status.
            RETURN (K_INS)          // Toggle insert mode indicator.
         CASE nKey == K_F2          // F2: generate notice.
            KEYBOARD '(c) Copyright 1994, AMULET Consulting'
            RETURN (ME_DEFAULT)
         OTHERWISE
            RETURN (ME_DEFAULT)
      ENDCASE
ENDIF

RETURN (ME_DEFAULT)

/***
*
*   EditStat() - Function display Row/Col/Ins screen status
*       at bottom
*
*/

STATIC FUNCTION EditStat( nRow, nCol )
@ MAXROW(), 0 SAY 'Row: ' + STR(nRow,3) + ;
        '  Col: ' + STR(nCol,3) +             ;
        ' ' +                                 ;
        IF( SET( _SET_INSERT ), 'INSERT ', 'REPLACE' )
RETURN NIL
```

Converting Summer '87 Memo Fields

There exists one slight difference in the treatment of memo field data between the Summer '87 release and CA-Clipper. When entering or editing text inside a memo window, and the text wraps onto more than one line, a soft carriage return character CHR(141) is inserted after the last word in the current line. In this way, the resulting text may be stored serially in the .DBT file while remembering the line break sequences. In Summer '87, whenever a line is broken up in this manner, a *single space* is removed at the point where the soft carriage return is inserted. Later, if you then rejustify the text, each soft carriage return is replaced by a single space character. This process normally works fine, but in CA-Clipper the removal and insertion of spaces no longer occurs. Instead, only the soft carriage returns are inserted and removed when needed.

This presents somewhat of a problem when accessing memo field data originally entered in a Summer '87 application from a CA-Clipper program. Once you rejustify the text, all soft carriage returns are simply removed, but no space inserted, causing some words to run together. In order to correct this situation, we can use the STRTRAN() function.

STRTRAN(Employee->Resume, CHR(141)+CHR(10), ' ')

In this example, all soft carriage returns found in the Resume memo field of the current database record will be replaced with a soft carriage return followed by a space. This way when rejustification happens, the space is already present and the words won't run together.

1. Prepare a MEMOEDIT() user function and an associated main program that disables the Esc key while inside the memo window. Normally, Esc is pressed to exit the memo window.
2. Write a MEMOEDIT() user function and an associated main program to remap the functionality of the Esc, Ctrl+Y, Ctrl+W, and Ctrl+T control keys to F2, F3, F4, and F5, respectively. Note, that once the remapping has been established, the control keys should no longer function.

1. The required user function for this example turns out to be quite simple. Basically, we're letting all keystrokes except Esc pass through by returning ME_DEFAULT back to MEMOEDIT(). With Esc, however, we return ME_IGNORE, which indicates to MEMOEDIT() that the user function has determined that the key is meaningless and should be ignored, thus Esc is disabled.

```
#include 'memoedit.ch'
#include 'inkey.ch'

FUNCTION Main
USE Employee NEW
Employee->Resume := ;
   MEMOEDIT(Employee->Resume,10,10,20,70,.T.,'UserFunc')
DBCLOSEAREA()

RETURN NIL

FUNCTION UserFunc(nMode, nLine, nCol)
LOCAL nRetVal

IF nMode == ME_INIT
   nRetVal := ME_DEFAULT
ELSEIF LASTKEY() == K_ESC
   nRetVal := ME_IGNORE
ELSE
   nRetVal := ME_DEFAULT
ENDIF

RETURN nRetVal
```

2. As seen in this solution, the ReMap() user function first disables the existing control keys by recognizing them and then returning ME_IGNORE back to MEMOEDIT(). Next, whenever any of the new function keys is pressed by the user, it is trapped and

then remapped to its default counterparts; that is, when the user presses F2, Esc is passed back to `MEMOEDIT()`.

```
#include 'memoedit.ch'
#include 'inkey.ch'

FUNCTION Main
USE Employee NEW
Employee->Resume := ;
   MEMOEDIT(Employee->Resume,10,10,20,70,.T.,'ReMap')
DBCLOSEAREA()

RETURN NIL

FUNCTION ReMap(nMode, nLine, nCol)
LOCAL nRetVal, nKey := LASTKEY()

IF nMode == ME_INIT
   nRetVal := ME_DEFAULT
ELSEIF nKey == K_ESC .OR. nKey == K_CTRL_Y .OR. ;
   nKey == K_CTRL_W .OR. nKey == K_CTRL_T
   nRetVal := ME_IGNORE
ELSEIF nKey == K_F2    // Remap Esc to F2
   nRetVal := K_ESC
ELSEIF nKey == K_F3    // Remap Ctrl+Y to F3
   nRetVal := K_CTRL_Y
ELSEIF nKey == K_F4    // Remap Ctrl+W to F4
   nRetVal := K_CTRL_W
ELSEIF nKey == K_F5    // Remap Ctrl+T to F5
   nRetVal := K_CTRL_T
ELSE
   nRetVal := ME_DEFAULT
ENDIF

RETURN nRetVal
```

Summary

In this chapter we've learned the basics of how to utilize CA-Clipper's memo field technology. Although the methodology hasn't changed much since Summer '87, applying CA-Clipper's other new constructs make memo fields much more appealing. We've also seen how to access memo field data with the `MEMOEDIT()` built-in function. There are many more advanced possibilities available using the `MEMOEDIT()` user-function parameter.

In the final analysis, however, memo fields need some updated technology in CA-Clipper, as well as all other Xbase dialects. This situation, however, has opened up an tremendous opportunity for third party firms who have filled a technological gap with several fine products that make memo fields much more attractive.

Exercise

1. Write a MEMOEDIT() user function that contains a simple, user-definable "macro" feature in which the user can press the F2 function key to pop-up a window to allow the entry of three values. The first value should be inserted in the memo text when the user presses the F3 function key. Additionally, the second and third values should be inserted in the memo text when the user presses the F4 and F5 function keys, respectively. Consider Figure 9.4 for an idea of how this feature should appear to the user.

Answer

1. In our solution, we have a main program called Main() that invokes MEMOEDIT() and replaces the edited contents of the memo field back into the original field. The key to the solution is the CASE statement inside UserUDF() which "traps" the F2 function key and presents the special macro definition window. Function keys F3, F4, and F5 are also trapped and the current values are KEYBOARDed into the MEMOEDIT() buffer.

```
#include 'memoedit.ch'
#include 'inkey.ch'
#include 'box.ch'

FUNCTION Main

Scroll(); SetPos(0,0) // Clear screen before beginning.

USE Employee

@ 5, 1, 15, 79 BOX B_SINGLE
Employee->Resume := MEMOEDIT(Employee->Resume, 6, 2, 14, 78, .T., ;
                  'UserUDF')
```

Figure 9.4 In Exercise 1, the system displays this MEMOEDIT screen with simple macro facility.

```
RESUME: WILLIAM CLAPROTH

EDUCATION: Harvard Medical School, 1993
           Specialty - Cardiology

PERSONAL:  Married, spouse: Jolande Claproth

EMPLOYMENT: Auto Club of Ca┌─────────────────────────┐
                           │ F3: EMPLOYMENT:         │
                           │ F4: 01/01/93            │
                           │ F5: Reference checked   │
                           └─────────────────────────┘
```

```
      DBCLOSEAREA()
      RETURN NIL

      /***
      *
      * UserUDF() - MEMOEDIT() user function to implement simple
      * macro facility
      *
      */

      FUNCTION UserUDF(nMode, nRow, nCol)

      STATIC aMacroText     // STATIC so macros will live longer.
      LOCAL nKey := LASTKEY(), cScrSave
      MEMVAR GetList        // Needed since GET issued later.

      IF nMode == ME_INIT
         * Only initialize macro storage once, during startup
         aMacroText := { SPACE(20), SPACE(20), SPACE(20) }
         RETURN ME_DEFAULT
      ELSE
         DO CASE
            CASE nKey == K_ESC .OR. nKey == K_CTRL_END
            RETURN nKey

            CASE nKey == K_F2
               * Display macro definition dialog box
               cScrSave := SAVESCREEN(13, 29, 17, 56)
               @ 13, 29 CLEAR TO 17, 56
               @ 13, 29, 17, 56 BOX B_DOUBLE_SINGLE
               @ 14,30 SAY 'F3: ' GET aMacroText[1]
               @ 15,30 SAY 'F4: ' GET aMacroText[2]
               @ 16,30 SAY 'F5: ' GET aMacroText[3]
               READ
               RESTSCREEN(13, 29, 17, 56, cScrSave)

            CASE nKey == K_F3     // Deposit MACRO 1 text
               KEYBOARD TRIM(aMacroText[1])

            CASE nKey == K_F4     // Deposit MACRO 2 text
               KEYBOARD TRIM(aMacroText[2])

            CASE nKey == K_F5     // Deposit MACRO 3 text
               KEYBOARD TRIM(aMacroText[3])
         ENDCASE
      ENDIF
      RETURN ME_DEFAULT
```

Standard Classes

Object-Based Technology: General Terms ➤ 266

Classes and Objects: The Basics ➤ 268

Instance Variables ➤ 269

Method Functions ➤ 272

Sending Messages ➤ 275

Clipper's OOP Limitations ➤ 275

Clipper Class Extensions Products ➤ 276

Summary ➤ 276

Exercise ➤ 277

With this chapter we'll make our initial entry into the world of objects by introducing the built-in CA-Clipper facilities for providing the basis of object technology. This is not to imply that Clipper is an object-oriented programming (OOP) language; it is not. A true OOP language requires the ability to define new classes and class relationships, and all that goes along with this ability: inheritance, polymorphism, and encapsulation. Clipper is however, an *object-based* language in that it comes with four predefined (standard) classes that may be manipulated in a manner similar to classes in traditional OOP languages.

Clipper's standard classes are: Error, Get, TBrowse, and TBColumn. This chapter will not focus on a specific Clipper class, but rather present the basics of how classes and objects are used in the current release of the compiler. Moreover, we'll be setting the stage for Chapter 11, which pertains to the use of the TBrowse and TBColumn classes. We need to now become acquainted with basic OOP terminology as it applies to CA-Clipper.

After completing this chapter, you will have learned:

- How the CA-Clipper language represents the first Xbase dialect to turn to object orientation
- What it means to be an *object-based* language
- The basic OOP components of CA-Clipper including: predefined classes, exported instance variables, constructor functions, and method functions
- How to "send" a message to an object
- What the future holds for Clipper and the OOP "paradigm-shift," and how to get started right away with these new concepts

Object-Based Technology: General Terms

What does it mean to be object based? The answer is found in an investigation of the underlying philosophy of several major ingredients of CA-Clipper. As we've seen in previous chapters, the Clipper language made bold steps in bringing about a "better way" of programming discipline. As hard as it was for many Summer '87 developers to accept these new ideas, the architectural basis for the improvements were sound and have survived the test of time. How does this apply to object technology? Let's see.

First, as previously mentioned, CA-Clipper has four standard classes. They are listed here along with a brief statement of their purpose:

Error class — This class provides for the creation and manipulation of objects containing information about run-time errors. ERROR.CH is a special header file for use with handling error objects. The purpose of the Error class is to provide for a means of custom handling of error conditions when they occur. Error objects do not have any method functions, only exported instance variables (terms we'll define shortly). When a run-time error happens, an Error object is constructed and then passed to the error handler block specified with the `ERRORBLOCK()` function. While the error handler is in control, the Error object may be interrogated to determine the cause of the error and appropriate actions taken.

Get class This class provides for the creation and manipulation of objects for interactive editing of database fields and/or memory variables. A Get object is a general purpose mechanism for editing data. Get objects are used to implement the commands that support full screen data entry: `@...GET` and `READ`. Get objects provide for the underlying support structure allowing for formatting data, editing data, cursor movement, as well as data validation.

TBrowse class This class provides for the creation and manipulation of objects used as the primary mechanism for browsing table-oriented data. TBrowse objects allow for the selection, formatting, and display of tabular data. A TBrowse object depends on one or more TBColumn objects.

TBColumn class This class provides for the creation and manipulation of objects used in conjunction with TBrowse objects. A TBColumn object contains all the specifications required to define a single column of a TBrowse object. TBColumn objects do not have method functions, only exported instance variables.

Why has Clipper taken the road towards object orientation? The reason these predefined classes exist is to provide the ultimate in flexibility for the areas of the language they target. This flexibility becomes obvious when you examine the benefits that become available when using any one of these classes. Take the browse system for example. Prior to the TBrowse and TBColumn classes, Clipper used the built-in `DBEDIT()` function to present data in a tabular fashion to the user. Even with its user-function feature, `DBEDIT()` could never provide for the flexibility that the two browse system classes yield. In fact, as a demonstration of just how flexible the Browse system can be, consider that the `DBEDIT()` built-in function is implemented using TBrowse and TBColumn objects in CA-Clipper.

Other Xbase dialects provided increased browsing power by introducing additional command syntax, a much more cluttered approach, resulting in longer, dialect specific constructs (as an example, take a look at dBASE IV's

BROWSE command definition with its numerous clauses). Clipper's object approach is much more elegant, relying upon one of the primary tenets of object technology: *reduce complexity* in program design by re-using commonly needed objects.

Probably the most important reason, however, that the Clipper architecture took a turn towards object technology was to pave a way towards the future. Object-oriented programming has taken the C world by storm with numerous C++ compilers and associated class libraries now available. Clipper, being the first in the Xbase world to move towards object technology has gained much respect in mainstream programming circles because of this direction. Note that all of the major Xbase vendors have made firm commitments to also include objects, making the Clipper move all the more insightful.

In this section, we've set the stage for Clipper's object-based technology. Next, let's look at a subset of OOP concepts that apply to what is currently available in Clipper.

Classes and Objects: The Basics

In order to utilize any of Clipper's standard classes, you must first construct an object of the class in question. This is called *instantiation* of the class, which yields an *object*. In the OOP world, the process of creating an object is performed by use of a special *constructor function* (we'll talk more about class method functions a bit later). Each of the four Clipper classes has at least one built-in constructor.

Once you have constructed an object of a particular class (multiple objects can then be created of a single class) you may manipulate it using instance variables and method functions (although the Error and TBColumn classes have no method functions). It is the interaction of these variables and functions that provide for this flexibility.

Here is a list of all currently available constructor functions:

```
TBrowseNew()     TBrowse class constructor
TBrowseDB()      TBrowse class constructor
TBColumnNew()    TBColumn class constructor
GetNew()         Get class constructor
ErrorNew()       Error class constructor
```

Whenever any of the above constructors is called, a new object (often called an instance of the class) of that class is created along with its own copy of instance variables defined for the class. You can then manipulate the object by calling a method function or assigning new values to instance variables.

Here are examples of using a constructor to build a new object:

```
LOCAL oNewBrowse, oNewColumn
```

```
* Use one of the TBrowse class's constructors
oNewBrowse := TBrowseDB(10, 10, 20, 60)
oNewColumn := TBColumnNew("Customer Name", {|| cname})
```

> **Note** The use of Hungarian notation dictates that the "o" data type prefix be added to each memory variable containing an object as its value.

Instance Variables

Once a given class has been instantiated with a new object of that class created, the object automatically has a unique set of *instance variables* initialized to default values. The term *exported instance variables* simply refers to those variables that are accessible to program use. This distinction is more pertinent to OOP languages, where user-defined classes are possible. For our discussion, exported and non-exported instance variables are virtually the same.

Instance variables are accessible in two ways. Some instance variables are assignable and others are not. For those that are not assignable, their values may only be examined and used elsewhere in the program. Assignable instance variables, however, allow their values to be changed from within a program, thus affecting the manner in which the object functions. You may not simply use the := assignment operator to give an instance variable a new value. Instead you must use the *send operator* (:) for this purpose.

The syntax for accessing the value of an instance variable is:

```
<ObjectName>:<InstanceVariableName>
```

And, the syntax for assigning a new value to an assignable exported instance variable is:

```
<ObjectName>:<InstanceVariableName> := <NewValue>
```

Here are examples of accessing instance variables:

```
LOCAL nLastRow

* Save bottom screen row used for the TBrowse object
nLastRow := oBrowser:nBottom

* Assign new value to TBColumn instance variable "block"
oColumn:block := {|| RECNO()}
```

Bear in mind that the names for all instance variables are predefined and cannot be changed. Also, new instance variables cannot be created in the current Clipper release. Instance variables normally have a certain data type associated with them. From the previous example, the `nBottom` instance variable requires a Numeric, whereas, `block` requires a Code Block. We assume that the objects `oBrowser` and `oColumn` have been previously created with an appropriate constructor.

> **Note** Each class also has an assignable instance variable named `cargo` that can contain user-defined data of any type. `Cargo` is meant to be used to store arbitrary information to be attached to an object and later retrieved.

The set of instance variables for an object persists as long as the object exists. Remember that since multiple instances (objects) of the same class may exist, this means that multiple and unique sets of instance variable may also exist.

Table 10.1 lists the collection of exported instance variables for each CA-Clipper predefined class along with a brief description of their purpose.

Table 10.1 Exported Instance Variables

ERROR CLASS

`args`	Array: containing function or operator arguments when an argument error occurs
`canDefault`	Logical: indicates whether or not default recovery is available for the error condition
`canRetry`	Logical: indicates whether or not a retry of the operation causing the error is possible
`canSubstitute`	Logical: indicates if a new result can be substituted for the operation causing the error
`cargo`	May contain a value of any type that shall be unused by the Error system; user-definable variable
`description`	Character: description of the error condition
`filename`	Character: filename used to open the file associated with the error
`genCode`	Numeric: Clipper error code number
`operation`	Character: description of the failed operation
`osCode`	Numeric: operating system error code number
`severity`	Numeric: severity indicator for error condition
`subCode`	Numeric: subsystem-specific error code number
`subSystem`	Character: description of the subsystem generating the error
`tries`	Numeric: number of times the failed operation has been attempted

(continued)

Table 10.1 Exported Instance Variables (Continued)

GET CLASS

badDate	Logical: indicates if the editing buffer contains an invalid date
block	Code Block: associates Get object with a variable
buffer	Character: defines the editing buffer used by the Get object
cargo	May contain a value of any type that shall be unused by the Get system; user-definable variable
changed	Logical: indicates whether the Get:buffer has changed
col	Numeric: column number where Get is displayed
colorSpec	Character: color string for Get object
decPos	Numeric: decimal point position within the editing buffer
exitState	Numeric: method by which the Get object was exited
hasFocus	Logical: indicates whether or not the Get object has input focus
name	Character: Get variable name
original	Contains the original value of the Get object
picture	Character: PICTURE string for Get object
pos	Numeric: current cursor position within the editing buffer
postBlock	Code block: validates a newly entered value
preBlock	Code block: decides if editing is permitted
reader	Code block: affects READ behavior of a Get object
rejected	Logical: indicates if last character specified by Get:insert/Get:overStrike character was rejected
row	Numeric: Get row number
subscript	Numeric/Array: information about array Get objects
type	Character: Get variable data type
typeOut	Logical: indicates attempt to move the cursor out of editing buffer

TBROWSE CLASS

autoLite	Logical: controls highlighting
cargo	May contain a value of any type that shall be unused by the Browse system; user-definable variable
colCount	Numeric: number of browse columns
colorSpec	Character: color string for TBrowse object
colPos	Numeric: column position of browse cursor
colSep	Character: column separator character
freeze	Numeric: number of columns to freeze on left side of display
goBottomBlock	Code block: executed in response to the TBrowse:goBottom() method function

(continued)

Table 10.1 Exported Instance Variables (Continued)

`goTopBlock`	Code block: executed in response to the `TBrowse:goTop()` method function
`headSep`	Character: heading separator character for TBColumn objects
`hitBottom`	Logical: indicates attempt to go past end of available data
`hitTop`	Logical: indicates attempt to go past beginning of available data
`leftVisible`	Numeric: position of left-most unfrozen column in display
`nBottom`	Numeric: bottom row number for the TBrowse display
`nLeft`	Numeric: left-most column for the TBrowse display
`nRight`	Numeric: right-most column for the TBrowse display
`nTop`	Numeric: top row number for the TBrowse display
`rightVisible`	Numeric: position of right-most unfrozen column in display
`rowCount`	Numeric: number of rows visible in the TBrowse display
`rowPos`	Numeric: row position of browse cursor
`skipBlock`	Code block: used to reposition within the data source
`stable`	Logical: indicates if the TBrowse object is stable
TBCOLUMN CLASS	
`block`	Code block: used to retrieve data for the column
`cargo`	May contain a value of any type that shall be unused by the Browse system; user-definable variable
`colorBlock`	Code block: used to determine color of data items
`colSep`	Character: column separator character
`defColor`	Array: of numeric indexes into the color table in the TBrowse object
`footing`	Character: column footing
`footSep`	Character: footing separator character
`heading`	Character: column heading
`headSep`	Character: heading separator character
`width`	Numeric: column display width

Method Functions

A *method function* enables operations to be defined for an object. For example, the `right()` method defined for the `TBrowse` class of objects causes the browse cursor to move right one column of data. As stated before, only the `TBrowse` and `Get` classes have methods. This is not to say you can't affect the operation of the `Error` and `TBColumn` classes, since you can modify any assignable exported instance variables defined for these classes to achieve different behavior.

Using OOP jargon, a method is the operation performed in response to a message *sent* to the object. For those of us using procedural programming terminology, we would speak of "the operation performed in response to a function call."

The `TBrowse` class contains many predefined method functions that affect the manner in which the browse operates and the way the data is displayed. These methods fall into two categories: cursor movement (allowing for operations such as: up/down, page up/down, top, bottom, pan, etc.) and miscellaneous methods (such as adding a column, stabilize, etc.).

The `Get` class has numerous exported method functions in the following groups: state change methods, cursor movement methods, editing methods, and text entry methods.

Tables 10.2 and 10.3 list the collection of exported method functions for each CA-Clipper predefined class.

Table 10.2   Exported Method Functions for the Get Class

GET CLASS

State Change Methods

`assign()`	Assigns the editing buffer contents to the Get variable
`colorDisp()`	Changes a Get object's color and then redisplays it
`display()`	Displays the Get on the screen
`killFocus()`	Takes input focus away from the Get object
`reset()`	Resets the internal state information of the Get
`setFocus()`	Gives input focus to the Get object
`undo()`	Sets the Get variable back to `Get:original`
`updateBuffer()`	Updates the editing buffer and redisplays the Get
`varGet()`	Returns the current value of the Get variable
`varPut()`	Sets the Get variable to the passed value

Cursor Movement Methods

`end()`	Moves the cursor to the right-most buffer position
`home()`	Moves the cursor to the left-most buffer position
`left()`	Moves the cursor left one character
`right()`	Moves the cursor right one character
`toDecPos()`	Moves the cursor to the immediate right of the decimal point position
`wordLeft()`	Moves the cursor left one word
`wordRight()`	Moves the cursor right one word

(continued)

Table 10.2 Exported Method Functions for the Get Class (Continued)

Editing Methods

`backspace()`	Moves the cursor to the left and deletes one character
`delLeft()`	Deletes the character to the left of the cursor
`delRight()`	Deletes the character to the right of the cursor
`delWordLeft()`	Deletes the word to the left of the cursor
`delWordRight()`	Deletes the word to the right of the cursor

Text Entry Methods

`insert()`	Inserts characters into the editing buffer
`overStrike()`	Overstrikes characters in the editing buffer

Table 10.3 Exported Method Functions for the TBrowse Class

TBROWSE CLASS

Cursor Movement Methods

`down()`	Moves the cursor down one row
`end()`	Moves the cursor to the right-most visible data column
`goBottom()`	Repositions the data source to the logical end-of-file
`goTop()`	Repositions the data source to the logical beginning-of-file
`home()`	Moves the cursor to the left-most visible data column
`left()`	Moves the cursor left one column
`pageDown()`	Repositions the data source downward
`pageUp()`	Repositions the data source upward
`panEnd()`	Moves the cursor to the right-most data column
`panHome()`	Moves the cursor to the left-most visible data column
`panLeft()`	Pans left without changing the cursor position
`panRight()`	Pans right without changing the cursor position
`right()`	Moves the cursor right one column
`up()`	Moves the cursor up one row

Miscellaneous Methods

`addColumn()`	Adds a TBColumn object to the TBrowse object
`colorRect()`	Alters the color of a rectangular group of cells
`colWidth()`	Returns the display width of a particular column
`configure()`	Reconfigures the internal settings of the TBrowse object
`deHilite()`	De-highlights the current cell

(continued)

Table 10.3 Exported Method Functions for the TBrowse Class (Continued)

`delColumn()`	Deletes a column object from a browse
`forceStable()`	Performs a complete stabilization of the TBrowse object
`getColumn()`	Gets a specific TBColumn object
`hilite()`	Highlights the current cell
`insColumn()`	Inserts a column object in a browse
`invalidate()`	Forces redraw during next stabilization
`refreshAll()`	Causes all data to be refreshed during the next stabilize
`refreshCurrent()`	Causes the current row to be refreshed on next stabilize
`setColumn()`	Replaces one TBColumn object with another
`stabilize()`	Performs incremental stabilization

Sending Messages

Sending a message is the way you request an object to perform a particular method. In procedural terms, this process is equivalent to a function call. In Clipper, you send a message via the *send* operator. The general syntax for sending a message to an object is

```
<ObjectName>:<Message>[(<ParmList>)]
```

where `<Message>` is the name of the message you wish to send to the object, specifically the name of the method function that causes an operation to be performed. Here is an example of sending a message to an object:

```
oBrowser:refreshAll() // Send the refreshAll() message
                      // to the object oBrowser
```

The OOP concept of *polymorphism* enters here since, for example, the `end()` method function is defined for both the `Get` and `TBrowse` classes. Polymorphism provides for the ability of objects of different classes to respond to the same message with different results. In the case of the `end()` method, entirely different things happen when this method is sent to a Get object versus a TBrowse object.

Clipper's OOP Limitations

If all of these OOP concepts apply to the current CA-Clipper release, you might wonder why Clipper isn't viewed as an OOP language? Basically, the reason lies in the fact that with the current CA-Clipper release you cannot define your own classes and use the OOP concepts normally associated with class definition and manipulation such as inheritance, polymorphism, and encapsulation. For now, we'll have to be satisfied with the "object-based" classification. Being object based has, however, indirectly done much for Clipper developers in that it has paved a path towards a new application development paradigm that has proven to yield many benefits as projects grow in magnitude.

CA-Clipper programmers represent the first group of Xbase enthusiasts to embrace the OOP paradigm, albeit in a limited fashion, given the limitations inherent in the current release. Application developers may, however, begin to use Clipper from a strictly OOP perspective and introduce strictly OOP concepts immediately. In fact, Clipper++ (denoting a language architecture parallel to the popular C++) is a term finding common use by some developers to describe "Clipper with Objects." Let's see how this is possible.

Clipper Class Extensions Products

Although not currently available from Computer Associates, Inc., CA-Clipper can be used in a strictly OOP fashion. This is possible through the use of any one of several object extension products that alter Clipper's current handling of objects to include *class definition*. The most notable of these products is Class(y) from ObjecTech, Inc. This product is basically a replacement for portions of CLIPPER.LIB (Clipper's primary link library) that handles message communication to and from objects, thus providing for user-created classes. Class(y) also provides for additional syntax that adheres to strict OOP guidelines, making "Clipper++" a reality now. This reality has manifested itself in a number of rather elegant user-interface "class libraries" based around Class(y) that allow for the building of event-driven, windows-like, GUI (graphical user interface) software applications.

If you are serious about becoming more fluent in object-oriented concepts, it is highly recommended that you get started with an OOP extension product such as Class(y) and begin reading one of many good books available on the subject that provide for a migration path towards this new programming paradigm. Indeed, there is a great deal of learning (or should we say "unlearning") that must accompany the pursuit of object orientation. This is due to the fact that more than a new programming direction must be learned. In addition, there is *object-oriented analysis* (OOA) and *object-oriented design* (OOD), which precede the actual coding of the application.

Summary

The future of CA-Clipper is now known through the introduction of a new product called Visual Objects for Clipper (previously known as Aspen from Nantucket Corp.) by Computer Associates, Inc. Although still under development VO-Clipper has been previewed publicly and numerous technical sessions have taken place describing its various components. One thing that becomes obvious with an investigation of VO is the serious OOP slant of the product. Consequently, it is a real good time to get started and prepare yourself for the future.

In the next chapter, we'll look at two of Clipper's predefined classes, `TBrowse` and `TBColumn` and see how to begin to apply some of the concepts we've talked about.

Exercise

1. Based on the concepts set forth in this chapter and while officially not knowing the definition and use of the OOP term *inheritance*, explain why you think it would be useful to be able to define new classes based upon the characteristics of existing classes, for example, defining a new class `TBrowse1M` based on the `TBrowse` class for implementing "one-to-many" browses.

Answer

1. As the complexity of software for contemporary applications continues to rise, developers are faced with making tough decisions with regard to combating the side effects of this complexity: higher development costs, longer development cycles, difficult maintenance, etc. In the past few years, object-oriented techniques have addressed these problems. By creating a generic set of base classes from which new functionality may be added later as new needs arise, the developer is saved from reinventing the world.

   Current procedural programmers may point out that well constructed libraries that allow you to change a few things here and there to suit new requirements exist today. This is true, but with OOP you don't have to change anything. The concept of inheritance lets you take existing functionality and allow it to trickle down to an application, while adding new behaviors and data to address more specific requirements and problems.

   For the case mentioned in this exercise, we could take the existing `TBrowse` and `TBcolumn` classes defined in CA-Clipper and inherit their characteristics to form a subclass that deals specifically with one-to-many browses. Here the data (instance variables) and behaviors (method functions) designed for generic data browsing would be inherited by the new subclass. At the same time, new data and behaviors would be added to tailor the class in order to solve a more specific problem. The point is that no code will need to be changed, just supplemented.

TBrowse

The TBrowse and TBColumn Classes ➤ 280

TBrowse Requirements ➤ 281

A Complete TBrowse ➤ 287

Speeding Up a TBrowse ➤ 289

Customizing a TBrowse ➤ 290

Array Browsing ➤ 293

Browsing Text Files ➤ 298

Other Topics ➤ 300

Summary ➤ 300

Exercise ➤ 300

This chapter applies the general object-based concepts defined in Chapter 10 by introducing the use and application of two CA-Clipper predefined classes: TBrowse and TBColumn. These classes have made obsolete Clipper's previous database browsing technology: DBEDIT(). This built-in function can still be used (in the manual it is listed as a Summer '87 compatibility function) but there is little reason to do so because CA-Clipper's current data browsing facilities far surpass anything previously in this language or any other Xbase dialect. The key here is the object-oriented direction that took place in enhancing the browsing technology with the Clipper 5 release.

We'll use the term *TBrowse* to encompass Clipper's browsing technology and it is understood that this includes both the TBrowse and TBColumn classes. Moreover, we understand that TBrowse can be used to browse more than just information coming from a database; any tabular data can be included in this group. For instance, arrays and DOS text files can be browsed using TBrowse (we'll see some of this later in this chapter).

After completing this chapter, you will have learned:

- Techniques for utilizing the object based technology inherent in CA-Clipper by using classes, objects, instance variables, constructor functions, method functions, and techniques for sending messages to objects
- All the basic ingredients of building a simple database browsing facility in the CA-Clipper language
- How to integrate the TBrowse and TBColumn predefined classes and make them work together
- Ways to use TBrowse to browse diverse data sources, such as arrays and DOS text files
- Techniques for customizing a TBrowse in order to achieve unique results

The TBrowse and TBColumn Classes

As we've said when introducing this chapter, in order to browse tabular data in CA-Clipper, the TBrowse and TBColumn predefined classes must be used. We use the TBrowse class to provide for the creation and manipulation of objects used as the primary mechanism for browsing table oriented data. Browsing in this sense means allowing for the selection, formatting, and display of tabular data.

A TBrowse object depends on one or more TBColumn objects. We use the TBColumn class to provide for the creation and manipulation of objects used in conjunction with TBrowse objects. A TBColumn object contains all the specifications required to define a single column of a TBrowse object.

Both classes have constructor functions used to create an instance, or object, of each class. For TBrowse there is the `TBrowseNew()` and `TBrowseDB()` constructors and for TBColumn there is `TBColumnNew()`.

In addition, there is a set of exported instance variables for both classes. Table 10.1 in Chapter 10 summarizes these variables including the variable's name, data type, and whether it's assignable or not. Think of the word *exported* to mean visible to the programmer for the purpose of assigning new values or accessing its value. In true OOP languages where you can create your own classes, *non-exported* instance variables become possible. In this case, the variables are used only internally by an object.

In the case of TBrowse, there are also several method functions available (TBColumn does not have any method functions). The TBrowse method functions are shown in Table 10.2 (in Chapter 10) along with a description of their purpose and return value.

TBrowse Requirements

Admittedly, generating even the most simple database browsing routine in CA-Clipper takes some effort, but it really is simple if you break the process down into component parts. We therefore define the four basic steps in programming a TBrowse:

1. Create a TBrowse object using either the TBrowseNew() or TBrowseDB() constructors.

2. Create multiple TBColumn objects, one for each column in the browse using the TBColumnNew() constructor.

3. Inform the TBrowse object of the columns in the browse by sending the addColumn() message for each TBColumn object previously created.

4. Set up the primary browse loop to display the data and handle keystroke exceptions.

For any browse to take place, you must first create at least one TBrowse and TBColumn object. The TBrowse object controls the browse in general and each TBColumn object is responsible for controlling a particular column of the display. Because of the nature of tabular data, a browse normally consists of a single TBrowse object and several TBColumn objects. To illustrate this concept, consider the following structure for the database EMPLOYEE.DBF:

Field Name	Field Type	Field Length	Decimal Places
Last	C	20	
First	C	15	
MI	C	C	

(continued)

Field Name	Field Type	Field Length	Decimal Places
Addr1	C	25	
Addr2	C	25	
City	C	15	
State	C	2	
ZIP	C	10	
HomePh	C	13	
WorkExt	C	5	
HireDate	D	8	
MoSal	N	7	2
FullPart	L	1	

Let's employ the steps in creating some sample code to do a browse of this database.

Step 1: Create a TBrowse Object

As with any object-oriented (or in our case, object-based) programming language, we must first instantiate the class, yielding an object from which we may gain functionality. Our immediate desire centers around the creation of a TBrowse object that will be the basis of the database browse. We do this by invoking either the TBrowseDB() or TBrowseNew() constructor functions. The syntax for calling these two constructors is

```
TBrowseDB( <nTop>, <nLeft>, <nBottom>, <nRight> ) –> oTBrowse
```

and

```
TBrowseNew( <nTop>, <nLeft>, <nBottom>, <nRight> ) –> oTBrowse
```

In both cases, we get a new TBrowse object. The difference between the constructors lies in their generality for browsing. You use TBrowseDB() when you need to browse database files, whereas TBrowseNew() doesn't make any assumptions about the data source of the browse. TBrowseDB() assigns default code blocks to the goBottomBlock, goTopBlock, and skipBlock instance variables, which are tailored for positioning in a database file. These defaults save you much time, since without them, you would have to provide TBrowse with this functionality yourself. We'll see a bit later how you go about developing these blocks.

In the case of both constructors, the passed calling parameters are mapped to similarly named instance variables in the newly created object. These instance variables are nTop, nLeft, nBottom, and nRight.

As an example of creating a TBrowse object for database browsing, let's say we wish to establish a browse for only the `Last`, `First`, `HireDate`, and `MoSal` fields of the EMPLOYEE database. The code required in this case becomes:

```
LOCAL oEmpBrowse, oColumn1, oColumn2, oColumn3, oColumn4
oEmpBrowse := TBrowseDB(5, 10, 20, 70)
```

Here, the `TBrowseDB()` constructor builds an instance (an object) of the `TBrowse` class and assigns it to a memory variable `oEmpBrowse`. We also define four `LOCAL` variables for storing new TBColumn objects created next in Step 2.

Once a TBrowse object has been created, you can assign some of its exported variables as appropriate in order to customize the operation of the browse.

Step 2: Create Multiple TBColumn Objects

Next, we must instantiate the `TBColumn` class once for each column in the browse, thus creating multiple TBColumn objects. To do this we must call the `TBColumnNew()` constructor function. The general form for calling this function is

```
TBColumnNew(<cHeading>, <bBlock>) --> oTBColumn
```

where `TBColumnNew()` returns a new TBColumn object `oTBColumn` using the specified column heading text `<cHeading>` and data retrieval code block `<bBlock>`. The heading text appears directly above the column's data when the browse is displayed. Notice the flexibility that using a code block for data retrieval purposes affords. Remember that any sequence of expressions may be embedded in a code block, including a call to a UDF. This implies that the data that populates a particular column in a browse can be arbitrarily complex.

Once a TBColumn object has been created, its exported instance variables can then be assigned. All TBColumn instance variables are assignable.

Here is the code to perform Step 2 for our example thus far:

```
oColumn1:=TBColumnNew('Last Name',{||Employee->Last})
oColumn2:=TBColumnNew('First Name',{||Employee->First})
oColumn3:=TBColumnNew('Hire Date',{||Employee->HireDate})
oColumn4:=TBColumnNew('Salary',{||Employee->MoSal})
```

This code creates four new TBColumn objects. The data retrieval blocks simply tell `TBColumn` in each case to get the field's contents and place it in the column.

At this point, the TBColumn objects are not yet connected to the TBrowse object. This will be done in Step 3. Note that depending on how many TBColumn objects are needed, you may wish to generalize the code by saving the objects in an array. Remember, CA-Clipper arrays can contain values of any type, including objects.

Step 3: Inform the TBrowse Object

Next, we need to inform the TBrowse object of the TBColumn object(s) just created. The general method of doing this is:

```
oTBrowse:addColumn(oTBColumn)
```

For some actual code, consider the following:

```
oEmpBrowse:addColumn(oColumn1)
oEmpBrowse:addColumn(oColumn2)
oEmpBrowse:addColumn(oColumn3)
oEmpBrowse:addColumn(oColumn4)
```

Using OOP jargon, each of the above syntax is read: "send the addColumn message to the oEmpBrowse object". Specifically, we are using the `addColumn()` method function to attach each TBColumn object with the TBrowse object. In doing so four times, each with a different TBColumn object, we can create a four column browse. If you save the objects in an array, a `FOR/NEXT` loop may be helpful here to avoid repetition of code.

As a generalization of the previous sample code, if you need all fields of the database included in the browse, the following UDF may prove useful:

```
/***
*
*   BrowseAll(<oBrowse>) -> oBrowse
*
*   Send addColumn() message to passed TBrowse object for
*   each field of currently selected database
*
*/

FUNCTION BrowseAll(oBrowse)
LOCAL nFld, oColumn

FOR nFld := 1 TO FCOUNT()
   /* Create TBColumn object for current field. Column heading shall
      be field name and retrieval block is {|| fieldname} */
   oColumn := TBColumnNew(FIELDNAME(nFld), ;
       FIELDBLOCK(FIELDNAME(nFld), SELECT()))
   oBrowse:addColumn(oColumn)
NEXT
RETURN (oBrowse) // Return newly "informed" object.
```

`BrowseAll()` assumes that the database is open and selected and that the TBrowse object already exists. The `FOR/NEXT` loop goes through each field of the database via the `FCOUNT()` built-in function that returns a numeric value indicating the number of fields in the current database. Since we are using `TBColumnNew()` to construct the new TBColumn object, we must establish the appropriate parameters. First, using the `FIELDNAME()` built-in function, which returns a Character value containing the field name of the specified field number, we define the heading text for the browse column. Next, we use `FIELDBLOCK()` to build the required data retrieval block. Finally, the `addColumn` message is sent to the browse object, passing to it multiple TBColumn objects. Notice that the TBColumn objects are never saved, just sent to the TBrowse object.

One last note about Step 3: this is a good place to tell the TBrowse basic things about the browse. Namely, you can specify what separator characters to use, what colors you want, and the like. To do this, you may assign new values to the appropriate exported `TBrowse` exported instance variables. You might find it helpful to review the table in Chapter 10 (Table 10.2) describing these instance variables.

Step 4: Establish the Primary TBrowse Loop

The last step, and probably the most crucial, requires you to build a loop structure to control the operation of the browse. This loop must perform several tasks. Let's define each now:

- First we must *stabilize* the browse. The process of stabilization involves sending the `stabilize()` message to a TBrowse object. This message tells the object to display current information on the screen. When you first create a TBrowse object, nothing is displayed on the screen. You must invoke the `stabilize()` method function which displays the headers. If you send the `stabilize()` message again, another row of the browse appears. This process proceeds until everything is displayed. The `stabilize()` method returns a .T. value when there is more to display and .F. when there is nothing left to display. The most basic form of stabilization is to enclose `stabilize()` in a tight loop as in:

    ```
    WHILE !oEmpBrowse:stabilize()
    END
    ```

    This stabilization loop simply updates the screen and when done, resumes inside the primary loop. Another way to perform stabilization is to use the `forceStable()` method as in:

    ```
    oEmpBrowse:forceStable()
    ```

- The second task is to get a keystroke from the user. A browse does no good unless we allow the user to move around in the data once we present the information. We need to trap keystrokes such as Up Arrow, Home, Escape, PgDn, etc. This task is achieved with the INKEY(0) function call as in:

```
nKey := INKEY(0)    // Get a keystroke.
```

- Next, we must act upon the entered keystroke, telling the browse how to respond to specific user requests. For example, if the user presses the Down Arrow key, we need to tell TBrowse what to do. Since we normally need to handle a wide variety of keystrokes, the usual way to satisfy this task is to construct one long DO CASE/ENDCASE statement in which each case identifies a keystroke (usually you pick them from the INKEY.CH header file). For example, the following code only allows the user to move up and down through records:

```
DO CASE
   CASE nKey == K_UP        // Up Arrow key.
      oEmpBrowse:up()       // Send up() message.

   CASE nKey == K_DOWN      // Down Arrow key.
      oEmpBrowse:down()     // Send down() message.
ENDCASE
```

We trap both the Up Arrow and Down Arrow keys in the CASE. When a key is recognized, we simply send the appropriate message to the TBrowse object. Changes to the browse will then be displayed during the next stabilization.

- The last step in the loop is to repeat everything inside the primary loop until an exit is requested by the user—the Esc key works well for this purpose.

1. Write the code to create a new TBColumn object that would display the Employee->MoSal field values in a column with leading dollar signs.

    1. In order to affect the manner in which a Numeric value appears in a column of a TBrowse, we would need to tell the TBColumn object how to do so by customizing the data retrieval code block parameter. Inside the block, we can use the built-in TRANSFORM() function to format the number.

        ```
        oColumn := TBColumnNew( 'MoSal', ;
            {|| TRANSFORM(Employee->MoSal, '$9,999.99')})
        ```

A Complete TBrowse

Now let's see one example that implements all four steps just defined. The following code segment shows a modular form of a primary TBrowse loop. Stabilization is done with a UDF call to `GenStab()`. This way, you can do any kind of stabilization. Next, we grab a keystroke and arbitrarily choose Esc to mean exit. Finally, we do a call to another UDF, `GenKey()`, which becomes a generic keystroke handler.

```
#define TRUE .T.
#define NUM_COLS 4
#include 'inkey.ch'

FUNCTION Main
LOCAL oEmpBrowse, aColObjects[NUM_COLS]
LOCAL nKey
LOCAL cScrSave, nCnt

USE Employee NEW
/* Use constructor function to create 1 TBrowse object */
oEmpBrowse := TBrowseDB( 5, 10, 20, 70 )

/* Use constructor function to create 4 new TBColumn objects */
aColObjects[1] := TBColumnNew('Last Name',   ;
         {|| Employee->Last} )
aColObjects[2] := TBColumnNew('First Name',  ;
         {|| Employee->First} )
aColObjects[3] := TBColumnNew('Hire Date',   ;
         {|| Employee->HireDate} )
aColObjects[4] := TBColumnNew('Salary' ,     ;
         {|| Employee->MoSal} )

/* Tell TBrowse object about the TBColumn objects */
FOR nCnt := 1 TO LEN(aColObjects)
   oEmpBrowse:addColumn(aColObjects[nCnt])
NEXT

/* Customize TBrowse object with separators */
oEmpBrowse:headSep := CHR(196)
oEmpBrowse:colSep  := CHR(179)

/* Save screen contents where browse will appear */
cScrSave := SAVESCREEN( 5, 10, 20, 70 )

/* Begin primary TBrowse loop */
WHILE TRUE
```

```
      GenStab(oEmpBrowse)          // Perform generic stabilization.
      nKey := INKEY(0)             // Get a keystroke.
      IF nKey == K_ESC             // Esc is a good exit key.
        EXIT
      ELSE
        GenKey(oEmpBrowse, nKey)   // Perform generic key handling.
      ENDIF
END
RESTSCREEN( 5, 10, 20, 70, cScrSave)

RETURN NIL

/***
 *
 * GenStab(<oTBObject>) -> NIL
 *
 */

FUNCTION GenStab( oTBObject )

WHILE !oTBObject:stabilize()
END

RETURN NIL

/***
 *
 * GenKey(<oTBObject>, <nKey> ) -> NIL
 *
 */

FUNCTION GenKey(oTBObject, nKey)

DO CASE
   CASE nKey == K_UP
     oTBObject:up()

   CASE nKey == K_DOWN
     oTBObject:down()

   CASE nKey == K_PGUP
     oTBObject:pageUp()

   CASE nKey == K_PGDN
     oTBObject:pageDown()

   CASE nKey == K_LEFT
     oTBObject:left()
```

```
      CASE nKey == K_RIGHT
         oTBObject:right()
   ENDCASE

RETURN NIL
```

After all this work we've achieved a simple browse, something done by one command in other Xbase dialects. Yes, this is true, but with the object orientation surrounding database browsing in CA-Clipper, we now have the framework to do much more than a complex browse command syntax can do in other languages. With this example, we're sure you get a feeling for how customizable browsing with TBrowse and TBColumn can be!

Before we go on, we should say a few words about several housekeeping chores that need be fulfilled. First, unless you specify otherwise, TBrowse builds a browse on the screen in a very vanilla manner—basically you get raw data underneath the column headings you specified in the calls to TBColumnNew(). There are no boxes or borders drawn by default. Moreover, the prior screen contents are not saved. This is a task you must perform. The browse's color is drab, but you can also specify these.

Speeding Up a TBrowse

In the previous sections, the method for stabilization that we used was adequate for our purposes at the time, but now let's look at a more efficient approach. Many times, when perusing data in a browse, you may wish to scroll quickly through the data as you scan the data displayed. Instead of waiting for the entire browse screen to stabilize before a key is recognized as in

```
WHILE !oBrowser:stabilize()
END
```

we need an alternate method in order to let the user press a positioning key—PgUp or PgDn—and have the action take effect immediately. With the above stabilization loop, a PageDown request for example, won't take place until after stabilization completes. Consider the alternate solution:

```
#include 'inkey.ch'
#define TRUE .T.
LOCAL nKey

/* Begin primary TBrowse loop */
WHILE TRUE
   nKey := 0
   /* Stabilize TBrowse until done or user key */
   WHILE nKey == 0 .AND. !oBrowser:stable
```

```
    oBrowser:stabilize()
    nKey := INKEY()  // Poll keyboard for user key.
  END
  /* If user pressed Esc to get out of stabilize loop
     then it's time to quit */
  IF nKey == K_ESC
    EXIT
  ELSE
    /* Call generic keystroke handler */
    GenKey( oBrowser, nKey )
  ENDIF
END
```

The difference between this TBrowse loop and the prior one comes in the stabilization loop. This time, the `stabilize()` message is sent to the TBrowse object inside the loop. Plus, we use an `INKEY()` function, which checks to see if the user has pressed a key, to save a possible keystroke. Lastly, notice the logical expression in the WHILE/END statement. We continue to stabilize while no key was pressed and while the *stable* exported instance variable of the TBrowse object remains .F.

Don't get confused with

oBrowser:stable
versus
oBrowser:stabilize()

which admittedly seems, at first glance, very close in function. The first simply interrogates an instance variable for its value. No action is performed on the TBrowse object just by getting the value of an instance variable. The second, on the other hand, uses a method function to affect the object.

Customizing a TBrowse

The flexible nature of data browsing in CA-Clipper, with its object-based technology promotes the ability to customize browsing operations in many very free-form ways. In this section, we'll consider a few topics dealing with making your TBrowses more hospitable.

Formatting Data

One addition that might come to mind concerns formatting data appearing in a TBColumn object. Say you have dollar amount numeric data in a column and you wish to format it appropriately. In this case, the built-in `TRANSFORM()` function comes in handy as in:

```
oColumn := TBColumnNew( 'Salary', ;
    {|| TRANSFORM(Employee->Salary, '99,999.99')})
```

Remember, the flexibility of code blocks allows you to embed built-in functions in this manner. In this case, as the TBColumn object uses the code block to populate the browse column with data, the `Salary` field contents pass through `TRANSFORM()` yielding a formatted number.

Freezing Columns

In a previous example, when we put together a sample TBrowse program, we assigned values to two TBrowse instance variables, `headSep` and `colSep`. We can further customize the browse by assigning other such variables. As another example, let's freeze a column in the browse window. To do this, you would assign a value to the `freeze` instance variable as in:

```
oBrowser:freeze := 1 // Freeze the first column.
```

Freezing a column is a useful user-interface technique in which a key database value, such as customer name, remains visible as you pan right through other data columns.

Using Color

If you're into pretty colors, the TBrowse instance variable `colorSpec` and TBColumn instance variables `colorBlock` and `defColor` will be of interest to you. Assigning standard color strings to these variables yields custom color combinations to give your TBrowse a polished look.

Limiting the Scope

Once you're browsing data, you'll need a way to limit the scope of the data presented. TBrowse is particularly well suited for doing custom filtering of data. The key components fall into three areas of movement: how to move to the top, how to move to the bottom, and how to move forward and backward through the records. Implementing these functions requires knowledge of the following TBrowse instance variables: `goTopBlock`, `goBottomBlock`, and `skipBlock`, respectively. As their names imply, all three of these instance variables contain a code block value. As we stated earlier, the `TBrowseDB()` constructor function creates defaults for each. For example, here are two code blocks equivalent to the default:

```
oBrowser:goTopBlock    := {|| DBGOTOP()}
oBrowser:goBottomBlock := {|| DBGOBOTTOM()}
```

Remembering back to *Chapter 8, Database Access Functions*, these code blocks are based on the built-in database functions, DBGOTOP() and DBGOBOTTOM().

The contents of the goTopBlock and goBottomBlock instance variables are used by TBrowse to position to the top and bottom, respectively, of the data being browsed. When the data is coming from a database, goTopBlock is equivalent to the GO TOP command and goBottomBlock is similar to GO BOTTOM. The beauty of CA-Clipper's browsing facility is that you define what it means to *go to the top of the data,* depending on what kind of data you happen to be browsing. If you're browsing an array, this concept has an entirely different meaning (go to the first element in the array). In OOP terms this capability is called *polymorphism*—responding to the same message in different ways depending on the characteristics of the object acted upon.

Once we have our custom goTopBlock and goBottomBlock code blocks ready, we must then attach them to the GenKey() UDF from the previous section. Just add the following lines to the CASE/ENDCASE statement:

```
CASE nKey == K_CTRL_PGUP
   oTBObject:goTop()    // Jump to top of data source.

CASE nKey == K_CTRL_PGDN
   oTBObject:goBottom() // Jump to bottom of data source.
```

If the user presses either Ctrl Pg Up/Dn the goTop() or goBottom() message is sent to the TBrowse object and the corresponding code block in goTopBlock or goBottomBlock is then performed.

The equivalent default for skipBlock, used to move forward and backward through the data source, is a bit more involved. In our next example, we see a generic *skipper function*:

```
/* Sample usage in the calling program */

oBrowser:skipBlock := {|nSkip| Skipper( nSkip )}

/***
*
*   Skipper(<nSkip>) -> nSkipped
*
*   Process database record movement requests from a TBrowse
*   object
*
*/
STATIC FUNCTION Skipper(nSkip)
LOCAL nSkipped := 0
```

```
  DO CASE
    /* 0 Skip amount */
    CASE nSkip == 0
      DBSKIP(0)    // Re-read current record.

    /* Process forward skip */
    CASE nSkip > 0
      WHILE nSkipped < nSkip .AND. !EOF()
        DBSKIP(FORWARD)
        IF !EOF()
          nSkipped++
        ENDIF
      END
      IF EOF()
        DBSKIP(BACKWARD)
      ENDIF

    /* Process backward skip */
    CASE nSkip < 0
      WHILE nSkipped > nSkip .AND. !BOF()
        DBSKIP(BACKWARD)
        IF !BOF()
          nSkipped--
        ENDIF
      END
  ENDCASE

RETURN nSkipped
```

Examining this sample skipper function verifies the level of customization that is possible. TBrowse calls `Skipper()` each time it needs to move forward or backward through the data source; this includes each time the stabilization process needs to traverse the database and whenever the `down()`, `up()`, `pageDown()`, or `pageUp()` messages are sent.

Array Browsing

Let's now turn our attention to browsing another type of data source. As alluded to before, we can use the flexible browsing technology of CA-Clipper to browse data other than that coming from a database file. When using TBrowse in this manner, you must customize the following areas in the TBrowse and TBColumn objects:

- The data selection code block `oCol:block` for the TBColumn object
- The `oBrowser:skipBlock` code block used by TBrowse for traversing the data source

- The `oBrowser:goTopBlock` code block used by TBrowse to jump to the top of the data source
- The `oBrowser:goBottomBlock` code block used by TBrowse to jump to the bottom of the data source

In this section, we'll consider arrays as an alternate data source (we'll limit the discussion to one-dimensional arrays). For example, suppose we have a ZIP code table loaded in an array. For test data, we can use the following code in `Main()` to generate a 100 element array:

```
#include 'inkey.ch'
#define TRUE .T.

FUNCTION Main
LOCAL aZipCodes[100], nIndex, nKey, nZip := 90000
LOCAL oArrayBrowser

/* Generate test data for ZIP array */
FOR nIndex := 1 TO 100
   aZipCodes[nIndex] := STR(nZip+nIndex)
NEXT

oArrayBrowser := TBrowseNew( 5, 35, 20, 45 )
oArrayBrowser:headSep := CHR(196)

/* Custom code blocks for positional control */
oArrayBrowser:goTopBlock := {|| nIndex := 1}
oArrayBrowser:goBottomBlock := {|| nIndex := LEN(aZipCodes)}
oArrayBrowser:skipBlock := {|nSkip| Skipper(nSkip, @nIndex, aZipCodes)}

/* In lieu of a "record pointer" we need a positional index
   for our new data source */
nIndex := 1

/* The TBColumn data retrieval code block simply returns
   the array element at nIndex */
oArrayBrowser:addColumn(TBColumnNew('Zip Codes', ;
   {|| aZipCodes[nIndex]}))

/* Primary TBrowse loop */
WHILE TRUE
   WHILE !oArrayBrowser:stabilize()
   END
   nKey := INKEY(0)
   IF nKey == K_ESC
     EXIT
   ELSE
```

```
         GenKey( oArrayBrowser, nKey )
      ENDIF
   END

RETURN NIL

/***
*
* Skipper(<nSkip>, <nIndex>, <aArray>) -> nSkipped
*
*/

STATIC FUNCTION Skipper(nSkip, nIndex, aArray)
LOCAL nTemp := nIndex

IF nIndex + nSkip > LEN(aArray)   // Skip past end?
   nIndex := LEN(aArray)          // Yes, point to end.
ELSEIF nIndex + nSkip < 1         // Skip before beginning?
   nIndex := 1                    // Yes, point to first.
ELSE
   nIndex += nSkip                // Simple case, bump index.
ENDIF

RETURN (nIndex - nTemp)           // Actual skipped.

/***
*
* GenKey( oTBObject, nKey ) -> NIL
*
*/

FUNCTION GenKey( oTBObject, nKey )

DO CASE
   CASE nKey == K_UP
      oTBObject:up()

   CASE nKey == K_DOWN
      oTBObject:down()

   CASE nKey == K_PGUP
      oTBObject:pageUp()

   CASE nKey == K_PGDN
      oTBObject:pageDown()

   CASE nKey == K_CTRL_PGUP
      oTBObject:goTop()
```

```
        CASE nKey == K_CTRL_PGDN
           oTBObject:goBottom()
ENDCASE

RETURN NIL
```

There are several key components in this example. First, the generic constructor `TBrowseNew()` is used. Next, the contents of `goTopBlock`, `goBottomBlock`, and `skipBlock` are crucial to the operation of any TBrowse whose data source is anything other than a database file. In this case, we define what it means to "go to the top, bottom, next, and last" element of an array. You achieve "going to the top" by setting the array index to 1. "Going to the bottom" means to position to the last element, namely `LEN(aZipCodes)`.

Finally, skipping forward and backward through elements requires a special `Skipper()` function that can handle arrays. We pass `Skipper()` the number of elements to skip (nSkip) the current element pointer (nIndex) and the array itself. Notice the index pointer is passed By Reference (@nIndex) so that it can be modified inside the UDF.

The code block passed to `TBColumnNew()` is also interesting:

```
oArrayBrowser:addColumn(TBColumnNew('Zip Codes', ;
   {|| aZipCodes[nIndex]}))
```

Here, we're doing a couple of things in one line. We give `TBColumnNew()` the code block `{|| aZipCodes[nIndex]}`, which selects array elements for display in the browse column. `TBColumnNew()` returns a TBColumn object, which is passed directly to the `addColumn()` method of the TBrowse object. This approach is more optimized but, unfortunately, a bit harder to understand.

`GenKey()` is similar to the previous version; the difference is that fewer keystrokes must be handled for a one-dimension array as the data source.

1. Rethink the array browsing technology defined in this section and come up with a browser that establishes a browse for the two-dimensional array returned by the built-in `DBSTRUCT()` function. This browse would enable you to view the structure of any database file. The resulting browse would necessarily consist of four columns: field name, data type, length, and decimals.

1. We can browse the contents of the `DBSTRUCT()` array by first creating four TBColumn objects, each containing a column in the array. We must also define custom code block values for `goTopBlock`, `goBottomBlock`, and `skipBlock`. This time, we'll experiment with defining the array skipping process without a skipper function, instead placing everything inside the code block itself.

```
#include 'dbstruct.ch'
#include 'common.ch'
```

```
#include 'inkey.ch'

STATIC nElem

FUNCTION Main

LOCAL aStruct, nElem := 1, nKey
LOCAL oSBrowse

USE Employee NEW
aStruct := DBSTRUCT()

oSBrowse := TBROWSENEW(1, 1, 23, 79)

// First column - field names
oSBrowse:addColumn(TBColumnNew('Field Name', ;
   {|| aStruct[nElem, DBS_NAME]}))

// Second column - field data types
oSBrowse:addColumn(TBColumnNew('Type',        ;
   {|| aStruct[nElem, DBS_TYPE]}))

// Third column - field lengths
oSBrowse:addColumn(TBColumnNew('Field Len',  ;
   {|| aStruct[nElem, DBS_LEN]}))

// Fourth column - field decimals
oSBrowse:addColumn(TBColumnNew('Field Dec',  ;
   {|| aStruct[nElem, DBS_DEC]}))

oSBrowse:goTopBlock    := {|| nElem := 1}
oSBrowse:goBottomBlock := {|| nElem := LEN(aStruct)}
oSBrowse:skipBlock     := {|i, j|  j := nElem, ;
         nElem := IIF(i > 0,                   ;
         MIN(LEN(aStruct), nElem + i),         ;
         MAX(1, nElem + i)),                   ;
         nElem - j }

WHILE TRUE
  oSBrowse:forceStable()

  nKey := INKEY(0)
  IF nKey == K_ESC
     EXIT
  ELSE
     GenKey(oSBrowse, nKey)
  ENDIF
END

RETURN NIL
```

Browsing Text Files

The last application of TBrowse that we will discuss concerns the use of TBrowse to browse DOS text files. As with array browsing, the first thing to consider is the characteristics of the data source. With text files, we need an underlying system of functions to support the traversal of lines in the file.

Luckily, we have the memo functions MEMOREAD(), MLCOUNT(), and MEMOLINE(). The following example uses these functions in conjunction with TBrowse to browse the contents of a text file.

Note there is one inherent limitation for this method: the contents of the file must be read into a character memory variable. A character memory variable has a maximum length of 64K bytes (precisely 65,535 characters in length). Therefore, the file size must be within this limit.

```
#include 'inkey.ch'
#define TRUE .T.

FUNCTION Main
LOCAL cTextFile, nLine := 1 ,nLastLine, nKey
LOCAL oTextBrowser
LOCAL cFileName := 'read.me'

/* Read a text file TBrowse */
cTextFile := MEMOREAD(cFileName)

oTextBrowser := TBrowseNew( 5, 10, 20, 70 )
oTextBrowser:headSep := CHR(196)

/* Determine number of lines given window width */
nLastLine := MLCOUNT(cTextFile,oTextBrowser:nRight - ;
   oTextBrowser:nLeft)
oTextBrowser:goTopBlock := {|| nLine := 1}
oTextBrowser:goBottomBlock := {|| nLine := nLastLine}
oTextBrowser:skipBlock := {|nSkip| Skipper(nSkip, @nLine, nLastLine)}
oTextBrowser:addColumn(TBColumnNew(cFileName, ;
   {|| MEMOLINE(cTextFile, oTextBrowser:nRight - oTextBrowser:nLeft,
   nLine)} ))

WHILE TRUE
   WHILE !oTextBrowser:stabilize()
   END

   nKey := INKEY(0)
   IF nKey == K_ESC
     EXIT
   ELSE
     GenKey( oTextBrowser, nKey )
```

```
      ENDIF
   END

   RETURN NIL



/***
*
*  Skipper( nSkip, nLine, nLastLine ) -> nSkipped
*
*/

STATIC FUNCTION Skipper( nSkip, nLine, nLastLine )
LOCAL nSkipped

IF nSkip >= 0                           // FORWARD skip through text
   IF (nLine + nSkip) > nLastLine       // Past last line?
      * Yes, skip as many as possible
      nSkipped := nLastLine - nLine
      nLine := nLastLine                // Move line pointer to last.
   ELSE
      nSkipped := nSkip                 // No, skip requested amount.
      nLine += nSkip                    // Advance line pointer.
   ENDIF
ELSE                                    // BACKWARD skip through text
   IF (nLine + nSkip) < 1               // Past first line?
      * Yes, skip as many as possible
      nSkipped := 1 - nLine
      nLine := 1                        // Move line pointer to first.
   ELSE
      nSkipped := nSkip                 // No, skip requested amount.
      nLine += nSkip                    // Back up line pointer
   ENDIF
ENDIF

RETURN nSkipped                         // Return number skipped.
```

Let's analyze this example. To begin with, MEMOREAD() loads the text from a file into a memory variable. Next, we calculate the number of lines in the text, given the line length of the TBrowse window. MLCOUNT() becomes useful for this purpose, using the nRight and nLeft instance variables to determine the line length. As with array browsing, we need a numeric pointer variable to track the line number position in the text file. nLine is used in the goTopBlock, goBottomBlock, and skipBlock positioning code blocks. The Skipper() UDF is particularly interesting since it simply manipulates nLine. The text is then pulled from cTextFile inside the data retrieval code block for TBColumn. Here, we use MEMOLINE() to extract a line at a time.

Being true to its name, the `GenKey()` generic keystroke UDF is the same as the one used in previous examples in this chapter.

Other Topics

For your learning enjoyment, let's list a few additional topics of interest that you may decide to investigate as a follow-up to our cursory look at TBrowse. If there is one area of CA-Clipper that has become the darling of the developer community, it is TBrowse. There are many reasons for this, but probably the most important is that TBrowse, and the underlying object-based technology that supports it, excites programmers due the elegance and simplicity of design it affords. For this reason and many others, TBrowse is capable of many interesting applications. Consider the following applications:

- Browsing with updates: editing and deleting data
- Colorful browses, for example: using red to indicate negative numbers
- Browsing two-dimensional (or even multi-dimensional) arrays
- Simultaneously browsing multiple data sources
- Browsing one-to-many relationships
- Multi-user browsing considerations
- Multi-line browses, for example: browsing a customer database in "mailing label" format

Summary

In this chapter, we've completed our discussion of TBrowse. From a beginner's perspective, the learning curve required to become productive with TBrowse is somewhat steep. Once mastered, however, much of the flexibility behind an object-based browsing system becomes evident. After using TBrowse for a while, you'll wonder how you once got by with only BROWSE commands and their many clauses and options!

Exercise

1. Based on your knowledge of arrays, functions, and code blocks, revise the methodology defined in the beginning of this chapter to parameterize the invocation of TBrowse method functions. To do this, use a two-dimensional array where the first column is a keystroke character and the second column is a code block that calls the associated method. Also revise the primary TBrowse loop to handle this array. (Hint: remember ASCAN() for the solution).

Answer

1. The key to this browsing methodology is the `aMethods` array, which has a subarray for each key/code block pair. The primary browse loop becomes streamlined using the array. In fact, the entire process is controlled by the `ASCAN()` and `EVAL()` functions. Please read closely the comment blocks embedded in the code in order to gain insight into how the method functions are determined and called.

```
#include 'inkey.ch'
#include 'common.ch'

FUNCTION Main

LOCAL aMethods
LOCAL oBrowse, oTBCol1, oTBCol2    // Define browse system objects.
LOCAL nMethPtr
LOCAL nLastKey

/* Use a two-dimensional array to define keys and their associated
   TBrowse cursor movement methods. Notice that the methods are
   invoked in code blocks where the object name is passed as a
   parameter. */

aMethods := { {K_DOWN,        {|object| object:down()}},     ;
              {K_UP,          {|object| object:up()}},       ;
              {K_PGDN,        {|object| object:pageDown()}}, ;
              {K_PGUP,        {|object| object:pageUp()}},   ;
              {K_CTRL_PGUP,   {|object| object:gotop()}},    ;
              {K_CTRL_PGDN,   {|object| object:gobottom()}}, ;
              {K_RIGHT,       {|object| object:right()}},    ;
              {K_LEFT,        {|object| object:left()}},     ;
              {K_HOME,        {|object| object:home()}},     ;
              {K_END,         {|object| object:end()}},      ;
              {K_CTRL_LEFT,   {|object| object:panLeft()}},  ;
              {K_CTRL_RIGHT,  {|object| object:panRight()}}, ;
              {K_CTRL_HOME,   {|object| object:panHome()}},  ;
              {K_CTRL_END,    {|object| object:panEnd()}}   }

USE Employee NEW             // Open EMPLOYEE database.

oTBCol1 := TBColumnNew('Employee Name', {|| Employee->Last})
oTBCol2 := TBColumnNew('City', {|| Employee->City})

oBrowse := TBrowseDB(5, 10, 20, 60)

oBrowse:addColumn(oTBCol1)
oBrowse:addColumn(oTBCol2)
```

```
WHILE TRUE
   oBrowse:forceStable()
   nLastKey := INKEY(0)

   /* In the following ASCAN(), aMethods is the array being scanned.
   The array is scanned, executing the block for each element. As
   each element is encountered, ASCAN() passes the element's value
   as an argument to the code block, and then performs an EVAL() on
   the block. ASCAN() stops when the code block returns .T. or
   reaches the last element. */

   nMethPtr := ASCAN(aMethods,{|elem|nLastKey==elem[1]})

   IF nMethPtr != 0
      /* Now that key was found, EVAL() method function passes the
      browse object as a parameter */
      EVAL(aMethods[nMethPtr,2], oBrowse)
   ELSE
      IF nLastKey == K_ESC
         EXIT
      ENDIF
   ENDIF
END

DBCLOSEAREA()

RETURN NIL
```

Low-Level
File Functions

A Review of the Functions ➤ 304

FILEIO.PRG ➤ 311

Low-Level File Example for Beginners ➤ 311

Summary ➤ 314

Exercise ➤ 314

This chapter deals with a topic important to many CA-Clipper developers, low-level file functions. These functions provide for direct read/write access to DOS files from a Clipper program, thus avoiding the necessity to write C or Assembler programs to achieve this purpose. With these functions, you may access both standard ASCII text and binary files. The low-level functions entered into the language with Summer '87 release but have undergone a few changes with CA-Clipper, so as a side benefit to Summer '87 programmers entering the Clipper language for the first time, we'll present the functions with a CA-Clipper flavor.

As Clipper beginners, you may need a little help visualizing why you might one day need to use the low-level file functions. Consider the situation where you may wish to generate a non-.DBF data file so that a non-Xbase program can read it. Possibly, this data may be destined for a mainframe computer or for data transmission to a branch office of an information service. Or consider that you may need to read and then parse some kind of foreign file format and stuff the data into .DBF format for further processing. Of course these are just two possible applications, but there are many more. Just bear in mind that with the low-level functions, anything is possible when it comes to accessing disk-based data because you are not restricted by the standard .DBF file format.

After you complete this chapter, you'll know how to:

- Access both ASCII text and binary DOS disk files directly from within a CA-Clipper program
- Use each of the low-level file functions available in CA-Clipper
- Put together the low-level file functions in order to implement a workable program module

A Review of the Functions

In this section, we'll step you through each of the low-level file functions by briefly discussing their purpose and by providing an example. Before we begin, you might find it helpful to review Table 12.1 for a complete list of the functions, along with their parameter lists and return values. Also, you might take a look at the standard FILEIO.CH Clipper header file, which contains frequently used manifest constants specifically for use in conjunction with the direct file functions. We'll present portions of this file as we use its various components in the examples that follow.

Create/Open DOS Files

We begin our discussion of the low-level file functions by seeing how to create/open a DOS disk file. There are two functions, FCREATE() and FOPEN(),

Table 12.1 Low-Level File Functions

Function Name/Parameters	Description
FCREATE(<cFileName> [,<nAttr>]) —> nFileHandle	Create a new file
FOPEN(<cFileName> [,<nOpenMode>]) —> nFileHandle	Open an existing file
FERASE(<cFileName>) —> nSuccess	Erase a file
FERROR() —> nErrorCode	Obtain file function error
FREAD(<nFileHandle>, @<cBufferVar>, <nBytesToRead>) —> nBytesRead	Read file including embedded nulls
FREADSTR(<nFileHandle>, <nBytesToRead>) —> cString	Read file until first null
FRENAME(<OldFile>, <cNewFile>) —> nSuccess	Rename a file
FSEEK(<nFileHandle>, <nOffset> [,<nOrigin>]) —> nPosition	Position within a file
FWRITE(<nFileHandle>, <cBufferVar> [,<nBytesToWrite>]) —> nBytesWritten	Write to a file
FCLOSE(<nFileHandle>) —> lError	Close a file
ERASE or DELETE FILE <cFileName>	Erase a file

which we can use to create a new file or open an existing file, respectively. As an example, the following code segment will attempt to create a new file:

```
#include 'fileio.ch'
LOCAL nFileHandle

nFileHandle := FCREATE('Report.TXT', FC_NORMAL)
IF nFileHandle == F_ERROR
   ? 'Unable to create file, error code is: ', FERROR()
ENDIF
```

Here, we call FCREATE() passing the filename to be created. The return value of FCREATE() is a *DOS file handle*. From your knowledge of DOS, you'll remember that any file opened by a program is assigned a file handle. A file handle is an positive integer value used to point to a file table entry created by DOS. When successful, both FCREATE() and FOPEN() return a handle that is then used for all subsequent access to the file. If an error occurs however, a value of -1 is returned instead.

The second parameter of `FCREATE()` contains the DOS file attributes, the default being read/write access. See the following portion of FILEIO.CH for other possible attributes. These are all standard DOS file attributes.

```
// FCREATE() file attribute modes
// NOTE:  FCREATE() always opens with (FO_READWRITE + FO_COMPAT)

#define FC_NORMAL    0 // Create normal read/write file (default).
#define FC_READONLY  1 // Create read-only file.
#define FC_HIDDEN    2 // Create hidden file.
#define FC_SYSTEM    4 // Create system file.

// Error value (all functions)
#define F_ERROR    (-1)
```

Notice that the code segment then checks the file handle returned by `FCREATE()` to see if it indicates that an error occurred. `F_ERROR` is a manifest constant used for this purpose. The specific error is supplied by the low-level file function `FERROR()`. See Table 12.2 for a list of possible error codes. The other way to detect an error condition would be to directly check for a non-zero return value from `FERROR()`.

Table 12.2   DOS Error Codes for FERROR()

Error	Description
0	Successful
2	File not found
3	Path not found
4	Too many files open
5	Access denied
6	Invalid handle
8	Insufficient memory
15	Invalid drive specified
19	Attempted to write to a write-protected disk
21	Drive not ready
23	Data CRC error
29	Write fault
30	Read fault
32	Sharing violation
33	Lock Violation

If there were no problems in creating the new file, processing may continue, presumably calling other file functions to read from or write to the new file.

Opening an existing file occurs in much the same manner as creating a new file. Here is a code sample, that asks `FOPEN()` to open an existing file, REPORT.TXT, for read/write access:

```
#include 'fileio.ch'

LOCAL nFileHandle

nFileHandle := FOPEN('Report.txt', FO_READWRITE)
IF FERROR() != 0
    ? 'Unable to open file, error code is: ', FERROR()
ENDIF
```

If there was an error opening a file, we can use `FERROR()` to allow us to find out more about the error. For example if the file was not found, `FERROR()` returns a 2.

Here is the portion of FILEIO.CH pertaining to `FOPEN()` access modes:

```
// FOPEN() access modes
#define FO_READ       0    // Open for reading (default).
#define FO_WRITE      1    // Open for writing.
#define FO_READWRITE  2    // Open for reading or writing.
```

One other topic should be discussed at this point. If you are operating in a network environment, `FOPEN()` needs to know how you wish to share the file as a resource. Listed here are the definitions in FILEIO.CH dealing with sharing modes:

```
// FOPEN() sharing modes (combine with open mode using +)
#define FO_COMPAT     0    // Compatibility mode (default).
#define FO_EXCLUSIVE  16   // Exclusive use (other processes have no
                           // access).
#define FO_DENYWRITE  32   // Prevent other processes from writing.
#define FO_DENYREAD   48   // Prevent other processes from reading.
#define FO_DENYNONE   64   // Allow other processes to read or write.
#define FO_SHARED     64   // Same as FO_DENYNONE.
```

When using the sharing modes, you should *add* them to an appropriate access mode. For example, to open a file for read/write shared access, you would use `FO_READWRITE + FO_SHARED`, yielding a value of 66.

Moving through the Data

One low-level file function that becomes useful when navigating through a DOS file is `FSEEK()`. With `FSEEK()` you may move the *file pointer* forward and backward through the file. The file pointer determines where the next read or write operation will occur in a manner similar to the record pointer used in a .DBF file. The difference here is that where a record pointer positions to a specific record in the file, a file pointer allows positioning at the byte level.

As indicated in Table 12.1, the second parameter for FSEEK() is <nOffSet>, which determines the direction and distance the file pointer should move. A positive value moves the file pointer in the forward direction and a negative one moves the file pointer in a backward direction. The third parameter, <nOrigin>, affects the movement too—it determines where the file pointer begins when FSEEK() performs its operation.

FILEIO.CH has several definitions used with the third parameter:

```
// FSEEK() modes
#define FS_SET      0    // Seek from beginning of file.
#define FS_RELATIVE  1   // Seek from current file position.
#define FS_END      2    // Seek from end of file.
```

Note that FSEEK() returns a value indicating the position of the file pointer *after* the seek operation. Here are some examples of using FSEEK():

```
#include 'fileio.ch'

FUNCTION Main
LOCAL nFileHandle, nFileLength, nFilePtr

/* Open file Read-Only */
nFileHandle := FOPEN('TempOut', FO_READ)
IF FERROR() != 0
   ? 'Unable to open file, error code is: ', FERROR()
   QUIT
ENDIF

/* Move forward 80 bytes from beginning of file */
nFilePtr := FSEEK(nFileHandle, 80, FS_SET)        // 80

/* Now move 80 more */
nFilePtr := FSEEK(nFileHandle, 80, FS_RELATIVE)   // 160

/* Finally, determine file length */
nFileLength := **FSEEK(nFileHandle, 0, FS_END)**
FCLOSE(nFileHandle)                               // Close the file.

RETURN NIL
```

Notice in the last call to FSEEK() that we define the origin to be FS_END, the last byte of the file, and then move 0 bytes. This technique allows us to retrieve the file length, which is the numeric value returned by FSEEK().

Also, notice that we use the low-level file function `FCLOSE()` to close the file before leaving.

Reading Data

Now let's turn our attention to reading and writing files. For this purpose, we have `FREAD()`, `FREADSTR()`, and `FWRITE()`. `FREAD()` and `FREADSTR()` both read bytes from a file into a buffer variable. The only difference between the two is how they handle the null character (CHR(0)). `FREAD()` reads bytes including any embedded null characters while `FREADSTR()` stops at the first null character encountered regardless of how many bytes were specified to read. Let's see some examples:

```
#define F_BLOCK_SIZE 256

LOCAL nFileHandle, nBytesRead
LOCAL cBuffer := SPACE(F_BLOCK_SIZE)

nFileHandle := FOPEN('TempIn')    // Open read-only.
IF nFileHandle == F_ERROR
  ? 'Error opening file, error was', FERROR()
ELSE
  nBytesRead := FREAD(nFileHandle, @cBuffer, F_BLOCK_SIZE)
  IF nBytesRead != F_BLOCK_SIZE
    ? 'Error occurred reading file'
  ENDIF
  FCLOSE(nFileHandle)
ENDIF
```

This example illustrates how you can open a file and read a number of characters on which to operate. Notice that we pass the buffer variable `cBuffer` to `FREAD()` By Reference since its value will be altered upon returning from `FREAD()`. `FREAD()` returns a numeric value indicating how many bytes were actually read. If this value differs from the number requested, it means that end-of-file was reached or some other error occurred.

Writing Data

Use `FWRITE()` to write to an open file. In the following code segment, we simply create a new file and write a report title line.

```
#include 'fileio.ch'
#define F_BLOCK_SIZE 132

FUNCTION Main
```

```
LOCAL nFileHandle, nBytesWritten, cBuffer := SPACE(F_BLOCK_SIZE)
LOCAL nPage := 1

nFileHandle := FCREATE('OrdRep.txt', FC_NORMAL)
IF nFileHandle == F_ERROR
   ? 'Unable to create file, error code is: ', FERROR()
ENDIF

/* Construct a report title line */
cBuffer := STUFF(cBuffer,1,8,DTOC(DATE()))
cBuffer := STUFF(cBuffer,120,10,'Page: '+STR(nPage,4))
cBuffer := STUFF(cBuffer,56,23,'Customer History Report')

/* Now write it to the new file */
nBytesWritten := FWRITE(nFileHandle, @cBuffer, F_BLOCK_SIZE)
IF nBytesWritten < F_BLOCK_SIZE
   ? 'Write error occurred', FERROR()
ENDIF

FCLOSE(nFileHandle)

RETURN NIL
```

In this program we begin by defining an empty buffer, `cBuffer`, which contains an amount of space equal to the block size. Next, we create a new file, ORDREP.TXT, then construct a line to write, and finally we call `FWRITE()` to write the line to the file. Notice that we pass `cBuffer` By Reference.

Note   One common technique used here to determine whether the write operation succeeded, is to check if the number of bytes actually written is equal to the block size.

1. Write a CA-Clipper UDF named `FCREATES()` that creates a new DOS disk file, but first checks to see if it exists. If the file exists, the function must prompt the user for confirmation to overwrite the old file.

   1. In our new low-level file function, the caller must pass the filename and attributes. The function then uses the built-in `FILE()` function to check for the file's existence. If the file exists, we call `ALERT()` to prompt the user to overwrite the old file.

      ```
      #include 'common.ch'
      #include 'fileio.ch'

      FUNCTION Main
      LOCAL cFileName := 'Report.TXT'
      LOCAL nHandle
      ```

```
    nHandle := FCREATES(cFileName, FC_NORMAL)
    IF nHandle == -1
       ? 'File not created'
    ENDIF

    FCLOSE(nHandle)

    RETURN NIL

    /***
    *
    * FCREATES( <cFileName>, <nAttr> ) -> nRetVal
    *
    */

    FUNCTION FCREATES(cFileName, nAttr)
    LOCAL nRetVal := 0
    LOCAL aOptions := {'Abort', 'Overwrite'}
    LOCAL nChoice

    IF FILE(cFileName) // File already exists.
       nChoice := ALERT('File aready exists', aOptions)
       IF nChoice == 2 // User says NO.
          nRetVal := FCREATE(cFileName, nAttr)
       ELSE
          nRetVal := -1 // Tell caller, not created.
       ENDIF
    ELSE
       nRetVal := FCREATE(cFileName, nAttr)
    ENDIF

    RETURN nRetVal
```

FILEIO.PRG

The low-level file functions we have discussed so far provide for a simple interface for accessing DOS files. The access method, however, requires you to do most of the work. There is an easier way! One very useful sample program that comes with CA-Clipper is FILEIO.PRG found in the \CLIPPER5\SOURCE\SAMPLE directory. This file contains the source code for a collection of UDFs that apply the low-level functions for more enhanced purposes. Table 12.3 shows these UDFs and a brief description of what they do.

Low-Level File Example for Beginners

Now let's get down to an integrated example of the kinds of things the direct file I/O functions can achieve. We'll use these functions to perform a common type of operation—copying a file. Consider the following complete program:

```
#include 'fileio.ch'
#define F_BLOCK_SIZE 512
#define TRUE  .T.
#define FALSE .F.

FUNCTION Main
LOCAL nSource, nDest

nSource := FOPEN('OldIn', FO_READ)
nDest := FCREATE('NewOut', FC_NORMAL)

IF !CopyFile( nSource, nDest )
   ? 'Copy operation failed'
ENDIF

FCLOSE(nSource)
FCLOSE(nDest)

RETURN NIL

/***
*
* CopyFile( nSource, nDest ) -> lSuccess
*
* Parameters:
*         nSource - file handle for source file
*         nDest   - file handle for destination file
*
*/

FUNCTION CopyFile( nSource, nDest )
LOCAL lRetVal := TRUE
LOCAL nBytesRead, nBytesWritten, cBuffer := SPACE(F_BLOCK_SIZE)

WHILE TRUE
   nBytesRead := FREAD(nSource, @cBuffer, F_BLOCK_SIZE)
   nBytesWritten := FWRITE(nDest, cBuffer, nBytesRead)
   IF nBytesWritten < nBytesRead
     ? 'Write error', FERROR()
     lRetVal := FALSE
     EXIT
   ELSEIF nBytesRead == 0
     EXIT
   ENDIF
END

RETURN (lRetVal)
```

Table 12.3 Extended Low-Level File Functions (FILEIO.PRG)

UDF	Description
FGets(<nFileHandle>, [<nLinesToRead>], [<nLineLength>], [<cDelim>]) —> cBuffer	Reads one or more lines from a text file; an alternate way of calling FReadLn()
FPuts(<nFileHandle>, <cString>, [<nLength>], [<cDelim>]) —> nBytes	Writes a line to a text file; an alternate way of calling FWriteLn()
DirEval(<cFileSpec>, <bAction>) —> aArray	Applies a code block to each file matching a given file specification (e.g. *.DBF)
FileTop(<nFileHandle>) —> nPosition	Positions the file pointer to the first byte in a file and returns the new file position (i.e., 0)
FileBottom(<nFileHandle>) —> nPosition	Positions the file pointer to the last byte in a file and returns the new file position (i.e. file size)
FilePos(<nFileHandle>) —> nPosition	Returns the current position of the file pointer in a file
FileSize(<nFileHandle>) —> nBytes	Returns the size of a file
FReadLn(<nFileHandle>, [<nLinesToRead>], [<nLineLength>], [<cDelim>]) —> cLines	Reads one or more lines from a text file
FileEval(<nHandle>, [<nLineLength>], [<cDelim>],; <bBlock>, [<bWhileCondition>], [<nNextLines>], [<nLine>], [<lRest>]) —> NIL	Applies a code block to a file similar in manner to the way DBEVAL() applies a code block to database records, and allows you to control—through the use of <bForCondition>, <bWhileCondition>, and <lRest>—the scope of records considered when <bBlock> is applied
FEof(<nFileHandle>) —> lBoundary	Determines if the current file pointer position is the last byte in the file
FWriteLn(<nFileHandle>, <cString>, [<nLength>], [<cDelim>]) —> nBytes	Writes a line to a text file at the current file pointer position

Let's take a minute to analyze this sample program. First, we have a driver program, `Main()`, that opens the source file and creates the destination file for the copy operation. Note, that for space considerations, all error checking, which should find its way into production code, is left out here. Next, we call the `CopyFile()` UDF, passing to it the file handles for the two files.

Once inside `CopyFile()`, we alternate calling `FREAD()` and `FWRITE()` by first filling the buffer variable with a block of data from the source file and then writing the same block out to the destination file. This process continues until the number of bytes read becomes 0, meaning that end-of-file for the source file has been reached. `CopyFile()` returns a logical value, indicating the success of the copy. We see that the return value is set to .F. if a write error occurs during the copy.

Summary

In this chapter, we've provided a beginner's overview of a potentially very useful capability of the Clipper language. There are many possible applications of the low-level file functions. As you gain experience with Clipper, keep in mind these possible uses for the functions we've discussed in this chapter:

- Translating all characters to uppercase
- Preparing a log of all user names of a network application
- Translating .DBF files to their DIF equivalents
- Protecting a .DBF file by changing its first byte
- Converting a straight ASCII file to a word processor's format

Exercise

1. Write a CA-Clipper user-defined function named `FAREAD()` that reads the contents of an ASCII text file and places its contents into the elements of an array. Each line of the text file should go into an element of the array. The function must accept one parameter, the name of the file and return the loaded array.

Answer

1. In this answer we provide one possible solution for `FAREAD()`. The heart of the function is the line that reads a line from the text file and adds it to the array with `AADD()`. We use the `FREADLN()` function from FILEIO.PRG to read the lines of the text file. In order to link a program that references any of the functions in this file, you must first compile FILEIO.PRG and then include the resulting .OBJ file in your link command as in:

```
rtlink fi test, fileio /pll:base52
```

The program loops through all lines found in the file, adding them to the array and then finally stops as the file pointer comes to the end of the file.

```
#include 'fileio.ch'

FUNCTION Main
LOCAL aTable

* Load spreadsheet into array
aTable := FAREAD('Spread.TXT', 80)

RETURN NIL

/***
*
* FAREAD( <cFileName>, <nLineLen> ) -> aLines
*
*/

FUNCTION FAREAD(cFileName, nLineLen)
LOCAL aLines := {}
LOCAL nHandle
LOCAL nPtr := 0
LOCAL nFileLen := 0

* Open Read-Only
IF (nHandle := FOPEN(cFileName, FO_READ)) != F_ERROR
   * Get number of bytes in file
   nFileLen := FSEEK(nHandle, FS_SET, FS_END)
   FSEEK(nHandle, FS_SET)
   WHILE nPtr < nFileLen
      * Read a line and insert into next element
      AADD(aLines, FREADLN(nHandle, 1, nLineLen))
      nPtr := FSEEK(nHandle, FS_SET, FS_RELATIVE)
   ENDFCLOSE(nHandle)
ENDIF

RETURN aLines    // Return loaded array.
```

13

Applications

Data Entry CA-Clipper Style ➤ 318

The GET System ➤ 325

Basic Reporting ➤ 331

Summary ➤ 340

Exercises ➤ 340

Throughout the previous chapters of this book, we have built quite a complement of language constructs and techniques with which to put together CA-Clipper applications. With this, the final chapter, we'll take a stab at applying this knowledge by implementing two primary components of most applications: *data entry* and *reporting*. To do this, we'll take a look at two simple, easy-to-use, and enhanceable groups of subprograms that define a style of data entry screens and reports. The style of data entry and reports that we present here is not meant to be a final solution but rather it should provide you a starting point from where you will begin building enhanced data entry and reporting components that satisfy more complex requirements.

After completing this chapter, you will have at your disposal:

- A complete library of functions that implement a simple data entry scheme
- An easy to understand framework for generating hard copy reports from within a CA-Clipper program
- Full working examples of real-life CA-Clipper programs

Data Entry CA-Clipper Style

In this section, we present a complete facility for entering data in a CA-Clipper application. All the usual features of a data entry screen are provided, including adding new records, editing and deleting existing records, moving through the existing records, and finding records. The specific style of data entry that we have chosen is but one of potentially unlimited styles and this specific style may not suit you. The bottom line is: this style works, it is relatively easy to use, and most importantly, it is easily enhanced and expanded. Before we present the collection of data entry routines, let's identify the specific areas of CA-Clipper that will become the basis for the software that follows. Here is a short list of language components that you should look for in the code:

- Modular structure using `FUNCTION` subprograms
- Preprocessor usage (`#include` and `#define`)
- `LOCAL`s and file-wide `STATIC`s
- `STATIC` functions
- Hungarian notation for memory variables
- Database functions, such as `DBAPPEND()`
- Simple menu using the `@ PROMPT` and `MENU TO` commands
- Scatter/Gather routines

There should be no surprises here, but since we're new to putting together cohesive programs with the CA-Clipper language, a simple road map might make the process a bit more tolerable and less intimidating. The sections that follow provide this map.

The Clipper code found in Listing 13.1 represents a collection of UDFs designed to provide for the data entry process. We base the code around a sample database, EMPLOYEE.DBF, whose structure is shown in Figure 13.1. You may substitute your own database(s) to achieve the same functionality. The individual functions, their purpose, and a complete description of how they operate is supplied in the following sections. We have also interjected comments recommending ways you might enhance these functions, making them more robust. You'll see too, in Listing 13.1, that we have a simple driver program, `Main()`, that initiates the data entry process by calling `Entry()`. Finally, as a point of reference, Figure 13.2 shows the data entry screen during execution. Let's now move on to the road map of the functions.

Entry()

The `Entry()` UDF is the entry point for the data entry routine collection and does several things in preparation for bringing up the data entry screen. From here, we perform the following housekeeping chores: save/restore the screen contents, define all appropriate SETs, activate any RDDs, open databases, open index files, set the screen mode, paint the "wallpaper" to act as a back-drop for the data entry screen, and display the screen and field titles. Lastly, we pass

Figure 13.1 This is EMPLOYEE.DBF database structure.

Field Number	Field Name	Field Type	Field Width	Dec
1	EmpNo	Character	5	
2	EmpName	Character	30	
3	HomeAddr	Character	35	
4	HomeCity	Character	15	
5	HomeSt	Character	2	
6	HomeZIP	Character	10	
7	HomePhone	Character	13	
8	Ext	Character	4	
9	HireDate	Date	8	
10	FullTime	Logical	1	
11	MoSAl	Numeric	7	2
12	SSN	Character	11	
13	Birthdate	Date	8	
		Total	150	

Figure 13.2 Clipper data entry screen.

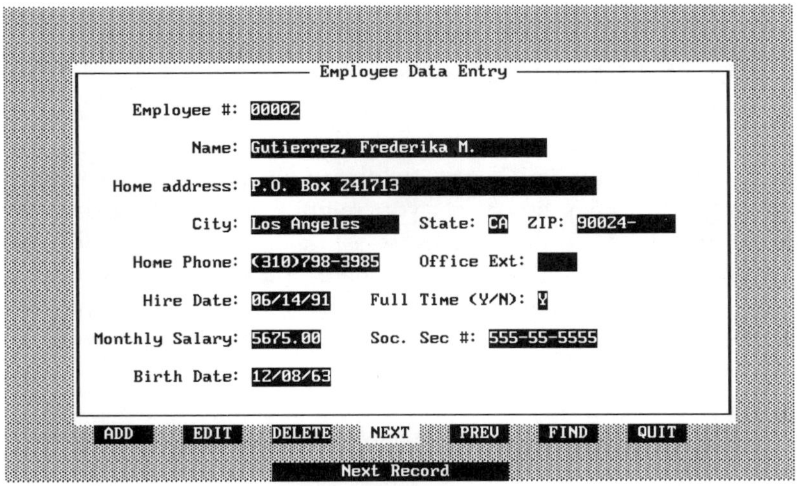

control to `SetVars()` and then to `GetScr()` in order to retrieve the contents of the first record for display purposes only. Notice that `GetScr()` contains no `READ` statement since the function needs to serve two purposes: display a record and perform data entry on a record. Here, we do the former so we issue a `CLEAR GETS` to flush all the pending `GETs`.

`Entry()` completes its job by calling `Menu()` to display a horizontal bar menu and let the user choose which option to perform. We'll discuss each option in detail a bit later.

GetScr()

As mentioned above, `GetScr()` actually has two distinct purposes. This is the routine that initiates data entry with the user, but it also serves as the vehicle whereby record data is displayed on the screen. In either case, `GetScr()` populates the `GetList` array by issuing a series of `@ GET` statements, one for each field on the screen. You can manually design the positioning of these fields and the `PICTURE` strings used to control the data entry, or you can use a screen design utility to generate this code (many commercial and shareware products provide this capability).

Notice that all data entry is done to memory variables, not the fields they parallel. The specific memory variable names referenced are determined by the `InitVars()` and `SetVars()` functions. Any routine that calls `GetScr()` must follow the call with either a `READ` (data entry) or a `CLEAR GETS` (display only).

Take note that `GetScr()`, as well as the other support functions that are part of this collection, are implemented as STATIC FUNCTIONs. This technique is necessary so that similarly named functions in other .PRG files will not conflict with these. We are, in effect, "hiding" the function from all program modules outside the current .PRG.

Note also that `GetScr()` is the function in which data validation must be performed on the data entered by the user. For this purpose, remember CA-Clipper has both the WHEN and VALID clauses for @ GET. In addition, we may call UDFs to implement any level of complex data checking. Consider the following enhancement to the GET for the state code field:

```
@ 11,49 GET cHomeSt PICTURE '@!' VALID CheckSt(cHomeSt)
```

In this example, the UDF `CheckSt()` does a table lookup presumably on a database or array containing all valid state codes.

InitVars()

The `InitVars()` function creates a parallel set of memory variables for the structure of the database and assigns initial values to each. We use a preprocessor pseudo function `CHARINIT()` for the purpose of generating a number of spaces equal to the length of a field of type Character. We'll see later that invoking `InitVars()` becomes necessary when adding new database records.

As a logical extension of this function, we could have developed an intelligent UDF designed to determine the data type of each field in a database and initialize a memory variable accordingly. For example, a Character field would yield a Character memory variable containing spaces, a Numeric field would result in a Numeric memory variable containing a 0. The initial value for a logical field we arbitrarily decide is .F. and the null date is assigned to memory variables for Date fields. Note that instead of using the traditional method of creating a null date with `CTOD(' / / ')`, we could have also used the following UDC to implement the more usable dBASE IV style date constants:

```
#xtranslate {<month>/<day>/<year>} => ;
    CTOD(#<month>+'/'+#<day>+'/'+#<year>)
#xtranslate { / / } => CTOD(' / / ')
#xtranslate { } => CTOD(' / / ')
```

This technique allows for easier specification of date constants. Therefore, we could have initialized the Date memory variable in the following way:

```
dSample := {10/27/55}// Easier than CTOD()
dHireDate := { }     // Assign null date.
```

SetVars()

The purpose of SetVars() is to copy the contents of each database field into a corresponding memory variable. This process is called *scattering* the fields, and SetVars() implements a simple "scatter" routine. This function is necessary for editing the current record since our style of data entry requires that we only directly change the contents of memory variables and then eventually copy those changes back to the database.

Note

> There are numerous reasons to scatter the data of a record prior to data entry. The most important of these reasons is that working with memory variables makes it easy to back out of the editing process. For example, imagine that the user is halfway through editing the fields and then wants to abort the process; the memory variable contents are simply discarded and the fields will not change.

As an extension of the scatter routine provided, we could have written a entirely generic version that uses array elements instead of specific memory variables to hold the field values. One possible solution is shown here:

```
/***
*
* Scatter() -> aScatterArray
*
*/

FUNCTION Scatter
LOCAL nFields := FCOUNT()  // Get number of fields.
LOCAL nCount
LOCAL aScatterArray := {}

/* Add element containing value of each field */
FOR nCount := 1 TO nFields
    AADD(aScatterArray, FIELDGET(nCount))
NEXT
RETURN (aScatterArray)     // Return field value array.
```

The function of Scatter() is to return an array whose elements contain the values stored in the fields of the current record of the open database. This way, your data entry program may reference array elements instead of memory variables in the @ GETs. Notice that we begin with an empty array and then use AADD() to create elements containing the values of the fields. The built-in function FIELDGET() accepts a single parameter, the field number, and returns the field's value.

ReplVars()

The reverse of a scatter routine is a *gather* function. Gathering a record's field values means to place the newly edited values from a group of memory variables or array elements back into the database record. Our ReplVars() function does this with memory variables created by either InitVars() or SetVars(). Notice that all database field names are aliased. Many Clipper developers consistently use this technique to avoid confusion when dealing with relational data entry programs involving more than one database.

Using the array approach once again, we can come up with the following gather routine:

```
/***
*
* Gather( <aGatherArray> ) -> NIL
*
*/

FUNCTION Gather( aGatherArray )
LOCAL nFields := FCOUNT()
LOCAL nCount

FOR nCount := 1 TO nFields
    FIELDPUT(nCount,aScatterArray[nCount])
NEXT
RETURN NIL
```

Here, the Gather() function takes array elements that have been previously entered or edited by the user and replaces them back in the record. The built-in FIELDPUT() is used here to replace the values instead of the REPLACE command since we readily have the field number and not the field name.

Menu()

As mentioned earlier, our data entry system consists of a simple horizontal bar menu enabling the user to specify the desired option to be performed. The function Menu() implements our menu. To present the menu to the user we use the @ PROMPT and MENU TO commands. Once the user selects the desired option, the DO CASE/ENDCASE construct decides where to go. As the code indicates, each option is implemented as a series of function calls to the various data entry support routines previously defined. Now, let's briefly go through each option to see what makes it tick.

ADD New Record

This option adds new records to the database. To do this we use InitVars() to initialize (or to re-initialize if the add option is used more than once) the memory variables to their initial values. Next, we display the initial values in their data entry boxes. The READ statement then initiates data entry and control of the screen is passed to the user. After satisfying the pending GETs, we use the UPDATED() built-in function to check if any of the GETs were changed, that is, if some new value(s) was entered. If so, we use the DBAPPEND() database function to add a null record and then we call ReplVars() to gather the memory variable data into the appropriate fields.

EDIT Existing Record

The EDIT option goes much the same way as the ADD New Record option except it begins with a call to SetVars(), which scatters the field values to memory variables. Notice that after the READ we don't invoke DBAPPEND() this time since we're only replacing the field values of an existing record.

This edit feature requires you to first position to the record to edit. An obvious enhancement would be to have an edit prompt (possibly with the aid of a picklist presenting name or other information) for a key value that we would use to position to the desired record prior to editing.

DELETE Existing Record

Deleting a record is simple. We just make sure we're positioned at the record to delete, choose the DELETE option, and confirm the delete operation. The program then calls the database function DBDELETE() to mark the record for deletion. The confirmation is very important here since, otherwise, it would be all too easy to delete a record by mistake. Given the way Xbase products handle record deletions, we would, of course, need a PACK process somewhere else in the application to physically delete all records previously marked.

For the deletion to be honored, you must be sure to issue a SET DELETED ON in the Entry() routine. Once you move forward or backward in the database and then try to return to the deleted record, with SET DELETED ON, this is not possible. Unfortunately, the record remains visible even after you've confirmed deletion. As an enhancement, we could automatically display the next record in sequence instead so the user will have the feeling that the record was really deleted.

NEXT/PREV Record

Moving forward (Pg Dn) and backward (Pg Up) through the records is simple, just use the DBSKIP() and DBSKIP(-1) database functions, respectively. The only hitch is what to do when we encounter EOF() or BOF(). No problem really, we just check the file position status after attempting to reposition and display a message box using the built-in ALERT() function.

FIND Record

The only function not implemented in our generic data entry process is the find function. This one was left out because there are so many different methods and so many diverse requirements when it comes to presenting a picklist to the user.

One preferred approach is to use a TBrowse and one or more TBColumn objects as the picklist mechanism. Let's list some hints as to how this might occur. The user would select Find and a TBrowse window would appear, consisting of the employee number and name fields, indexed by name. The user scrolls through the list, hunting for the desired name. Once the user locates the record and presses Enter, the record appears on the screen.

The GET System

With all we've said thus far about data entry potential with CA-Clipper, we've only scratched the surface of what can be accomplished. CA-Clipper is extremely flexible when it comes to data entry techniques. Underlying each and every @ GET command that you include in your application is something called the GET system. The way a GET behaves is determined by the GET system. Luckily, if you wish to change or customize how GETs work, you can do so yourself by modifying the GETSYS.PRG program located in the \CLIPPER5\SOURCE\SYS directory. GET system programming is an advanced topic and beyond the scope of this book. Just bear in mind that anything is possible when it comes to data entry in Clipper. It may just take an extra bit of education and work. Please do review the various general purpose commercial libraries that contain features using of a custom GET system.

Listing 13.1 Data Entry UDF Collection

```
/***
*
* Main() -> NIL
*
*/

FUNCTION Main
   Entry(3, 7, 21, 73)
RETURN NIL


/***
*
* ENTRY.PRG - Simple data entry library
*
*/

#include 'box.ch'
#define CHARINIT(c) SPACE(LEN(c))
#define TRUE .T.
#define FALSE .F.
```

```
STATIC cEmpNo
STATIC cEmpName, cHomeAddr, cHomeCity, cHomeSt
STATIC cHomeZip, cHomePhone, cExt, dHireDate
STATIC lFullTime, nMoSal, cSSN, dBirthDate

/***
*
* Entry( <nTopRow>, <nLeftCol>, <nBottomRow>,
*        <nRightCol> ) -> NIL
*
*/

FUNCTION Entry( nTopRow, nLeftCol, nBottomRow, nRightCol )
LOCAL cScreenSave := SAVESCREEN(0, 0, 24, 79)
LOCAL cWallPaper := '', nRow
MEMVAR GetList

CLEAR ALL
SET ESCAPE OFF
SET BELL OFF
SET SCOREBOARD OFF
SET DELETED ON

* Open EMPLOYEE.DBF file
*       EMPLOYEE.NTX, Key: Employee->EmpName

USE Employee INDEX Employee NEW

SETMODE(25,80)          // Plain old 25x80 display.
SETCOLOR('B/N')         // Blue on black for effect.
FOR nRow := 0 TO 25     // Paint the wallpaper.
   @ nRow,0 SAY PADC(cWallPaper, 80, CHR(176))
NEXT
SETCOLOR('W/B,N/W,,,N/W')
@ nTopRow, nLeftCol CLEAR TO nBottomRow, nRightCol
@ nTopRow, nLeftCol, nBottomRow, nRightCol ;
     BOX B_SINGLE COLOR 'W/B'

@  3,31 SAY ' Employee Data Entry '
@  5,13 SAY 'Employee #:'
@  7,19 SAY 'Name:'
@  9,11 SAY 'Home address:'
@ 11,19 SAY 'City:'
@ 11,42 SAY 'State:'
@ 11,53 SAY 'ZIP:'
@ 13,13 SAY 'Home Phone:'
@ 13,42 SAY 'Office Ext:'
@ 15,14 SAY 'Hire Date:'
@ 15,37 SAY 'Full Time (Y/N):'
```

```
    @ 17, 9 SAY 'Monthly Salary:'
    @ 17,37 SAY 'Soc. Sec #:'
    @ 19,13 SAY 'Birth Date:'

    SetVars() // Load memory variables with contents of first record.
    GetScr()  // Display record.
    CLEAR GETS
    Menu()    // Prompt user for option.

    RESTSCREEN(0, 0, 24, 79, cScreenSave)
    RETURN NIL




/***
*
* GetScr() -> NIL
*
* Purpose: Issue GETs for data entry screen
*
*/

STATIC FUNCTION GetScr

MEMVAR GetList

@  5,25 GET cEmpNo     PICTURE '@!'
@  7,25 GET cEmpName
@  9,25 GET cHomeAddr
@ 11,25 GET cHomeCity
@ 11,49 GET cHomeSt    PICTURE '@!'
@ 11,58 GET cHomeZip   PICTURE '99999-9999'
@ 13,25 GET cHomePhone PICTURE '(999)999-9999'
@ 13,54 GET cExt       PICTURE '9999'
@ 15,25 GET dHireDate
@ 15,54 GET lFullTime  PICTURE 'Y'
@ 17,25 GET nMoSal     PICTURE '9999.99'
@ 17,49 GET cSSN       PICTURE '999-99-9999'
@ 19,25 GET dBirthDate

RETURN NIL

/***
*
* InitVars() -> NIL
*
* Purpose: Initialize all static variables for
*          data entry
```

```
*
*/

STATIC FUNCTION InitVars
cEmpNo      := CHARINIT(Employee->EmpNo)
cEmpName    := CHARINIT(Employee->EmpName)
cHomeAddr   := CHARINIT(Employee->HomeAddr)
cHomeCity   := CHARINIT(Employee->HomeCity)
cHomeSt     := CHARINIT(Employee->HomeSt)
cHomeZip    := CHARINIT(Employee->HomeZip)
cHomePhone  := CHARINIT(Employee->HomePhone)
cExt        := CHARINIT(Employee->Ext)
dHireDate   := CTOD('  /  /  ')
lFullTime   := FALSE
nMoSal      := 0.00
cSSN        := CHARINIT(Employee->SSN)
dBirthDate  := CTOD('  /  /  ')

RETURN NIL

/***
*
* SetVars() -> NIL
*
* Purpose: Assign database field values to
*          static memory variables
*
*/

STATIC FUNCTION SetVars

cEmpNo      := Employee->EmpNo
cEmpName    := Employee->EmpName
cHomeAddr   := Employee->HomeAddr
cHomeCity   := Employee->HomeCity
cHomeSt     := Employee->HomeSt
cHomeZip    := Employee->HomeZip
cHomePhone  := Employee->HomePhone
cExt        := Employee->Ext
dHireDate   := Employee->HireDate
lFullTime   := Employee->FullTime
nMoSal      := Employee->MoSal
cSSN        := Employee->SSN
dBirthDate  := Employee->BirthDate

RETURN NIL

/***
*
```

```
* ReplVars() -> NIL
*
* Purpose: Replace database field values with memory variable contents
*
*/

STATIC FUNCTION ReplVars

REPLACE Employee->EmpNo      WITH cEmpNo      ,;
        Employee->EmpName    WITH cEmpName    ,;
        Employee->HomeAddr   WITH cHomeAddr   ,;
        Employee->HomeCity   WITH cHomeCity   ,;
        Employee->HomeSt     WITH cHomeSt     ,;
        Employee->HomeZip    WITH cHomeZip    ,;
        Employee->HomePhone  WITH cHomePhone  ,;
        Employee->Ext        WITH cExt        ,;
        Employee->HireDate   WITH dHireDate   ,;
        Employee->FullTime   WITH lFullTime   ,;
        Employee->MoSal      WITH nMoSal      ,;
        Employee->SSN        WITH cSSN        ,;
        Employee->BirthDate  WITH dBirthDate
RETURN NIL

/***
*
* Menu() -> NIL
*
* Purpose: Present menu and prompt user for option
*
*/

STATIC FUNCTION Menu

MEMVAR GetList
LOCAL nOption, lDelete := FALSE

SET ESCAPE OFF
SET MESSAGE TO 24 CENTRE

WHILE TRUE
   SETCOLOR('R/W,W/R,,,N/W')
   @ 22, 9 PROMPT ' ADD  ' MESSAGE ' Add new record '
   @ 22,18 PROMPT ' EDIT ' MESSAGE ' Edit existing record '
   @ 22,27 PROMPT 'DELETE' MESSAGE ' Delete existing record '
   @ 22,36 PROMPT ' NEXT ' MESSAGE ' Next Record '
   @ 22,45 PROMPT ' PREV ' MESSAGE ' Previous Record '
   @ 22,54 PROMPT ' FIND ' MESSAGE ' Search for item '
   @ 22,63 PROMPT ' QUIT ' MESSAGE ' Return to main menu '
   MENU TO nOption
```

```
         DO CASE
           CASE nOption == 1      // ADD
             InitVars()
             GetScr()
             READ
             IF UPDATED()
               DBAPPEND()
               ReplVars()
             ENDIF

           CASE nOption == 2      // EDIT
             SetVars()
             GetScr()
             READ
             IF UPDATED()
               ReplVars()
             ENDIF

           CASE nOption == 3      // DELETE
             IF ALERT('Confirm delete?', ;
                {'Yes', 'No'}) == 1
               ALERT('Record deleted, key: '+ ;
                  Employee->EmpNo)
               DBDELETE()
             ENDIF

           CASE nOption == 4      // NEXT
             DBSKIP()
             IF EOF()
               ALERT('End of file')
             ELSE
               SetVars()
               GetScr()
               CLEAR GETS
             ENDIF

           CASE nOption == 5      // PREV
             DBSKIP(-1)
             IF BOF()
               ALERT('Beginning of file')
             ELSE
               SetVars()
               GetScr()
               CLEAR GETS
             ENDIF

           CASE nOption == 6      // FIND

           CASE nOption == 7      // QUIT
```

```
            EXIT
      ENDCASE
END
RETURN NIL
```

Basic Reporting

Next we'll examine another important program group: reporting. In a manner similar to the previous section, we'll pull together our newfound knowledge of CA-Clipper by writing a generic multi-table report program that you can use as a model for future reporting requirements.

A Formula for Reporting

Before we look at some actual code, let's define some simple goals for our report program. We'll begin by providing an easy-to-follow, five-step formula for putting together a simple report program in CA-Clipper. The formula is presented in time sequence order, meaning that the report should proceed with each item in the sequence given in order to achieve the desired results. Later, as we go through the sample report code, we'll see how each of these ingredients of the formula has been implemented.

1. **Establish the environment:** This step includes opening the files and indexes required by the report. You might also consider building temporary index files on-the-fly. Since you are generally less concerned about the speed of a report than, say, an interactive query, creating new, special purpose indexes is not a problem. At this stage, you will also set any relations and filters. Finally, you may also activate any of the available replaceable database drivers (RDDs) available with CA-Clipper version 5.2 in order to access data coming from diverse database environments.

2. **Prompt for selection criteria:** Such criteria might be nothing more than a date or account number range, but it could also be much more ad-hoc in the sense that the user has more control over how the data is selected. A good report is one that allows the user to obtain the information from many different perspectives. A flexible selection criteria process makes this possible. Many times a picklist or series of picklists is an appropriate means of selecting report criteria. Be sure to validity check all user inputs—nonsensical report criteria can wreak havoc in a report.

3. **General Report Setup:** This area includes several items required before the report actually begins reading data and producing output. For example, you might check the status of the printer (see if the printer port is accepting data). You might also display a friendly message on the screen advising the user to sit back and enjoy the ride as the report prints. This is certainly necessary as

some reports produce sizable quantities of output and a blank screen could cause the user great concern; displaying a "Please be patient" message lets the user know that something is happening. You might find that a message is especially helpful if the program runs on a network and the printed output is directed to a centrally located network printer.

Also, if the report program does considerable processing before any output appears, you might try displaying something on the screen such as customer names or account numbers being read by the program, so the user can see something is happening.

Next in the setup area, any necessary escape sequences (commands to activate various printer modes) to the printer should be sent now. Of course, additional printer commands will normally be sent during the processing of the report, but these sequences are the ones that affect the whole report.

The last item you would need to include during setup is a command to redirect all @ SAY output to the printer. The manner in which you do this depends on whether you've written a ? or an @ SAY style report. For ? reports, you would use a SET PRINTER ON/OFF and SET CONSOLE ON/OFF combination. With @ SAY reports, however, you would use SET DEVICE TO PRINTER/SCREEN.

Some other possibilities you might consider in this step would be to prompt the user to specify which printer port should be used. You might even choose to write the output to a disk file.

4. **Start the main report loop:** This is the area of the program that actually produces output. Here, you would traverse the various database files and generate report detail lines. For the main report loop you have a couple of choices. You may choose to use the standard WHILE/END loop for controlling the database traversal process or you might try a CA-Clipper specific methodology, namely the DBEVAL() database function. If you recall, this built-in function sequentially selects records from a database under control of a code block. The result tends to be a very elegant solution for report generation.

Of course, most reports need to contain an end-of-page routine, a separate UDF that handles when the report has printed all the information possible for a single page and then prepares for the next page.

One feature any good report program should have is the ability to "listen" to the Escape key, allowing the user to stop the report at any time and optionally continue or abort the reporting process.

5. **Clean-up, close files, etc.:** Here we need to tidy up after ourselves before returning to the main program. We need to redirect output to the screen, close all databases, indexes, relations, filters, etc., restore the screen's contents and colors, and reset the printer to its prior mode.

A Simple Style of Report

The CA-Clipper code found in Listing 13.2 represents a model report program along with several support UDFs. You may use the program "straight out of the box" if you wish, modifying it only to suit your own purposes. A complete description of how the primary report module functions and each associated UDF is supplied in the remainder of this section.

The `ClipRep()` UDF is the entry point for the reporting module and is called from the `Main()` program. Each major code section corresponding to our earlier discussion of the five-step formula is clearly labeled with comments. Let's now analyze each of these code sections to see how we've implemented the report with CA-Clipper.

Establish Environment

In this section of the program, we centrally define the various database environment elements needed by the report. We begin by opening two databases EMPLOYEE and DEPT (along with an existing index file DEPT.NTX). The structure for EMPLOYEE.DBF (see Figure 13.1) has one addition. The new field DeptNo (CHAR 3) acts as the link field for the one-to-many relation of these databases. See Figure 13.3 for the structure of DEPT.DBF. For this report, a temporary index is required that orders EMPLOYEE by the `EmpName` field. Notice that to provide you with practice in using database functions, we use the `DBCREATINDEX()` function instead of the `INDEX ON` command to build this index. Lastly, we link up the two databases with a one-to-many relationship (EMPLOYEE is the parent and DEPT is the child) with `DBSETRELATION()`.

Report Selection Criteria

The criteria section of `ClipRep()` prompts the user for a hire date range. We present a dialog box to the user, allow the entry of two date values, and then validity check the input to make sure that only appropriate dates are used for the selection process. We finish up by building a code block, `bCond`, that

Figure 13.3 This is the database structure for DEPT.DBF.

Field Number	Field Name	Field Type	Field Width
1	DeptNo	Character	3
2	DeptName	Character	25
3	Manager	Character	25
4	Bldg	Character	2
		Total	55

contains the logical expression needed to select the desired records for the report. We'll see later how the code block drives the entire reporting process.

Report Setup

In this section, we have included several of the items identified in our generic formula discussion earlier. First, we test if the printer is ready. For this purpose, we use the built-in `ISPRINTER()` function that returns a logical value .T. if the printer is ready and .F. if not. Our example attempts 30 times and if at the end of that time the printer is still not ready, the program notifies the user and then returns to `Main()`. Next, we display a "please wait" box while saving the current color setting and screen contents.

We then send the printer command sequence to tell an HP laser printer to go to landscape mode. To do this, we use the UDF `ToPrinter()`, which does nothing more than send a command string to the printer. Lastly, we activate the printer with `SET DEVICE TO PRINTER`.

Main Report Loop

The main report loop section is the most interesting part of `ClipRep()` since it uses neither of Clipper's looping constructs, `WHILE/END` or `FOR/NEXT`. Instead, we simply call a series of UDFs—`EndPage()`, `PrintDet()`, and `CheckAbort()`—under the control of `DBEVAL()`. Remember that `DBEVAL()` processes records by considering each record according to the code block given as the function's second parameter. The first code block, in our case, is mostly a sequence of UDF calls.

The positioning of the call to `EndPage()` in this sequence is important since it must handle the initial page heading in addition to end-of-page processing. We force an initial page heading by initially setting `nLineNo` to 99. Notice the use of file-wide `STATIC`s for several report variables, thus allowing easy access from all report modules.

The `PrintDet()` function handles printing of one detail line on the report. As indicated, `PrintDet()` also increments running totals.

Notice that the call to `DBEVAL()` is inside a `BEGIN/END SEQUENCE` structure. This structure is the Clipper mechanism that allows for the report to be interrupted. We check inside of `CheckAbort()` to see if a key has been pressed and, if so, the function prompts the user to continue or to abort the report. If the user chooses to abort, we issue a `BREAK` command. `BREAK` transfers control to the statement immediately after `END SEQUENCE`. In the case of an aborted report, the program still prints the totals accumulated thus far.

Housekeeping

In our sample report program, the housekeeping chores amount to re-directing @ SAY output to the screen with SET DEVICE TO SCREEN, resetting the laser printer to portrait mode, restoring the prior color settings and screen contents, and closing all databases, indexes and the relation.

Listing 13.2   Multi-Table Report Program

```
/***
*
* Main() -> NIL
*
*/

FUNCTION Main

    ClipRep()      // Print the report.

RETURN NIL

/***
*
* CLIPREP.PRG - Simple multi-table reporting
*
* Contains:     ClipRep()
*
*  Purpose:     Print Employee List by Hire Date
*
*/

#define TRUE .T.
#define FALSE .F.
#define NULL_DATE CTOD('  /  /  ')
#define PAGE_LENGTH 55
#define PAGE_WIDTH 100
#define PRINTER_RETRY 30
#define REPORT_TITLE 'EMPLOYEE LIST BY NAME REPORT'
#define RCENTER(string) (PAGE_WIDTH - LEN(string)) / 2

* Define file-wide STATICs
STATIC nTotalSal := 0
STATIC nPageNo:= 1
STATIC nLineNo:= 99
STATIC dBegDate, dEndDate
```

```
/***
*
* ClipRep() -> NIL
*
*/

FUNCTION ClipRep

MEMVAR GetList

LOCAL cScreen, cColor
LOCAL nReTry
LOCAL lPrinterReady := FALSE
LOCAL bCond

CLEAR ALL
SET ESCAPE OFF
SET BELL OFF
SET SCOREBOARD OFF

       /* ———————————————————————————————————————————— */
       /*       E S T A B L I S H   E N V I R O N M E N T       */
       /* ———————————————————————————————————————————— */

* Open all files

USE Employee NEW           // Open EMPLOYEE.DBF file.

USE Dept INDEX Dept NEW    // Open DEPT.DBF file.
                           // Key: Dept->DeptNo


* Build report-specific index

SELECT Employee
DBCREATEINDEX('EmpName', 'EmpName', {|| Employee->EmpName})

* Establish 1:M relation from Employee to Dept

DBSETRELATION('Dept', {|| Employee->DeptNo}, ;
     'Employee->DeptNo')

       /* ———————————————————————————————————————————— */
       /*    P R O M P T   F O R   S E L E C T   C R I T E R I A    */
       /* ———————————————————————————————————————————— */

Scroll()                         // Clear the screen.
SetPos(0,0)
```

```
cScreen := SAVESCREEN(5,20,11,60)    // Save screen contents.
cColor  := SETCOLOR('W+/G')          // Save current color setting.
@ 5, 20 CLEAR TO 11,60               // Clear the window.
@ 5, 20 TO 11, 60 DOUBLE             // Draw a border.

dBegDate := dEndDate := CTOD('  /  /  ')
WHILE TRUE                           // Loop until good data.
   @ 7,25 SAY 'Enter beginning date: ' GET dBegDate
   @ 9,25 SAY '   Enter ending date: ' GET dEndDate
   READ

   /* Provide a way out of prompt */
   IF dBegDate == NULL_DATE .OR. dEndDate == NULL_DATE
     DBCLOSEALL()
     SETCOLOR(cColor)            // Restore color setting.
     RESTSCREEN(5,20,11,60,cScreen)
     RETURN NIL
   ENDIF

   IF dBegDate > dEndDate    // Invalid date range.
     ALERT('Invalid hire date range')
   ELSE
     EXIT
   ENDIF
END

SETCOLOR(cColor)                     // Restore color setting.
RESTSCREEN(5,20,11,60,cScreen)

* Establish a filter to make report streamlined
bCond := {|| Employee->HireDate >= dBegDate .AND. ;
    Employee->HireDate <= dEndDate}

         /* ─────────────────────────────────────────── */
         /*              R E P O R T   S E T U P        */
         /* ─────────────────────────────────────────── */

* Check printer status
FOR nReTry := 1 TO PRINTER_RETRY
   IF ISPRINTER()
     lPrinterReady := TRUE
     EXIT
   ENDIF
NEXT

IF !lPrinterReady
   ALERT('Printer Not Ready')
   RETURN NIL
ENDIF
```

```
* Display a "please be patient" message
cScreen := SAVESCREEN(5,20,9,60)
cColor  := SETCOLOR('W+/B')     // Save current color setting.
@ 5, 20 CLEAR TO 9,60           // Clear the window.
@ 5, 20 TO 9, 60 DOUBLE         // Draw a border.
@ 7, 23 SAY 'Please Wait For Report to Complete'

ToPrinter(CHR(27) + '&l1O')     // HP LaserJet landscape.

SET DEVICE TO PRINTER           // Redirect @ SAY output

        /* ─────────────────────────────────────────────── */
        /*              M A I N   R E P O R T   L O O P    */
        /* ─────────────────────────────────────────────── */

SELECT Employee
BEGIN SEQUENCE
   DBEVAL( {|| EndPage(), PrintDet(), nLineNo++, ;
      CheckAbort()}, bCond)
END SEQUENCE

* Print report totals
@ nLineNo+1, 87 SAY REPLICATE('-',9)
@ nLineNo+2, 87 SAY nTotalSal PICTURE '99,999.99'
@ nLineNo+3, 87 SAY REPLICATE('=',9)
EJECT

        /* ─────────────────────────────────────────────── */
        /*              H O U S E K E E P I N G             */
        /* ─────────────────────────────────────────────── */

SET DEVICE TO SCREEN

ToPrinter(CHR(27) + '&l1O')  // HP LaserJet portrait.

SETCOLOR(cColor) // Restore color setting.
RESTSCREEN(5,20,9,60,cScreen)

DBCLOSEALL()     // Close all databases, indexes, relations, and filters.

RETURN NIL

/***
*
* ToPrinter( <cCmdString> ) -> NIL
*
*/

STATIC FUNCTION ToPrinter(cCmdString)
```

```
   SET PRINTER ON
   SET CONSOLE OFF
   ?? cCmdString      // Send command string to printer.
   SET CONSOLE ON
   SET PRINTER OFF

RETURN NIL

/***
*
* PrintDet() -> NIL
*
*/

STATIC FUNCTION PrintDet

* Print a detail line
@ nLineNo,  0 SAY Employee->EmpName PICTURE '@!'
@ nLineNo, 31 SAY Employee->EmpNo
@ nLineNo, 37 SAY Employee->DeptNo
@ nLineNo, 44 SAY Dept->Manager
@ nLineNo, 70 SAY Dept->Bldg
@ nLineNo, 77 SAY IIF(Employee->FullTime, 'Full Time', 'Part Time')
@ nLineNo, 88 SAY Employee->MoSal PICTURE '9,999.99'
nTotalSal += Employee->MoSal

RETURN NIL

/***
*
* EndPage() -> NIL
*
*/

STATIC FUNCTION EndPage

IF nLineNo > PAGE_LENGTH
   IF nLineNo != 99     // No eject first time.
     EJECT
   ENDIF
   @ 0, RCENTER(REPORT_TITLE) SAY REPORT_TITLE
   @ 0, PAGE_WIDTH-10 SAY 'Page: '+STR(nPageNo,2)
   @ 2, 30 SAY 'Hire Date Range: '+DTOC(dBegDate)+ ;
        ' - '+DTOC(dEndDate)
   @ 4,  0 SAY 'Employee Name'
   @ 4, 31 SAY 'Emp #'
   @ 4, 37 SAY 'Dept #'
   @ 4, 44 SAY 'Supervisor Name'
   @ 4, 70 SAY 'Bldg #'
   @ 4, 77 SAY 'Status'
```

```
     @ 4, 87 SAY 'Salary'

     @ 5,  0 SAY REPLICATE('-', LEN(Employee->EmpName))
     @ 5, 31 SAY REPLICATE('-', LEN(Employee->EmpNo))
     @ 5, 37 SAY REPLICATE('-', 6)
     @ 5, 44 SAY REPLICATE('-', LEN(Dept->Manager))
     @ 5, 70 SAY REPLICATE('-', 6)
     @ 5, 77 SAY REPLICATE('-', 9)
     @ 5, 87 SAY REPLICATE('-', 9)
     nLineNo := 7
     nPageNo++
ENDIF

RETURN NIL

/***
*
*  CheckAbort() -> NIL
*  Routine to pause and alternately abort or continue a report.
*
*/

FUNCTION CheckAbort()

IF INKEY() != 0       // Check for key press.
   IF ALERT('List/Letter paused', {'Abort','Continue'}) == 1
      BREAK           // Report aborted.
   ENDIF
ENDIF

RETURN NIL
```

Summary

As we come to a wrap on the subject of applications, this chapter provided you with a simple framework from which you may begin to develop custom data entry screens and reports using the CA-Clipper style of coding. Please take the enhancement hints provided in the chapter and see what kind of innovative end results you can come up with.

You should now be well postured to construct entire applications, including a complete menuing system, interactive queries, and update processes as well as the program groups addressed in this chapter.

Exercises

1. Based on the sample data entry code in Listing 13.1, modify the Menu() function's ADD and EDIT options to automatically transfer control to each

other depending on whether the key value entered was found or not. For example, if ADD was selected and the employee number entered was already in the database, prompt the user to see if the existing record should be edited. Similarly, if EDIT was selected and the employee number entered was not found, then prompt the user to see if a new record should be added.

2. Enhance the sample report code in Listing 13.2 to produce the same report except broken down by Department #. That is to say, each department group sould be preceded by a report line showing the department number, name, and manager name. Following the department group line should be a list of all the employees in that department, ordered by name. Each department group should end with a department monthly salary sub-total. And finally, the report must have a grand salary total for all departments.

Answers

1. In order to give the data entry program shown in Listing 13.1 the ability to automatically transfer to either the ADD or EDIT modes depending on whether the key value entered exists, involves a reworking of the code that implements these functions. (Take particular note of the CASE statement in the revised code.) Using an additional index file, EMPNUM.NTX, based on the employee number, we are able to immediately check the record's existence as the key is entered by the user. Also, to eliminate code redundancy, we have created two new functions, AddRec() and EditRec().

```
#include 'box.ch'
#define CHARINIT(c) SPACE(LEN(c))
#define TRUE  .T.
#define FALSE .F.

STATIC cEmpNo
STATIC cEmpName, cHomeAddr, cHomeCity, cHomeSt, cHomeZip
STATIC cHomePhone, cExt, dHireDate, lFullTime, nMoSal, cSSN
STATIC dBirthDate

/***
*
* Entry( <nTopRow>, <nLeftCol>, <nBottomRow>, <nRightCol> ) ->
*     NIL
*
*/

FUNCTION Entry( nTopRow, nLeftCol, nBottomRow, nRightCol )

LOCAL cScreenSave := SAVESCREEN(0, 0, 24, 79)
LOCAL cWallPaper := '', nRow
MEMVAR GetList
```

```
CLEAR ALL
SET ESCAPE OFF
SET BELL OFF
SET SCOREBOARD OFF
SET DELETED ON

/* Open EMPLOYEE.DBF file EMPNUM.NTX, Key: Employee->EmpNo
   EMPLOYEE.NTX, Key: Employee->EmpName */

USE Employee INDEX Employee, EmpNo NEW

/* The following code does the following:
   (1) Sets standard display mode
   (2) Paints the wallpaper for entry screen backdrop
   (3) Draws a simple box around entry surface
   (4) Displays the screen title
   (5) Displays field titles
*/

SETMODE(25,80)           // Plain old 25x80 display.

SETCOLOR('B/N')          // Blue on black for effect.
FOR nRow := 0 TO 25      // Paint the wallpaper.
   @ nRow,0 SAY PADC(cWallPaper, 80, CHR(176))
NEXT

SETCOLOR('W/B,N/W,,,N/W')
@ nTopRow, nLeftCol CLEAR TO nBottomRow, nRightCol
@ nTopRow, nLeftCol, nBottomRow, nRightCol BOX ;
        B_SINGLE COLOR 'W/B'

@ 3,31 SAY ' Employee Data Entry '

@  5,13 SAY 'Employee #:'
@  7,19 SAY 'Name:'
@  9,11 SAY 'Home address:'
@ 11,19 SAY 'City:'
@ 11,42 SAY 'State:'
@ 11,53 SAY 'ZIP:'
@ 13,13 SAY 'Home Phone:'
@ 13,42 SAY 'Office Ext:'
@ 15,14 SAY 'Hire Date:'
@ 15,37 SAY 'Full Time (Y/N):'
@ 17, 9 SAY 'Monthly Salary:'
@ 17,37 SAY 'Soc. Sec #:'
@ 19,13 SAY 'Birth Date:'

SetVars()   // Load memory variables with contents of first record.
GetScr()    // Display record.
```

```
CLEAR GETS
Menu()          // Prompt user for option.

RESTSCREEN(0, 0, 24, 79, cScreenSave)

RETURN NIL

/***
*
* GetScr() -> NIL
*
* Purpose: Issue GETs for data entry screen.
*
*/

STATIC FUNCTION GetScr

MEMVAR GetList

@  5,25 SAY cEmpNo      // Just display the key.
@  7,25 GET cEmpName
@  9,25 GET cHomeAddr
@ 11,25 GET cHomeCity
@ 11,49 GET cHomeSt     PICTURE '@!'
@ 11,58 GET cHomeZip    PICTURE '99999-9999'
@ 13,25 GET cHomePhone  PICTURE '(999)999-9999'
@ 13,54 GET cExt        PICTURE '9999'
@ 15,25 GET dHireDate
@ 15,54 GET lFullTime   PICTURE 'Y'
@ 17,25 GET nMoSal      PICTURE '9999.99'
@ 17,49 GET cSSN        PICTURE '999-99-9999'
@ 19,25 GET dBirthDate

RETURN NIL

/***
*
* InitVars() -> NIL
*
* Purpose: Initialize all static variables for data entry.
*
*/

STATIC FUNCTION InitVars

cEmpNo     := CHARINIT(Employee->EmpNo)
cEmpName   := CHARINIT(Employee->EmpName)
cHomeAddr  := CHARINIT(Employee->HomeAddr)
cHomeCity  := CHARINIT(Employee->HomeCity)
```

```
cHomeSt      := CHARINIT(Employee->HomeSt)
cHomeZip     := CHARINIT(Employee->HomeZip)
cHomePhone   := CHARINIT(Employee->HomePhone)
cExt         := CHARINIT(Employee->Ext)
dHireDate    := CTOD('  /  /  ')
lFullTime    := FALSE
nMoSal       := 0.00
cSSN         := CHARINIT(Employee->SSN)
dBirthDate   := CTOD('  /  /  ')

RETURN NIL

/***
*
* SetVars() -> NIL
*
* Purpose: Assign database field values to static memory variables.
*
*/

STATIC FUNCTION SetVars

cEmpNo       := Employee->EmpNo
cEmpName     := Employee->EmpName
cHomeAddr    := Employee->HomeAddr
cHomeCity    := Employee->HomeCity
cHomeSt      := Employee->HomeSt
cHomeZip     := Employee->HomeZip
cHomePhone   := Employee->HomePhone
cExt         := Employee->Ext
dHireDate    := Employee->HireDate
lFullTime    := Employee->FullTime
nMoSal       := Employee->MoSal
cSSN         := Employee->SSN
dBirthDate   := Employee->BirthDate

RETURN NIL

/***
*
* ReplVars() -> NIL
*
* Purpose: Replace database field values with memory variables contents.
*
*/

STATIC FUNCTION ReplVars

REPLACE   Employee->EmpNo     WITH cEmpNo      ,;
```

```
            Employee->EmpName     WITH cEmpName    ,;
            Employee->HomeAddr    WITH cHomeAddr   ,;
            Employee->HomeCity    WITH cHomeCity   ,;
            Employee->HomeSt      WITH cHomeSt     ,;
            Employee->HomeZip     WITH cHomeZip    ,;
            Employee->HomePhone   WITH cHomePhone  ,;
            Employee->Ext         WITH cExt        ,;
            Employee->HireDate    WITH dHireDate   ,;
            Employee->FullTime    WITH lFullTime   ,;
            Employee->MoSal       WITH nMoSal      ,;
            Employee->SSN         WITH cSSN        ,;
            Employee->BirthDate   WITH dBirthDate

RETURN NIL

/***
 *
 * Menu() -> NIL
 *
 * Purpose: Present menu and prompt user for option.
 *
 */

STATIC FUNCTION Menu

MEMVAR GetList

LOCAL nOption, lDelete := FALSE

SET ESCAPE OFF
SET MESSAGE TO 24 CENTRE

WHILE TRUE
   SETCOLOR('R/W,W/R,,,N/W')
   @ 22, 9 PROMPT ' ADD  ' MESSAGE ' Add new record '
   @ 22,18 PROMPT ' EDIT ' MESSAGE ' Edit existing record '
   @ 22,27 PROMPT 'DELETE' MESSAGE ' Delete existing record '
   @ 22,36 PROMPT ' NEXT ' MESSAGE ' Next Record '
   @ 22,45 PROMPT ' PREV ' MESSAGE ' Previous Record '
   @ 22,54 PROMPT ' FIND ' MESSAGE ' Search for record '
   @ 22,63 PROMPT ' QUIT ' MESSAGE ' Return to main menu '
   MENU TO nOption

   DO CASE
      CASE nOption == 1  // ADD mode
         InitVars()
         GetScr()            // Display fresh screen before
                             // ADDing new record.
         CLEAR GETS
```

```
         @ 5,25 GET cEmpNo PICTURE '@!'
         READ              // Prompt for key value.
         SET ORDER TO 2    // Activate EmpNo index.
         SEEK cEmpNo       // Key found?
         IF FOUND()        // Yes, cannot add another.
            IF ALERT('Employee already exists,edit?',;
               {'Yes', 'No'}) == 1
            EditRec()       // Just edit the record.
            ENDIF
         ELSE
            AddRec(cEmpNo)// OK to add new key.
         ENDIF
         SET ORDER TO 1    // Back to EmpName index.

      CASE nOption == 2     // EDIT mode
         @ 5,25 GET cEmpNo PICTURE '@!'
         READ
         SET ORDER TO 2
         SEEK cEmpNo
         IF !FOUND()
            IF ALERT('Employee does not exist,add?',;
               {'Yes', 'No'}) == 1
               AddRec(cEmpNo)
            ENDIF
         ELSE
             EditRec()
            ENDIF
            SET ORDER TO 1     // Back to EmpName index.

      CASE nOption == 3    // DELETE mode
         IF ALERT('Confirm delete?', {'Yes', 'No'}) == 1
            ALERT('Record deleted, key: ' + ;
               Employee->EmpNo)
            DBDELETE()
         ENDIF

      CASE nOption == 4    // NEXT mode
         DBSKIP()
         IF EOF()
            ALERT('End of file encountered')
         ELSE
            SetVars()
            GetScr()
            CLEAR GETS
         ENDIF

      CASE nOption == 5    // PREV mode
         DBSKIP(-1)
         IF BOF()
```

```
              ALERT('Beginning of file encountered')
           ELSE
              SetVars()
              GetScr()
              CLEAR GETS
           ENDIF

      CASE nOption == 6     // FIND mode

      CASE nOption == 7
         EXIT
   ENDCASE
END

RETURN NIL

/***
*
* AddRec( <cNewKey> ) -> NIL
*
* Purpose: Add a record using passed key value.
*
*/

STATIC FUNCTION AddRec(cNewKey)

MEMVAR GetList

InitVars()
cEmpNo := cNewKey      // Display new key value.
GetScr()
READ
IF UPDATED()
   DBAPPEND()
   ReplVars()
ENDIF

RETURN NIL

/***
*
* EditRec() -> NIL
*
* Purpose: Edit a record
*
*/

STATIC FUNCTION EditRec

MEMVAR GetList
```

```
SetVars()
GetScr()
READ
IF UPDATED()
   ReplVars()
ENDIF

RETURN NIL
```

2. This problem represents a typical scenario when developing report programs, that is, changing requirements. Once the user reviews the report originally specified, new ideas surface, indicating a re-programming exercise. The report program shown in Listing 13.2 is enhanced in the following code to add department breaks. To do this, we needed to use a 1:M relationship between DEPT.DBF (parent) and EMPLOYEE.DBF (child). Due to the smaller amount of information on this version of the report, we leave the report in portrait mode.

The major differences in this version are: a new `DeptBrk()` UDF for handling the department breaks, a revised method for performing the primary report loop processing, and the accumulation of the salary amounts for department sub-totals and the grand total.

```
#define TRUE .T.
#define FALSE .F.
#define NULL_DATE CTOD('  /  /  ')
#define PAGE_LENGTH 55
#define PAGE_WIDTH 80
#define PRINTER_RETRY 30
#define REPORT_TITLE 'EMPLOYEE LIST BY DEPARTMENT REPORT'
#define RCENTER(string) (PAGE_WIDTH - LEN(string)) / 2

* Define file-wide STATICs
STATIC nGrandTotalSal := 0
STATIC nDeptTotalSal := 0
STATIC nPageNo    := 1
STATIC nLineNo    := 99
STATIC dBegDate, dEndDate
STATIC cCurDept := ''

/***
*
* ClipRep() -> NIL
*
*/

FUNCTION ClipRep

MEMVAR GetList
```

```
LOCAL cScreen, cColor
LOCAL nReTry
LOCAL lPrinterReady := FALSE
LOCAL bCond
LOCAL lFirst := TRUE

CLEAR ALL
SET ESCAPE OFF
SET BELL OFF
SET SCOREBOARD OFF

      /* ─────────────────────────────────────────────── */
      /*         E S T A B L I S H   E N V I R O N M E N T       */
      /* ─────────────────────────────────────────────── */

* Open all files

USE Employee NEW           // Open EMPLOYEE.DBF file.

USE Dept INDEX Dept NEW    // Open DEPT.DBF file.
                           // Key: Dept->DeptNo




* Build report-specific index

SELECT Employee
DBCREATEINDEX('NameDept', 'DeptNo+EmpName', ;
     {|| Employee->DeptNo+Employee->EmpName})

* Establish 1:M relation from DEPT (parent) to EMPLOYEE (child)

SELECT Dept
DBSETRELATION('Employee', {|| Dept->DeptNo})

      /* ─────────────────────────────────────────────── */
      /* P R O M P T   F O R   S E L E C T   C R I T E R I A */
      /* ─────────────────────────────────────────────── */

Scroll()        // Clear the screen.
SetPos(0,0)

cScreen := SAVESCREEN(5,20,11,60)    // Save screen contents.
cColor  := SETCOLOR('W+/G')          // Save current color setting.
@ 5, 20 CLEAR TO 11,60               // Clear the window.
@ 5, 20 TO 11, 60 DOUBLE             // Draw a border.

dBegDate := dEndDate := CTOD('  /  /  ')
```

```
      WHILE TRUE                            // Loop until good data.
        @ 7,25 SAY 'Enter beginning date: ' GET dBegDate
        @ 9,25 SAY '   Enter ending date: ' GET dEndDate
        READ

          /* Provide a way out of prompt */
        IF dBegDate == NULL_DATE .OR. dEndDate == NULL_DATE
          DBCLOSEALL()
          SETCOLOR(cColor)                  // Restore color setting.
          RESTSCREEN(5,20,11,60,cScreen)
          RETURN NIL
        ENDIF

        IF dBegDate > dEndDate              // Invalid date range.
          ALERT('Invalid hire date range')
        ELSE
          EXIT
        ENDIF
      END

      SETCOLOR(cColor)                      // Restore color setting.
      RESTSCREEN(5,20,11,60,cScreen)

      * Establish a filter to make report streamlined
      bCond := {|| Employee->HireDate >= dBegDate .AND. ;
          Employee->HireDate <= dEndDate}


          /* ─────────────────────────────────────────────── */
          /*                R E P O R T   S E T U P          */
          /* ─────────────────────────────────────────────── */

      * Check printer status
      FOR nReTry := 1 TO PRINTER_RETRY
        IF ISPRINTER()
          lPrinterReady := TRUE
          EXIT
        ENDIF
      NEXT

      IF !lPrinterReady
        ALERT('Printer Not Ready')
        RETURN NIL
      ENDIF

      * Display a "please be patient" message
      cScreen := SAVESCREEN(5,20,9,60)
      cColor := SETCOLOR('W+/B')   // Save current color setting.
      @ 5, 20 CLEAR TO 9,60        // Clear the window.
```

```
@ 5, 20 TO 9, 60 DOUBLE       // Draw a border.
@ 7, 23 SAY 'Please Wait For Report to Complete'

SET DEVICE TO PRINTER         // Redirect @ SAY output.

      /* ─────────────────────────────────────────────── */
      /*           M A I N   R E P O R T   L O O P       */
      /* ─────────────────────────────────────────────── */
SELECT Dept
BEGIN SEQUENCE
   EndPage()              // First time logic.
   WHILE !EOF()           // Loop for all department records.
      DeptBrk(@lFirst)
      cCurDept := Dept->DeptNo
      SELECT Employee     // Relation points us to right place.
      WHILE cCurDept == Employee->DeptNo .AND. !EOF()
         * Select only qualifying records
         IF EVAL(bCond)
            EndPage()
            PrintDet()     // Print detail line.
            CheckAbort()
         ENDIF
         DBSKIP()        // Next employee.
      END
      SELECT Dept
      DBSKIP()           // Next department record.
   END
END SEQUENCE

* Print report grand totals
@ nLineNo+1, 47 SAY REPLICATE('-',10)
@ nLineNo+2, 15 SAY 'All Dept. Salary Total:'
@ nLineNo+2, 47 SAY nGrandTotalSal PICTURE '999,999.99'
@ nLineNo+3, 47 SAY REPLICATE('=',10)
EJECT

      /* ─────────────────────────────────────────────── */
      /*            H O U S E K E E P I N G              */
      /* ─────────────────────────────────────────────── */

SET DEVICE TO SCREEN

SETCOLOR(cColor)     // Restore color setting.
RESTSCREEN(5,20,9,60,cScreen)

DBCLOSEALL()// Close all databases, indexes, relations, and filters.

RETURN NIL
```

```
/***
*
* PrintDet() -> NIL
*
*/

STATIC FUNCTION PrintDet

* Print a detail line
@ nLineNo,  0 SAY Employee->EmpName PICTURE '@!'
@ nLineNo, 31 SAY Employee->EmpNo
@ nLineNo, 38 SAY IIF(Employee->FullTime, 'Full Time', 'Part Time')
@ nLineNo, 49 SAY Employee->MoSal PICTURE '9,999.99'
nGrandTotalSal += Employee->MoSal
nDeptTotalSal  += Employee->MoSal
nLineNo++

RETURN NIL

/***
*
* DeptBrk( <lFirst> ) -> NIL
*
*/

STATIC FUNCTION DeptBrk(lFirst)

* Time for department break
IF !lFirst
   nLineNo++
   @ nLineNo, 48 SAY REPLICATE('-',9)
   nLineNo++
   @ nLineNo, 15 SAY 'Dept. Salary Sub-total: '
   @ nLineNo, 48 SAY nDeptTotalSal PICTURE '99,999.99'
ENDIF
nLineNo := nLineNo + 3
@ nLineNo,  0 SAY 'Dept: ' + Dept->DeptNo
@ nLineNo, 10 SAY LEFT(Dept->DeptName,25)
@ nLineNo, 36 SAY 'Mgr: ' + Dept->Manager
@ nLineNo, 67 SAY 'Bldg#: ' + Dept->Bldg
nLineNo := nLineNo + 2
lFirst := FALSE

RETURN NIL

/***
*
* EndPage() -> NIL
*
```

```
*/

STATIC FUNCTION EndPage

IF nLineNo > PAGE_LENGTH
   IF nLineNo != 99   // No eject first time.
      EJECT
   ENDIF
   @ 0, RCENTER(REPORT_TITLE) SAY REPORT_TITLE
   @ 0, PAGE_WIDTH-10 SAY 'Page: '+STR(nPageNo,2)
   @ 2, 22 SAY 'Hire Date Range: '+;
        DTOC(dBegDate)+' - '+DTOC(dEndDate)
   @ 4,  0 SAY 'Employee Name'
   @ 4, 31 SAY 'Emp #'
   @ 4, 38 SAY 'Status'
   @ 4, 49 SAY 'Salary'

   @ 5,  0 SAY REPLICATE('-', LEN(Employee->EmpName))
   @ 5, 31 SAY REPLICATE('-', LEN(Employee->EmpNo))
   @ 5, 38 SAY REPLICATE('-', 9)
   @ 5, 49 SAY REPLICATE('-', 9)
   nLineNo := 7
   nPageNo ++
ENDIF

RETURN NIL

/***
*
*  CheckAbort() -> NIL
*  Routine to pause and alternately abort or continue a report.
*
*/

FUNCTION CheckAbort()

IF INKEY() != 0
   IF ALERT('Report paused', {'Abort','Continue'}) == 1
      BREAK
   ENDIF
ENDIF

RETURN NIL
```

Index

#command, 89-90
#define, 71
#error, 82-83
#stdout, 83
#translate, 89-90
#xcommand, 89-90
#xtranslate, 89-90
& macro operator, 41
&& (Xbase), 33
.CLP files, 12
!= (not equal operator), 41
/*, 33
//, 33
/a, 9
/b, 9
/d, 9, 69
/ES, 9
/ES1, 9
/ES2, 9
/ESO, 9
/i, 9
/l, 9
/m, 10
/n, 10, 131
/o, 10
/p, 10
/q, 10-11
/r, 11
/s, 11
/t, 11
/U, 75
/u, 11
/v, 11
/w, 11
/z, 11
\ backward slash, 69
—, 38
++, 38
: send operator, 269
:= assignment operator, 38
=, 40
= overloaded operator, 38, 163
== exactly equal operator, 40, 157
? <expr>, 23

?? <expr>, 23
@ BOX, 52-54
@ prompt, 54-55
@ SAY GET, 51-52

A

AADD(), 160-61
ACHOICE(), 166
ACLONE(), 161
ACOPY(), 161
Actual parameters, 113
Add new record, 323
addColumn(), 274
ADEL(), 162
AEVAL(), 169
AFILL(), 162
AINS(), 162
Alias functions, 42-43
ALIAS(), 199
Alternate command set, 88
Animate, 23
ANNOUNCE, 131
APPEND FROM, 193
Appendices Guide, 8
Applications, 317-18
    data entry, 318
        Entry(), 319-20
        GetScr(), 320-21
        InitVars(), 321
        Menu(), 323-25
        ReplVars(), 323
        SetVars(), 322
    GET system, 325-31
    reporting, 331-40
    summary, 340
args, 270
Array(s), 151-53
    applying in everyday coding, 158-59
    browsing, 293-97
    code block related, 169
    database related, 167-68
    declaring and using, 153
        array references, 156-57
        assigning values to array elements, 156

comparing arrays, 157-58
  dynamic declarations, 155-56
  fixed-size declarations, 155
  literal declarations, 154-55
 environment, 169-72
 functions, 159-60
 global variables, 175-76
 manipulation, 160
    AADD(), 160-61
    ACLONE(), 161
    ACOPY(), 161
    ADEL(), 162
    AFILL(), 162
    AINS(), 162
    ARRAY(), 163
    ASCAN(), 163
    ASIZE(), 164
    ASORT(), 164-65
    ATAIL(), 165
    LEN(), 165
 passing as parameters, 172-74
 recursion, 174
 references, 156-57
 return values, 173-74
 summary, 176
 user interface, 165-66
ARRAY(), 163
ASCAN(), 163
Ashton-Tate, i
ASIZE(), 164
ASORT(), 164-65
Assertions, 83-84
assign(), 273
Assigning values to array elements, 156
Assignment operator, 38
ATAIL(), 165
autoLite, 271

B

backspace(), 274
Backward pointer, 241
Backward slash \, 69
badDate, 271
BEGIN/END SEQUENCE, 47-50
Blank spaces, 70
block, 271-72
Blockify result marker, 103-04
Breakpoint, 23-24, 27-28
Browsing text files, 298-300
buffer, 271
Buffered screen output, 57
By reference, 115
By value, 115

C

CALLSTACK, 23
canDefault, 270
canRetry, 270
canSubstitute, 270
cargo, 270–72
Carriage returns, 244-46, 260
Case sensitive, 23, 69
Chained relationship, 229
changed, 271
Class definition, 276
Class extensions products, 276
Classes, 268-69
CLEAR SCREEN, 56
Code block(s), 139-41, 225
    array, 169
        AEVAL(), 169
    data type, 141
    definition, 141
    evaluation, 141-43
    Get/Set block functions, 147-50
    parameter passing, 146-47
    programming applications, 143-46
    summary, 150
Code hiding, 130
Coding style, 32-35
colorBlock, 272
colorDisp(), 273
colorRect(), 274
colorSpec, 271
colorSpec, 271
Column(s)
    addColumn(), 274
    col, 271
    colCount, 271
    colPos, 271
    colSep, 271-72
    colWidth(), 274
    delColumn(), 275
    freezing, 291
    getColumn(), 275
    insColumn(), 275
    setColumn(), 275
Command line features, 23-25
Comment block, 33
Comments, 33
Compact indexes, 189
Comparing arrays, 157-58
Comparison operator, 40, 157
Compilers, 5-7
    macros, 81
    switches, 8-11
Compiling with CA-Clipper, 8-12
    .CLP files, 12

Computer Associates, Inc., xii, 3, 28, 73, 107, 276
Conditional compilation, 64, 76-79
configure(), 274
Constants, manifest, 9, 64, 68-73
Constructor function, 268
Controlling order, 185
COPY TO, 193-94
Cursor movement, 273-74

D

Data entry, 318-25
    screen, 320
Data hiding, 129-30
Data types, 35-37
Database access, 179-82
    code blocks, 225
    commands, 192
        APPEND FROM, 193
        COPY TO, 193-94
        GO, 194-95
        INDEX, 195-96
        SEEK, 196-97
        SET INDEX TO, 197
        SET ORDER TO, 198-99
    database traversal and DBEVAL(), 225-27
    functions, 199
        ALIAS(), 199
        DBAPPEND(), 199-200
        DBCLEARFILTER(), 200
        DBCLEARINDEX(), 200-01
        DBCLEARRELATION(), 201
        DBCLOSEALL(), 201
        DBCLOSEAREA(), 202
        DBCOMMIT(), 202
        DBCOMMITALL(), 202
        DBCREATE(), 167-68, 202-03
        DBCREATEINDEX(), 203-04
        DBDELETE(), 204
        DBEVAL(), 204, 225-27
        DBFILTER(), 204-05
        DBGOBOTTOM(), 205
        DBGOTO(), 205
        DBGOTOP(), 205-06
        DBRECALL(), 206
        DBREINDEX(), 206
        DBRELATION(), 206-07
        DBRSELECT(), 207
        DBSEEK(), 207-08
        DBSELECTAREA(), 208
        DBSETDRIVER(), 208
        DBSETFILTER(), 208-09
        DBSETINDEX(), 209
        DBSETORDER(), 209-10
        DBSETRELATION(), 210
        DBSKIP(), 210
        DBSTRUCT(), 168
        DBUNLOCK(), 210-11
        DBUNLOCKALL(), 211
        DBUSEAREA(), 211
        HEADER(), 211
        INDEXEXT(), 211-12
        INDEXKEY(), 212
        INDEXORD(), 212-13
        LASTREC(), 213
        RECNO(), 213
        RECSIZE(), 213-14
    RDD commands, 214
        DELETE TAG, 214
    RDD functions, 214
        DBRLOCK(), 214
        DBRLOCKLIST(), 215
        DBRUNLOCK(), 216
        ORDBAGEXT(), 216
        ORDBAGNAME(), 217
        ORDCREATE(), 217
        ORDDESTROY(), 218
        ORDFOR(), 219
        ORDKEY(), 219
        ORDLISTADD(), 220
        ORDLISTCLEAR(), 220
        ORDLISTREBUILD(), 220
        ORDNAME(), 221
        ORDNUMBER(), 221
        ORDSETFOCUS(), 222
        RDDLIST(), 222
        RDDNAME(), 223
        RDDSETDEFAULT(), 223
    RDD technology, 182
        architecture overview, 182-84
        DBFCDX RDD, 189-90
        DBFMDX RDD, 188-89
        DBFNDX RDD, 187-88
        DBFNTX RDD, 187
        DBPX RDD, 190-91
        installing RDD files, 192
        linking, 192
        order management system, 186-87
        overview, 182
        terminology, 184-86
    setting relations, 228-30
    summary, 237
Database related arrays, 167-68
Database utility (DBU), 3-4, 16-18
dBase II, i
Debugger, 21
    /b option, 9

basics, 22-28
command line features, 23-25
features, 22
Declaring and using arrays, 153
assigning values to array elements, 156
comparing, 157-58
dynamic declarations, 155-56
fixed-size declarations, 155
literal declarations, 154-55
references, 156-57
decPos, 271
Decrement operator, 38-39
defColor, 272
deHilite(), 274
delColumn(), 275
DELETE, 305
DELETE ALL, 23
Delete existing record, 324
DELETE TAG, 214
delLeft(), 274
delRight(), 274
delWordLeft(), 274
delWordRight(), 274
Demonstration versions, 77
Dependency rules, 14
Description, 270
Development cycle, 6-8
DEVOUT(), 57
DEVOUTPIC(), 57
DEVPOS(), 57-58
Directories, setup, 3-5
DIRECTORY(), 170
DirEval, 313
DISPBEGIN(), 57
DISPBOX(), 58
DISPCOUNT(), 58
DISPEND(), 57
display(), 273
DISPOUT(), 58-59
DO CASE/ENDCASE, 46-47
DO WHILE, 44-45
DOS environment variables, 5-8
DOS error level, 9
down(), 274
Dumb stringify result marker, 102
Dynamic declarations, 155-56
Dynamic typing, 35

E

Edit existing record, 324
Embedded line numbers, 9
end(), 273–74
Entry(), 319-20

Environment, 169
DIRECTORY(), 170
jump tables, 171-72
ERASE, 305
Error class, 266-67
Error codes, 306
Error level, DOS, 9
Error Messages and Appendices Guide, 8
Error System, 4
ErrorNew(), 268
exactly equal operator, 40
Exception handling, 47
Execution, 16
Exit list, 136
EXIT procedures, 133-37
exitState, 271
Exported instance variables, 269-72
Extended expression, 41-42, 193-94
match marker, 94-95
translations, 95
External references, 12

F

FCLOSE(), 305
FCREATE(), 304-07
FEof, 313
FERASE(), 305
FERROR(), 305-06
FGets, 313
FIELD/MEMVAR statements, 37
FIELDBLOCK(), 147-48
FIELDWBLOCK(), 148-49
FILE DOS, 23
FILE EXIT, 23
FILE OPEN, 23
FILE RESUME, 23
File handle, 305
File pointer, 307-08
File-wide static, 10, 82, 121, 127-28
FileBottom, 313
FileEval, 313
FILEIO.PRG, 311
filename, 270
FilePos, 313
FileSize, 313
FileTop, 313
Find record, 324-25
Fixed-size declarations, 155
Flow-of-control, 43
footing, 272
footSep, 272
FOPEN(), 304-07
FOR/NEXT, 46

forceStable(), 275
Formal parameters, 113
Formatting data, 290-91
FoxPro, ii
FPuts, 313
FREAD(), 309
FReadLn, 313
FREADSTR(), 309
freeze, 271
Freezing columns, 291
FRENAME(), 305
FSEEK(), 307-09
Full screen editor, 250
Function keys, 17-18
Function prototype, 199
Function string, 52
Function-style procedure structure, 114
Functions, 117-19, 313
FWRITE(), 309-11
FWriteLn, 313

G

Gather, 323
genCode, 270
GET PICTURE functions, 53
GET PICTURE templates, 53
GET system, 4, 325-31
Get class, 267
Get/Set block functions, 147
    FIELDBLOCK(), 147-48
    FIELDWBLOCK(), 148-49
    MEMVARBLOCK(), 149-50
getColumn(), 275
GetNew(), 268
GetScr(), 320-21
Global scope, 129
Global variables, 175-76
Globals, 121
GO, 194-95
goBottom(), 274
goBottomBlock, 271
goTop(), 274
goTopBlock, 272

H

Hard carriage returns, 244-46
hasFocus, 271
Header files, 4, 9, 64, 74
HEADER(), 211
heading, 272
headSep, 272
HELP, 23
Hiding, 129-30

hilite(), 275
hitBottom, 272
hitTop, 272
home(), 273-74
Hungarian notation, 32-33, 36, 153, 269

I

Identity, 185
Identity order, 185
IF statement, 43-44
Implants, 26
Include files, 64, 73-76
Increment operator, 38-39
Indenting, coding style, 33-34
INDEX, 195-96
INDEXEXT(), 211-12
INDEXKEY(), 212
INDEXORD(), 212-13
Inference rules, 15
Inheritance, 120
INIT procedures, 133-37
Initialization list, 135
InitVars(), 321
insColumn(), 275
insert(), 274
Installation, 2-5
Instance variables, 269-72
Instantiation, 268
Interpreters, 5-6
invalidate(), 275

J

Jump tables, 171-72

K

Key expression, 184
Key value, 184
Keyboard, 59-60
Keyed-pair, 185
killFocus(), 273

L

Language basics, 31
    & macro operator, 41
    alias functions, 42-43
    assignment operator, 38
    BEGIN/END SEQUENCE, 47-50
    coding style, 32-35
    data types, 35-37
    DO CASE/ENDCASE, 46-47
    DO WHILE, 44-45
    extended expressions, 41-42
    FIELD/MEMVAR statements, 37

FOR/NEXT, 46
IF statement, 43-44
increment and decrement, 38-39
relational operators, 40-41
screen input/output, 51
    @ BOX, 52-54
    @ Prompt, 54-55
    @ SAY GET, 51-52
    buffered screen output, 57
    DEVOUT(), 57
    DEVOUTPIC(), 57
    DEVPOS(), 57-58
    DISPBOX(), 58
    DISPCOUNT(), 58
    DISPOUT(), 58-59
    saving/restoring screen contents, 55-57
    stuffing the keyboard, 59-60
LASTREC(), 213
left(), 273-74
leftVisible, 272
LEN(), 165
Lexical scoping, 120
Library files directory, 3
lifetime, 119, 130
Lifetime rules, 131
Limited scope, 128
Line numbers, embedded, 9-10
Linkage database, 231
Linking, 12-13
List match marker, 97-98
Literal declarations, 154-55
Literal name, 194
Local scope, 123-25
LOCATE CASE, 23
LOCATE FIND, 23
LOCATE GOTO, 23
LOCATE NEXT, 23
LOCATE PREVIOUS, 23
Lock list, 186
Logify result marker, 99, 103
Low-level file functions, 303-04
    example, 311-14
    FCLOSE(), 305
    FCREATE(), 304-07
    FERASE(), 305
    FERROR(), 305
    FILEIO.PRG, 311
    FOPEN(), 304-07
    FREAD(), 309
    FREADSTR(), 309
    FRENAME(), 305
    FSEEK(), 307-09
    FWRITE(), 309-11
    summary, 314

M

Macro, 81
Macro operator, 41
Main report loop, 334
Maintainable scoped orders, 186
Make file, 14
Manifest constants, 9, 64, 68-73
Many-to-many relationship, 230
Match markers, 89, 91
    extended, 94-95
    list, 97-98
    optional clauses, 95-97
    regular, 93-94
    restricted, 98-99
    wild, 100-01
    word, 92
Memo field(s), 239-42
    basics, 242-43
    character string functions, 243-50
    converting summer '87 memo fields, 260-62
    MEMOEDIT(), 250-52
        editing text disk files, 256-60
        getting memo fields, 255-56
        memo field access, 253-54
        user function, 252-53
    summary, 262
Memo functions, 244-45
MEMOEDIT() parameters, 251
Memory variables, 9
MEMVARBLOCK(), 149-50
Menu(), 323-25
Method functions, 272-75
Microsoft, ii, 7
Mnemonics, 67
MONITOR ALL, 23
MONITOR LOCAL, 23
MONITOR PRIVATE, 23
MONITOR PUBLIC, 23
MONITOR SORT, 23
MONITOR STATIC, 24
Multiple children, 230
Multiple-order bag, 186

N

name, 271
Nantucket Corporation, i, 276
Native code compiler, 7
nBottom, 272
Next/prev record, 324
NG files, 28
nLeft, 272
Non-maintainable/temporary orders, 186
Non-selected work area, 42
Normal stringify result marker, 104-05

Norton Guides, 5, 28-29
not equal operator, 41
nRight, 272
nTop, 272
Null character, 309
Null string, 102
NUM ON|off, 24

O

Object files, 4
Object-based, 266
Object-oriented analysis, 276
Object-oriented design, 276
Objects, 268-69
One-way link, 241
OOP limitations, 275-76
operation, 270
Operators
    assignment, 38
    comparison, 40, 157
    decrement, 38-39
    exactly equal, 40, 157
    increment, 38-39
    macro, 41
    not equal, 41
    overloaded, 38, 163
    relational, 40-41
    send operator, 269
Optional clauses, 95-97
OPTIONS CODEBLOCK, 24
OPTIONS COLOR, 24
OPTIONS EXCHANGE, 24
OPTIONS LINE, 24
OPTIONS MENU, 24
OPTIONS MONO, 24
OPTIONS PATH, 24
OPTIONS PREPROCESSED, 24
OPTIONS RESTORE, 24
OPTIONS SAVE, 24
OPTIONS SWAP, 24
OPTIONS TAB, 24
ORD, 187
ORDBAGEXT(), 216
ORDBAGNAME(), 217
ORDCREATE(), 217
ORDDESTROY(), 218
Order, 185
Order expression, 186
Order list, 185
Order list focus, 185
Order name, 186
Order number, 185
ORDFOR(), 219
ORDKEY(), 219
ORDLISTADD(), 220
ORDLISTCLEAR(), 220
ORDLISTREBUILD(), 220
ORDNAME(), 221
ORDNUMBER(), 221
ORDSETFOCUS(), 222
original, 271
osCode, 270
overloaded operator, 38
overStrike(), 274

P

pageDown(), 274
pageUp(), 274
panEnd(), 274
panHome(), 274
panLeft(), 274
panRight(), 274
Parameter passing techniques, 118
Parameter passing, code block, 146-47
Passed by reference, 115
Passed by value, 115
Passing arrays as parameters, 172-74
PE, 16, 19
picture, 271
POINT BREAKPOINT, 24
POINT DELETE, 24
POINT TRACEPOINT, 24
POINT WATCHPOINT, 24
Polymorphism, 275, 292
pos, 271
Post-validation, 51
postBlock, 271
PPO, 10, 65, 71, 90
Pre-linked libraries, 4
Pre-validation, 51
preBlock, 271
Preprocessor, 63-67
    assertions, 83-84
    conditional compilation, 64, 76-79
    directives, 8
    #error, 82-83
    include files, 64, 73-76
    manifest constants, 64, 68-73
    pseudo functions, 64, 80-82
    #stdout, 83
    summary, 85
Private scope, 120-23
Procedures, 113-17
Program module, compile only, 10
Program units, 112-13
Programmer's Editor, iii, 4, 6, 16
Pseudo functions, 64, 80-82
Public scope, 125-27

Q

Quotation marks, 69
Quiet display, 10

R

Ragged arrays, 152
RDD commands, 214
    DELETE TAG, 214
RDD files, 192
RDD functions, 214
    DBRLOCK(), 214
    DBRLOCKLIST(), 215
    DBRUNLOCK(), 216
    ORDBAGEXT(), 216
    ORDBAGNAME(), 217
    ORDCREATE(), 217
    ORDDESTROY(), 218
    ORDFOR(), 219
    ORDKEY(), 219
    ORDLISTADD(), 220
    ORDLISTCLEAR(), 220
    ORDLISTREBUILD(), 220
    ORDNAME(), 221
    ORDNUMBER(), 221
    ORDSETFOCUS(), 222
    RDDLIST(), 222
    RDDNAME(), 223
    RDDSETDEFAULT(), 223
RDD technology, 182
    architecture overview, 182-84
    DBFCDX RDD, 189-90
    DBFMDX RDD, 188-89
    DBFNDX RDD, 187-88
    DBFNTX RDD, 187
    DBPX RDD, 190-91
    installing RDD files, 192
    linking, 192
    order management system, 186-87
    terminology, 184-86
RDDLIST(), 222
RDDNAME(), 223
RDDSETDEFAULT(), 223
reader, 271
RECNO(), 213
Record, 186
RECSIZE(), 213-14
Recursion, 174
Recursive function call, 174
refreshAll(), 275
refreshCurrent(), 275
Regular match marker, 93-94
Regular result marker, 101
Regular static, 127

rejected, 271
Relational operators, 40-41
Repeating clauses, 105-06
ReplVars(), 323
Report and label, 16, 18
Report and label designer utility, 4
Reporting, 331-40
REQUEST, 131
RESERVED.CH, 76
reset(), 273
Restricted match marker, 98-99
RESTSCREEN(), 55
Result markers, 89, 101
    blockify, 103-04
    dumb stringify, 102
    logify, 103
    normal stringify, 104-05
    regular, 101
    repeating clauses, 105-06
    smart stringify, 102-03
Reverse compiler, 6
right(), 273–74
rightVisible, 272
RL, 16, 18-19
RMAKE, 14-16
row, 271
rowCount, 272
rowPos, 272
RUN ANIMATE, 24
RUN GO, 24
RUN NEXT, 24
RUN RESTART, 25
RUN SPEED, 24
RUN STEP, 24
RUN TO, 24
RUN TRACE, 24

S

Sample programs directory, 4
SAVESCREEN(), 55
Saving/restoring screen contents, 55-57
Scattering, 322
Scope and lifetime, 119, 130
    global scope, 129
    local scope, 123-25
    private scope, 120-23
    public scope, 125-27
    static scope, 127-29
Screen input/output, 51
    @ BOX, 52-54
    @ prompt, 54-55
    @ SAY GET, 51-52
    buffered screen output, 57

DEVOUT(), 57
DEVOUTPIC(), 57
DEVPOS(), 57-58
DISPBOX(), 58
DISPCOUNT(), 58
DISPOUT(), 58-59
    saving/restoring screen contents, 55-57
    stuffing the keyboard, 59-60
SEEK, 196-97
SELECT, 42
Semicolon, 34, 93
Send operator, 269
Set colors, 24
Set exact, 163
SET INDEX TO, 197
SET ORDER TO, 198-99
SET WRAP, 55
setColumn(), 275
setFocus(), 273
SetVars(), 322
severity, 270
Shortcutting optimizations, 11
Single-order bag, 186
skipBlock, 272
Skipper function, 292
Smart stringify result marker, 102-03
Soft carriage returns, 244-46, 260
Source code directory, 3
Square brackets, 95
Stabilization, 285
stabilize(), 275
stable, 272
Standard classes, 265-68
    class extensions products, 276
    classes and objects, 268-69
    instance variables, 269-72
    method functions, 272-75
    OOP limitations, 275-76
    sending messages, 275
    summary, 276-77
Static, 10, 82, 121, 127-28
Static functions and procedures, 129
Static scope, 127-29
Static variables, 127
Stuffing the keyboard, 59-60
subCode, 270
Subprograms, 111-12
    ANNOUNCE, 131
    EXIT procedures, 133-37
    functions, 117-19
    INIT procedures, 133-37
    procedures, 113-17
    programs units, 112-13
    REQUEST, 131
    scope and lifetime, 119, 130
        global scope, 129
        local scope, 123-25
        private scope, 120-23
        public scope, 125-27
        static scope, 127-29
    static functions and procedures, 129
    summary, 137
subscript, 271
subSystem, 270
Symantec, 28
Symbol table, 120
Syntax definition, 193
Syntax-only, 11

T

Table driven, 65
Table driven syntax, 88
Tag, 185
TBColumn class, 267
TBColumnNew(), 268
TBrowse, 279-81
    array browsing, 293-97
    browsing text files, 298-300
    complete, 287-89
    customizing, 290
        color, 291
        formatting data, 290-91
        freezing columns, 291
        limiting the scope, 291-93
    requirements, 281-86
    speeding up, 289-90
TBrowse class, 267
TBrowseDB(), 268
TBrowseNew(), 268
Template string, 52
Temporary files, 11
Text entry methods, 274
Third-party utilities, 19-21
toDecPos(), 273
Tracepoint, 23-24, 28
Tries, 270
Two-way communication, 257
type, 271
typeOut, 271

U

Undelimited comments, 45
undo(), 273
up(), 274
updateBuffer(), 273
User interface, 165-66
    ACHOICE(), 166
User-defined commands, 64, 87-89

COMMON.CH, 106-08
match markers, 89, 91-101
    extended expression, 94-95
    list, 97-98
    optional clauses, 95-97
    regular, 93-94
    restricted, 98-99
    wild, 100-01
    word, 92
preprocessor operations, 89-91
result markers, 89, 101-06
    blockify, 103-04
    dumb stringify, 102
    logify, 103
    normal stringify, 104-05
    regular, 101
    repeating clauses, 105-06
    smart stringify, 102-03
summary, 108
User-defined functions, 313
Utilities, 16
    DBU, 17-18
    PE, 19
    RL, 18-19
    third-party, 19-21

V

varGet(), 273
Variables, automatically declaring, 9

varPut(), 273
VIEW, 24
VIEW APP, 24
VIEW CALLBACK, 24
VIEW SETS, 24
VIEW WORKAREAS, 24
Visibility, 12
Visual Objects, 276

W

Watchpoint, 23-24, 28
Whitespace, 100
width, 272
Wild match marker, 100-01
WINDOW ICONIZE, 24
WINDOW MOVE, 24
WINDOW NEXT, 24
WINDOW PREV, 24
WINDOW SIZE, 24
WINDOW TILE, 24
WINDOW ZOOM, 24
Word match marker, 92
wordLeft(), 273
wordRight(), 273

X

Xbase, 33

Clipper: Step By Step Disk Offer!

The companion disk for CA-Clipper: Step by Step includes all program listings, sample code, and answers to exercises contained in this book, organized by chapter, and pre-tested and debugged.

You may order the companion disk in two different ways:

- Fill out the coupon below, telling us how many diskettes you want. Include your personal check, bank check, or money order.
- Order via modem by calling our BBS system, AMULET:vc. Just dial (310) 453-7705 where you may use your credit card and download the complete source code directly.

Mail the coupon to:

AMULET Consulting
P.O. Box 241713
Los Angeles, CA 90024

You may also call AMULET Consulting at (310) 798-3985 (voice/FAX) for more information.

Shipping and handling is $5 for first item, $1 for each additional item for orders shipped to the U.S. Order for Canada and Mexico, add $10 for first item, $2 for each additional item. Foreign orders, add $15 per item. Standard shipping is U.S. mail. Allow 3 to 4 weeks. Prices subject to change.

All funds should be made payable to AMULET Consulting.

Qty	Disk for:	Each	Total
___	*CA-Clipper Companion Disk(s)*	$19.95	_____
	California orders please add 8.25% sales tax:		_____
	Shipping and handling:		_____
	Total due, in U.S. funds:		_____

Disk Type: ☐ 5.25"   ☐ 3.5"

Name _____
Company _____
Address _____
City/State/ZIP _____
Daytime Phone _____

(John Wiley & Sons, Inc., is not responsible for orders placed with AMULET Consulting)